# THE REGION AND TRADE

New Analytical Directions

# THE REGION AND TRADE

## New Analytical Directions


Editors

**Amitrajeet A. Batabyal**
Rochester Institute of Technology, USA

**Peter Nijkamp**
VU University Amsterdam, The Netherlands



World Scientific

NEW JERSEY • LONDON • SINGAPORE • BEIJING • SHANGHAI • HONG KONG • TAIPEI • CHENNAI

*Published by*

World Scientific Publishing Co. Pte. Ltd.
5 Toh Tuck Link, Singapore 596224
*USA office:* 27 Warren Street, Suite 401-402, Hackensack, NJ 07601
*UK office:* 57 Shelton Street, Covent Garden, London WC2H 9HE

**Library of Congress Cataloging-in-Publication Data**
The region and trade : new analytical directions / edited by Amitrajeet A Batabyal, Peter Nijkamp.
pages cm
Includes index.
ISBN 978-9814520157 (alk. paper)
1. International trade. 2. Regional economics. I. Batabyal, Amitrajeet A., 1965–
II. Nijkamp, Peter.
HF1379.R4393 2015
382--dc23

2014041846

**British Library Cataloguing-in-Publication Data**
A catalogue record for this book is available from the British Library.



In-house Editor: Qi Xiao

Typeset by Stallion Press
Email: enquiries@stallionpress.com

My limbs are bow'd, though not with toil,
But rusted with a vile repose,
For they have been a dungeon's spoil,
And mine has been the fate of those
To whom the goodly earth and air
Are bann'd, and barr'd—forbidden fare;
But this was for my father's faith
I suffer'd chains and courted death;
That father perish'd at the stake
For tenets he would not forsake.

*The Prisoner of Chillon*, Lord Byron

## Contents

## Acknowledgments

This book would not have been possible without the assistance of several researchers dispersed throughout the world. Therefore, we would like to thank the contributors of the individual chapters of this book for their enthusiastic participation in this laborious project. The enthusiasm of the contributors is amply on display in the high quality chapters they have written on alternate aspects of the region and trade that comprise the subject matter of this book.

Batabyal would like to acknowledge the support he received during the long gestation period of this book from Swapna B. Batabyal and Sanjana S. Batabyal. In addition, he would also like to acknowledge the financial support he received from the Gosnell endowment at the Rochester Institute of Technology. Finally, he would like to dedicate this book to the memory of Balarka A. Batabyal (1966–2010). Nijkamp thanks members of the Department of Spatial Economics at VU University and the Tinbergen Institute, Amsterdam for providing an excellent supporting environment during the preparation of this book.



Amitrajeet A. Batabyal
*Rochester, New York*

Peter Nijkamp
*Amsterdam, The Netherlands*


September 2014

## Contributors

**Arnab K. Basu**

C.H. Dyson School of Applied Economics and Management. Cornell University, Ithaca, New York, USA. E-mail: arnab.basu@cornell.edu

**Amitrajeet A. Batabyal**

Department of Economics, Rochester Institute of Technology, Rochester, New York, USA. E-mail: aabgsh@rit.edu

**Hamid Beladi**

Department of Economics, University of Texas, San Antonio, Texas, USA. E-mail: Hamid.Beladi@utsa.edu

**Benjamin Brown-Steiner**

Department of Biological and Environmental Engineering, Cornell University, Ithaca, New York, USA. E-mail: beb83@cornell.edu

**Alecia W. Cassidy**

Department of Economics, University of Michigan, Ann Arbor, Michigan, USA. E-mail: aawaite@umich.edu

**Mehmet G. Celbis**

UNU-MERIT, Maastricht Graduate School of Governance, Maastricht University, Maastricht, The Netherlands. E-mail: celbis@merit.unu.edu

**Jialie Chen**

S.C. Johnson School of Management, Cornell University, Ithaca, New York, USA. E-mail: jc2428@cornell.edu

**Tomaz P. Dentinho**

Universidade dos Acores, Angra do Heroismo, Portugal. E-mail: tomazdentinho@uac.pt

**Kieran P. Donaghy**

Department of City and Regional Planning, Cornell University, Ithaca, New York, USA. E-mail: kpd23@cornell.edu

**Simon Falck**

Department of Urban Planning and Environment, Royal Institute of Technology, Stockholm, Sweden. E-mail: Simon.Falck@me.com

**Mauricio R. Grajeda**

Departmento de Metodos Cuantitativvos, Universidad de Guadalajara, Jalisco, Mexico. E-mail: ramirez-grajeda.1@osu.edu

**Eduardo Haddad**

Departamento de Economia, Universidade de Sao Paulo, Sao Paulo, Brazil. E-mail: ehaddad@usp.br

**Geoffrey J.D. Hewings**

Regional Economics Applications Laboratory, University of Illinois, Urbana, Illinois, USA. E-mail: hewings@illinois.edu

**Saibal Kar**

Center for Studies in Social Sciences, Calcutta, India; IZA, Bonn, Germany. E-mail: saibal@cssscal.org

**Jee-Sun Lee**

Korea Transport Institute, Sejong-City, 339-007, Korea. E-mail: jeeslee@koti.re.kr

**Peter Nijkamp**

Department of Spatial Economics, VU University, Amsterdam, The Netherlands. E-mail: p.nijkamp@vu.nl

**Ryoichi Nomura**

Department of Economics, Ritsumeikan University, Kusatsu, Shiga, Japan. E-mail: rnt21840@fc.ritsumei.ac.jp

**Takao Ohkawa**

Department of Economics, Ritsumeikan University, Kusatsu, Shiga, Japan. E-mail: toto6878@gmail.com

**Makoto Okamura**

Economics, Department Hiroshima University, Higashi-Hiroshima, Japan. E-mail: okamura.makoto@sepia.plala.or.jp

**Jacques Poot**

National Institute of Demographic and Economic Analysis, University of Waikato, Hamilton, New Zealand. E-mail: jpoot@waikato.ac.nz

**Alexandre A. Porsse**

Department of Economics, Federal University of Parana, Curitiba, Brazil. E-mail: porsse@ufpr.br

**Ian Sheldon**

Department of Agricultural, Environmental, and Development Economics, Ohio State University, Columbus, Ohio, USA. E-mail: sheldon.1@osu.edu

**Folke Snickars**

Department of Urban Planning and Environment, Royal Institute of Technology, Stockholm, Sweden. E-mail: folke.snickars@abe.kth.se

**Vasco M. Silva**

Servico Regional de Estatistica does Acores, Angra do Heroismo, Portugal. E-mail: vrms76@gmail.com

**Makoto Tawada**

Faculty of Economics, Aichi Gakuin University, Nisshin-shi, Aichi-ken, Japan. E-mail: mtawada2@dpc.agu.ac.jp

**Henry Thompson**

Department of Economics, Auburn University, Auburn, Alabama, USA. E-mail: henry.thompson@auburn.edu

**Edward Tower**

Department of Economics, Duke University, Durham, North Carolina, USA. E-mail: tower@duke.edu

**Xiaolu Wang**

Department of Economics, Cornell University, Ithaca, New York, USA. E-mail: xiaolu.wang0702@gmail.com

# Part I
# Introduction

# Chapter 1

# Introduction to "The Region and Trade: New Analytical Directions"*

*Amitrajeet A. Batabyal*[†] *and Peter Nijkamp*[‡]
[†]*Rochester Institute of Technology*
[‡]*VU University, Amsterdam*

## 1.1. Preliminaries

A reasonable case can be made to support the proposition that the formal study of trade began with the publication of the essay *Of the Balance of Trade* by the Scottish philosopher David Hume in 1758. Almost two decades later, Adam Smith published his magisterial *The Wealth of Nations* in 1776. As noted by Krugman *et al.* (2012, p. 1), these two publications, along with the many disputes about British trade policy in the 19th century helped convert economics from a largely descriptive and informal subject into a mathematically rigorous and model oriented one.

Within economics, the recent history of the study of models in *trade* can be traced back to the pioneering work of David Ricardo who published his justly famous tome *The Principles of Political Economy and Taxation* in 1817. In its simplest version, the eponymous Ricardian model analyzes a world consisting of two countries (Home and Foreign), each producing two goods (cheese and wine), with a single factor of production called labor. There are no demand-side differences in these two countries and the differences that matter are supply related. Specifically, production possibilities

*The first author acknowledges financial support from the Gosnell endowment at RIT. The usual absolution applies.

in each country are determined by the *productivity* of the existing labor. In turn, this productivity is measured by the so called unit labor requirements in cheese and wine. The unit labor requirement refers to the number of units of labor needed to produce one unit of either cheese or wine.

The key question in this setting concerns the desirability of trade between Home and Foreign. The key insight from the Ricardian model is that even if one country is able to produce both cheese and wine more efficiently than the other country in *absolute* terms, the opportunity cost of producing the goods will typically be different in the two countries. As a result, one country will tend to have a *comparative advantage* in the production of cheese and the other country in the production of wine. This notion of comparative advantage is one of the most salient ideas in trade and the significant prediction of the Ricardian model is that when nations export (or import) goods in which they have a comparative advantage (or disadvantage), there are gains from trade and hence trade benefits both trading nations.

Although there are a couple of misconceptions about the concept of comparative advantage,[1] the central prediction of the Ricardian model stated above has stood the test of time. Even so, it is important to comprehend that with only a single factor of production, the Ricardian model predicts that *every* individual in a nation benefits from trade driven by the principle of comparative advantage. This is because in the Ricardian world, trade does *not* alter the existing distribution of income. This prediction is clearly at odds with what we observe in the real world. In fact, in the real world, trade tends to result in non-trivial income distribution effects and therefore produces clear winners and losers. Because of the inability of the Ricardian model to address income distribution issues, economists have come up with alternate models that address income distribution effects or, to put it plainly, the "who wins and who loses from trade" question.

[1]See Krugman *et al.* (2012, pp. 37–40) for a lucid discussion of these misconceptions.

The most prominent of these alternate models is the one formulated by Eli Heckscher and Bertil Ohlin and hence called the Heckscher–Ohlin model.[2] In addition to addressing income distribution issues, this model has an added advantage. It emphasizes the fact that resource differences between nations can be a source of trade and that comparative advantage is affected by the interaction between the relative *abundance* of the factors of production and the *intensity* with which they are used to produce different goods.

The simplest version of the Heckscher–Ohlin model analyzes a world of two countries (Home and Foreign), each producing two goods (cloth and food), with two factors of production (physical capital and labor). As in the Ricardian model, there are no demand-side differences between the two countries and all the trade related differences between these two nations are supply based. Four results concerning trade are associated with the Heckscher–Ohlin model. The first result follows from the work of the Polish economist T.M. Rybczynski (1955) and it is known as the Rybczynski theorem. This theorem says that changes in resources lead to *biased* effects on a nation's production possibilities. An implication of this theorem is that countries tend to be better at producing goods that are intensive in the factors with which the country is well endowed. The second result is the well-known Heckscher–Ohlin theorem. This theorem states that nations export (or import) those goods that use their abundant (or scarce) factor intensively.[3]

The third result is the Stolper–Samuelson theorem named after Wolfgang Stolper and Paul Samuelson who first stated this theorem in a now prominent paper in 1941. The theorem says that under certain circumstances, a rise in the relative price of a good will lead to a rise in the return to the factor which is used most *intensively* in the production of the good, and conversely, to a fall in the return to the other factor. This result shows that changes in relative goods prices have significant income distribution effects. In particular, not

[2]The Heckscher–Ohlin model is also known as the factor proportions model.

[3]The validity of this result is not limited to the case of two countries. Deardorff (1982) has shown that this result can be extended to the case of multiple goods, factors of production, and countries.

"only does a change in the prices of goods change the distribution of income; it always changes it so much that owners of one factor of production gain while owners of the other are made worse off" (Krugman *et al.*, 2012, p. 92).

The fourth and final result stems from the fact that free trade in the Heckscher–Ohlin model leads to the equalization of goods prices. The factor price equalization theorem simply says that this goods price equalization leads to the equalization of *factor* prices as well. Although this last result has some theoretical appeal, it is important to point out that in the real world, trade between nations does *not* lead to the equalization of factor prices. The Heckscher–Ohlin model has been a standard workhorse in modern trade theory for many years. Even so, it is not without shortcomings.[4] Having said this, our goal now is to point to some general features of the two models we have discussed thus far and then to use this commentary to segue to a discussion of *inter-regional* trade.

The two models we have discussed above concern trade between nations and *not* between regions where the word region refers to a geographical entity that is smaller than a nation.[5] In addition, these models emphasize either technological differences (Ricardian model) or resource differences (Heckscher–Ohlin model) between nations. Finally, firms in both models are assumed to be *competitive* with production functions characterized by constant returns to scale. As such, these models are good at explaining *inter-industry* trade between nations which involves, for instance, Home exporting cheese to and importing wine from Foreign. However, even if we focus attention on nations, these models are unable to explain the fact that a significant proportion of all trade in the world today is *intra-industry*

[4]See Krugman *et al.* (2012, pp. 103–110) and Hewings and Oosterhaven (2014) for a discussion of these shortcomings.

[5]Although this is the usual interpretation of the word region, it is not the only such interpretation. Researchers have sometimes used the word region to refer to a nation and, on occasion, this word has also been used to refer to supranational geographic entities such as the European Union or North America.

trade.[6] An example of intra-industry trade is when the United States exports and imports automobiles from Japan. To explain the phenomenon of intra-industry trade — which often takes place between regions — we will need to dispense with the competition and the constant returns to scale assumptions.

This means that we permit firms to operate with *economies of scale* or, equivalently, with increasing returns to scale. The existence of economies of scale means that it often makes sense for a nation or a region to specialize in a limited range of goods and services and then trade with other nations or regions for goods and services, the first nation or region does not produce. Even though the existence of scale economies does not inevitably lead to imperfect competition between firms,[7] the models that comprise the "new trade theory" typically involve an imperfectly competitive industry structure.[8]

Since the traditional factors of production such as physical capital and labor are mobile within nations, they frequently move to where the industries are within a nation. As a result, these traditional factors of production are of secondary importance in explaining inter-regional trade. Instead, what drives specialization and trade between regions is the presence of economies of scale. The most common way to model these scale economies is to posit that the firms in the pertinent industries in the regions being studied produce *heterogeneous* products and that the utility functions of consumers in these regions display a love of *variety*. This basic schema is operationalized by working with a model of monopolistic competition due to Dixit and Stiglitz (1977). In the Dixit–Stiglitz

[6]See Krugman *et al.* (2012, pp. 178–179) for more on the numerical significance of intra-industry trade in the world today.

[7]When the cost per unit of output depends on the size of an individual firm and not the size of the industry, we say there are internal economies of scale. In contrast, when the cost per unit of output depends on the size of the industry and not the size of an individual firm, we say there are external economies of scale. With external economies of scale, a competitive industry structure may be possible. See Krugman *et al.* (2012, pp. 147–148) for additional details on this point.

[8]See Schmutzler (1999) for a competent review of the literature on "new trade theory".

model, consumers possess a constant elasticity of substitution (CES) utility function and they derive utility by consuming goods of all possible varieties.

The study of inter-regional trade using the theoretical framework delineated in the preceding two paragraphs has now attracted a lot of attention from economists and regional scientists in the last three decades. Even so, this study has definitely lagged the study of international trade which has been ongoing for over three centuries. Put differently, although international trade has been studied extensively by economists, inter-regional trade has received much less attention from both economists and regional scientists. Given this state of affairs, it is fair to say that there are several theoretical and empirical questions in inter-regional trade that have received little or no attention in the literature. Therefore, the purpose of this book is to provide an *analytic* perspective on some of these outstanding research questions. We now proceed to a more detailed and systematic discussion of the contents of this book.

Following this introductory chapter which comprises Part I of the book, there are 11 chapters and each of these chapters — written by an expert or by a team of experts — discusses a particular research question in inter-regional trade. For ease of comprehension, we have divided these 11 chapters into three parts. Part II of this book focuses on theoretical research questions and this part consists of three chapters that provide a detailed discussion of trade between a Northern and a Southern region (Chapter 2), regional trade in a three-country model (Chapter 3), and the formation of a free trade area in a three-country market model (Chapter 4), respectively.

Part III is concerned with empirical research questions and this part consists of five chapters. Chapter 5 uses data for 1993, 1997, 2002, 2007, and discusses the spatial structure of inter-regional trade within the United States. Chapter 6 first constructs five specific datasets and then uses these datasets to study whether it is true that a nation cannot develop without a strong manufacturing base and that trade restrictions are necessary to facilitate the development of this manufacturing base and hence stimulate economic growth. Chapter 7 utilizes data from 1977 to 2007 to analyze the evolution of freight movement and the related non-point source pollution emissions in the Midwest–Northeast transport corridor in the United States. Chapter 8 uses input–output analysis to study the economies of the nine islands that together comprise the Azores archipelago in Portugal. Finally, Chapter 9 utilizes a database about the European Incoherent Scatter (EISCAT) Scientific Association to shed new light on both international and inter-regional trade. Iron ore and knowledge are traded across nations and regions in this chapter.

The three chapters that comprise Part IV of this book are devoted to a discussion of theoretical and empirical approaches to the analysis of research questions in inter-regional trade. Specifically, Chapter 10 utilizes theoretical and spatial econometric approaches to ascertain the effects of trade openness on the size of what it considers to be the most important cities in 84 countries of the world. Chapter 11 first focuses on the Anderson and van Wincoop (2003) gravity model. It then uses this model to explain the extent to which the recent expansion and the sub-regional differences in Turkey's export performance can be attributed to the creation of trade related infrastructure. Finally, Chapter 12 discusses a theoretical model of trade and then connects this model to the regional specialization of trade in health services in India. With this preliminary discussion out of the way, we now proceed to comment on the intellectual contributions of the individual chapters in this book.

## 1.2. Theory

### 1.2.1. *North–South trade*

Consider trade between a Northern and a Southern region where the Northern region is developed and the Southern region is underdeveloped. In this setting, will import penetration from the Northern region into the Southern region eliminate lower quality manufacturing products in the latter region? Recently, Amiti and Khandelwal (2013) have shed some empirical light on this question but there are relatively *few* theoretical analyses of this question.

Therefore, Chapter 2 constructs and analyzes a model of quality perceptions to shed theoretical light on the above general question. A specific question that is well addressed in this chapter is the following: What precise mechanism leads manufacturers in the Southern region to upgrade their product quality when faced with increasing competition from Northern imports? The chapter answers this question by first supposing that the quality of the Southern experience good cannot be observed prior to purchase. Given this supposition, the chapter shows that Southern manufacturers face an information barrier because consumers in the Southern region utilize country-of-origin labels to statistically discriminate between the Southern product and a Northern import. The key point to comprehend in this regard is that Southern consumer perceptions about product quality can be self-fulfilling. In other words, the perception of a lower average quality for the domestic product *vis-a-vis* imports can translate into a lower willingness to pay and this, in turn, relegates Southern import competing industries into a low quality level equilibrium *trap*.

Because of the salience of self-fulfilling perceptions and the resulting low equilibrium trap, we can ask whether there is a role for intervention designed to improve the quality of the domestically produced and heterogeneous Southern good. By way of answering this question, Chapter 2 focuses on four possible policy interventions. These are a tariff on the Northern import, a quota on the Northern import, a subsidy to the domestically produced Southern good, and an export subsidy. For each policy intervention, the chapter derives conditions under which a temporary restriction has a permanent effect on the inter-temporal path of quality perceptions. In this way, a temporary intervention can move the pertinent Southern industry *away* from a low quality level equilibrium trap.

One issue raised by the analysis of product quality and trade in Chapter 2 is the potential nexus between the productivity of firms in a particular region and trade. In particular, what is the nature of trade in a world in which there are three countries? This question is interestingly addressed in Chapter 3.

### 1.2.2. *Regional trade*

This third chapter focuses on a world in which, initially, there are two countries. The analysis is then extended to account for a third country. There are two final goods and within each country, there is a constant cost production possibility frontier. Each nation maximizes utility subject to its constant cost production possibility frontier.

In the two-country version of the model being studied, competitive trade between a small and a large nation occurs at the large nation autarky price and, consistent with one's intuition, the small nation enjoys the standard gains from trade. When there is an arbitrarily small cost of adjusting output along the small country's production possibility frontier, specific gains are needed for trade to occur. These gains arise when the second country exports at least as much as what it would consume in autarky.

In what ways are the above results affected by the introduction of a third country into the model? The analysis undertaken in Chapter 3 shows that several outcomes are now possible. Therefore, this chapter delineates some of these possibilities using the word "regional" in the supranational sense described in footnote 5. Specifically, we see that trade between all the countries in the model — or global trade — arises in a relatively small number of scenarios. Instead, regional trade in which trade is limited to a *subset* of the total number of countries under study arises in several scenarios. The motivation for this kind of regional trade is the geographical distribution of productivity and country sizes. In particular, regional trade frequently arises when the countries involved are located *close* to each other.

Chapter 3 notes that when contemplating the nature of this regional trade, it is important to keep two facts in mind. First, a small country may produce too little to offer gains from trade to the other two nations under study. Second and in contrast, it is possible for a country to be too productive and hence not gain from trade.

### 1.2.3. *Free trade areas*

In contemporary times, many nations have either attempted to or have actually formed free trade agreements which are regional in the sense that the number of nations that are signatories to the agreement is relatively small and the agreement in question does *not* include every nation in the world.[9] Narrow bilateral free trade agreements may well lead eventually to broad multilateral free trade agreements. Chapter 4 points out that using this line of thinking, the World Trade Organization (WTO) has, in fact, encouraged the creation of regional free trade agreements. However, from a theoretical perspective, does it make sense to believe that bilateral free trade agreements will lead to the formation of multilateral free trade agreements? Like Chapter 3, Chapter 4 also uses a model with three countries to shed light on this salient question.

The specific model that is analyzed is game-theoretic in nature and it builds on the prior work of Brander and Spencer (1985). The focus in Chapter 4 is on a stylized world consisting of three countries in which two countries are exporters and the remaining country is an importer. The number of firms in each of the exporting nations is different. The importing nation imposes tariffs on the imports from the two exporting nations and it is possible for the relevant authorities in the two exporting nations to use production subsidies.

In the first stage of the three stage game that is analyzed, governments in the importing and in an exporting nation decide whether to form a bilateral free trade agreement or not. If the bilateral free trade agreement is formed, then in the second stage, free trade prevails between the two members of the free trade agreement. When this happens, the importing nation stops using its tariff and the exporting nation eschews its production subsidy. As far as trade between the importing nation and the non-member exporting nation is concerned, tariffs and subsidies remain in place. Given the preceding description

[9]The reader will note that the word "regional" is, once again, being used in the supranational sense mentioned in footnote 5.

of events in the first and in the second stages, in the third stage, firms in the exporting nations export a homogeneous good to the importing nation in the presence of Cournot competition in this latter nation.

In this stylized setting, the analysis in Chapter 4 demonstrates that a bilateral free trade agreement can be formed between the importing nation and *the* exporting nation with the *larger* number of domestic firms. However, this bilateral free trade agreement *cannot* be extended to include the other exporting nation in the model. This saturnine result notwithstanding, Chapter 4 does demonstrate a more positive result. Specifically, it shows that when both exporting nations subsidize their domestic firms, a multilateral free trade agreement *can* be formed by gradually extending the bilateral free trade agreement. With this discussion of the three theoretical chapters that comprise Part II of this book out of the way, we now turn to the five chapters that together make up the empirical Part III of this book.

## 1.3. Empirics

### 1.3.1. *Spatial connectivity of states*

There is no gainsaying the fact that one kind of inter-regional trade, i.e., trade between the various states, has increased significantly in the United States in the last three decades. This has happened because the states themselves have become more integrated as a result of the decline in transport costs, alterations in the spatial organization of production systems, and the opportunity to take advantage of scale economies. This state of affairs calls for a systematic scrutiny of the spatial connectivity of the various US states and this task is competently undertaken in Chapter 5 of this book.

The specific question asked in this chapter is the following: Where are the principal sources of inputs and markets for each region in the US and how have these changed over time? To answer this question, the chapter conducts exploratory data analysis by utilizing commodity flow survey (CFS) data. In the US, such data have been surveyed and compiled by the US Census Bureau and the Bureau of Transportation Statistics (BTS) every year since 1993. The analysis conducted in Chapter 5 utilizes all the four-year CFS data sets to discern the geographic patterns of US interstate commodity flows between 1993 and 2007.

The two main methods employed in this chapter are trade Gini measures and dyadic factor analysis of commodity flows. The ensuing analysis shows that since 1993, the complete interstate commodity flow system in the US has become *less* spatially focused. The chapter points out that this happened because of the deregulation of the US railroads. This action resulted in a significant decline in transport costs and this decline, in turn, resulted in what the chapter calls the "hollowing-out effect" and the fragmentation of production.

Does the spatial structure of interstate trade in the US demonstrate a contiguity effect? The analysis in Chapter 5 shows that this question can be answered affirmatively. The reasons for this contiguity effect stem not only from geography but also from the effect of *increased* energy costs. This general result notwithstanding, there is a noteworthy exception to the contiguity effect story and this concerns the state of California. With regard to California, we learn that this state is the *most* salient trading entity in the US interstate trading system for all the years covered by the data.

More generally, the analysis in this chapter shows that interstate commodity flows in the US can be grouped into five major geographical clusters. First, California serves the western US and the entire nation. Second, Texas serves primarily the south–western US. Third, trade in the Midwest of the US is represented by Illinois, Indiana, Michigan, and Ohio. Fourth, trade in the Middle Atlantic region is represented mainly by New York and New Jersey. Finally, Georgia and Florida serve the south-eastern part of the US.

### 1.3.2. *Protection of manufacturing*

Both the general public and even some analysts believe that a nation cannot possibly develop and thrive without a strong manufacturing base. This perspective which privileges manufacturing over other economic activities is termed "manufacturing fetishism" in Chapter 6 of this book. This chapter concentrates on answering four queries. First, does a strong manufacturing share of gross domestic product (GDP) aid economic growth? Second, do trade restrictions ensure the development of a strong manufacturing base? Third, how can governance influence the manufacturing share? Finally, are the relationships determined in the analysis of the preceding three questions, robust across regions? The chapter uses five comprehensive datasets from the National Bureau of Economic Research (NBER) in the US, the World Bank, and the United Nations to shed light on the four queries stated above.

In its analysis of the statistical relationship between living standards and the manufacturing share, Chapter 6 points out that for the world as a whole, a one percent increase in the manufacturing share is associated with an insignificant increase in per capita income. More interestingly, for the Asia, Europe, and North America regions, this relationship is negative. In other words, there is *no* robust positive relationship between the manufacturing share and per capita GDP.

Of the six performance indicators studied in Chapter 6, government effectiveness *positively* affects manufacturing. This finding holds across all four model specifications that are studied. Also, the impact of government effectiveness is the same, irrespective of whether additional controls and/or dummy variables are included in the analysis or not. This tells us that a negative shock that reduces the manufacturing share can be offset by an apposite *improvement* in government effectiveness and regulatory quality.

This chapter's analysis of the factors that are responsible for promoting economic growth yields interesting findings. First, poorer nations tend to grow *faster*. Second, for the European region, political stability and the absence of violence have noteworthy effects on long term economic growth. Finally, higher control of corruption raises long term economic growth in Europe but it decreases short term economic growth in North America.

Finally, with regard to the effects of trade restrictions, the results are noteworthy. For instance, home and foreign barriers to imports have *negative* effects on economic growth. Similarly, manufacturing trade barriers at home and abroad also retard economic growth. In Asia, a 10 percentage point increase lowers economic growth by 6.6% per year. The key point made in this chapter concerning the impact of trade restrictions is that to the extent that domestic protection increases the likelihood of a trade war, it reduces both the manufacturing sector and economic growth.

### 1.3.3. *Freight movement and emissions*

The phenomenon that we now call globalization has led to the increased movement of people, goods, money, and information over time and across space. As noted by Levinson (2008), one striking way in which this increased mobility has manifested itself is the significant growth in the movement of freight involving the transport of final and intermediate goods. These developments have been accompanied by the exploitation of economies of scale by firms and this, in turn, has led to the *fragmentation* of production processes in such a way that many production related activities are now dispersed in least-cost locations.

Given this scenario, Chapter 7 rightly points out that although there now exist some empirically supported theoretical explanations of fragmentation, theories and models that directly connect the decision-making of shippers and carriers with impacts on nodes and links in transportation networks are largely absent in the literature. Furthermore, what is needed is time series data on inter- and intra-industry trade that can help us comprehend and forecast future developments in the transport sector. To this end, Chapter 7 first uses a particular methodology to generate such data and then it demonstrates how this data can be utilized to shed light on interstate inter-industry freight flows in the Midwest–Northeast transport corridor of the US. An additional objective of this chapter is to simulate the connections between local air quality, the meteorological system, the global economy, and economic activities in the Northeast region of the US.

How salient is *intra-industry* trade in the Midwest–Northeast corridor of the US? The analysis conducted in this chapter yields a number of interesting findings about this question. First, we learn that for some sectors and between some states, there is considerable variation in intra-industry trade. Second, across all states in the study region, in industries where there is a significant amount of specialization, intra-industry trade is limited. Third, in the 31-year time period of the study, dramatic changes in intra-industry trade have not occurred. Finally, in the case of some goods such as agriculture and food product manufacturing, clear regional trade patterns in the Midwest–Northeast corridor of the US can be discerned.

This chapter concludes its empirical analysis by focusing on the emissions of black carbon from commodity shipping from all sectors in the 13 states under study and in the rest of the US. The analysis undertaken shows that the northernmost and the southernmost grid cells under study have comparable emissions because these grid cells are either outside or on the outskirts of the pertinent transportation corridor. In contrast, the innermost grid cells have multiple transportation corridors within their boundary and hence these cells have the highest emissions — emissions that are three to four times the emissions of the northernmost and the southernmost grid cells.

### 1.3.4. *An island economy*

Chapter 8 studies the Azores which are nine small islands that spread out over 600 kilometers in an east–west direction, in the Atlantic Ocean, about half-way between Portugal and Newfoundland. The Azores are a part of Portugal and the nine islands are quite different from each other. Less than a quarter million people inhabit these islands. The economy of the Azores depends on its human, social, and productive capital, and the usefulness of these three forms of capital is governed by favorable agricultural conditions, strategic location, physical beauty, and a rather large exclusive economic zone.

The main objective of this chapter is to produce an inter-regional input–output system for all the Azores islands by estimating inter-industry and inter-island economic flows and then looking at the relationship between these flows and the existing structure of the communication and transport system. A related objective is to study the impacts of economic insularity by looking at the input–output multiplier effects of the economic base in the nine islands comprising the Azores.

The analysis of an elaborate input–output model shows that even though agriculture related exports and external public transfers are the two main components of the economic base in the Azores, the multiplier effects of these two items are quite different. In particular, the multipliers associated with agricultural exports to Portugal and to other nations are *higher* and this demonstrates the relative salience of the agricultural cluster and particularly the cluster associated with dairy exports. This relatively high multiplier finding suggests that economic policy ought to attempt to expand agricultural exports to other nations.

The discussion in this chapter of the economics of the individual islands that together comprise the Azores is interesting. *Inter alia*, we learn that because of high multiplier effects, an island such as Graciosa ought to continue to focus on agricultural exports. In contrast, an island such as Corvo ought not to be similarly focused on agricultural exports because this island is significantly more dependent on external public transfers. In addition to this discussion of the island specific multiplier effects in the Azores, this chapter also points out that consistent with our intuition, spatial spillovers between individual islands are strong when the pertinent islands are geographically *close* and hence connected by frequent ferryboat services.

### 1.3.5. *Trade in knowledge*

The EISCAT Scientific Association has, over the last three decades, been providing the scientific community in general with a significant amount of high latitude data for conducting research on the atmosphere and the ionosphere using the incoherent scatter radar technique. The EISCAT Scientific Association research facilities are located in Finland, Norway, and in the town of Kiruna in Sweden. In addition to this research facility, Kiruna is also home to prominent iron ore mines which have been in operation for over a hundred years.

Given the above state of affairs, Chapter 9 begins by pointing out that there are two kinds of trade present in the region surrounding and including Kiruna. First, there is international and inter-regional trade in iron ore. The chapter notes that this kind of trade is well explained by the classical theories of trade — see Section 1.1 — with transport costs. Second, in addition to this trade in iron ore, there is also trade in *knowledge* involving researchers in different nations who have contracted to perform experiments within the purview of modern space physics.

Because very little is known about the knowledge trade mentioned in the preceding paragraph, the primary objective of Chapter 9 is to use a database on research — including journal articles and doctoral theses — conducted at the EISCAT radar system to shed new light on the empirical aspects of this inter-regional knowledge trade. The dataset in question looks at both forward and backward linkages. Here, forward linkages refer to the flow of knowledge from the EISCAT experiments to researchers in various universities. Backward linkages pertain to the cooperation of researchers at EISCAT Scientific Association across their inter-regional and international networks.

The analysis of knowledge trade conducted in Chapter 9 yields several noteworthy findings. For instance, we learn that the presence of EISCAT Scientific Association leads to a more diversified local labor market, it positively influences the formation of human capital, and it serves as an effective magnet for highly skilled professionals. In addition, EISCAT Scientific Association provides salient infrastructure that effectively *interconnects* knowledge networks with a global reach. One way to see this interconnection is through memberships in scientific communities that lead to the dynamism and the renewal of local knowledge. Finally, even though the main impacts of the knowledge trade lie within the academic system, this knowledge trade has the potential to significantly enhance the competitiveness and the desirability of what would otherwise be a relatively desolate region in northern Sweden. This completes our discussion of the five empirical chapters that comprise Part III of this book. We now proceed to discuss the three theoretical and empirical chapters that together make up Part IV of this book.

## 1.4. Theory and Empirics

### 1.4.1. *Cities and trade*

What are the effects of openness to trade on the size of the most important cities in 84 countries in the world? This is the central question that is answered from both a theoretical and an empirical perspective in Chapter 10. The theoretical framework in this chapter is based on the prior work of Krugman and Livas (1996) and Fujita *et al.* (1999). Specifically, the theoretical model that is analyzed embeds imperfect competition into an inter-temporal general equilibrium setting and the model supposes that there exists an exogenous congestion cost that explicitly influences real wages.

This chapter initially states three specific hypotheses. The first hypothesis is that openness to trade reduces the size of main cities and increases the size of secondary cities. The second hypothesis states that openness to trade diminishes the size of the main city and increases the size of secondary cities given that these cities represent a significant proportion of the urban population. The third and final hypothesis is that openness to trade reduces the size of the main city and increases the size of secondary cities given that these cities are heavily populated. Next, the chapter sets out three straightforward reduced form specifications to test the above three hypotheses.

To resolve the definitional issue concerning what it actually means for a city to be open to trade, this chapter utilizes several metrics of trade openness. These include the weighted share of trade with the US, the share of trade with Germany, Japan, and the US, and an instrumental variable. The dataset used in this chapter provides information on 84 nations during two distinct time periods, namely, 1970–1985 and 1985–2000.

The detailed empirical analysis conducted in this chapter yields thought provoking results about the nexuses between city size and openness to trade. In this regard, let us briefly consider the first and third hypotheses stated above. The first hypothesis is validated as long as, in the language of Chapter 10, cities can be "top ranked". As the chapter helpfully points out, an implication of this result is that problems stemming from crime, pollution, and poverty in top ranked cities can be partially dealt with by *promoting* international trade. With regard to the third hypothesis, we are told that heavily populated cities are more sensitive to trade because economies of scale play a *more* salient role.

More generally, with regard to the impact of trade openness on the entire urban system, we learn that there are two points to comprehend. First, greater openness to trade substantially *reduces* the incentives to cluster together. Put differently, agglomeration economies (centripetal forces) are now offset by the high congestion costs (centrifugal forces). Second, the size of a particular city well explains the size of other cities. In other words, there are clear interaction effects among cities.

### 1.4.2. *Infrastructure and exports in Turkey*

The focus of Chapter 11 is on Turkey. The chapter begins by pointing out that since the early 2000s, Turkey has embarked on an ambitious program whose goal has been to improve the nation's transport infrastructure. The implementation of this ambitious program has been accompanied by a rise in export performance. As a result, researchers have now begun to investigate the possible existence of a *causal connection* between countrywide highway infrastructure improvements and trade in Turkey.

This chapter seeks to contribute to this burgeoning literature by shedding light on two questions. First, to what extent can one attribute the recent expansion and the sub-regional differences in Turkey's export performance to the growth of trade related infrastructure? Second, what is the impact of alternate kinds of infrastructure on exports? To answer these two questions, this chapter first builds a theoretical edifice that is based on the gravity model of trade due to Anderson and van Wincoop (2003). The analysis of this edifice yields a regression equation that the chapter then estimates using regional output data for Turkey. The spatial scale of this data is altered from NUTS3 to NUTS2[10] and the indicator of output is changed as well. As a result of these changes, the pertinent dataset is winnowed down from 186 nations to 180 nations.

With regard to transport costs and export capacity, the empirical analysis leads to some interesting results. For instance, the analysis does *not* find conclusive evidence that economies that are located further away from airports export less than economies that are close to what the chapter calls "exit nodes". Even so, robust evidence *is* obtained to support the proposition that the transport capacity at these "exit nodes" is an important predictor of regional exports. With regard to port infrastructure, the results suggest that port capacity and the number of private ports are both salient determinants of regional exports. In particular, distance to ports has a *negative* impact on regional exports, possibly because of transport related difficulties posed by the movement of bulky and heavy goods.

From a policy perspective, the analysis in this chapter suggests that from a trade promotion perspective, with the possible exception of some port infrastructure, investments in transport infrastructure are very desirable. In addition, we see that, *ceteris paribus*, agglomerated economies export more. Finally and as expected, the larger the value of the Turkish Lira in the currency of a trading partner, the *lower* are the flows of exports.

### 1.4.3. *Services and regional specialization in India*

There is no denying the fact that a key feature of contemporary globalization is the growing scope and the quantitative salience of cross-border commercial service transactions and, more generally, investments in the services sector. As such, Chapter 12 examines the

[10]The acronym NUTS stands for Nomenclature of Units for Territorial Statistics.

regional specialization in service trade in India. More specifically, the kind of trade that is looked at is trade in health services and medical tourism is an important part of this trade. We are told that the subject of service trade in India is worth studying because of two reasons. First, the demand for health tourism in India arises from specific *regional* blocs. Second, the supply of health tourism in India is very *region* specific.

The relatively straightforward theoretical model in this chapter delineates a stylized developing country with multiple regions. In each region, there exists an industrial sector and a service sector and the outputs in each sector are produced with a combination of skilled and unskilled labor. Unlike the region specific endowment of unskilled labor, the supply of skilled labor in any particular region depends on the infrastructure present in that region. A key theoretical finding in this chapter is that in the presence of trade, all regions that possess *higher* skill endowments are the ones that supply the output of the service sector. This essentially means that the regional concentration of the service facility is a result of the higher returns to this sector, supported by the presence of the relevant infrastructure.

The empirical analysis in this chapter is based on a pilot survey that was conducted in eight cities in India in the 2009–2010 time period. These cities were chosen because they are the key locations for the export of health services from India. The analysis of the collected survey data results in a number of noteworthy findings and, in the remainder of this section, we briefly highlight three such findings. First, the total export earnings from the health service sector was approximately US$ 200 million in the time period of interest. The trading partners of — or the medical tourists to — the eight identified cities originate from five blocs and these blocs are classified as America, Africa, Europe, West Asia and Australia.

Second, the principal reason for being a medical tourist in India is the significantly lower *cost* of this medical care, as compared to the cost of similar care in what Chapter 12 calls the "advanced countries" of the world. This finding holds despite the fact that, on occasion, the quality of the received medical care in India is lower than what it would be in the so called advanced nations. Finally, catering to foreign medical tourists certainly creates pressure on the ability of the various facilities under study to serve local patients in India. As such, there has been an *upward* movement in the price of medical care. Even so, it is important to comprehend that the existing price differential is large enough to sustain trade in the provision of health care services.

## 1.5. Conclusions

In recent times, the study of interregional trade, from both theoretical and empirical standpoints, has attracted a considerable amount of attention from economists and regional scientists. Even so, as pointed out in Section 1.1, this study has certainly lagged the study of international trade which has been ongoing for over three hundred years. In other words, although international trade has been analyzed extensively by economists and regional scientists, inter-regional trade has received much *less* attention in the scholarly literature. Therefore, it is fair to say that there are several theoretical and empirical questions in inter-regional trade that have received little or no attention in the literature.

Given this state of affairs, our objective in this book is to provide analytic accounts of some of these outstanding research questions that are written by experts. These experts have tremendous credibility because of two important reasons. First, they are active researchers themselves. Second, they are also some of the leading contemporary voices on public policy concerning inter-regional trade and its effects.

In this introductory chapter, we have attempted to provide a holistic and coherent context within which one may view the emergence and the study of the various research questions that are addressed here. In addition, a perusal of the independent chapters clearly demonstrates the salience and the policy relevance of these research questions that are analytically studied in this book. Therefore, in the coming years, one may look forward to many interesting and policy relevant developments in inter-regional trade that are directly or indirectly related to the questions dealt with in this tome.

## References


Amiti, M and A Khandelwal (2013) Import competition and quality upgrading, *Review of Economics and Statistics* 95, 476–490.

Anderson, JE and E van Wincoop (2003) Gravity with gravitas: a solution to the border puzzle, *American Economic Review* 93, 170–192.

Brander, JA and BJ Spencer (1985) Export subsidies and international market share rivalry, *Journal of International Economics* 18, 83–100.

Deardorff, A (1982) The general validity of the Heckscher–Ohlin theorem, *American Economic Review* 72, 683–694.

Dixit, A and J Stiglitz (1977) Monopolistic competition and optimum product diversity, *American Economic Review* 67, 297–308.

Fujita, M, PR Krugman and AJ Venables (1999) *The Spatial Economy*. Cambridge, Massachusetts: MIT Press.

Hewings, GJD and J Oosterhaven (2014) Inter-regional trade models. In *Handbook of Regional Science*. MM Fischer and P Nijkamp (Eds.). Berlin: Springer, 903–925.

Hume, D (1758) Of the balance of trade. In *Essays and Treatises on Several Subjects*. A Millar, A Kincaid and A Donaldson, London and Edinburgh, UK. The text is available at www.davidhume.org/texts/etss.html. Accessed on December 22, 2014.

Krugman, PR and R Livas (1996) Trade policy and the third world metropolis, *Journal of Development Economics* 49, 137–150.

Krugman, PR, M Obstfeld and MJ Melitz (2012) *International Economics*, 10th edition. Upper Saddle River, New Jersey: Pearson.

Levinson, M (2008) *The Box*. Princeton, New Jersey: Princeton University Press.

Ricardo, D (1817) *The Principles of Political Economy and Taxation*. London, UK: John Murray.

Rybczynski, TM (1955) Factor endowments and relative commodity prices, *Economica* 22, 336–341.

Schmutzler, A (1999) The new economic geography, *Journal of Economic Surveys* 13, 355–379.

Smith, A (1776) *An Inquiry into the Nature and Causes of the Wealth of Nations*. London, UK: Strahan and Cadell.

Stolper, W and P Samuelson (1941) Protection and real wages, *Review of Economic Studies* 9, 58–73.

# Part II
# Theory

# Chapter 2

## Statistical Discrimination, Endogenous Quality and North–South Trade

*Arnab K. Basu*
*Charles H. Dyson School of Applied Economics and Management, Cornell University, Ithaca, NY 14850*

We consider a Southern industry engaged in the production of an experience good whose quality cannot be observed prior to purchase. Consequently, Southern consumers rely on the *country-of-origin* labels to statistically discriminate between a Northern import and the Southern product. We provide a framework to analyze the formation of such quality perceptions and point out its self-fulfilling nature when consumers' willingness to pay and interact with producers' incentive to determine equilibrium average quality of the Southern product. As a theory of the determination of trade volume, our framework shows that the sign of the income effect of import demand is endogenously determined, depending only on the *relative* perceived quality of the Northern *vis-à vis* the Southern product. We also derive conditions under which *temporary* import restrictions may have a *permanent* effect on the dynamic path of quality perceptions and thus alleviate the Southern industry from a low quality-trap.

### 2.1. Introduction

Does import penetration from developed (Northern) countries eliminate lower quality manufacturing products in the developing (Southern) world? The answer seems to be a simple yes, and examples abound. Two of the more recent examples involve the end of the road for India's ubiquitous passenger car, Ambassador — the first car to be made in India and a status symbol of pre-liberalization India[1] and the closing of piano manufacturing firms in Russia.[2] While standard neoclassical trade theory would suggest that inefficient import-competing industries (those producing poorer quality products on average) are bound to disappear once trade is liberalized, a recent paper by Amiti and Khandelwal (2013) analyze specifically how tougher import competition affects firms' decisions to upgrade the quality of their goods. They show that for firms already producing very high-quality goods, lower tariffs induce them to produce goods of even higher quality. But for firms producing very low-quality goods, lower tariffs actually discourage quality upgrading. Fernandes and Paunov (2013), in a study of Chilean manufacturing firms however find that stronger import competition leads to significant quality upgrading for domestic firms.

Casual observations and empirical findings notwithstanding, a valid question remains as to what precise mechanism might be at play that leads Southern manufacturing industries to upgrade product quality when faced with stiffer competition from Northern imports. In this chapter, we focus on a particular type of information barrier faced by manufacturing industries in developing countries — one that is generated through statistical discrimination on the part of consumers whose willingness to pay is based on their perception about *average* product quality bearing a particular *country-of-origin* label. To fix ideas, surely not all Ambassador cars are of inferior quality compared to imports (at least accounting for durability on Indian road conditions), and not all Russian made pianos are of inferior quality as compared to the imported ones. The *average* quality may well be, and it is precisely this idea of statistical discrimination by Southern consumers that we exploit in this chapter to highlight cases where consumers perceptions about product quality can be self-fulfilling — perception of a lower average quality

[1]The Guardian (2014), May 25.

[2]*The Baltimore Sun* (2006), May 19. Russia's oldest manufacturer, J. Bekker of St. Petersburg ceased operations in 2004 as did the Yartsevskaya Piano Factory near Moscow. Since 2004, the bulk of pianos for sale in Russia are better-known imports, which typically have better sound, and are of higher quality.

*vis-à-vis* imports translates into lower willingness to pay, which ultimately dooms domestic Southern import-competing industries into a low equilibrium trap. We also discuss the effectiveness of policy interventions, as well as explore an issue of practical concern — the impact of rising consumer income on manufacturing product quality in the South.

The idea that consumers view *identical* goods produced in different countries as imperfect substitutes of one another can be traced back to Armington (1969). However, theoretical research on the effectiveness of state interventions in raising *average* quality in the presence of such statistical discrimination is sparse with Mayer (1984) and Chiang and Masson (1988), being exceptions. Mayer points out that if consumers' expectation of product quality varies positively with cumulative sales, then a subsidy stimulates the volume of sales and engenders an upward revision of quality expectations by consumers. Hence, infant industry subsidization has the effect of speeding up the process of consumer learning. On the other hand, Chiang and Masson (1988), in a partial equilibrium framework, show that statistical discrimination introduces moral hazard in a firm's choice of quality. In particular, an individual firm lacks the incentive to undertake quality improvements since the gains from doing so spillover to benefit all other firms bearing the same *country-of-origin* label. Accordingly, government intervention either through a minimum quality standard or restrictions on the number of firms within the infant industry leads to improvements in both product quality and national welfare by altering the incentive of individual firms in favor of high quality products.[3]

[3]It is important to distinguish information barriers caused by statistical discrimination based on the *country-of-origin* labels from the one caused by the inability of consumers to distinguish between reputable and *fly-by-night* firms. The later scenario has been extensively analyzed by Grossman and Horn (1988), Bagwell and Staiger (1989) and more recently, Creane (1999). Grossman and Horn (1988) point out that the inability of consumers to identify reputable firms give rise to the problem of moral hazard in an individual firm's choice of quality and adverse selection amongst potential entrants into the industry. As such, temporary protection worsens welfare as it leaves unaffected the problem of moral hazard while exacerbating the problem of adverse selection by encouraging lower quality

Indeed, a number of empirical studies have confirmed that infant export industry assistance leads to improvements in product quality and national welfare. Notable examples include the textile industry in Taiwan and a range of manufacturing products in Japan. In particular, industrial consolidation of export industries in Taiwan and subsidies to selective industries by the Ministry of Trade and Industry (MITI) in Japan had a major role to play in the East Asian miracle. Such precedents for infant export industries notwithstanding long periods of protection to infant import-competing industries has generated mixed results insofar as product quality improvements are concerned. While evidence from South Korean industries producing integrated circuits, machining centers and computer numerically controlled (CNC) lathes show improvements in product quality in response to protection (Jacobsson, 1993), evidence from the metalworking and microcomputer industry in Brazil (Fleury, 1995), and Luzio and Greenstein (1995) show a decline in product quality, where a protection induced captive market acted as a dis-incentive for firms to improve quality.

As the primary objective, we identify the conditions under which intervention does indeed lead to improvements in product quality and national welfare in the South. In particular, we are interested in (i) analyzing whether factor intensities of firms within the Southern import-competing industry play any role in determining the response of average product quality to interventions, and (ii) whether the seemingly contradictory empirical evidence on import-competing infant industry protection can be also reconciled through a unified framework. In order to proceed with the task at hand, we formalize a general equilibrium model of a small open economy with the

firms to enter. Bagwell and Staiger (1989), on the other hand, focuses purely on the adverse selection problem and considers a situation where the absence of subsidies inhibits entry of high quality firms since they are unable to sell at a price that reflects their true quality. In a recent paper, Creane (1999) unifies Grossman and Horn and Bagwell and Staiger's framework and posits that governments should impose a tax on entrants in the first period to prevent adverse selection and subsidize firms in the second period, since only those firms that have established quality reputations survive.

following features. On the demand side, consumers within the economy statistically discriminate against the domestically produced import-competing product based on *country-of-origin* labels.[4] On the supply side we assume, unlike earlier models of statistical discrimination with homogeneous firms, that (a) individual firms within the infant industry differ according to their endowment of *knowledge* capital, which is indispensable for the production of the quality good, (b) firms are free to choose between the production of either the high or the low quality product, that is, there is free entry into the production of each quality type and (c) there exists a foreign competing product with an established average quality. As we shall point out in the sequel, the supply side of Mayer's (1984) model turns out to be a special case of ours when all firms are identical in their endowment of knowledge capital.

We show that if individual Southern consumers differ in their valuation of quality, then both the domestically produced and the imported good coexist in a segmented market where consumers are divided into two identifiable subgroups: Buyers of the Southern import-competing product and buyers of Northern imports, even though relative perceptions about product quality render the two competing products imperfect substitutes *ex-ante*. Thus relative quality perceptions of the Northern import *vis-à-vis* the Southern experience good determines the price of the latter and accordingly, its average quality and output in equilibrium. Once the commodity price is determined by relative perceptions, Southern firms self-select into the production of either the high or the low quality product. Hence, in equilibrium, a low perception regarding the quality of the domestically produced good translates into a lower willingness to pay, which in turn, implies that a higher proportion of Southern firms have the incentive to produce the lower quality of the product. We focus on the multiple equilibria arising from the self-fulfilling nature of quality perceptions on the part

[4]It should be noted that even though our analysis pertains to an import-competing industry, it is easily amenable to study the case of statistical discrimination against export industries.

of rational consumers to underscore the existence of quality-traps. Pessimistic perception about average quality of the Southern good leads to a low level quality-trap rendering the long run equilibrium sub-optimal, in so far as average product quality and national income is concerned.

Perhaps more interestingly, our results pertaining to the Southern quality response to import protection is mixed, providing credence to the empirical evidence of both improvement and deterioration of product quality (*à la* Amiti and Khandelwal, 2013). In particular, whether interventions engender improvements in product quality and national income depends on two effects: (i) the relative increase in output of the *intra-marginal* firms in the production of the high quality *vis-à-vis* the low quality type of the product and (ii) the quality choice of the *marginal* firm. The former effect depends on the relative share of labor in total output and the elasticity of labor demand in response to the price increase for firms engaged in the production of the two quality types, while the latter depends on the relative output–capital ratio for the marginal firm in the production of the two quality types. Therefore, temporary protection may increase or decrease average product quality and national welfare permanently depending on the interaction of these two opposing effects.[5]

By highlighting the role of statistical discrimination based on *country-of-origin* labels, this chapter also contributes to the literature on infant industry argument in the following ways. First, *à la* Donnenfeld (1986), statistical discrimination based on the *country-of-origin* label is a sufficient condition for a violation of the *law of one price* — identical products are priced differently in the same market. Second, the sign of the income effect of import demand is

[5]The interested reader is referred to Das and Donnenfeld (1987) and Krishna (1987) for a discussion on the role of trade policies in determining a foreign monopolist's decision on price, quality and quantity. Also, Das and Donnenfeld (1987) analyze trade restrictions on imports in an oligopolistic industry consisting of foreign and domestic firms with the number of firms (domestic and foreign) producing each quality type constant.

endogenously determined, depending only on the relative perceived quality of the foreign and import-competing products. Further, we find that the product with the lower perceived quality behaves as though it is an *inferior* good in consumption. For instance, if the domestic product is perceived to be of lower quality, then an increase in consumers' income through a boom in the exportable sector, might lead to the incidence of *Dutch Disease* (Krugman, 1987) and van Wijnbergen (1984) which adversely affects the infant import-competing sector — price and output decline as do average product quality and national income. Lastly, unlike earlier literatures, the response of average quality to state interventions is shown to depend crucially on the output–capital ratios of firms producing high and low quality products.

The plan of the chapter is as follows: Section 2.2 develops a model of quality perceptions, determines the product and factor market equilibrium and depicts how relative quality perceptions affect the balance of trade. Section 2.3, analyzes the causality between quality perceptions and equilibrium price, quantity and quality of the Southern product and discusses the sub-optimality of average product quality insofar as national income is concerned. Section 2.4, analyzes the effect of commercial policies in improving average product quality and national income while Section 2.5 concludes the paper.

## 2.2. A Model of Quality Perceptions

To capture the factors influencing the interactions between consumers' quality perceptions and Southern firms' incentive to produce high quality products, we consider a general equilibrium model of a small Southern open economy in discrete time. The economy consists of three groups of decision makers: (1) consumers who desire two goods: a homogeneous product with fixed quality and a heterogeneous product that is either of high ($h$) or low ($l$) quality, (2) producers of the homogeneous product and (3) producers of the heterogeneous product who determine the quality and quantity of their output.

### 2.2.1. *Consumers' preferences and market segmentation in the south*

The Southern economy is populated by a large and constant number of individuals, $\mathcal{L}$. In any given time period, an individual supplies one unit of labor inelastically and earns a wage $w$. This income is allocated between the consumption of one unit of either the Northern (foreign) or the Southern (domestically produced) heterogeneous product ($X$) and $y$ units of the homogenous product ($Y$).[6] The per period utility function of a representative consumer is written as $U(a^i, y) = \alpha \log a^i + (1 - \alpha) \log y$, $i = h, l$ where $a^i > 0$ is a taste parameter which denotes the private valuation of one unit of the heterogeneous product of quality type $i$ and $y$ and denotes the consumption of the homogeneous commodity with quality index unity. We shall assume that $a^h > a^l$ so that every consumer prefers the high quality product to the low quality one.[7] We further allow for the possibility that the ratio of taste parameters $a^h/a^l \equiv a \in [a^-, a^+]$, referred to in the sequel as the *taste bias*, differ across consumers. The fraction of total population with a *taste bias* $a \leq \bar{a}$ is given by a cumulative distribution function $F(\bar{a})$ with $\frac{\partial F(a)}{\partial a} = f(a) > 0$ as the associated density function.

The information available to a consumer prior to allocating $w$ to the consumption of $X$ and $Y$ is summarized as follows:

1. Consumers cannot decipher the true quality of the heterogeneous product prior to purchase.
2. There are two identifiable groups of products, Northern and Southern produced. All Southern $X$-sector products are identical

---

[6]Since the decision calculus of agents is identical across all time periods, the time subscripts for all variables are suppressed. Further, to focus on the issue on hand, we refrain from incorporating the possibility of savings in a consumer's decision calculus.

[7]In effect, we consider a model of *vertical* differentiation where a good is said to have higher quality if *all* consumers prefer it to another good of the same general type, prices being equal. This is distinct from *horizontal* differentiation where buyers differ as to their most preferred choice, when all goods in question are offered at the same price.

prior to purchase. Similarly, imported high and low quality Northern products are indistinguishable *ex-ante*.

3. A representative Southern consumer's perception regarding the *average quality of Northern and Southern products are summarized by a pair* $\{\pi^*, \pi\}$ *where* $\pi\,(\pi^*) \in [0,1]$ *represents a consumer's subjective probabilistic belief: with probability* $\pi$ $(\pi^*)$, *a randomly selected heterogeneous good produced in the South (North) is of high quality.*

Let $P$ and $P^*$ respectively be the price of an unit of the Southern (domestic) and Northern (foreign) heterogeneous good and let $Y$ be the Southern numeraire good whose international price ($P_Y$) normalized to unity. From points 1–3 above, the expected utility from purchasing a Southern $X$-sector good ($U^d(a^h, a^l, P, \pi)$) at any given time period can be written as[8]:

$$\begin{aligned} U^d(a^h, a^l, P, \pi) &= \pi[\alpha \log a^h + (1-\alpha)\log(w-P)] \\ &\quad +(1-\pi)[\alpha \log a^l + (1-\alpha)\log(w-P)] \\ &= \pi\alpha \log \frac{a^h}{a^l} + \alpha \log a^l + (1-\alpha)\log(w-P). \end{aligned} \tag{2.1}$$

Similarly, the expected utility from purchasing an imported Northern heterogeneous good ($U^f(a^h, a^l, P^*, \pi^*)$) can be

[8]It can be readily shown that there can only be one uniform price of the Southern product and one for the Northern product which may support positive demand for the heterogeneous good produced in the South and the North. To see this, let $P^1, P^2$, be two different prices of the Southern output. Hence,

$$\begin{aligned} U^d(a^h, a^l, P^1, \pi) - U^d(a^h, a^l, P^2, \pi) &= \pi[\alpha \log a^h + (1-\alpha)\log(w-P^1)] \\ &\quad + (1-\pi)[\alpha \log a^l + (1-\alpha)\log(w-P^1)] \\ &\quad - \pi[\alpha \log a^h + (1-\alpha)\log(w-P^2)] \\ &\quad - (1-\pi)[\alpha \log a^l + (1-\alpha)\log(w-P^2)] \\ &= (1-\alpha)\log \frac{w-P^1}{w-P^2} > (\leq)\, 0 \end{aligned}$$

if and only if $P^1 < (\geq) P^2$. Simply put, it never pays to purchase the higher priced product when two products are indistinguishable *ex-ante*.

written as:

$$
\begin{aligned}
U^f(a^h, a^l, P^*, \pi^*) &= \pi^*[\alpha \log a^h + (1-\alpha)\log(w - P^*)] \\
&\quad + (1-\pi^*)[\alpha \log a^l + (1-\alpha)\log(w - P^*)] \\
&= \pi^* \alpha \log \frac{a^h}{a^l} + \alpha \log a^l + (1-\alpha)\log(w - P^*).
\end{aligned}
\tag{2.2}
$$

A consumer with taste bias $a$ is better off purchasing the Northern product at any time period if and only if $U^f(a^h, a^l, P^*, \pi^*) \geq U^d(a^h, a^l, P, \pi)$ or

$$
\begin{aligned}
\pi^* \alpha \log \frac{a^h}{a^l} + (1-\alpha)\log(w - P^*) &\geq \pi \alpha \log \frac{a^h}{a^l} + (1-\alpha)\log(w - P) \\
(\pi^* - \pi)\alpha \log \frac{a^h}{a^l} &\geq (1-\alpha)\log \frac{(w-P)}{(w-P^*)} \\
\log a &\geq \frac{1}{(\pi^* - \pi)} \frac{(1-\alpha)}{\alpha} \log \frac{(w-P)}{(w-P^*)} \\
&\equiv \log a^*(\pi, \pi^*, P, P^*) \qquad (2.3)
\end{aligned}
$$

if $\pi^* > \pi$. Therefore, if imported Northern products are expected to be of higher quality on average, then, $U^f(a^h, a^l, P^*, \pi^*) > U^d(a^h, a^l, P, \pi)$ for consumers with *taste bias* $a \geq a^* = a^*(\pi, \pi^*, P, P^*, w)$. In particular, $a > 1$ if and only if $P < P^*$.

Hence, the fraction of total population with *taste bias* $a \geq a^*$ demands the imported heterogeneous product. Demand for imports at any time period therefore equals $C^* = C^*(\pi, \pi^*, P, P^*, w)$ where $C^* = [1 - F(a^*)]\,\mathcal{L}$. It can be readily confirmed that $C^*$ is decreasing in $P^*$ and increasing in $P$ and $w$ as long as $\pi^* > \pi$. Meanwhile, the demand for domestic $X$-sector products $C = C(\pi, \pi^*, P, P^*, w)$ is given by $F(a^*)\mathcal{L}$. Note in particular that $C$ is decreasing in $P$, increasing in $P^*$ and *decreasing* in $w$. In other words, the product with an average lower quality will respond to income changes as if it is an inferior good.[9]

[9]See Appendix for a proof. Note also that if imported Northern products are expected to be of lower quality on average (i.e., $\pi^* < \pi$), then, $U^f(a^h, a^l, P^*, \pi^*)$

### 2.2.2. *Production*

Production in the homogeneous goods sector $Y$ exhibits constant returns to scale, perfect competition and follows the production function $Y = \beta L_y$, where $L_y$ denotes the number of workers employed in sector $Y$ and $\beta > 1$. It therefore follows that the competitively determined real wage in the $Y$-sector is equal to $\beta$ as long as positive amounts of $Y$ is produced. Since laborers are perfectly mobile between the $Y$ and the heterogeneous $X$-sector, the Southern economy wide wage rate is fixed once the price of $Y$ is internationally given.

There are a large number of Southern producers ($M$) of the heterogeneous output $X$. Each individual producer is endowed with some amount of firm specific knowledge capital $K \in [\underline{K}, \bar{K}]$. Let $\lambda(\tilde{K})$ be a cumulative distribution function which represents the fraction of $X$-sector producers endowed with $K \leq \tilde{K}$. At any time period, a firm in the $X$-sector may choose to produce either high or low quality type of $X$. Production of high quality type of $X$, ($x^h$), entails a fixed per period cost $c^h$ where $c^h$ is identical for all firms.[10] Once the fixed cost of production is incurred, output of a firm producing high quality products takes the firm specific capital ($K$) and labor ($L^h$) as inputs with $x^h = F^h(K, L^h)$, where $F^h(K, L^h)$ is twice differentiable and exhibits constant returns to scale with diminishing marginal productivity to the inputs. Production of the low quality product requires no fixed cost. Given the firm specific knowledge capital $K$ and $L^l$ amount of labor inputs, output of a firm producing low quality products follows $x^l = F^l(K, L^l)$, where $F^l(K, L^l)$ satisfies all the general properties of $F^h$.

---

$> U^d(a^h, a^l, P, \pi)$ for consumers with *taste bias* $a \leq a^* = a^*(\pi, \pi^*, P, P^*, w)$. It thus follows that the demand for Northern imports is captured by $C^* = F(a^*)\mathcal{L}$. Again, it can be readily confirmed that $C^*$ is decreasing in $P^*$, increasing in $P$ and decreasing in $w$. Meanwhile, the demand for the Southern $X$-sector product, $C = [1 - F(a^*)]\mathcal{L}$, is decreasing in $P$, increasing in $P^*$ and *increasing* in $w$. Note, however, that if $(\pi^* - \pi) > (<)0$ then $(P^* - P) > (<)0$ otherwise *all* Southern consumers will demand the Northern (Southern) product.

[10]One can interpret $c^h$ as the cost incurred in setting up a specific plant or machinery indispensable to the production of the high quality type of $X$.

At the beginning any time period, each firm in the Southern $X$-sector solves a two stage maximization problem. In the first stage, the firm chooses product quality[11] while in the second stage, the amount of labor input to be used in the production of the chosen quality type is determined. Consider first the second stage problem of a firm. The amount of labor input to be hired ($L^i(K,P,w)$) given $K$ amount of knowledge capital, domestic price $P$ and wage rate $w$ for a firm producing quality type $i$ is determined by

$$PF_L^i(K, L^i(K,P,w)) = w \tag{2.4}$$

It follows, therefore, that the production of high quality products yields no less profits than the production of low quality products if and only if $\Pi^h(K,P) \geq \Pi^l(K,P)$ which by virtue of the linear homogeneity of the production functions reduces to

$$\begin{aligned} PF^h(K, L^h(K,P,w)) - wL^h(K,P,w) - c^h \\ \geq PF^l(K, L^l(K,P,w)) - wL^l(K,P,w) \\ P[F_K^h(K, L^h(K,P,w)) - F_K^l(K, L^l(K,P,w))]K \geq c^h. \end{aligned}$$

Let $K^* = K^*(c^h, P, w)$ be the implicit solution to

$$P[F_K^h(K^*, L^h(K^*,P,w)) - F_K^l(K^*, L^l(K^*,P,w))]K^* = c^h. \tag{2.5}$$

We now turn to the determination of $K^*$. By virtue of the constant returns to scale technologies and Equation (2.5), $r^h = PF_K^h$ and $r^l = PF_K^l$ are both constants as the capital–labor ratio's in the production of the two quality types are uniquely determined once $w$ and $P$ are given. Thus, equating $r^hK - c^h$ and $r^lK$ solves for $K^*$ in Equation (2.6) as long as $r^h > r^l$. Hence, the fraction of firms in the $X$-sector which produces the high quality product is just $1 - \lambda(K^*)$. Based on the forgoing analysis, it should be clear that if all firms had identical endowment of the knowledge capital, then the equilibrium self-selection criterion above would imply a corner solution — all Southern firms would choose to produce either the low or the high quality of the product.

[11]Clearly, in the presence of fixed cost of production, it is never optimal for a firm to be incompletely specialized in both quality types.

Before proceeding to analyze the effect of an increase in the domestic price, $(P)$, the wage rate, $(w)$, and the cost of producing the high quality type of the product, $(c^h)$, on the marginal firm's choice of product quality, it is important to pin down the following relationship between the output–capital and labor–capital ratio's of firms engaged in the production of either the high or the low quality type of the heterogeneous good. In particular, if $\frac{L^h}{K} > \frac{L^l}{K}$ and $r^h > r^l$, then $\frac{x^h}{K} > \frac{x^l}{K}$.[12] Consider then the following proposition:

**Proposition 1.**

1. *The fraction of low quality firms,* $\lambda(K^*)$ *is decreasing in* $P$ *if and only if* $\frac{L^h}{K} > \frac{L^l}{K}$.
2. $\lambda(K^*)$ *is increasing in* $w$ *if and only if* $\frac{L^h}{K} > \frac{L^l}{K}$.
3. $\lambda(K_t^*)$ *is increasing in* $c^h$.

The reason behind the response of the *marginal* firm (with capital endowment $K^*$) to changes in $P$, $w$ and $c^h$ is as follows: As $P$ rises, profits for firms producing either quality type rises. If, however, the labor–capital and hence output–capital ratio of high quality firms is higher than low quality ones, it follows that profits of the former increase proportionately more than the latter. The resulting shift in $K^*$ in favor of high quality production increases the fraction of firms producing high quality products as well. Upon an increase in $w$, *ceteris paribus*, profits of firms producing both quality types decrease. However, if the labor–capital and hence the output–capital ratio in the production of the high quality type is higher than the corresponding ratio for the low quality type, then, the decline in profit is relatively higher if the marginal firm produces the high quality type. The latter in turn implies that the number of firms producing the low quality type increases. Finally, an increase in the cost of producing the high quality type automatically reduces the marginal firm's profit leading to a higher number of firms producing the low quality type.

[12] A derivation of this result is provided after the proof for proposition 1 in the Appendix.

To characterize the supply side of the market for any given values of $\pi$, $\pi^*$, $w$, and $c^h$, denote $X^i = X^i(\pi, \pi^*, P, P^*, w, c^h)$ as the total supply of the $i$th quality type $i = h, l$. Aggregate supply of the $X$-sector output, at given time period, is then given by $X = X^h + X^l$, where $X^l = M \int_{\underline{K}}^{K^*} F^l(K, L^l(K, P, w)) d\lambda(K)$ and $X^h = M \int_{K^*}^{\bar{K}} F^h(K, L^h(K, P, w)) d\lambda(K)$. In order to determine the response of aggregate $X$-sector output to changes in $P$, $w$ and $c^h$ we need to consider not only the response of the marginal firm to changes in these parameters but also the response of the intra-marginal firms producing both quality types. Suppose, for instance, that the labor–capital (and hence the output–capital) ratio is relatively higher for high quality firms. In this case an increase in $P$ would not only increase the number of firms producing high quality but would also increase output of the intra-marginal firms of both quality types. Thus, even though the supply of $X$ unambiguously rises, the effect on the *proportion* of high quality products is ambiguous.

The response of $X$ to an increase in $w$ can similarly be ascertained. First, an increase in the wage rate reduces profits for intra-marginal producers of both quality types and induces producers to reduce labor employment. This leads to a fall in $X$. Second, from proposition (1), if $\frac{L^h}{K^*} > \frac{L^l}{K^*}$ then $K^*$ rises in response to an increase in $w$, increasing the number of firms engaged in the production of the low quality type. Thus, even though the output–capital ratio for the high quality type is relatively higher, the labor–capital ratio is also higher, leading to a fall in profit for the marginal firm. As a result, output of the marginal producer declines and the second effect reinforces the first, leading to a decline in aggregate supply of the heterogeneous good. An increase in $c^h$ may not, however, reduce aggregate supply of $X$. The intuition here is that even though profits of the high quality intra-marginal producers unambiguously falls, the marginal producer shifts to the production of the low quality thereby increasing the output of the latter. Consequently, aggregate output may still rise. If, however, the labor–capital (and hence the output–capital) ratio for the low quality type is relatively lower for the marginal producer then the increase in output of the low quality type is insufficient to counter the decline of the high quality type and aggregate supply falls. We therefore have the following proposition:

**Proposition 2.**

1. *$X$ is strictly increasing in $P$.*
2. *$X$ is decreasing in $w$ if $\frac{L^h}{K^*} > \frac{L^l}{K^*}$.*
3. *$X$ is decreasing in $c^h$ if and only if $\frac{L^h}{K^*} > \frac{L^l}{K^*}$.*

### 2.2.3. *Determination of equilibrium southern price and quality*

We are now in a position to complete the specification of the model by combining the consumption and production side of the Southern economy elaborated above to determine the equilibrium price, the quantity as well as the quality of the Southern heterogeneous good. Recall that the small open economy in question takes as given by the price of the Northern heterogeneous good $P^*$ as well as $\pi^*$. Assuming $\pi < \pi^*$, the output market for the Southern good clears whenever $X(P, P^*, w, M) = C(P, P^*, \pi, \pi^*, w, \mathcal{L})$, or

$$M \int_{\underline{K}}^{K^*} F^l(K, L^l(K, P, w))d\lambda(K)$$

$$+ M \int_{K^*}^{\bar{K}} F^h(K, L^h(K, P, w))d\lambda(K) = F(a^*)\mathcal{L} \qquad (2.6)$$

Denoting $|\eta_w^C|$ and $|\eta_w^X|$ respectively as the absolute value of the elasticity of demand and supply of the heterogeneous $X$-sector good with respect to the wage rate, we have

**Proposition 3.**

1. *$P$ and $X$ are increasing in $P^*$ and $(\pi - \pi^*)$.*
2. *If $\pi < \pi^*$, an increase in $w$ leads to a decrease in $P$, a reduction in $X$ and an increase in imports if and only if $|\eta_w^C| > |\eta_w^X|$.*

3. *If* $\pi < \pi^*$, *then an increase in* $c^h$ *increases* $P$, *reduces* $X$ *and increases imports if and only if* $\frac{x^h}{K^*} > \frac{x^l}{K^*}$.

Proposition 3 shows the possible impact of perception differences on the determination of equilibrium price and the quantity of the Southern heterogeneous good. Since Southern and Northern products are substitutes, an increase in either $P^*$ or a relative improvement in the perceived quality of the Southern product raises the demand for the domestically produced heterogeneous product. Perhaps more interesting is the effect of an increase in $w$ or the income of Southern consumers through an increase in wages, on the equilibrium price and quantity of the Southern heterogeneous good. In particular, when $\pi < \pi^*$, an increase in $w$ has the effect of shifting consumers' demand in favor of Northern imports. Meanwhile, since an increase in wages exerts downward pressure on the production of the Southern heterogeneous good. The combined result is a reduction in both the quantity and the price of $X$ if the former effect dominates. Finally, an increase in $c^h$ may lead to a decline in $X$ if the increase in output of the low quality type is insufficient to overweigh the decline in output of the high quality type. The ensuing reduction in supply then leads to an increase in $P$.

Once the domestic price $P$ is determined, the threshold level of knowledge capital which divides domestic firms in the $X$-sector into high and low quality firms can be determined as well by Equation (2.6). Denote the fraction of high quality domestically produced heterogeneous product at any time period as $\mu$, we have

$$\mu = \frac{X^h}{X} \tag{2.7}$$

Define the share of labor in the total value of output for the $i$th quality type, $i = h, l$; as $\theta_L^i$ and the elasticity of labor demand with respect to $P_t$ as $\eta_P^i$ for quality type $i$. We have, then, under the conditions (i) $\theta_L^h \eta_P^h > \theta_L^l \eta_P^l$ and (ii) $\frac{x^h}{K^*} > \frac{x^l}{K^*}$, the following proposition:

**Proposition 4.**

1. $\mu$ *is increasing in* $P^*$ *and* $(\pi - \pi^*)$.

2. *If $\pi < \pi^*$, an increase in $w$ leads to a reduction in $\mu$ if and only if the income elasticity of demand is strictly higher than the elasticity of $X$ with respect to $w$.*
3. *$\mu$ is decreasing in $c^h$.*

To trace out the dependence of $\mu$ on the foreign price, $P^*$, and the relative quality perceptions, $(\pi^* - \pi)$, note from Equation (2.7) that the Southern domestic price $P$ always adjusts the market for the Southern $X$-sector output as soon as the Northern price $P^*$ and $\pi^*$ and $\pi$ are given. In particular, from proposition 1, an increase in $P^*$ shifts Southern domestic demand in favor of the $X$-sector good. The attendant increase in $P$ affects the proportion of high quality output $\mu$ depending on the relative size of the following effects: (i) the output response of intra-marginal Southern firms engaged in the production of the two quality types and (ii) the quality choice of the marginal firm, which determines in turn the number of firms engaged in the production of each quality type. Consider now the condition $\theta_L^h \eta_P^h > \theta_L^l \eta_P^l$. Under this condition, an increase in the price of the Southern heterogeneous good leads to a relatively higher demand for labor by the intra-marginal producers of the high quality type, and thus, an increase in the proportion of high quality type of the product in equilibrium. Further, if $\frac{x^h}{K^*} > \frac{x^l}{K^*}$ then the marginal producer finds it relatively more profitable to produce the high quality type leading to an increase in $K^*$ and therefore, the number of producers in the production of the high quality type. The two effects thus reinforce each other to guarantee an increase in $\mu$ in response to an increase in $P$.

Turning now to the effect of an increase in $(\pi - \pi^*)$ on domestic quality, a decline in $\pi^*$ causes demand to shift away from imports and leads to an increase in $P$. It follows, therefore, that the attendant variation in $\mu$ depends once again on the interaction of the two effects above. An increase in $w$, on the other hand, shifts demand away from the domestically produced $X$-sector product if the latter is deemed to be an inferior good. From proposition 3, there will be an excess supply of $X$ if $|\eta_w^C| > |\eta_w^X|$. The result is thus a reduction in $P$ as well as the proportion of high quality type of the product. An increase in

$c^h$ leads to an unambiguous decline in $\mu$ since the number of firms producing the high quality type declines.

### 2.2.4. *Southern labor market equilibrium*

Before ending this section we need to depict the labor market equilibrium and the balance of trade. In particular, we are interested in the effect of changes in $P^*$, $w$ and $(\pi^* - \pi)$ on the output of the exported good and hence on the volume of trade. Consider therefore the following material balance equation:

$$M \int_{\underline{K}}^{K^*} L^l(K, P, w) d\lambda(K) + M \int_{K^*}^{\bar{K}} L^h(K, P, w) d\lambda(K) + L_y = \mathcal{L} \tag{2.8}$$

First, an increase in $P^*$ leads to an increase in $P$ and an increase in $X$. Therefore, labor flows out of the Southern export sector into the $X$-sector leading to a decline in exports and imports. An increase in $\pi^* - \pi$ leads to a decline in $P$ and $X$ and an inflow of labor into the export sector increasing its output. An increase in $w$ leads to a decline in $P$ and $X$ if $(\pi^* - \pi) > 0$. In this case imports increase, as does exports since a decline in production of $X$ entails an outflow of labor from the $X$-sector into the $Y$-sector.

### 2.2.5. *Balance of trade*

Consider now the equilibrium in the balance of trade under the situation $\pi^* > \pi$.

$$\begin{aligned} P^*[1 - F(a^*)]\mathcal{L} + c^h M[1 - \lambda(K^*)] \\ = wL_y - F(a^*)\mathcal{L}(w - P) - [1 - F(a^*)]\mathcal{L}(w - P^*) \\ -M \int_{\underline{K}}^{K^*} (P_t x^l - wL^l) d\lambda(K) \\ -M \int_{K^*}^{\bar{K}} (Px^h - wL^h - c^h) d\lambda(K) \end{aligned}$$

The left-hand side of the above equation is the value of imports from the North, while the right-hand side is the value of Southern exports. Using the goods and labor market equilibrium conditions (Equations (2.7) and (2.9)) the above equation reduces to

$$P^*[1 - F(a^*)]\mathcal{L} + Mc^h[1 - \lambda(K^*)] = 0.$$

Clearly, relative perceptions regarding the Northern *vis-à-vis* the Southern heterogeneous good determines the volume of trade through the dependence of $P$, $K^*$ and $a^*$ on $\pi^*$ and $\pi$.

## 2.3. Self-Fulfilling Quality Perceptions

Consider any time period $t$. The Southern small open economy in question takes the international price of imports $P_t^*$ as well as $\pi_t^*$ as given with $P_t^* = P_{t+i}^* = P^*$, $i = 1, 2, \ldots$, and $\pi_t^* = \pi_{t+i}^* = \pi^*$, $i = 1, 2, \ldots,$. The interpretation here is standard, changes in the Southern demand for the imported product has no influence on the internationally determined $P^*$ and $\pi^*$. For the Southern heterogeneous product, however, propositions 1 through 4 show that the quality composition and prices of the Southern heterogeneous product interact. In addition, the quality composition of Southern products also interact with consumers' perception about product quality, $\pi_t$. Recall, from Equation (2.8) that

$$\mu_t = \phi(\pi_t, \pi^*, P_t^*) \equiv \frac{X_t^h(\pi_t, \pi^*, P_t^*)}{X_t(\pi_t, \pi^*, P_t^*)}.$$

Hence, a subjective perception $\tilde{\pi}$ confirms itself if and only if $(\tilde{\pi}, \pi^*, P^*) = \tilde{\pi}$. In other words, a self-fulfilling quality perception $\tilde{\pi}$ indeed coincides with the actual probability of purchasing a high quality Southern heterogeneous product given $\tilde{\pi}$. Consider therefore two possible scenarios where: (i) the relationship between $\phi(\pi_t)$ and $\pi_t$ as obtained in proposition 5 is monotonically increasing when $\mu_t$ is increasing in $\pi_t$ subject to the conditions that $\theta_L^h \eta_P^h > \theta_L^l \eta_P^l$ and $\frac{x^h}{K^*} > \frac{x^l}{K^*}$ and (ii) the relationship between $\phi(\pi_t)$ and $\pi_t$ as obtained in proposition 5 is monotonically decreasing when $\mu_t$ is decreasing in $\pi_t$ subject to the conditions that $\theta_L^h \eta_P^h < \theta_L^l \eta_P^l$ and $(\frac{\tilde{x}^h}{\tilde{K}^*} < \frac{\tilde{x}^l}{\tilde{K}^*})$.

For case (i), since $\phi(\pi_t)$ is monotonically increasing in $y_t$, there can be, in general, a multiple number of self-fulfilling equilibria. For instance, if consumers have low expectations of the average quality of Southern products, the market clearing price for Southern products are low. The lack of incentives for Southern firms to produce high quality products accordingly impinge on the actual fraction of Southern firms producing the high quality product. It follows that a pessimistic belief fulfills itself. Similarly, optimistic beliefs depicts another possible steady state outcome with a high and sustainable average quality of the Southern product.

The discussion above highlights the existence of quality-traps. In this context, a natural question arises as to whether the decentralized equilibrium is efficient or can national welfare be improved through a change in $\pi$. To answer this question, denote $\mathcal{W}$ as the gross national income of the economy and let a $\sim$ denote equilibrium values of all the endogenous variables. Then,

$$\mathcal{W} = \tilde{P}M\int_{\underline{K}}^{\tilde{K}^*}\tilde{x}^l d\lambda(K) + \tilde{P}M\int_{\tilde{K}^*}^{\bar{K}}(\tilde{x}^h - \frac{c^h}{\tilde{P}})d\lambda(K) + \tilde{w}\tilde{L}_Y$$
$$= \tilde{P}\tilde{X}^l + \tilde{P}\tilde{X}^h + \tilde{w}\tilde{L}_Y - M[1-\lambda(\tilde{K}^*)]c^h \tag{2.9}$$

Differentiating with respect to $\pi$ and utilizing the labor market equilibrium condition, (Equation (2.9)), we have

$$\frac{\partial\mathcal{W}}{\partial\pi} = (\tilde{X}^l + \tilde{X}^h)\frac{\partial\tilde{P}}{\partial\pi} + M\lambda'(\tilde{K}^*)(\tilde{P}\tilde{x}^l - (\tilde{P}\tilde{x}^h - c^h))\frac{\partial\tilde{K}^*}{\partial\pi}$$
$$= \Big[(\tilde{X}^l + \tilde{X}^h) + M\lambda'(\tilde{K}^*)\{(\tilde{P}\tilde{x}^l - r^l\tilde{K}^*)$$
$$-(\tilde{P}\tilde{x}^h - r^h\tilde{K}^*)\}\frac{\partial\tilde{K}^*}{\partial\tilde{P}}\Big]\frac{\partial\tilde{P}}{\partial\pi}$$
$$= \Bigg[(\tilde{X}^l + \tilde{X}^h) + \frac{M\lambda'(\tilde{K}^*)(\tilde{K}^*)^2\tilde{w}}{(r^h - r^l)}$$
$$\times\left(\frac{\tilde{L}^h}{\tilde{K}^*} - \frac{\tilde{L}^l}{\tilde{K}^*}\right)\left(\frac{\tilde{x}^h}{\tilde{K}^*} - \frac{\tilde{x}^l}{\tilde{K}^*}\right)\Bigg]\frac{\partial\tilde{P}}{\partial\pi}$$

First note that the potential welfare gain from an increase in $\pi$ is $(\tilde{X}^l + \tilde{X}^h)\frac{\partial\tilde{P}}{\partial\pi}$, while the potential welfare loss is $M\lambda'(\tilde{K}^*)(\tilde{P}\tilde{x}^l - (\tilde{P}\tilde{x}^h - c^h))\frac{\partial\tilde{K}^*}{\partial\pi}$. Since producers only account for the difference $(r^h\tilde{K}^* - c^h) - r^l\tilde{K}^*$ in their quality choice, the social gain from having an additional high quality firm is $\tilde{P}\tilde{x}^h - c^h$, while the social loss from having one more low quality firm is $\tilde{P}\tilde{x}^l$. In particular, if $\frac{\tilde{L}^h}{\tilde{K}^*} > \frac{\tilde{L}^l}{\tilde{K}^*}$, then Southern national income is increasing in $\pi$ and any policy interventions which increases $\mu$ in period $t$ can improve both $\pi$ and $\mathcal{W}$ from period $t+1$ onwards.

For case (ii) — when $\mu$ is monotonically decreasing in $\pi$, any government intervention to increase $\pi$ results in a lower $\mu$, and therefore $\mathcal{W}$. In this case, any intervention to increase $\pi$ results in a lower $\mu$.[13]

## 2.4. Commercial Policies

As noted in the previous section, temporary intervention may have a permanent impact on the quality of the domestically produced heterogeneous good. Here, we focus on four such interventions: (i) a tariff on the imported heterogeneous good, (ii) quota on imports, (iii) a subsidy to the domestically produced heterogeneous good and (iv) an export subsidy. Our aim is to delineate the mechanism through which such interventions may lead to improvements in $\mu_t$ and $\mathcal{W}$. In what follows we shall focus only on the case where $\pi_t < \pi_t^*$.

### 2.4.1. *Tariff on the imported heterogeneous good*

An *ad valorem* tariff, $\tau$, imposed on the imported good raises the price of imports to $P_t^*(1+\tau)$. From proposition 1, an increase in the price of imports leads the marginal consumer to substitute away from Northern imports towards the Southern heterogeneous good. This is the substitution effect. Now two cases can arise: (i) the tariff revenue is redistributed back to the consumers or (ii) the government appropriates the revenue. In the first instance, tariff revenue equals $P_t^*\tau[1 - F(a^*t)]\mathcal{L}$, therefore, each consumer gets an amount $P_t^*\tau[1 - F(a_t^*)]$. This increase in income leads the marginal

[13]Note that this mechanism through which national income improvements in our model occur is distinct from that of Bond (1984) where labeling of inferior quality foreign and superior quality domestic products leads to welfare improvement for the home country as domestic products can then be sold at a higher price.

consumer to shift demand toward the Northern imported good, since domestic goods are deemed inferior. This is the income effect. For the marginal consumer, however, it can be verified that the substitution effect overweighs the income effect, leading to an increase in $C_t$ and hence $P_t$. In the case where the government appropriates the tariff revenue, the income effect is absent and as a result, demand for the Southern heterogeneous good and hence its price rises unambiguously.

An increase in $P_t$ triggers two effects on the average quality of the Southern heterogeneous good. While both high and low quality firms find it profitable to increase output, high quality firms increase output relatively more if $\theta^h_L\eta^h_P > \theta^l_L\eta^l_P$. In addition, if $\frac{x^h_t}{K^*_t} > \frac{x^l_t}{K^*_t}$, then the marginal firm shifts to the production of the high quality product thereby increasing the number of firms engaged in the production of the latter in equilibrium. As a consequence, the second effect reinforces the first entailing an increase in the proportion of high quality type of the product. Note that national income increases when $\mu_t$ responds positively to an increase in $P_t$, irrespective of whether the tariff revenue is redistributed or appropriated by the domestic government. In the case where the tariff revenue is redistributed the result is similar to that derived for Equation (2.9). When tariff revenue is appropriated, $\mathcal{W}$ is written as:

$$\mathcal{W} = P_tX^l_t + P_tX^h_t + w_tL_Y - M[1-\lambda(K^*_t)]c^h + P^*_t\tau[1-F(a^*_t)]\mathcal{L},$$

where the last term is the tariff revenue. Differentiating with respect to $\tau$, we have

$$\frac{d\mathcal{W}}{d\tau} = \left\{\left[X_t + \frac{M\lambda'(K^*_t)(K^*_t)^2w_t}{(r^h-r^l)}\left(\frac{L^h_t}{K^*_t} - \frac{L^l_t}{K^*_t}\right)\left(\frac{x^h_t}{K^*_t} - \frac{x^l_t}{K^*_t}\right)\right]\right.$$
$$\left.\times\frac{\partial P_t}{\partial \pi_t}\frac{\partial \mu_t}{\partial P_t} - P^*_t\tau f(a)\frac{\partial a^*_t}{\partial P_t}\mathcal{L}\right\}\frac{\partial P_t}{\partial \tau} + P^*_tC^*_t.$$

The right-hand side of he above expression is positive if (i) $\theta^h_L\eta^h_P > \theta^l_L\eta^l_P$ and if (ii) $\frac{x^h_t}{K^*_t} > \frac{x^l_t}{K^*_t}$.

However, if (i) $\theta^h_L\eta^h_P < \theta^l_L\eta^l_P$ and if (ii) $\frac{x^h_t}{K^*_t} < \frac{x^l_t}{K^*_t}$, then an increase in $P_t$ engenders a lower proportion of high quality type in equilibrium, while unambiguously worsening welfare when tariff revenue is redistributed. In the event where the tariff revenue is appropriated, welfare would worsen provided the increase in tariff revenue is "small" such that the income loss engendered by a decrease in the proportion of high quality type of the product overweighs the income gain from the tariff revenue. Sufficient conditions for such an event to occur are that the own price elasticity of demand for the Southern heterogeneous good is small and that the difference in $P_t^*$ and $P_t$ is small. We have, therefore, the following proposition:

**Proposition 5.**

1. *Imposition of a tariff on the imported heterogeneous good increases* $\mu_t$ *if* (i) $\theta_L^h \eta_P^h > \theta_L^l \eta_P^l$ *and* (ii) $\frac{x_t^h}{K_t^*} > \frac{x_t^l}{K_t^*}$.
2. *When tariff revenue is either redistributed or appropriated by the government,* $\mathcal{W}$ *increases if* $\theta_L^h \eta_P^h > \theta_L^l \eta_P^l$ *and if* $\frac{x_t^h}{K_t^*} > \frac{x_t^l}{K_t^*}$. *If* $\theta_L^h \eta_P^h < \theta_L^l \eta_P^l$ *and if* $\frac{x_t^h}{K_t^*} < \frac{x_t^l}{K_t^*}$, *then* $\mathcal{W}$ (i) *decreases when tariff revenue is redistributed and* (ii) *is ambiguous when tariff revenue is appropriated.*

### 2.4.2. *Quota*

Consider now the case where a quota $\mathcal{Q}$, is imposed on Northern imports and for simplicity, assume that the quota rent accrues to foreign producers. In this case, the price of imports $\tilde{P}_t^*$ is no longer given to domestic consumers, but endogenously determined along with $P_t$. The market clearing equations for the domestically produced heterogeneous good and imports are summarized by

$$C_t(P_t, \tilde{P}_t^*, \pi_t, \pi_t^*, w_t) = X_t(P_t, w_t, c^h), \tag{2.10}$$

$$C_t^*(P_t, \tilde{P}_t^*, \pi_t, \pi_t^*) = \mathcal{Q}, \tag{2.11}$$

which can be simultaneously solved to yield the equilibrium values of $P_t$ and $P_t^*$. First, the imposition of a quota (a reduction in $\mathcal{Q}$) increases the price of Northern imports $(P_t^*)$ through a reduction in its supply. Since Northern imports and the Southern heterogeneous good are substitutes, $P_t$ rises as well. The increase in $P_t$, again, leads to an increase in $\mu_t$ and $\mathcal{W}$ if (i) $\theta_L^h \eta_P^h > \theta_L^l \eta_P^l$ and if (ii) $\frac{x_t^h}{K_t^*} > \frac{x_t^l}{K_t^*}$. Therefore, the welfare effects of a quota is similar to that of a tariff. It should be noted that our focus on a small open economy precludes the response of $\pi^*$ to changes in $P_t^*$.[14] We have then the following proposition:

**Proposition 6.** *A quota on imports increases $P_t^*$ and increases $\mu_t$ and $\mathcal{W}$ if,* (i) $\theta_L^h \eta_P^h > \theta_L^l \eta_P^l$ *and if* (ii) $\frac{x_t^h}{K_t^*} > \frac{x_t^l}{K_t^*}$.

Our results regarding the effect of tariff and quota on Northern imports of quality differentiated products conforms closely to that observed for the US auto industry where perceptions about product quality render competing autos imperfect substitutes of one another *ex-ante*. For example, car imports from Japan has been subject to a quota restraint since 1981, while compact trucks have faced an *ad-valorem* tariff of 25% since 1980. The effect of quotas on the quality of US made cars is ambiguous (Nelson, 1996), while US made trucks show improvements in quality in response to the tariff.[15] However, as Feenstra (1988) notes, the quality of Japanese cars has risen in response to the quota which, in terms of our model, translates into an increase in $\pi_t^*$. Therefore, consumers' relative perception of Japanese *vis-à-vis* US cars ($\pi_t^* - \pi_t$) might have also changed in favor of the former thereby impinging on the incentive of US producers to produce higher quality cars.

[14] The interested reader is referred to Basu and Chau (1998) for a two country model of intra-industry trade in quality products that endogenizes the determination of $\pi_t^*$. See also Chisik (2003) for impact of differing perceptions of the *country-of-origin* labels on export performance and national welfare.

[15] Nelson (1996) notes that even though the quality of Chrysler cars improved during the period, Ford and GM cars show no clear trend. A word of caution should be used in applying our analysis to the auto industry. First, brand names matter in addition to *country-of-origin* labels and secondly, the market structure for autos is oligopolistic rather than a perfect competitive one, even though the assumption of perfect competition is the one commonly used (see Feenstra, 1988).

### 2.4.3. *Subsidy to the Southern heterogeneous good*

We shall assume that the subsidy to producers of the Southern heterogeneous good is raised through a lump-sum tax $\bar{T}$ on the consumers. The direct effect of the subsidy is to raise the price received by $X$-sector producers to $P_t(1+s)$. This leads to both the high and the low quality producers increasing their outputs, resulting in an increase in $X_t$. As before, the proportion of high quality type in equilibrium and national income increases if (i) $\theta_L^h \eta_s^h > \theta_L^l \eta_s^l$ and (ii) $\frac{x_t^h}{K_t^*} > \frac{x_t^l}{K_t^*}$, where $\eta_s^i$ is the elasticity of output of quality type $i = h, l$ with respect to the subsidy rate. The indirect effect of an increase in $s$ can be decomposed in two effects. First, note that since the subsidy is financed through a lump-sum tax on consumers and since $\pi_t < \pi_t^*$, the decrease in consumers' income translates into an increased demand for $X_t$. Therefore, whether $P_t$ increases or not, depends on whether the elasticity of demand with respect to the subsidy rate, $\eta_s^C$, is greater (less) than the elasticity of output with respect to the subsidy rate $\eta_s^X$. The price of the domestically produced heterogeneous good increases if and only if $\eta_s^C > \eta_s^X$. Secondly, the increase in $P_t$ would again increase $\mu_t$ if (i) $\theta_L^h \eta_P^h > \theta_L^l \eta_P^l$ and (ii) $\frac{x_t^h}{K_t^*} > \frac{x_t^l}{K_t^*}$. The net effect on $\mu_t$ and $\mathcal{W}$ depends, therefore, on the interaction of the direct and the indirect effects. Proposition 7 summarizes the cases that may arise.

**Proposition 7.**

1. *If $\eta_s^C > \eta_s^X$, then an increase in the subsidy rate to producers in the $X$-sector leads to an increase in $\mu_t$ and $\mathcal{W}$ if* (i) $\theta_L^h \eta_s^h > \theta_L^l \eta_s^l$, (ii) $\theta_L^h \eta_P^h > \theta_L^l \eta_P^l$ *and* (iii) $\frac{x_t^h}{K_t^*} > \frac{x_t^l}{K_t^*}$.
2. *If $\eta_s^C < \eta_s^X$, then an increase in the subsidy rate to producers in the $X$-sector has an ambiguous effect on $\mu_t$ and $\mathcal{W}$.*

#### 2.4.3.1. *Subsidy to high quality producers*

If the government were able to correctly identify the high quality producers and provide an *ad valorem* production subsidy $\delta$, then the direct effect of the subsidy is to increase the production of $X_t$.

Also, $X_t^h$ increases relative to $X_t^l$, thereby increasing $\mu_t$. However, if the subsidy is financed through a lump-sum tax on the consumers, then $P_t$ increases if and only if $\eta_\delta^C > \eta_\delta^X$. The increase in $P_t$ will again trigger an indirect effect on $\mu_t$. If $P_t$ increases then the indirect effect reinforces the direct effect to engender an increase in $\mu_t$ and $\mathcal{W}$. However, if $\eta_\delta^C < \eta_\delta^X$, then the direct and the indirect effects conflict, rendering the effect of an increase in $\delta$ on $\mu_t$ and $\mathcal{W}$ ambiguous. Note that $\mu_t$ can increase even when (i) $\theta_L^h \eta_P^h < \theta_L^l \eta_P^l$ and (ii) $\frac{x_t^h}{K_t^*} < \frac{x_t^l}{K_t^*}$, provided $P_t$ declines.

### 2.4.4. *Subsidy to the southern export sector*

An *ad valorem* subsidy, $\gamma$, to the export sector leads to an increase in the wage rate. If, $\pi_t < \pi_t^*$, then an increase in the wage rate leads consumers to shift to imports, thereby leading to a decline in the demand for the Southern heterogeneous good (proposition 1). However, if the subsidy is again raised through a lump-sum tax on consumers, the ensuing decline in income leads to an increase in demand for the Southern heterogeneous good. The net effect on demand depends then on the elasticity of the $Y$-sector output with respect to the subsidy rate and the relative levels of employment across the two sectors ($X$ and $Y$) of the economy. Therefore, necessary and sufficient condition for a decline in demand for the Southern heterogeneous good is $\eta_\gamma^Y < \frac{L_{X_t}}{L_{y_t}}$, where $\eta_\gamma^Y$ is the elasticity of the $Y$-sector output with respect to the subsidy rate and $L_{X_t}$ is number of laborers employed in the production of the Southern heterogeneous good at time $t$. *Ceteris paribus*, the lower the proportion of labor employed in the $Y$-sector, the higher is the possibility that an increase in the subsidy rate to the $Y$-sector financed through a lump-sum tax on consumers will lead to a decline in demand for the Southern heterogeneous good. The latter effect would, in turn, lead to a decline in $P_t$ and hence in $\mu_t$ and $\mathcal{W}$ if (i) $\theta_L^h \eta_P^h > \theta_L^l \eta_P^l$ and (ii) $\frac{x_t^h}{K_t^*} > \frac{x_t^l}{K_t^*}$. Thus, subsidization of the $Y$-sector leads to the incidence of the *Dutch Disease* — not only does $X_t$ decline but $\mu_t$ and $\mathcal{W}$ declines as well.

**Proposition 8.**

1. *If* $\eta_{\gamma}^{Y} < \frac{L_{X_t}}{L_{y_t}}$ *and if* (i) $\theta_{L}^{h}\eta_{P}^{h} > \theta_{L}^{l}\eta_{P}^{l}$ *and* (ii) $\frac{x_t^h}{K_t^*} > \frac{x_t^l}{K_t^*}$, *then an increase in the subsidy rate to the* $Y$*-sector financed through a lump-sum tax on consumers leads to a decrease in* $P_t$, $X_t$, $\mu_t$, *and* $\mathcal{W}$.
2. *If* $\eta_{\gamma}^{Y} < \frac{L_{X_t}}{L_{y_t}}$ *and if* (i) $\theta_{L}^{h}\eta_{P}^{h} < \theta_{L}^{l}\eta_{P}^{l}$ *and* (ii) $\frac{x_t^h}{K_t^*} < \frac{x_t^l}{K_t^*}$, *then an increase in the subsidy rate to the* $Y$*-sector financed through a lump-sum tax on consumers leads to an increase in* $P_t$, $X_t$, $\mu_t$ *and* $\mathcal{W}$.

Apart from relating the incidence of the *Dutch Disease*, affecting the quality of the import-competing good, to the relative levels of employment in the two sectors of the economy, proposition 8 has interesting policy implications. In South Korea and Taiwan, during the early part of industrialization (1950–1970), multiple exchange rates and import controls were used to protect the import-competing sector, while the export sector was subsidized (Hughes, 1988). As our analysis points out, the protection of the import-competing sector in the face of export subsidization is a logical policy — import controls prevent demand from shifting in favor of better quality imports as income increases in response to the export subsidy.

## 2.5. Conclusion

In this chapter, we have shown how consumers' perception of product quality impinge on firms' incentive to produce the high quality product thereby leading to the prevalence of quality-traps. Our analysis provides a theory based on statistical discrimination of quality products that shows the existence of quality-traps engendered by rational expectations equilibria. Further, in the light of such quality-traps, our theory helps explain when infant import-competing industries are likely to show improvements in product quality in response to protection. As it turns out, when domestic products are perceived to be of inferior average quality, sufficient conditions for quality improvements of infant industries are that

(i) labor's share in the total value of output of the high quality type (ii) the elasticity of labor demand in response to the domestic price for the high quality type and (iii) the output–capital ratio of the marginal producer in the production of the high quality type of the product has to be relatively higher than their counterparts in the production of the low quality type. Finally, we highlight the role of the marginal consumer and producer in determining the volume of trade and, in particular, point out that if the domestic good is perceived to be of lower quality, then it is deemed as an inferior good in consumption and as such, the import-competing sector is susceptible to the *Dutch Disease*.

## References

Amiti, M and A Khandelwal (2013) Import competition and quality upgrading, *Review of Economics and Statistics* 95, 476–490.

Armington, PS (1969) A theory of demand for products distinguished by place of production, *IMF Staff Papers* 16, 159–178.

Bagwell, K and R Staiger (1989) The role of export subsidies when product quality is unknown, *Journal of International Economics* 27, 69–89.

Basu, AK and NH Chau (1998) Asymmetric country-of-origin effects on intra-industry trade and international quality race, *Review of Development Economics* 2, 140–166.

Bond, EW (1984) International trade with uncertain product quality, *Southern Economic Journal* 51, 196–207.

Chiang, S-C and RT Masson (1988) Domestic industrial structure and export quality, *International Economic Review* 29, 261–269.

Chisik, R (2003) Export industry policy and reputational comparative advantage, *Journal of International Economics* 59, 423–451.

Creane, A (1999) Trade policy with risky investment in quality, *Canadian Journal of Economics* 32, 39–54.

Das, SP and S Donnenfeld (1987) Trade policy and its impact on quality of imports: A welfare analysis, *Journal of International Economics* 23, 77–95.

Donnenfeld, S (1986) Intra-industry trade and imperfect information about product quality, *European Economic Review* 1986, 401–417.

Erika, N (2006) *The Baltimore Sun*, Music Fades for Russian Pianos, May 19 http://articles. baltimoresun.com/2006–05–19/news/0605190167_1_lira-piano-factory.

Feenstra, RC (1988) Quality change under trade restraints in Japanese autos, *Quarterly Journal of Economics* 103, 131–146.

Fernandes, AM and C Paunov (2013) Does trade stimulate product quality upgrading? *Canadian Journal of Economics* 46, 1332–1364.

Fleury, A (1995) Quality and productivity in the competitive strategies of Brazilian industrial enterprises, *World Development* 23, 73–85.

Grossman, GM and H Horn (1988) Infant industry protection reconsidered: The case of informational barriers to entry, *Quarterly Journal of Economics* 103, 767–787.

Hughes, H (Ed.) (1988) *Achieving Industrialization in East Asia*, Cambridge: Cambridge University Press.

Jacobsson, S (1993) The length of the infant industry period: Evidence from the engineering industry in South Korea, *World Development* 21, 407–419.

Krishna, K (1987) Tariffs versus quotas with endogenous quality, *Journal of International Economics* 23, 97–122.

Krugman, P (1987) The narrow moving band, the dutch disease, and the competitive consequences of Mrs. Thatcher, *Journal of Development Economics* 27, 41–55.

Luzio, E and S Greenstein (1995) Measuring the performance of a protected infant industry: The case of brazilian microcomputers, *Review of Economics and Statistics* 77, 622–633.

Mayer, W (1984) The infant export industry argument, *Canadian Journal of Economics* 16, 249–269.

Nelson, D (1996) The Political Economy of U.S. Automobile Protection. In *The Political Economy of American Trade Policy*. K Anne (Ed.). Chicago: The University of Chicago Press.

Nelson, P (1970) Information and consumer behavior, *Journal of Political Economy* 78, 311–329.

The Guardian (2014) End of the road for the Ambassador as India carmaker halts production, May 25 http://www.theguardian.com/world/2014/may/25/india-ambassador-car-hindustan-motors-production.

van Wijnbergen, S (1984) The 'Dutch Disease': A disease after all? *The Economic Journal* 94, 41–55.

## Appendix

### 2.A1. Consumer Preferences and Market Segmentation

Aggregate demand for the Southern heterogeneous product is

$$\begin{aligned} C &= F(a^*)\mathcal{L}, \qquad \pi^* > \pi;\ \ P^* > P \\ &= [1 - F(a^*)]\mathcal{L}, \qquad \pi^* < \pi;\ \ P^* < P. \end{aligned}$$

Given

$$\log a^* = \frac{1}{(\pi^* - \pi)} \frac{(1-\alpha)}{\alpha} \log\left(\frac{w - P}{w - P^*}\right),$$

We have,

$$\frac{\partial a^*}{\partial P} = -\frac{a^*}{(\pi^* - \pi)} \frac{(1-\alpha)}{\alpha} \frac{1}{(w-P)} < 0,$$

$$\frac{\partial a^*}{\partial P^*} = \frac{a^*}{(\pi^* - \pi)} \frac{(1-\alpha)}{\alpha} \frac{1}{(w-P^*)} > 0,$$

$$\frac{\partial a^*}{\partial w} = \frac{a^*}{(\pi^* - \pi)} \frac{(1-\alpha)}{\alpha} \left[\frac{1}{(w-P)} - \frac{1}{(w-P^*)}\right] < 0,$$

$$\frac{\partial a^*}{\partial(\pi^* - \pi)} = -\frac{1}{(\pi^* - \pi)^2} \frac{(1-\alpha)}{\alpha} \log\left(\frac{w-P}{w_t - P^*}\right) < 0,$$

which in turn implies:
1. $\frac{\partial C}{\partial P} < 0, \ \forall \{\pi^*, \pi\}$ 2. $\frac{\partial C}{\partial P^*} > 0, \ \forall \{\pi^*, \pi\}$ 3. $\frac{\partial C}{\partial w} < 0, \ \text{if} f \ \pi^* > \pi$
4. $\frac{\partial C}{\partial(\pi^* - \pi)} < 0, \ \text{if} f \ \pi^* > \pi$.
The response of $C^*$ to changes in $P^*$, $P$, $w$ and $\pi^* - \pi$ can be similarly calculated.

**Proof of Proposition 1:**
Totally differentiating Equation (2.6) and noting that $PF_L^i = w$ and $PF_K^i = r^i$, $i = h,\ l$; we have:

$$(r^h - r^l)\partial K^* = \partial c^h - (x^h - x^l)\partial P + (L^h - L^l)dw.$$

Therefore,

1. $$\frac{\partial K^*}{\partial P} = -\frac{K^*}{(r^h - r^l)} \left(\frac{x^h}{K^*} - \frac{x^l}{K^*}\right) < (>)\, 0.$$

2. $$\frac{\partial K^*}{\partial w} = \frac{K^*}{(r^h - r^l)} \left(\frac{L^h}{K^*} - \frac{L^l}{K^*}\right) > (<)\, 0.$$

3. $$\frac{\partial K^*}{\partial c^h} = \frac{1}{(r^h - r^l)} > 0.$$

It is important to note that even though the return from investing in high quality is higher than the corresponding return for low quality $((r^h - r^l) > 0)$, there is no guarantee that a higher output–capital ratio for high quality firms (as compared to the low quality types) also implies that they have a higher labor–capital ratio. To see this, define $\frac{x^i}{K}$, $i = h, l$; as the output–capital ratio for quality type $i$

and $\frac{L^i}{K}$ as the labor–capital ratio in the production of quality type $i$. By virtue of constant returns to scale, we have

$$\frac{PF_L^i L^i + PF_K^i K}{K} = w\frac{L^i}{K} + r^i = \frac{Px^i}{K}.$$

Therefore,

$$P\left(\frac{x^h}{K} - \frac{x^l}{K}\right) = w\left(\frac{L^h}{K} - \frac{L^l}{K}\right) + (r^h - r^l).$$

If $r^h > r^l$ and $\frac{L^h}{K} > \frac{L^l}{K}$, then the right-hand side of the above equation is strictly positive implying that $\frac{x^h}{K} > \frac{x^l}{K}$. It should be noted that $\frac{L^l}{K} > \frac{L^h}{K}$ does not imply that $\frac{x^l}{K} > \frac{x^h}{K}$. However, if $\frac{x^l}{K} > \frac{x^h}{K}$ and $r^h > r^l$, then it must be true that $\frac{L^l}{K} > \frac{L^h}{K}$.

**Proof of Proposition 2:**

Note that

$$X^l = M\int_{\underline{K}}^{K^*} F^l(K,\ L^l(K,P,w))d\lambda(K).$$

Totally differentiating the above equation and noting that (i) $KF_{KK}^i + LF_{LK}^i = 0,\ i = h,\ l$ and (ii) $F_K^i + F_L^i\frac{dL^i}{dK} = 0,\ i = h,\ l,$ we have

$$\partial X^l = M\int_{\underline{K}}^{K^*} F_L^l \partial L^l d\lambda(K) + MF^l\lambda'(K^*)\partial K^*.$$

Again,

$$F_L^i(K,\ L^i) = \frac{w}{P}.$$

Totally differentiating the above equation we have,

$$F_{LK}^i \partial K + F_{LL}^i \partial L^i = \frac{1}{P}\partial w - \frac{w}{P^2}\partial P,$$

which in turn implies

$$\frac{\partial L^i}{\partial w} = \frac{1}{PF_{LL}^i} < 0,$$

$$\frac{\partial L^i}{\partial P} = -\frac{w}{P^2 F_{LL}^i} > 0.$$

Utilizing the above derivatives we have,

$$\frac{\partial X^l}{\partial P} = M \int_{\underline{K}}^{K^*} F_L^l \frac{\partial L^l}{\partial P} d\lambda(K) + MF^l \lambda'(K^*) \frac{\partial K^*}{\partial P},$$

$$\frac{\partial X^l}{\partial w} = M \int_{\underline{K}}^{K^*} F_L^l \frac{\partial L^l}{\partial w} d\lambda(K) + MF^l \lambda'(K^*) \frac{\partial K^*}{\partial w},$$

$$\frac{\partial X^l}{\partial c^h} = MF^l \lambda'(K^*) \frac{\partial K^*}{\partial c^h}.$$

Therefore we have,

$$\frac{\partial X^l}{\partial P} > 0 \leftrightarrow \frac{x^l}{K^*} > \frac{x^h}{K^*}; \quad \frac{\partial X^l}{\partial w} > 0 \leftrightarrow \frac{L^l}{K^*} > \frac{L^h}{K^*}; \quad \frac{\partial X^l}{\partial c^h} > 0.$$

Similarly since,

$$\partial X^h = M \int_{K^*}^{\bar{K}} F_L^h \partial L^h d\lambda(K) - MF^h \lambda'(K^*) \partial K^*.$$

$$\frac{\partial X^h}{\partial P} > 0 \leftrightarrow \frac{x^l}{K^*} < \frac{x^h}{K^*}; \quad \frac{\partial X^h}{\partial w} > 0 \leftrightarrow \frac{L^l}{K^*} < \frac{L^h}{K^*}; \quad \frac{\partial X^h}{\partial c^h} < 0.$$

Note that since $X = X^l + X^h$,

$$\frac{\partial X}{\partial P} = M \int_{\underline{K}}^{K^*} F_L^l \frac{\partial L^l}{\partial P} d\lambda(K) + M \int_{K^*}^{\bar{K}} F_L^h \frac{\partial L^h}{\partial P} d\lambda(K)$$
$$+ \frac{M\lambda'(K^*)(K^*)^2}{(r^h - r^l)} \left( \frac{x^h}{K^*} - \frac{x^l}{K^*} \right)^2 > 0,$$

$$\frac{\partial X}{\partial w} = M \int_{\underline{K}}^{K^*} F_L^l \frac{\partial L^l}{\partial w} d\lambda(K) + M \int_{K^*}^{\bar{K}} F_L^h \frac{\partial L^h}{\partial w} d\lambda(K)$$

$$-\frac{M\lambda'(K^*)(K^*)^2}{(r^h - r^l)}\left(\frac{x^h}{K^*} - \frac{x^l}{K^*}\right)\left(\frac{L^h}{K^*} - \frac{L^l}{K^*}\right) > (<)\, 0,$$

$$\frac{\partial X}{\partial c^h} = \frac{M\lambda'(K^*)}{(r^h - r^l)}\left(\frac{x^l}{K^*} - \frac{x^h}{K^*}\right) > (<)\, 0.$$

**Proof of Proposition 3:**
Consider the goods market equilibrium for the Southern heterogeneous product for $\pi^* - \pi > 0$. The results for $\pi^* < \pi$ can easily be checked by the interested reader.

$$F(a^*)\mathcal{L} = M\int_{\underline{K}}^{K^*} x^l d\lambda(K) + M\int_{K^*}^{\bar{K}} x^h d\lambda(K).$$

Totally differentiating the above equation we get

$$\frac{dP}{dP^*} = \frac{\partial C/\partial P^*}{\partial X/\partial P - \partial C/\partial P} > 0,$$

$$\frac{dX}{dP^*} = \frac{\partial X}{\partial P}\frac{dP}{dP^*} > 0,$$

$$\frac{dP}{d(\pi^* - \pi)} = -\frac{F'(a^*)(\partial a^*/\partial(\pi^* - \pi))\mathcal{L}}{F'(a^*)(\partial a^*/\partial P)\mathcal{L} - \partial X/\partial P} > 0,$$

$$\frac{dP}{dw} = \frac{(\partial C/\partial w - \partial X/\partial w)}{(\partial X/\partial P - \partial C/\partial P)} = \frac{C}{w}\frac{(|\eta_w^C| - |\eta_w^X|)}{(\partial X/\partial P - \partial C/\partial P)} > (<)\, 0,$$

$$\frac{dP}{dc^h} = \frac{\partial X/\partial c^h}{\partial C/\partial P - \partial X/\partial P} < (>)\, 0 \leftrightarrow \frac{x^l}{K^*} > (<) \frac{x^h}{K^*}.$$

Imports, $(\mathcal{I})$, equals $[1 - F(a^*)]\mathcal{L}$. Therefore,

$$\frac{d\mathcal{I}}{dw} = -F'(a^*)\mathcal{L}\frac{\partial a^*}{\partial P}\frac{\partial P}{\partial w} > (<)\, 0,$$

$$\frac{d\mathcal{I}}{dc^h} = -F'(a^*)\mathcal{L}\frac{\partial a^*}{\partial P}\frac{\partial P}{\partial c^h} > (<)\, 0.$$

**Proof of Proposition 4:**
Total differentiation of Equation (2.8) yields

$$d\mu_t = \frac{dX_t^h}{X_t} - \frac{(dX_t^h + dX_t^l)}{X_t^2}$$

$$\leftrightarrow \frac{d\mu_t}{dP_t} = \frac{X_t^h X_t^l}{X_t^2}\left[\frac{1}{X_t^h}\frac{dX_t^h}{dP_t} - \frac{1}{X_t^l}\frac{dX_t^l}{dP_t}\right],$$

$$= \frac{X_t^h X_t^l}{P_t X_t^2}\left\{\frac{P_t F_L^h L_t^h}{P_t x_t^h M[1-\lambda(K_t^*)]}\frac{\partial L_t^h}{\partial P_t}\frac{P_t}{L_t^h}M[1-\lambda(K_t^*)]\right.$$

$$\left. - \frac{P_t F_L^l L_t^l}{P_t x_t^l M\lambda(K_t^*)}\frac{\partial L_t^l}{\partial P_t}\frac{P_t}{L_t^l}M\lambda(K_t^*)\right\}$$

$$- \frac{X_t^h X_t^l}{X_t^2}M\lambda'(K_t^*)\frac{\partial K_t^*}{\partial P_t}\left(\frac{x_t^h}{X_t^h} + \frac{x_t^l}{X_t^l}\right),$$

$$= \frac{X_t^h X_t^l}{P_t X_t^2}(\theta_L^h \eta_P^h - \theta_L^l \eta_P^l) + \frac{X_t^h X_t^l}{X_t^2}\frac{M\lambda'(K_t^*)K_t^*}{(r^h - r^l)}$$

$$\times \left(\frac{x_t^h}{X_t^h} + \frac{x_t^l}{X_t^l}\right)\left(\frac{x_t^h}{K_t^*} - \frac{x_t^l}{K_t^*}\right).$$

The last two terms are positive (negative), if (i) $\theta_L^h \eta_P^h > (<)\, \theta_L^l \eta_P^l$ and if (ii) $\frac{x_t^h}{K_t^*} > (<) \frac{x_t^l}{K_t^*}$. Therefore, proposition 4 follows from the fact that $\frac{d\mu_t}{dj} = \frac{\partial \mu_t}{\partial P_t}\frac{\partial P_t}{\partial j}$; $j = w_t, c^h$.

**Proof of Proposition 5:**
Consider first the case where the tariff revenue is redistributed back in a lump-sum fashion. Since total tariff revenue is $[1 - F(a_t^*)]\mathcal{L}P_t^*\tau$, each consumer in the economy gets $[1 - F(a_t^*)]P_t^*\tau$. Therefore Equation (2.3) is rewritten as:

$$\log a_t^* = \frac{1}{(\pi_t^* - \pi_t)}\frac{(1-\alpha)}{\alpha}\log\frac{(w_t + [1 - F(a_t^*)]P_t^*\tau - P_t)}{(w_t + [1 - F(a_t^*)]P_t^*\tau - P_t^*(1+\tau))}.$$

Therefore,

$$\frac{\partial a_t^*}{\partial \tau} = \frac{1}{(\pi_t^* - \pi_t)} \frac{(1-\alpha)}{\alpha} \frac{a_t^*}{\Delta\Delta^*}(P_t^*\Delta^* + P_t^* F(a_t^*)[P_t^*(1+\tau) - P_t]) > 0,$$

where $\Delta = w_t + [1 - F(a_t^*)]P_t^*\tau - P_t > 0$ and $\Delta^* = w_t + [1 - F(a_t^*)]P_t^*\tau - P_t^* > 0$.

If tariff revenue is appropriated then

$$\log a_t^* = \frac{1}{(\pi_t^* - \pi_t)} \frac{(1-\alpha)}{\alpha} \log \frac{(w_t - P_t)}{(w_t - P_t^*(1+\tau))}.$$

Therefore,

$$\frac{\partial a_t^*}{\partial \tau} = a_t^* \frac{1}{(\pi_t^* - \pi_t)} \frac{(1-\alpha)}{\alpha} \frac{P_t^*}{(w_t - P_t^*(1+\tau))} > 0.$$

Using the relationship $C_t = X_t$ we have,

$$\frac{dP_t}{d\tau} = \frac{F'(a_t^*)\mathcal{L}\frac{\partial a_t^*}{\partial \tau}}{\frac{\partial X_t}{\partial P_t} - \frac{\partial C_t}{\partial P_t}} > 0.$$

Therefore, $P_t$ increases irrespective of whether the tariff revenue is redistributed in a lump-sum fashion or appropriated by the government. Finally $\frac{d\mu_t}{d\tau} = \frac{\partial \mu_t}{\partial P_t}\frac{\partial P_t}{\partial \tau} > (<)\, 0$.

**Proof of Proposition 6:**
Totally differentiating Equations (2.11) and (2.12) and applying Cramer's rule we get,

$$\begin{bmatrix} C_P - X_P & C_{P^*} \\ C_P^* & C_{P^*}^* \end{bmatrix} \begin{bmatrix} dP \\ dP^* \end{bmatrix} = \begin{bmatrix} 0 \\ dQ \end{bmatrix}.$$

The determinant of the above matrix is $(C_P - X_P)C_{P^*}^* - C_{P^*}C_P^*$, where $C_P = \frac{dC_t}{dP_t}$ and $C_{P^*} = \frac{dC_t}{dP_t^*}$, with $C^*$ being the import demand at time $t$. Now utilizing the condition $C_t^* + C_t = \mathcal{L}$, the determinant of the above matrix reduces to $-X_P C_{P^*}^* > 0$. Thus, $\frac{dP_t}{dQ} < 0$ and $\frac{dP_t^*}{dQ} < 0$.

**Proof of Proposition 7:**
First consider Equation (2.6). Since the *ad-valorem* subsidy $s$ raises the price received by producers in the $X$-sector to $P_t(1+s)$, we have

$$\frac{\partial K_t^*}{\partial s} = -\frac{P_t K_t^*}{(r^h - r^l)} \left( \frac{x_t^h}{K_t^*} - \frac{x_t^l}{K_t^*} \right) > (<)\, 0.$$

Therefore,

$$\frac{\partial X_t}{\partial s} = \frac{x_t^h}{s} \theta_L^h \eta_s^h M \left[1 - \lambda(K_t^*)\right] + \frac{x_t^l}{s} \theta_L^l \eta_s^l M \lambda(K_t^*)$$
$$+ \frac{M\lambda'(K_t^*) P_t (K_t^*)^2}{(r^h - r^l)} \left( \frac{x_t^h}{K_t^*} - \frac{x_t^l}{K_t^*} \right) > 0.$$

Now if the subsidy is raised through a lump-sum tax ($\bar{T}$) on the consumers, then $\bar{T}\mathcal{L} = sP_t X_t$. Therefore,

$$\frac{d\bar{T}}{ds} = \frac{P_t X_t + sP_t \frac{\partial X_t}{\partial s}}{\mathcal{L}} = \phi > 0.$$

Now

$$\log a_t^* = \frac{1}{(\pi_t^* - \pi_t)} \frac{(1-\alpha)}{\alpha} \log \frac{(w_t - \bar{T} - P_t)}{(w_t - \bar{T} - P_t^*)}.$$

Therefore,

$$\frac{\partial a_t^*}{\partial s} = -\frac{1}{(\pi_t^* - \pi_t)} \frac{(1-\alpha)}{\alpha} \frac{a_t^* \phi}{\tilde{\Delta}\tilde{\Delta}^*} (P_t^* - P_t) > 0,$$

where $\tilde{\Delta} = w_t - \bar{T} - P_t$ and $\tilde{\Delta}^* = w_t - \bar{T} - P_t^*$. Therefore, $\frac{\partial C_t}{\partial s} > 0$.

Now since $C_t = X_t$ is in equilibrium,

$$\frac{dP_t}{ds} = \frac{(\eta_s^X - \eta_s^C) C_t / s}{\frac{\partial C_t}{\partial P_t} - \frac{\partial X_t}{\partial P_t}} > (<) 0 \leftrightarrow \eta_s^C > (<) \eta_s^X,$$

where $\eta_s^m = \frac{\partial m}{\partial s}\frac{s}{m} > 0$; $m = C, X$. Since $\mu_t = \mu_t(P_t, s)$, total differentiation yields,

$$\begin{aligned}
\frac{d\mu_t}{ds} &= \frac{X_t^h X_t^l}{X_t^2}\left[\frac{1}{X_t^h}\frac{\partial X_t^h}{\partial s} - \frac{1}{X_t^l}\frac{\partial X_t^l}{\partial s}\right] \\
&\quad + \frac{X_t^h X_t^l}{X_t^2}\left[\frac{1}{X_t^h}\frac{\partial X_t^h}{\partial P_t} - \frac{1}{X_t^l}\frac{\partial X_t^l}{\partial P_t}\right]\frac{\partial P_t}{\partial s} \\
&= \frac{X_t^h X_t^l}{sX_t^2}(\theta_L^h \eta_s^h - \theta_L^l \eta_s^l) + \frac{X_t^h X_t^l}{X_t^2}\frac{M\lambda'(K_t^*)P_t K_t^*}{(r^h - r^l)} \\
&\quad \times \left(\frac{x_t^h}{X_t^h} + \frac{x_t^l}{X_t^l}\right)\left(\frac{x_t^h}{K_t^*} - \frac{x_t^l}{K_t^*}\right) \\
&\quad + \left\{\frac{X_t^h X_t^l}{P_t X_t^2}(\theta_L^h \eta_P^h - \theta_L^l \eta_P^l) + \frac{X_t^h X_t^l}{X_t^2}\frac{M\lambda'(K_t^*)K_t^*}{(r^h - r^l)}\right. \\
&\quad \left. \times \left(\frac{x_t^h}{X_t^h} + \frac{x_t^l}{X_t^l}\right)\left(\frac{x_t^h}{K_t^*} - \frac{x_t^l}{K_t^*}\right)\right\}\frac{\partial P_t}{\partial s}.
\end{aligned}$$

## 2.A2. Subsidy to High Quality Producers

In this case, Equation (2.6) is written as $(r^h - r^l)K_t^* = c^h(1 - \delta)$. Therefore, $\frac{\partial K_t^*}{\partial \delta} = -\frac{c^h}{(r^h - r^l)} < 0$. Again,

$$\frac{\partial X_t}{\partial \delta} = \frac{M\lambda'(K_t^*)K_t^* c^h}{(r^h - r^l)}\left(\frac{x_t^h}{K_t^*} - \frac{x_t^l}{K_t^*}\right) > 0.$$

With the budget constraint, $\bar{T}\mathcal{L} = M[1 - \lambda(K_t^*)]\delta c^h$, one can easily check that $\frac{d\bar{T}}{d\delta} > 0$. As a result, $\frac{\partial C_t}{\partial \delta} > 0$ with $\frac{dP_t}{d\delta} > (<) \leftrightarrow \eta_\delta^C > (<)\eta_\delta^X$. Therefore,

$$\begin{aligned}
\frac{d\mu_t}{d\delta} &= \frac{X_t^h X_t^l}{X_t^2}\left\{\frac{M\lambda'(K_t^*)K_t^* c^h}{(r^h - r^l)}\left[\frac{x_t^h}{K_t^*}\left(\frac{1}{X_t^h} - \frac{1}{X_t}\right) + \frac{x_t^l}{K_t^*}\frac{1}{X_t}\right]\right. \\
&\quad \left. + \left[\left[\frac{1}{X_t^h}\frac{\partial X_t^h}{\partial P_t} + \frac{1}{X_t}\frac{\partial X_t}{\partial P_t}\right]\frac{\partial P_t}{\partial \delta}\right]\right\}.
\end{aligned}$$

The above expression is positive if $\eta_\delta^C > \eta_\delta^X$.

**Proof of Proposition 8:**
Consider first the equation $\beta(1+\gamma) = w_t$. Therefore, $\frac{\partial w_t}{\partial \gamma} = \beta > 0$. Now since the subsidy to the export sector is financed through a lump-sum tax, $\bar{T}$, on consumers, the following relationship must hold in equilibrium: $\gamma P_Y Y_t = \bar{T}\mathcal{L}$ which again implies that $\frac{\partial \bar{T}}{\partial \gamma} = \frac{Y_t}{\mathcal{L}}(1+\eta_\gamma^Y)$ and where $\eta_\gamma^Y > 0$ is the elasticity of the $Y$-sector output with respect to the subsidy rate.

Now

$$\log a_t^* = \frac{1}{(\pi_t^* - \pi_t)} \frac{(1-\alpha)}{\alpha} \log \frac{(w_t - \bar{T} - P_t)}{(w_t - \bar{T} - P_t^*)}.$$

Therefore,

$$\frac{\partial a_t^*}{\partial \gamma} = -\frac{1}{(\pi_t^* - \pi_t)} \frac{(1-\alpha)}{\alpha} \frac{a_t^*}{\tilde{\Delta}\tilde{\Delta}^*}(P_t^* - P_t)\beta \times \left[1 - \frac{L_{y_t}}{\mathcal{L}}(1+\eta_\gamma^Y)\right] > (<)0,$$

where $\tilde{\Delta} = w_t - \bar{T} - P_t$ and $\tilde{\Delta}^* = w_t - \bar{T} - P_t^*$. Hence, $\frac{\partial a_t^*}{\partial \gamma}$ is positive if the term within the square brackets in the above equation is negative. A necessary and sufficient condition for that to happen is $(1+\eta_\gamma^Y) > \frac{\mathcal{L}}{L_{y_t}}$ or $\eta_\gamma^Y > \frac{L_{X_t}}{L_{y_t}}$.

Once again, utilizing the equilibrium condition $C_t = X_t$, we get

$$\frac{dP_t}{d\gamma} = -\frac{F'(a_t^*)\mathcal{L}\frac{\partial a_t^*}{\partial \gamma}}{\frac{\partial C_t}{\partial P_t} - \frac{\partial X_t}{\partial P_t}} > (<)\,0,$$

if and only if $\eta_\gamma^Y > (<)\frac{L_{X_t}}{L_{y_t}}$.

# Chapter 3

## Regional Trade in a Three Country Model*

*Henry Thompson*

*Department of Economics, Auburn University, AL 36849, USA*

*This chapter develops a three country model of constant cost production and trade based on productivity and country size. Trade may be limited to two of the countries assuming that gains from trade are necessary for trade to take place. A small country may produce too little to offer gains from trade to the other two. At the other extreme, a country may be too productive to gain from trade. Regional trade is observed if the countries with similar productivities are located closer together, a testable hypothesis.*

Regional trade in the literature is based on various forms of imperfect competitions. In contrast, trade may be limited to two to three countries in the present competitive model due to their productivity and size. Each country maximizes identical Cobb–Douglas utility subject for constant cost production and balanced trade. Gains from trade are necessary for trade assuming a cost of adjusting production along the production frontier. A country that is too unproductive is not able to offer gains from trade. At the other extreme, a country may be too productive to gain from trade. Regional trade is observed if countries with similar productivity happen to be located closer together.

*Roy Ruffin provided key comments and suggestions as this paper developed. Hyeongwoo Kim, Charlie Sawyer, Farhad Rassekh, John Gilbert, Randy Beard, Ghislain Nono Gueye, and Henry Kinnucan also provided comments that focused the analysis.

Regional trade in the literature arises due to various forms of market imperfections including the differential tariffs and trade diversion of Viner (1950); game theoretic optimal tariffs of Johnson (1953); policy credibility of Staiger and Taellini (1987), Whalley (1996), Hamilton and Whalley (1983), and Keenan and Riezman (1990); increasing returns of Krugman (1991); insurance against trade wars of Peronni and Whalley (2000); border effects of Engel and Rogers (1996), Helliwell (1998), and Anderson and van Wincoop (2003); various non-traditional issues of Fernández and Portes (1998); geographic barriers of Eaton and Kortum (2002); and production externalities of Rossi-Hansberg (2005). The present model is based on the competitive Torrens–Ricardo–Mill trade model developed by McKenzie (1954), Chipman (1965), and Eaton and Kortum (2012).

The first section presents the classical constant cost trade model with two countries and two goods, followed by a section adding the third country. The third section extends the model to more goods and more countries.

## 3.1. Trade in the 2 × 2 Model

Countries are represented by $k$ = A, B and goods by $j = 1, 2$. Unit input coefficients $a_{jk}$ imply the constant cost production frontier $E_k = \Sigma_j a_{jk} x_{jk}$ where $E_k$ is the factor endowment and $x_{jk}$ the output of good $j$. Complete specialization in good $j$ occurs at $E_k/a_{jk}$.

Each country maximizes utility subject to its production frontier in autarky with consumption $c_{jk}$ of good $j$ equal to output $x_{jk}$. Assume the utility functions $u_k = c_{1k}c_{2k}$ implying marginal utilities $u_{1k} = c_{2k}$ and $u_{2k} = c_{1k}$. The autarky relative price of good 1 is $a_{1k}/a_{2k}$. Utility maximization implies equal consumption shares, $a_{1k}c_{1k} = a_{2k}c_{2k}$ with half the factor endowment employed producing each good, $E_k/2a_{jk} = c_{jk} = x_{jk}$.

Assuming country A has the comparative advantage in good 1,

$$\frac{a_{1\mathrm{B}}}{a_{2\mathrm{B}}} > \frac{a_{1\mathrm{A}}}{a_{2\mathrm{A}}}. \tag{3.1}$$

It would specialize and export good 1, and country B good 2, if

$$\frac{a_{1\mathrm{B}}}{a_{2\mathrm{B}}} > p > \frac{a_{1\mathrm{A}}}{a_{2\mathrm{A}}}, \tag{3.2}$$

where $p \equiv p_1/p_2$ is the terms of trade. Prices are determined in the producing country, $p_1 = a_{1\mathrm{A}}w_\mathrm{A}$ and $p_2 = a_{2\mathrm{B}}w_\mathrm{B}$, where $w_k$ represents the factor price. It follows that $p = (a_{1\mathrm{A}}/a_{2\mathrm{B}})\,(w_\mathrm{A}/w_\mathrm{B})$ limiting relative factor prices from Equation (3.2) according to $a_{1\mathrm{B}}/a_{1\mathrm{A}} > w_\mathrm{A}/w_\mathrm{B} > a_{2\mathrm{B}}/a_{2\mathrm{A}}$.

Total consumption with trade equals specialized production,

$$c_{1\mathrm{A}} + c_{1\mathrm{B}} = \frac{E_\mathrm{A}}{a_{1\mathrm{A}}} \quad \text{and} \quad c_{2\mathrm{A}} + c_{2\mathrm{B}} = \frac{E_\mathrm{B}}{a_{2\mathrm{B}}}. \tag{3.3}$$

Each country consumes the same amount of each good $c_{j\mathrm{A}} = c_{j\mathrm{B}}$ equal to half the specialized output. Trade is balanced with export revenue equal to import spending, $(E_\mathrm{A}/a_{1\mathrm{A}}) - c_{1\mathrm{A}} = c_{2\mathrm{A}}/p$ and $(E_\mathrm{B}/a_{2\mathrm{B}}) - c_{2\mathrm{B}} = pc_{1\mathrm{B}}$ implying $p = c_{2k}/c_{1k}$.

Figure 3.1 pictures production frontiers and autarky consumption at $U_\mathrm{A}$ and $U_\mathrm{B}$. Consumption with trade is $T_\mathrm{A}$ and $T_\mathrm{B}$ with increased consumption of the import, but consumption of the export remaining at the autarky level. The terms of trade depend on productivity and country size from Equation (3.3) according to $p = (a_{1\mathrm{A}}/a_{2\mathrm{B}})(E_\mathrm{B}/E_\mathrm{A})$.

If a country is small, competitive trade would occur at the large country's autarky price as it is forced to partially specialize and trade

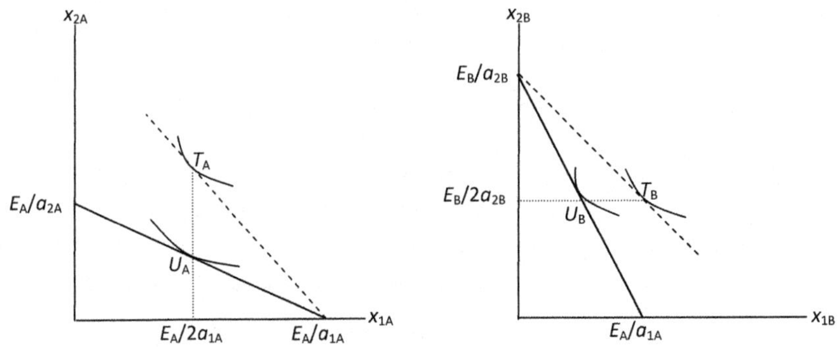


**Figure 3.1.** Gains from trade in the 2 × 2 model.

back to its autarky consumption. The small country enjoys the gains from trade, a well-known property of trade theory. To avoid trade without gains, assume an arbitrarily small cost of adjusting output along the production frontier,

$$C_{jk} = \gamma_{jk} dx_{jk}. \tag{3.4}$$

Gains from trade are then necessary to offset this arbitrarily small $C_{jk}$ as an economy specializes. Partial specialization and trade with a small country are ruled out.

The condition for gains from trade is that the other country would export at least as much as would be consumed in autarky. Gains from trade for country A require $E_{\mathrm{B}}/2a_{2\mathrm{B}} > E_{\mathrm{A}}/2a_{2\mathrm{A}}$. For the two countries, conditions for gains from trade can be stated

$$\mathrm{A}_1 > \mathrm{B}_1 \quad \text{and} \quad \mathrm{B}_2 > \mathrm{A}_2, \tag{3.5}$$

where $\mathrm{A}_j \equiv E_{\mathrm{A}}/a_{j\mathrm{A}}$ and $\mathrm{B}_j \equiv E_{\mathrm{B}}/a_{j\mathrm{B}}$. Specialized production must be larger in a different good for each country given the necessity of gains from trade. The production conditions in Equation (3.5) imply the weaker comparative advantage in Equation (3.1). Productivity and size restrictions for gains from trade are

$$\frac{a_{2\mathrm{A}}}{a_{2\mathrm{B}}} > \frac{E_{\mathrm{A}}}{E_{\mathrm{B}}} > \frac{a_{1\mathrm{A}}}{a_{2\mathrm{B}}}. \tag{3.6}$$

Similar restrictions in the following three country model lead to the possibility that trade may be limited to two countries.

## 3.2. Trade in the 2 × 3 Model

Assume the third country C has constant cost production $E_{\mathrm{C}} = \Sigma_j a_{j\mathrm{C}} x_{j\mathrm{C}}$ and the same utility function. Its autarky production $x_{j\mathrm{C}}$ and consumption $c_{j\mathrm{C}}$ equals $E_{\mathrm{C}}/2a_{j\mathrm{C}} = \frac{1}{2}\mathrm{C}_j$. Assume it has the comparative advantage in good 2 with country B in the middle,

$$\frac{a_{1\mathrm{C}}}{a_{2\mathrm{C}}} > \frac{a_{1\mathrm{B}}}{a_{2\mathrm{B}}} > \frac{a_{1\mathrm{A}}}{a_{2\mathrm{A}}}. \tag{3.7}$$

Limits to the terms of trade similar to Equation (3.2) are $a_{1\mathrm{C}}/a_{2\mathrm{C}} > p > a_{1\mathrm{A}}/a_{2\mathrm{A}}$ with country A exporting good 1, country C good 2, and middle country B either good.

Production conditions extend Equation (3.5) to the third country. One possibility is the mirror image condition

$$\mathrm{A}_1 > \mathrm{B}_1 > \mathrm{C}_1 \quad \text{and} \quad \mathrm{C}_2 > \mathrm{B}_2 > \mathrm{A}_2, \tag{3.8}$$

implying

$$\frac{a_{1\mathrm{B}}}{a_{1\mathrm{A}}} > \frac{E_\mathrm{B}}{E_\mathrm{A}} > \frac{a_{2\mathrm{B}}}{a_{2\mathrm{A}}} \quad \text{and} \quad \frac{a_{1\mathrm{C}}}{a_{1\mathrm{B}}} > \frac{E_\mathrm{C}}{E_\mathrm{B}} > \frac{a_{2\mathrm{C}}}{a_{2\mathrm{B}}}, \tag{3.9}$$

extending Equation (3.6). The conditions in Equation (3.9) imply $a_{1\mathrm{C}}/a_{1\mathrm{A}} > E_\mathrm{C}/E_\mathrm{A} > a_{2\mathrm{C}}/a_{2\mathrm{A}}$ and the comparative advantage in Equation (3.7), but include restrictions on relative country sizes. The potential competition in an export market may lead to losses from trade for one country.

Country A exports and consumes $a_1 \equiv \frac{1}{2}\mathrm{A}_1$ in Equation (3.8) and similarly $c_2 \equiv \frac{1}{2}\mathrm{C}_2$ for country C. Country B specializing in good 1 would compete with country A for $c_2$, earning its share $s_{\mathrm{B}1}c_2$, where $s_{\mathrm{B}1} \equiv \mathrm{B}_1/(\mathrm{A}_1+\mathrm{B}_1)$ is its portion of the good 1 market. The utility of B would then be $u_{\mathrm{B}1} = s_{\mathrm{B}1}b_1c_2$, while utility specializing in good 2 would be $u_{\mathrm{B}2} = s_{\mathrm{B}2}a_1b_2$, where $b_2 \equiv \frac{1}{2}\mathrm{B}_2$ and $s_{\mathrm{B}2} \equiv \mathrm{B}_2/(\mathrm{B}_2 + \mathrm{C}_2)$. Assume $u_{\mathrm{B}1} > u_{\mathrm{B}2}$ with country B specializing in good 1.

Table 3.1 reports consumption levels for autarky $K$ and global specialization $G$ as well as three situations $R_{kh}$ of trade limited to countries $k$ and $h$. With utility the product of consumption levels, country C ranks global trade highest $G > R_{\mathrm{AC}} > R_{\mathrm{BC}} > K = R_{\mathrm{AB}}$.

**Table 3.1.** Trade in the 2 × 3 model.

| | A | | B | | C | |
|---|---|---|---|---|---|---|
| | 1 | 2 | 1 | 2 | 1 | 2 |
| $K$ | $a_1$ | $a_2$ | $b_1$ | $b_2$ | $c_1$ | $c_2$ |
| $R_{\mathrm{AB}}$ | $a_1$ | $b_2$ | $a_1$ | $b_2$ | $c_1$ | $c_2$ |
| $R_{\mathrm{AC}}$ | $a_1$ | $c_2$ | $b_1$ | $b_2$ | $a_1$ | $c_2$ |
| $R_{\mathrm{BC}}$ | $a_1$ | $a_2$ | $b_1$ | $c_2$ | $b_1$ | $c_2$ |
| $G$ | $a_1$ | $s_{\mathrm{A}1}c_2$ | $b_1$ | $s_{\mathrm{B}1}c_2$ | $a_1 + b_1$ | $c_2$ |

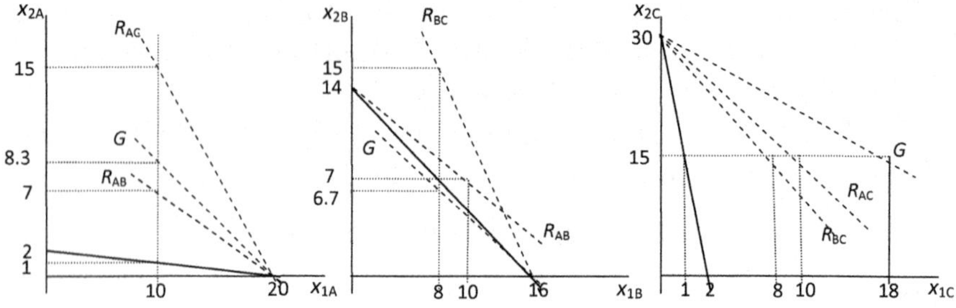


**Figure 3.2.** Trade in the $2 \times 3$ model.

The terms of trade for C are best in $G$ as the other two specialize in its imported good 1. Country A ranks $R_{\mathrm{AC}} > G$ consuming $c_2$ in $R_{\mathrm{AC}}$ but only its share $s_{\mathrm{A1}} = 1 - s_{\mathrm{B1}}$ in $G$. Country A also ranks $R_{\mathrm{AC}} > R_{\mathrm{AB}} > K = R_{\mathrm{BC}}$.

Country B would export good 1 to country C in $R_{\mathrm{BC}}$ that it ranks ahead of autarky, $R_{\mathrm{BC}} > K$. Country B also ranks $R_{\mathrm{BC}}$ ahead of $G$, as it avoids competing in the good 1 export market. Its ranking of $G$ and $K$ are ambiguous. Countries A and B both prefer trading with only C, while it prefers global trade.

As an example, Figure 3.2 pictures production for $\mathrm{A}_1 = 20$, $\mathrm{B}_1 = 16, \mathrm{C}_1 = 2, \mathrm{A}_2 = 2, \mathrm{B}_2 = 14$, and $\mathrm{C}_2 = 30$ with comparative advantage in Equation (3.7) and production condition in Equation (3.8). Country A ranks $R_{\mathrm{AC}} > G > R_{\mathrm{AB}}$ while C ranks $R_{\mathrm{AC}} > R_{\mathrm{BC}}$. Country B ranks $K > G$ due to global competition with country A in good 1 ruling out global trade. Countries A and C would trade with each other in $R_{\mathrm{AC}}$.

Production conditions other than Equation (3.8) lead to different trade patterns. For instance $\mathrm{A}_2 > \mathrm{C}_2 > \mathrm{B}_2$ replacing the second condition in Equation (3.8) implies country A would not gain from trade since it produces more of both goods, than either of the other countries can offer in trade. Comparative advantage in Equation (3.7) cannot be ruled out but country A is too large to trade as seen in the implied conditions $a_{1\mathrm{B}}/a_{1\mathrm{A}} > a_{2\mathrm{B}}/a_{2\mathrm{A}} > E_{\mathrm{B}}/E_{\mathrm{A}}$ and $a_{1\mathrm{C}}/a_{1\mathrm{A}} > a_{2\mathrm{C}}/a_{2\mathrm{A}} > E_{\mathrm{C}}/E_{\mathrm{A}}$. There are six similar conditions with a country too large to gain from trade.

At the other extreme $B_2 > A_2 > C_2$ as the second condition in Equation (3.8) implies country C is too small to offer gains from trade to the other two. There are six such rankings with a small economy excluded from trade. Global autarky would result with $A_2 > B_2 > C_2$ as the second condition in Equation (3.8).

A third good allows each country to have the highest production potential in its own particular good. Under a wide range of production conditions, however, trade would be limited to two countries.

## 3.3. Trade with More Countries and Goods

Gains from trade with three goods depend on production conditions extending Equation (3.8) to the third good. Thompson (2001) identifies the general trade patterns in the $3 \times 3$ model. Utility maximization implies each country in autarky produces and consumes a third of each output, $a_h \equiv A_h/3$ for $h = 1, 2, 3$ and similarly for $b_h$ and $c_h$. Each country can export one third of its output of up to two goods in exchange for one third of the outputs of other goods.

Each country has a unique advantage in

$$\begin{aligned} &A_1 > B_1 > C_1, \\ &B_2 > C_2 > A_2 \quad \text{and} \\ &C_3 > A_3 > B_3. \end{aligned} \tag{3.10}$$

Each country also has a unique disadvantage in Equation (3.10) consistent with the assignment of Jones (1961). Country A specializes in good 1, country B good 2, and country C good 3. Utility $a_1b_2c_3$ of each country with global trade is illustrated in Figure 3.3a by the dashed terms of trade, plane beyond the three production frontiers.

There are a total of $6^3 = 216$ production conditions. In 48, each country ranks first for a different good as in Equation (3.10) leading to unique specialization. There are another 24 rankings with one country first for every good resulting in autarky. In another 24, a country ranking last for every good is excluded from trade. An example is country B in Figure 3.3b facing $R_{AC}$ and the dashed terms of trade between goods 1 and 3.

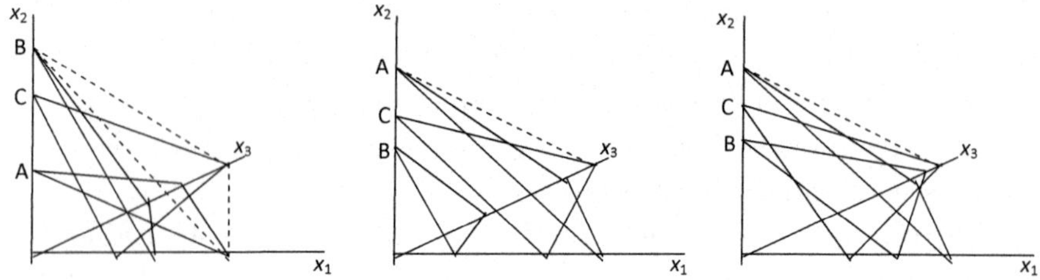


(a) Global trade in Equation (8) (b) Small unproductive B (c) $R_{AC}$ in Equation (9)

**Figure 3.3.** Trade in the 3 × 3 model.

**Table 3.2.** Trade in the 3 × 3 model.

| | A | | | B | | | C | | |
|---|---|---|---|---|---|---|---|---|---|
| | 1 | 2 | 3 | 1 | 2 | 3 | 1 | 2 | 3 |
| $K$ | $a_1$ | $a_2$ | $a_3$ | $b_1$ | $b_2$ | $b_3$ | $c_1$ | $c_2$ | $c_3$ |
| $R_{AB}$ | $a_1$ | $a_2$ | $b_3$ | $a_1$ | $b_2$ | $b_3$ | $c_1$ | $c_2$ | $c_3$ |
| $R_{AC}$ | $a_1$ | $a_2$ | $c_3$ | $b_1$ | $b_2$ | $b_3$ | $a_1$ | $c_2$ | $c_3$ |
| $R_{BC}$ | $a_1$ | $a_2$ | $a_3$ | $b_1$ | $b_2$ | $c_3$ | $b_1$ | $c_2$ | $c_3$ |
| $G$ | $a_1$ | $b_2$ | $c_3$ | $a_1$ | $b_2$ | $c_3$ | $a_1$ | $b_2$ | $c_3$ |

The other possibility is that one country does not rank highest for any good, accounting for a majority of the possible production conditions. Table 3.2 reports the outcomes of

$$\begin{aligned} A_1 > B_1 > C_1, \\ A_2 > C_2 > B_2, \\ C_3 > B_3 > A_3, \end{aligned} \tag{3.11}$$

assuming $A_1 > A_2$ with country A specialized in good 1. Rankings for country A are $R_{AC} > G$ and $R_{AC} > R_{AB} > R_{BC} = K$. Similarly country C ranks $R_{AC} > G$ and $R_{AC} > R_{BC} > R_{AB} = K$. Country B ranks $G > R_{BC}$ and $R_{AB} > R_{AC} = K$, but is isolated by $R_{AC}$ as shown in Figure 3.3c.

There is global trade for only 22% of the possible production conditions. With an equal number of countries and goods, each country could rank highest in a unique good resulting in global trade.

Countries that do not rank highest for any good, however, would be excluded from trade. Countries that rank highest for all goods would not gain from trade.

Extending the model to more countries and goods, Graham (1948) argues that trade may be limited to a subset of countries when there are more countries than goods, as in the present $2 \times 3$ model. With more goods than countries, each country may have the highest production potential for at least one good, but the above results imply trade may be limited. This result extends to the continuum goods model of Dornbusch *et al.* (1977).

## 3.4. Conclusion

The present competitive model offers an alternative motivation for regional trade, namely the geographical distribution of productivity and country size. Trade limited to a subset of countries is unexceptional in the present model. If trading countries were located closer together, regional trade would be observed.

The extent to which observed regional trade patterns are explained by the distribution of productivity and country size becomes an empirical issue. The present results would apply directly to factor proportion models and the factor income distribution within countries with regional *versus* global trade.

Regarding policy implications, the various assumptions of imperfect competitions in the regional trade literature lead to second best policy recommendations that would ease symptoms of assumed market imperfections. In the present competitive model, policy focus shifts to productivity and production potential.

## References

Anderson, J and E van Wincoop (2003) Gravity with gravitas: A solution to the border puzzle, *American Economic Review* 93, 170–192.

Chipman, J (1965) A survey of the theory of international trade: Part 1, the classical theory, *Econometrica* 33, 477–519.

Dornbusch, R, S Fischer and P Samuelson (1977) Comparative advantage, trade, and payments in a Ricardian model with a continuum of goods, *American Economic Review* 67, 823–839.

Eaton, J and S Kortum (2002) Technology, geography and trade, *Econometrica* 70, 1741–1779.

Eaton, J and S Kortum (2012) Putting Ricardo to work, *Journal of Economic Perspectives* 26, 65–90.

Engel, C and J Rogers (1996) How wide is the border? *American Economic Review* 86, 1112–1125.

Fernández, R and J Portes (1998) Returns to regionalism: An analysis of non-traditional gains from regional trade agreements, *The World Bank Economic Review* 12, 197–220.

Graham, F (1948) *The Theory of International Values.* Princeton, New Jersey: Princeton University Press.

Hamilton, B and J Whalley (1983) Optimal tariff calculations in alternative trade models and some possible implications for current world trading arrangements, *Journal of International Economics* 15(3–4), 323–348.

Helliwell, J (1998) *How Much Do National Borders Matter?* Washington: Brookings Institution Press.

Johnson, H (1953) Optimum tariffs and retaliation, *Review of Economic Studies* 21, 142–163.

Jones, R (1961) Comparative advantage and the theory of tariffs: A multi-country, multi-commodity model, *Review of Economic Studies* 28, 161–175.

Keenan, J and R Riezman (1990) Optimal tariff equilibria with customs unions, *Canadian Journal of Economics* 23, 70–83.

Krugman, P (1991) Increasing returns and economic geography, *Journal of Political Economy* 99, 483–499.

McKenzie, L (1954) Specialization in production and the production possibility locus, *Review of Economic Studies* 21, 165–180.

Peronni, C and J Whalley (2000) The new regionalism: Trade liberalization or insurance? *Canadian Journal of Economics* 33(1), 1–24.

Rossi-Hansberg, E (2005) A spatial theory of trade, *American Economic Review* 95, 1464–1491.

Staiger, R and G Taellini (1987) Discretionary trade policy and excessive protection, *American Economic Review* 77, 823–837.

Thompson, H (2001) International trade with three factors, goods, or countries, *Keio Economics Studies* 38, 43–52.

Viner, J (1950) *The Customs Union Issue.* Lancaster PA: Carnegie Endowment for International Peace.

Whalley, J (1996) Why do countries seek regional trade agreements? *NBER Working Paper 5552*, Cambridge MA: National Bureau of Economic Research.

# Chapter 4

## Voluntary Formation of Free Trade Area in a Third Country Market Model

*Ryoichi Nomura*, Takao Ohkawa†, Makoto Okamura‡ and Makoto Tawada§*

**Department of Economics, Ritsumeikan University*
*†Department of Economics, Ritsumeikan University*
*‡Economics Department, Hiroshima University*
*§Faculty of Economics, Aichi Gakuin University*

This chapter investigates the formation of a multilateral free trade agreement (FTA) through the extension of bilateral FTAs in a third country market model of the Brander and Spencer (1985) type. Two exporting countries are different in their number of domestic firms. The importing country imposes tariff on the imports from the exporting countries. Then, we investigate the possibility of the bilateral FTA in the sense that the importing country agrees to abolish the tariff policy against the country forming the agreement. Our main result is that, in the case where each exporting country adopts a subsidization policy on its domestic firms, it is possible to make a voluntary multilateral FTA by the gradual extension of bilateral FTAs under the assumption that the subsidization policy is also resigned in the country reaching the agreement. However, if there is no subsidization policy in the exporting countries, any bilateral FTA cannot be established voluntarily. Thus, it is impossible to form a multilateral FTA by the gradual extension of bilateral FTA.

## 4.1. Introduction

Recently, many countries have been trying to form free trade agreements (FTAs). For example, Japan has been forming or negotiating FTAs with Singapore, Mexico, Thailand, Chile, Korea and so on. The World Trade Organization (WTO) admitted member countries to make a regional or bilateral FTA quite freely, since the gradual development of those FTAs among countries may be expected to build a free trade area including many countries. Thus many countries have attempted to make FTAs actively in these decades. These attempts however, do not seem to be going well in the sense of the establishment of a multilateral FTA. This guides us to the question that under what circumstances a multilateral FTA is successfully formed by the step by step extension of bilateral FTAs.

There are several literatures examining some aspects of FTAs and customs unions (CUs). For example, Yi (1996) examined the endogenous stability properties of CUs using the coalition formation game. Freund (2000) examined the interaction between preferential trade agreements (PTAs) and multilateral tariff reduction in a repeated game framework. Mukunoki (2004) investigated how the formation of an FTA affects optimal tariffs against the non-member country using an oligopoly model with product differentiation. One of the common feature of these papers is that they assumed that all countries have a local market and local firms, and trade each other, and that all governments impose an import tariff only as trade policies. These papers focused mainly on the effects of FTAs/CUs on the level of tariffs and welfare, but not on the voluntary formation of FTAs. Concerning the voluntary formation of an FTA, Nomura *et al.* (2013) investigated how a multilateral FTA is formed by the gradual extension of bilateral FTAs among countries, each having a domestic market of different size.

In the present chapter, we tackle the same topic but with different type of world economy. We consider the Brander and Spencer (1985) type of the world economy, where there are two exporting countries having no domestic market and one importing country having no production firm. Then we investigate the FTAs between the exporting countries and importing country. We suppose that the number of domestic firms in each exporting country is different between countries. The importing country is supposed to impose the import tariffs on imports from the exporting countries. In addition to this, we introduce the production subsidies in each exporting country. In reality, the governments can take various policies which affect the international trade. For example, production subsidy seriously affects international trade as seen in the European agriculture.

We consider the following three-stage game: In the first stage, the governments determine whether they form an FTA. In the second stage, if the FTA is formed between countries, whether free trade prevails between these member countries. Here we assume that, once the agreement is established, not only the importing country abolishes the import tariff but also the exporting country gives up the use of the production subsidy. In trade with a non-member country, tariffs and subsidies are available. In the third stage, given those policies, the firms in the exporting countries export a homogenous commodity under the Cournot competition in the importing country market. Our main conclusion is that FTA is possible only between the importing country and the exporting country with larger number of domestic firms, and this FTA cannot extend to involve the other exporting country.

## 4.2. Model

Consider a world economy where one commodity and three countries exist. Three countries are countries $L$ and $S$, and a third country. Countries $L$ and $S$ produce the commodity through the domestic firms $n_L$ and $n_S$, respectively, and export it to the third country, where we assume $n_L > n_S$. There is no production in the third country and no consumption in countries $L$ and $S$. All firms in both exporting countries are supposed to have an identical production cost function with constant marginal cost $c$.

Let an inverse demand function of the third country market be $p = P(Q) \equiv A - Q$, where $Q$ shows the demand for the commodity, $p$ is the commodity price and $A$ indicates market scale and is assumed to be greater than $c$. All firms in both exporting countries behave as the Cournot oligopolist in the third country market. The government of exporting country $i$ gives a production subsidy of $s_i (i = L, S)$ per output so as to maximize country $i$'s national welfare, while the government of the importing country imposes a tariff $t_i$ on the imports from country $i$, where $i = L$ and $S$.

We consider the following three-stage game: In the first stage, the governments of three countries determine whether they form an FTA or not simultaneously. If two of them agree to form an FTA with each other, then the tariff and subsidy are abolished between those two countries. The countries which do not have an FTA with each other can freely make use of tariff and subsidy between the two countries. Thus, in the second stage, if an exporting country has no agreement with the third country, the government of the exporting country chooses the level of the production subsidy in order to maximize its national welfare and the third country imposes the level of the tariff on the imports from that country in order to maximize its national welfare. In the third stage, each Cournot firm, facing the given production subsidy and tariff, decides the production amount in the third country market.

### 4.2.1. *The third and second stage of the game*

We solve this game by backward induction. In the third stage, each firm decides its level of outputs so as to maximize its profit under the given subsidy and tariff. The profit of each firm in country $i$ is given by $\pi_i = P(Q)q_i - (c - s_i + t_i)q_i$ where $q_i$ is each firm's output in country $i$. The equilibrium output level of each firm in country $i$ is given by

$$q_i = \frac{1 - (t_j - s_j)(n_j + 1) + (t_i - s_i)n_j}{n_i + n_j + 1}, \quad i, j = L, S, \quad i \neq j. \tag{4.1}$$

Therefore, assuming $A - c = 1$ without loss of generality, we obtain the total amount of output in the equilibrium as follows:

$$Q = \frac{(1 - t_L + s_L)n_L + (1 - t_S + s_S)n_S}{n_L + n_S + 1}. \tag{4.2}$$

In the second stage, the government of each exporting country $i$ sets the level of production subsidy $s_i$, in order to maximize its national welfare, defined as the sum of the domestic firms' net profits on the cost for production subsidies, which is

$$W_i = n_i(\pi_i - s_i q_i). \tag{4.3}$$

On the other hand, the third country's government determines the level of tariff $t_i$ in order to maximize its national welfare, defined as the sum of the consumer surplus and tariff revenue, which is shown as

$$W_I = \frac{1}{2}Q^2 + t_L n_L q_L + t_S n_S q_S. \tag{4.4}$$

### 4.2.2. *The first stage of the game*

Concerning the first stage of the game, we have to compare each country's welfare between two different regimes, distinguished by the formation of FTA.

First of all, we consider the regime where there is no FTA in the world economy. In this economy, each exporting country's government and the importing country's government can make use of a production subsidy and import tariff, respectively. For simplicity, we make the following two assumptions:

***Assumption* 1**

The third country imposes a uniform tariff on the imports from the countries with which it has no FTA.

***Assumption* 2**

$n_L \geq n_S + 2 \geq 5$

Under this assumption, we have $t_L = t_S = t$. Through Equations (4.1) to (4.4), we obtain the equilibrium levels of subsidies and tariff as

$$s_i = (n_j + 1 - n_i)(n_i + n_j)/n_i\Omega, \tag{4.5}$$

$$t = (n_i + n_j + 2)/\Omega, \tag{4.6}$$

where $\Omega = (n_i + n_j)^2 + 2(2n_i + 2n_j + 1)$.[1] Equations (4.5) and (4.6) yield the following lemma.

***Lemma* 1**

*Under Assumptions 1 and 2, the following (i) and (ii) hold.*

*(i) The government of country L imposes the production tax, while that of country S gives the production subsidy.*
*(ii) The importing country imposes a positive tariff.*

An intuitive explanation of (i) is that, if the country which has a larger number of firms encourages its domestic firms to export, the commodity price in the third market declines severely under the Cournot competition and the monopoly rent earned in this market reduces. Thus, in order to protect the firms from this situation, the government of the large country chooses the production tax to control the production amount of the domestic firms. More detailed explanation is given in Ohkawa *et al.* (2002).

Substituting Equations (4.5) and (4.6) into Equations (4.3) and (4.4), we obtain each country's welfare as

$$W_i = (n_i + 1)(n_i + n_j)^2/\Omega^2, \tag{4.7}$$

$$W_I = (n_i + 1)(n_i + n_j + 2)^3/2\Omega^2. \tag{4.8}$$

Then, in view of Equations (4.4), (4.7) and (4.8), the world welfare is calculated as

$$W = (n_i + n_j)(n_i + n_j + 2)((n_i + n_j)^2 + 2(3n_i + 3n_j + 2))/2\Omega^2. \tag{4.9}$$

[1]The detailed calculation is available from the authors upon request.

Next, we consider the regime where an FTA is formed between the importing country and the exporting country $i$. Hence $t_i = 0$ and $s_i = 0$. Making use of Equations (4.1) to (4.4), we have the equilibrium levels of the subsidy and tariff between the other exporting country $j$ and the importing country as

$$s_j^F = \frac{(2n_i + 1)(n_i - n_j + 1)}{(n_i + 1)\Phi}, \tag{4.10}$$

$$t_j^F = \frac{(n_i + 1)^2 - n_i n_j}{(n_i + 1)\Phi}, \tag{4.11}$$

where $\Phi = (n_i + 1)^2 + (3n_i + 2)n_j$. Equations (4.10) and (4.11) establish the following lemma.

***Lemma 2***

*Under Assumption 2, suppose that the FTA is formed between the exporting country $L$ and the importing country. Then, the other exporting country's government gives a production subsidy to its domestic firms and the importing country's government imposes a positive tariff on the imports from the other exporting country. On the contrary, under Assumption 2, suppose that the FTA is formed between the exporting country $S$ and the importing country. Then, the other exporting country's government imposes a production tax on its domestic firms and the importing country's government likely imposes a negative tariff on the imports from the other exporting country.*

In the case where the FTA is formed between the exporting country $S$ and the importing country, the reason why the third country's government likely imposes a negative tariff on the imports from the other exporting is as follows: The exporting country's government discourages its domestic firm production by imposing the production tax and thus the exports to the third country decrease. Therefore, the government of the third country uses a negative tariff to the imports from the country $L$ to recover its import level.

Substitution of Equations (4.10) and (4.11) into Equations (4.3) and (4.4) gives each country's welfare as follows:

$$W_i^F = \frac{n_i(n_i + n_j + 1)^2}{\Phi^2}, \tag{4.12}$$

$$W_j^F = \frac{(2n_i + 1)^2 n_j^2}{(n_i + 1)\Phi^2}, \tag{4.13}$$

$$W_I^F = \frac{\begin{array}{c} n_i^5 + 3n_i^4(2n_j + 1) + 3n_i^3(3n_j^2 + 6n_j + 1) \\ + n_i^2(11n_j^2 + 20n_j + 1) + (5n_i + 1)(n_j + 2)n_j \end{array}}{2(n_i + 1)\Phi^2}. \tag{4.14}$$

We can also derive the world welfare as

$$W^F = \frac{\begin{array}{c} (n_i + 1)(n_i^3 + 3n_i^2(2n_j + 1) \\ + n_i(9n_j^2 + 10n_j + 2) + (3n_j + 2)n_j) \end{array}}{2\Phi^2}, \tag{4.15}$$

from Equations (4.12), (4.13) and (4.14).

Using Equations (4.5), (4.6), (4.10), and (4.11), we obtain $t - t_j^F > 0$ and $s_j - s_j^F > 0$, from which we have the following proposition:

***Proposition* 1**

*Under Assumptions 1 and 2, suppose that the FTA is formed between the exporting country L(S) and the importing country. Then, (i) the importing country's government always reduces the tariff level against the other exporting country, and (ii) the other exporting country's government reduces the subsidy (increases the tax) level.*

Now we are in a position to inspect the first stage of the game, that is, to see whether an FTA is formed between one of the exporting country and the importing country. This can be done by a comparison of the level of each country's welfare between the "No FTA regime" and the "FTA regime". An FTA is supposed to be formed only when both countries become better off through the formation of FTA.

First, we consider whether the importing government has an incentive to form the FTA with one of the exporting countries.

Through the subtraction of Equation (4.8) from Equation (4.14), we can show that $W_I^F - W_I > 0$ if $n_i \geq n_j + 2 \geq 5$, and $W_I^F - W_I < 0$ if $n_j \geq n_i + 2 \geq 5$. So we have

***Lemma* 3**

*Under the Assumptions 1 and 2, the importing country's government has an incentive to form the FTA with country L, but does not with country S.*

The formation of FTA has two effects on the importing country's welfare: the effect on consumer surplus and tariff revenue. If the importing country forms an FTA with country $L$, the commodity price goes down drastically. Hence the consumer surplus greatly increases, which covers a loss in the revenue of the import tariff on the commodity from country $L$. In the case of an FTA with country $S$, however, the commodity price does not fall heavily. Thus an increase in the consumer surplus cannot cover a loss in the revenue of the import tariff on the commodity from country $S$.

So our next step is to inspect the possibility of country $L$ to form FTA with the importing country. Subtraction of Equation (4.7) from Equation (4.12) implies $W_L^F - W_L > 0$, which obviously establish

***Lemma* 4**

*Under Assumptions 1 and 2, the government of country L has an incentive to form the FTA with the importing country.*

The intuitive explanation of Lemma 4 is as follows: In the case where no FTA exists, the firms in country $L$ face export tax and import tariff and the firms in country $S$ face export subsidy and import tariff. But, in the case where country $L$ and the third country form an FTA with each other, the firms in country $L$ face no trade barriers, while the firms in country $S$ still face an import tariff. Thus, the firms in country $L$ can extend the market share in the third country after the FTA, so that even if the domestic policy is given up, the welfare of country $L$ goes up.

Combining Lemma 3 together with Lemma 4, we can conclude

***Proposition 2***

*Under Assumptions 1 and 2, the bilateral FTA between country L and the third country can be formed but not between country S and the third country.*

Finally, we consider how the FTA between the third country and counry $L$ affects the world welfare and the welfare of the non-member country $S$. Subtracting Equation (4.9) from Equation (4.15), we have $W^F - W > 0$. We also have $W_S^F - W_S < 0$ from Equations (4.7) and (4.13). Hence we can state

***Proposition 3***

*Under Assumptions 1 and 2, the FTA between the importing country and country L increases the world welfare but hurts the non-member country S.*

When an FTA is formed between the importing country and country $L$, the world output increases and the commodity price goes down heavily. This implies the world economy will have a benefit from the FTA as a whole. However, the FTA hurts the non-member country, because the firms of the country lose the market share in the third country.

Our final step is to investigate the possibility of a multilateral FTA by extending the bilateral FTA between the third country and country $L$. In our model, once the FTA is formed between third country and country $L$, the multilateral FTA is completed by the formation of a bilateral FTA between the third country and country $S$. Therefore we examine the possibility of this FTA under the existence of the FTA between the third country and country $L$. If the FTA is formed between the third country and country $S$, free trade is established in the whole world. Then, a simple calculation yields the welfare of each country as

$$W_i^{FT} = \frac{n_i}{(n_i + n_j + 1)^2}, \quad W_I^{FT} = \frac{(n_i + n_j)^2}{2(n_i + n_j + 1)},$$

where $W_i^{FT}$, for $i = L, S$, and $W_I^{FT}$ are, respectively, the welfare of country $i$ and the world welfare. Thus, under Assumption 2, it is clear that $W_I^{FT} - W_I^F < 0$. This means that the formation of an FTA between the third country and country $S$ is not possible even under the existence of FTA between the third country and country $L$. This is stated as

***Proposition* 4**

*Under Assumptions 1 and 2, the gradual extension of bilateral FTAs fail to build the multilateral FTA, where free trade is dominant.*

The same reason as that of Lemma 3 can be applied to this proposition.

## 4.3. Concluding Remarks

We have examined the possibility of the endogenous formation of FTA in a third country market model of the Brander and Spencer (1985) type. Under the circumstances where the importing third country uses a tariff policy to maximize its national welfare and the two exporting countries adopt the production subsidy policy for their domestic firms, so as to maximize their national welfares, it is revealed that the FTA is successfully formed only between the importing country and the exporting country where more firms exist. For this proposition to hold, we assumed that the establishment of an FTA requires not only the tariff free but also the abandonment of the production subsidy.

Some remarks may be in order.

***Remark* 1** The production subsidy can be interpreted as the export subsidy in our model, since both exporting countries have no domestic markets.

***Remark* 2** If we suppose that neither of the exporting country uses the subsidy policy, no bilateral FTA is possible. This is obvious for the FTA necessarily hurting the importing country.

***Remark* 3** Even if we allow the exporting countries to use the production subsidy, no bilateral FTA is possible under the circumstances, wherein exporting country can maintain the subsidy policy after the formation of FTA. This is a simple extension of Remark 2.

***Remark* 4** Since we focused on the FTA, we did not consider the possibility of the FTA between two exporting countries. However, if we extend the analysis to the economic partnership agreement (EPA), we need to think about the EPA between two exporting countries. In that case, we can show that EPA is not formed between the two countries since the large exporting country becomes worse off by this EPA.

Finally we should point out that our results are based on the assumption of a uniform tariff. However, even if this assumption is abandoned and a differential tariff is applied to each exporting country, the basic results seem to carry over. We need a precise analysis for this, though tough calculation is required.

## References

Brander, JA and BJ Spencer (1985) Export subsidies and international market share rivalry,*Journal of International Economics* 18, 83–100.

Freund, CL (2000) Multilateralism and the endogenous formation of preferential trade agreements, *Journal of International Economics* 52, 359–376.

Mukunoki, H (2004) On the optimal external tariff of a free trade area with internal market integration, *Japan and the World Economy*, 16, 431–448.

Nomura, R, T Ohkawa, M Okamura and M Tawada (2013) Does a bilateral FTA pave the way for multilateral free trade? *Review of International Economics* 21, 164–176.

Ohkawa, T, M Okamura and M Tawada (2002) Endogenous timing and welfare in the game of trade policies under international oligopoly. In *Economic Theory and International Trade*. A Woodland (Ed.). UK: Edward Elgar, 218–231.

Yi, SS (1996) Endogenous formation of customs unions under imperfect competition: Open regionalism is good, *Journal of International Economics* 41, 153–177.

# Part III
# Empirics

# Chapter 5

# Exploring the Spatial Connectivity of US States, 1993–2007

*Jee-Sun Lee* and Geoffrey J.D. Hewings†*

**Korea Transport Institute, Sejong-City, 339-007, Korea*

*†Regional Economics Applications Laboratory, University of Illinois, Urbana, IL 61801-3671, USA*

*After a hiatus of almost 30 years, the publication of the interstate commodity flow data for 1993 afforded the first opportunity to examine the nature and strength of interstate connectivity in the US. While the New Economic Geography has provided new stimulus to understanding the spatial economy, complemented by new developments in trade theory that have highlighted geographical proximity, relatively little attention has been paid to the spatial structure of trade, especially at the inter-regional scale. Using data of 1993, 1997, 2002 and 2007, this paper explores various features of the spatial connectivity of the US states. The initial explorations focus on the concentration of the interstate trade system using simple Gini measures and then exploring the flow patterns with principal component analyses to examine the degree to which states share similar product origins or shipment destinations. Thereafter dyadic factor analysis is used to explore the flow structure for an aggregation of 13 commodities. One of the important findings from the analyses is that the general spatial pattern of interstate trade still reflects a geographical structure based on contiguity, with the notable exception of California.*

## 5.1. Introduction

Inter-regional trade has increased as regions within a country have rapidly integrated with each other in response to decreases in transportation costs, the opportunity to exploit scale economies and changes in the spatial organization of production systems. According to new estimates from Commodity Flows Survey (CFS) published by the Bureau of Transportation Statistics (BTS) of the US Department of Transportation and US Census Bureau, over 12.2 billion tons of freight, valued at $11.5 trillion, was carried over 3.3 trillion ton-miles in the United States in 2007 (see Table 5.1). In particular, CFS data shows commodity flow growth exceeded growth of gross domestic product (GDP) in each time period of 1993, 1997, 2002 and 2007, and dependence on interstate flows had remarkably increased over the last decade (see Table 5.2). In addition to the increased inter-regional trade, the structure of inter-regional trade has been changing and becoming more complex.

Understanding of the nature of economic interactions as well as the relevant changes in production processes across different levels of geographic space contribute to the explanation of the transforming structure and system of inter-regional trade. In the past, the majority of firms comprised one or at most two establishments; however, multi-establishment firms were far more common by the mid-2000s. The effects of mergers and acquisitions together with the usual processes of entry and exit have promoted the presence of multi-establishment firms in recent years (Parr *et al.*, 2002). With this changing system, new ownership patterns have become the norm

**Table 5.1.** Total shipment of all the commodities, 1993–2007.

| Year | Value ($ Million) | Ton (Thousand tons) |
|---|---|---|
| 1993 | 5,846,334 | 9,688,493 |
| 1997 | 6,943,988 | 11,089,733 |
| 2002 | 8,397,210 | 11,667,919 |
| 2007 | 11,476,086 | 12,173,993 |

*Data source*: BTS, CFS 1993, 1997, 2002 and 2007.

**Table 5.2.** Comparison of growth rates of national GDP and commodity flows, 1993–2007.

| | Growth rates | | |
|---|---|---|---|
| | GDP | Commodity flows (Value) | Difference in percentage points |
| 1993–1997 | 15.54% | 18.78% | 3.23% |
| 1997–2002 | 15.46% | 20.93% | 5.47% |
| 2002–2007 | 14.68% | 36.67% | 21.99% |
| 1993–2002 | 33.40% | 43.63% | 10.23% |
| 1993–2007 | 52.98% | 96.30% | 43.32% |

*Source*: BTS, CFS 1993, 1997, 2002 and 2007.
BEA, *Real GDP (chained dollars)*, 1990–2008.

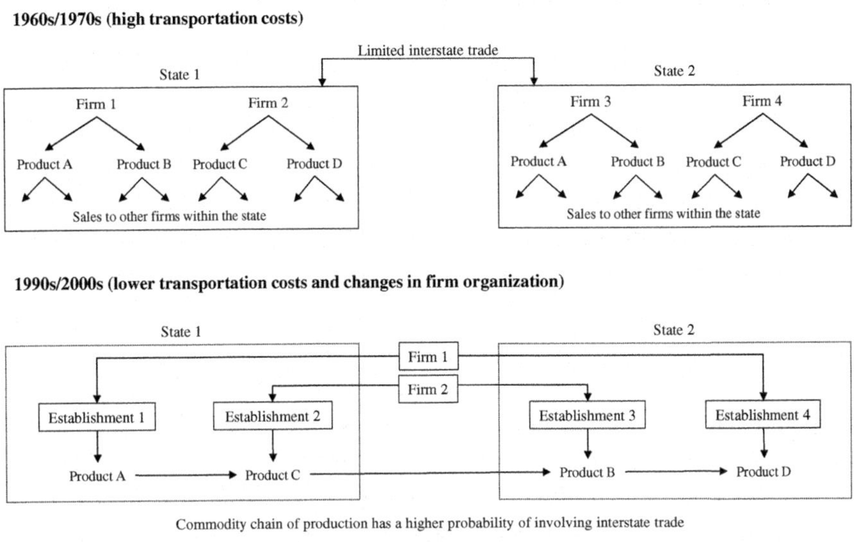


**Figure 5.1.** Changing spatial organization of firms (from four firms to two firms/four establishments).

*Source*: Parr *et al.*, 2002.

with firms owning a diverse portfolio of establishments. Figure 5.1 summarizes the changes in a stylized fashion. Establishments owned by a firm are more often located in many different states and even in multiple countries. Decreased transportation costs, advanced

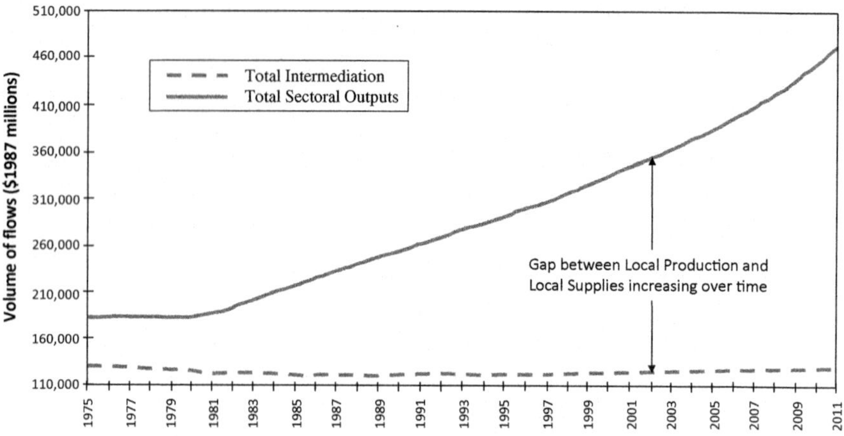


**Figure 5.2.** Values of total sectoral outputs and total intermediation in the changing economy, 1975–2011.

*Source*: Hewings *et al.*, 1998.

technology in communications and changing system of production have promoted this change in the spatial organization of firms. Therefore, it is important to investigate what is actually produced within the establishments, how and where inputs are sourced and output products are distributed to the market, within the transformed spatial organization of production to understand the changing structure and system of inter-regional trade.

Israilevich and Mahidhara (1991) and Hewings *et al.* (1998) detected that while output in most sectors was increasing for the period 1970–1987, and 1975–2011, respectively, in the Chicago region, the degree of interdependence was decreasing (see Figure 5.2). This process was referred to earlier as 'hollowing-out' by Okazaki (1989), and implies a relative decrease in the density of intermediate transactions. In other words, establishments are buying less from other establishments within the region and selling less within the region; as a result, the typical establishment is involved in a wider geographical search for their new sources of inputs and markets for their products, generating in the process more interstate trade.

Another challenging and significant change in production structure is represented by the fragmentation of production processes. The whole production process has been fragmented into smaller and more specialized production components; each specialized sub-production process is often located in different parts of the economy. The result of this new mechanism in the production process is that the commodity value chain now involves more interstate or inter-regional movements. In particular, more vertical intra-industry trade between smaller and more specialized production components have been observed. The service links such as transportation infrastructure and communication networking have encouraged the production process to become more fragmented and vertically integrated.

The present paper has as its main objective an understanding of the changing nature and structure of inter-regional trade within a country. Each region's economic structural changes and the new spatial organization of production, generated by the fragmented production process, made possible by an open economy with significantly lower transportation costs have resulted in a complex and changing pattern of inter-regional trade. Such changes in the inter-regional or interstate trade pattern raise the question: *where are the main sources of inputs and markets for each region and how have they changed over time*? In order to seek the answer to this question, exploratory spatial data analyses using the US CFS data are conducted to explore the spatial connectivity of US interstate trade. The chapter is organized as follows: a literature review follows prior to a presentation of the data sources in Section 5.3 together with some exploratory analysis of interstate commodity flows. Section 5.4 examines the spatial patterns of these flows and the presentation of trade regions. The final section offers some concluding remarks.

## 5.2. Literature Review

Commodity flows reflect differences in regional economic structure as well as differences in the tastes and preferences of consumers. Nevertheless, very little work has been directed to exploring the spatial or geographical patterns of trade. While the New Economic Geography has provided new stimuli to understanding the spatial economy, complemented by new developments in trade theory that have highlighted geographical proximity, relatively little attention has been paid to the *spatial structure* of trade, especially at the inter-regional scale (see Hewings and Oosterhaven, 2013 for a review). Frankel (1998) noted that (international) trade theorists and researchers have ignored the geographical dimension so that they treated countries as disembodied entities that lacked a physical location in geographical space. This reawakened interest in the geographical dimensions of trade has focused attention on the factors that influence the amount and type of commodities shipped between regions, paying special attention to the nature of spatial interdependence.

Krugman (1979) developed the New Economic Geography as a new trade theory that attempted to explain why trade occurred in the first place and to provide a better explanation for the specialization and trade between regions. This new theory does not depend on comparative advantage for explaining trade; the key to understanding the rationale for trade in Krugman's (1979) model is the combination of increasing returns to scale at the firm level and the love-of-variety effect in consumers' preferences. The introduction of increasing returns to scale implies a market structure of imperfect competition. In Krugman's (1979) model, little is said about the role of geography: the location of economic activity is not really an issue. Firms are indifferent about the location of their production sites since trade costs are zero. Even if there were positive trade costs, the market size is evenly distributed between two countries, which preclude any agglomeration of economic activity. It is indeterminate which country ends up producing which varieties. All one can say is that countries produce different varieties and the pattern of trade is indeterminate. Krugman (1979) developed his 1979 model keeping the same rationale for intra-industry trade but employing several different assumptions: (1) the opening up of trade does not lead to an increase in the scale of production, instead, more varieties are produced under trade than under autarky, (2) transport costs exist, which is obviously relevant from a geographical point of view, (3) demand per variety is no longer symmetric as countries differ in market size. Krugman and Venables (1990) refined previous models by allowing countries to differ in size, so that they addressed the agglomeration of economic activity better by means of introducing an uneven overall distribution. New Economic Geography emphasizes the need for a formal consideration of the geographical location to understand trade.

Such reawakened interests in the geographical dimensions of trade have focused attention on the factors that influence the amount and type of commodities shipped between regions, paying special attention to the nature of inter-regional trade. Studies on spatial pattern of inter-regional trade or commodity flows from the perspective of transportation or economic geography and regional science can be categorized into three main subjects.

The first category focuses on the exploratory spatial data analysis of the flows. This realm is associated with several quantitative approaches that analyze the geographical or spatial patterns with indices based on mathematical or statistical methods with the goal of depicting the detected phenomena in the geographical context in more effective ways. The second category has endeavored to detect and sort out the underpinning reasons or factors that determine the observed spatial pattern or structure of trade flows. For this division, various spatial interaction modeling approaches have been developed. While the first approach only portrays the observed phenomenon, the second approach tries to discover what kinds of forces determine the observed patterns or structure in the space. However, the second field can be developed based on the results extracted from the first category of analysis. The final topic is the estimation of trade flows; this third field is very much dependent on some of the findings and insights generated from the second field. Reliable estimation or forecast for the trade flows can be possible through the development of spatial interaction models that explain the reality in plausible ways. After all, the exploratory spatial data analysis of trade flows that can be categorized as the first subject in the field of inter-regional trade study, can be considered as the cornerstone for understanding the underlining regional economic structure.

Graphical presentations of commodity movements have been the most common tools to examine the pattern of trade flows among regions (Ullman, 1957; Smith, 1964; Cox, 1965; Berry, 1966; Rodgers, 1971; Tobler, 1975, 1981, 1987). Ullman (1957) examined the spatial pattern of commodity flows in US domestic and foreign trade mainly through railroads in order to explain the spatial connections in the US economy. He produced a series of maps demonstrating state-to-state freight movements of selective commodities for 20 representative states based on the Carload Waybill Statistics published by Interstate Commerce Commission for 1948. A study of the state-to-state trade flow maps enabled him to capture specialized production and consumption areas and the effect of distance on spatial interaction between regions. In this landmark study of his on the US commodity flows, Ullman explains flows as being determined by notions of complementarity, intervening opportunity, and transferability. According to his three bases of spatial interaction, trade takes place when there are two regions providing a market, clearing demand and supply of a shippable product (complementarity), when there is no other alternative source of supply (intervening opportunity), and when transport costs or friction is not too great (transferability). Several studies on spatial interaction between regions which had been built on Ullman's ideas are discussed next.

Smith (1964) examined the agricultural commodity flow by rail to the six New England states in the US in 1959. He devised an index based on one of Ullman's notions of spatial interaction, 'complementarity,' to depict the spatial pattern of shipments of agricultural commodities to New England from 34 states. His index of complementarity indicates the relative importance of trading partners. Knudsen (1988) also utilized Ullman's concept of complementarity to analyze the patterns of trade partnerships in the US interstate commodity flows for the period 1972–1981, and revealed that trade partnerships had been predominantly stable over time, despite rapidly fluctuating flow volumes. Further, he concluded that partnerships involving large volumes are much more stable than those involving small volumes.

Berry (1962, 1966) introduced factor analysis to the field of flow analysis. Berry (1966) conducted a study on the Indian commodity flows to depict the pattern of flows as well as to identify the factors determining the pattern of connections within the Indian economy. First, he illustrated the spatial patterns of commodity flows in India. His study produced a large volume of maps of Indian commodity flows that provide a vivid cartographic portrayal of the principal patterns of spatial interaction in India in 1960. This atlas of Indian commodity flows covers 63 commodity items shipped within India. For each commodity, a set of maps contains 12 characteristics indicating shipment quantity and value of flows to or from main metropolitan centers (Calcutta, Bombay, Madras, and Delhi) as well as non-metropolitan areas, major producing areas, main transportation routes, major origins and destinations in the trade partnership, major regional flows and hinterland, and urban population density as a potential demand factor. Although such descriptive maps provide a quick glimpse of the pattern of commodity flows, more detailed and supplementary measures are required to enrich the studies of trade flows among regions in the field of transportation geography and regional science. Hence, Berry (1966) employed a general field theory-based analysis on the relationship between commodity flows and spatial structure. To accomplish this analysis, dyadic factor analysis with a flow data matrix of 1,260 rows (36 by 36 for 36 major trade blocks) and 63 columns (for 63 commodity items) were made. Black (1973) also conducted dyadic factor analysis of a series of 24 commodity groups for the nine US census divisions. He detected five significant factors and discovered each of these was centered on a different geographic region. Factor analysis of commodity flow data may be basic in any description of the geography of inter-regional flows for a set of regions.

Recent efforts have been made in applying the exploratory spatial data analysis on the inter-regional trade. Perobelli and Haddad (2003) employed Local Indicators of Spatial Association (LISA) statistics to explore the spatial distribution of the inter-regional trade among the 27 Brazilian states for years of 1985–1996. They detected the presence of spatial heterogeneity in the inter-regional trade during the period of analysis. Based on this result, they concluded that the regional disparities in Brazil have persisted over time.

Compared to the field of inter-regional trade study, more work has been focused on inter-regional migration studies for analyzing the spatial pattern of inter-regional migration (see, for example, Plane and Isserman, 1983; Ellis *et al.*, 1993; Pandit, 1994; Plane and Mulligan, 1997; Rogers *et al.*, 2002). Although trade in goods and trade in people (migration) have different characteristics and motivations, similar approaches might be applicable, since both interactions are produced based on human economic and social behavior.

Now, after a hiatus of almost 30 years, commodity flows within the United States since 1993 have been surveyed and compiled in a series of reports for every five years by the US Census Bureau and the BTS. This publication of the interstate commodity flow data afforded the opportunity to examine the nature and strength of interstate connectivity in the US. This study replicates Berry's dyadic flow factor analysis and trade Gini measures to explore the spatial pattern of the US interstate commodity flows. The analyses investigate the temporal changes in spatial patterns of trade flows in terms of spatial connectivity in the distribution of interstate trade, trading partnership, and the spatial extent of trading zones over time.

## 5.3. Data and Methods

### 5.3.1. *Commodity flow survey (CFS) data*

Commodity flows within the United States have been surveyed and compiled in a series of reports by US Census Bureau in the US Department of Commerce and the Research and Innovative Technology Administration (RITA) in BTS every five years since 1993. This study utilizes all the four-year CFS datasets to identify the geographical patterns of US interstate commodity flows so as to explore their spatial shifts between 1993 and 2007. Table 5.3 provides a summary of the data collection process, sample sizes, transportation modes and commodity classifications. The commodity classification used in this chapter is shown in Table 5.4; for this level of aggregation, Tables 5.5 and 5.6 provide summaries of the

**Table 5.3.** Comparison among datasets of CFS 1993, 1997, 2002 and 2007.

| | 1993 | 1997 | 2002 | 2007 |
|---|---|---|---|---|
| Geographical coverage | 50 states & DC<br>89 NTARs[1] | | 4 census regions<br>9 census divisions<br>50 states & DC<br>Selected metropolitan areas | |
| Industry coverage | Based on 1987 SIC[2] | | Based on 1997 NAICS[3] | |
| Commodity Classification system | STCC<br>(33 commodities)[4] | SCTG<br>(41 commodities)[5] | SCTG<br>(41 commodities)[5] | SCTG<br>(41 commodities)[5] |
| Transportation mode | 17 modes[6] | 13 modes[6] | 13 modes[6] | 13 modes[6] |
| Sample size | About 200,000 establishments | About 100,000 establishments | About 50,000 establishments | About 100,000 establishments |
| Additional special reports | None | Export<br>hazardous materials | Export<br>hazardous materials | Export<br>hazardous materials |

*Notes*: Summary based on overview information for each CFS report.
1. National Transportation Analysis Regions defined in a basis of the BEA regions.
2. Standard Industry Classification.
3. North America Industry Classification System.
4. Standard Transportation Commodity Classification; number in the parenthesis is based on 2-digit SCTG code.
5. Standard Classification of Transported Goods; number in the parenthesis is based on 20-digit SCTG code; from the 2002 CFS, retail electronic shopping and mail-order houses are newly added.
6. Excludes "other and unknown modes"; figures include the number of single modes as well as multiple modes.

**Table 5.4.** Commodity classification for CFS analysis in this study.

| Code | Sector description | SCTG (1997, 2002, 2007) | STCC (1993) |
|---|---|---|---|
| 01 | Agriculture, forestry and fisheries | 1–4, 25 | 1, 8–9 |
| 02 | Mining | 10–16 | 10–11, 13–14 |
| 03 | Construction | None | None |
| 04 | Food, beverage, and tobacco products | 5–9 | 20, 21 |
| 05 | Textile, apparel, and leather products | 30 | 22, 23, 31 |
| 06 | Paper and printing related products | 27, 28, 29 | 26, 27 |
| 07 | Chemical and allied products | 17–24, 31 | 28–30, 32 |
| 08 | Primary metals products | 32 | 33 |
| 09 | Fabricated metal products | 33, 38 | 19, 34, 38 |
| 10 | Industrial machinery and equipment | 34 | 35 |
| 11 | Electronic and electric equipment | 35 | 36 |
| 12 | Transportation equipment | 36, 37 | 37 |
| 13 | Wood, furniture & misc. manufacturing products | 26, 29, 40 | 24, 25, 39 |
| 14 | TCU, services, and government enterprises | 41, 43, 99 | 40, 41, 42, 48, 99 |

*Note*: No commodities shipped in the sector of construction (03).

total value and tonnage of commodities shipped over the four observation years. The CFS data provides information on shipment characteristics such as type, value, weight, distance, origins and destinations, and transportation modes for commodities shipped in the 50 states and the District of Columbia (DC).[1] This study

[1]These state-to-state commodity flow movement information commonly used for regional transportation-related research and policy making has a couple of inherent problems: one main limitation is the data disclosure issue due to an unacceptably high statistical variability and the resulting lack of confidence in the estimate, and the other one is the limited industry coverage of survey. While the CFS covers shipments generated from mining, manufacturing, wholesale, and selected retail and services trade industries, commodity shipments from farms, fisheries, transportation, construction, and most government-owned establishments and many other retail and services industry-related establishments are excluded from the CFS.

**Table 5.5.** Value of shipment by commodity group, 1993, 1997, 2002, and 2007 (unit: million $).

| | 1993 | | 1997 | | 2002 | | 2007 | |
|---|---|---|---|---|---|---|---|---|
| Commodity | Value | Rank | Value | Rank | Value | Rank | Value | Rank |
| 01 | 125,762 | 11 | 187,157 | 11 | 114,311 | 11 | 251,953 | 11 |
| 02 | 41,321 | 12 | 47,100 | 12 | 36,576 | 12 | 79,037 | 12 |
| 04 | 855,005 | 2 | 650,620 | 3 | 590,903 | 3 | 1,005,265 | 2 |
| 05 | 351,666 | 6 | 302,927 | 9 | 312,562 | 7 | 348,722 | 10 |
| 06 | 185,720 | 10 | 353,553 | 7 | 242,567 | 9 | 358,588 | 9 |
| 07 | 1,017,600 | 1 | 1,156,792 | 1 | 1,234,678 | 1 | 2,765,197 | 1 |
| 08 | 206,116 | 9 | 251,882 | 10 | 198,434 | 10 | 432,696 | 8 |
| 09 | 371,532 | 4 | 323,361 | 8 | 294,230 | 8 | 564,295 | 6 |
| 10 | 360,360 | 5 | 363,248 | 6 | 360,486 | 6 | 555,574 | 7 |
| 11 | 348,926 | 7 | 734,938 | 2 | 602,977 | 2 | 879,577 | 3 |
| 12 | 502,301 | 3 | 527,563 | 5 | 557,228 | 4 | 788,757 | 4 |
| 13 | 569,522 | — | 301,503 | — | 491,624 | — | 708,510 | — |
| 14 | 71,708 | — | 650,620 | — | 590,903 | — | 917,136 | — |

*Notes* 1. Only 48 US states are considered for calculations.
2. For the rankings, sectors 13 and 14 are excluded due to their composition characteristics.
*Data source*: BTS, CFS 1993, 1997, 2002 and 2007.

**Table 5.6.** Tonnage of shipment by commodity group, 1993, 1997, 2002, and 2007 (unit: thousand tons).

| | 1993 | | 1997 | | 2002 | | 2007 | |
|---|---|---|---|---|---|---|---|---|
| Commodity | Ton | Rank | Ton | Rank | Ton | Rank | Ton | Rank |
| 01 | 525,984 | 4 | 966,203 | 3 | 504,135 | 3 | 790,010 | 3 |
| 02 | 2,602,296 | 2 | 3,101,830 | 1 | 2,768,892 | 2 | 3,668,875 | 1 |
| 04 | 832,836 | 3 | 575,422 | 4 | 494,483 | 4 | 703,793 | 4 |
| 05 | 35,334 | 9 | 39,028 | 11 | 33,054 | 10 | 34,252 | 11 |
| 06 | 199,341 | 6 | 244,023 | 6 | 162,365 | 6 | 226,173 | 6 |
| 07 | 2,853,626 | 1 | 2,813,131 | 2 | 2,770,650 | 1 | 3,561,016 | 2 |
| 08 | 245,258 | 5 | 286,966 | 5 | 224,704 | 5 | 304,608 | 5 |
| 09 | 84,318 | 7 | 83,176 | 8 | 66,089 | 8 | 106,093 | 8 |
| 10 | 28,521 | 10 | 41,608 | 9 | 43,457 | 9 | 52,910 | 9 |
| 11 | 25,811 | 11 | 33,085 | 11 | 28,375 | 11 | 34,675 | 10 |
| 12 | 74,235 | 8 | 83,950 | 7 | 87,796 | 7 | 116,984 | 7 |
| 13 | 99,585 | — | 219,074 | — | 295,300 | — | 387,396 | — |
| 14 | 656,793 | — | 338,235 | — | 312,856 | — | 384,718 | — |

*Notes* 1. Data calculated for 48 US states.
2. Rankings for sectors 13 and 14 are not considered.
*Data source*: BTS, CFS 1993, 1997, 2002 and 2007.

focuses on 48 contiguous US states and excludes Alaska and Hawaii. All the analyses in this study are basically conducted for all aggregated commodities and with greater attention to the values of shipments.

### 5.3.2. *Exploratory spatial data analysis of interstate commodity flows*

#### 5.3.2.1. *Gini index of concentration in the interstate trade system*

Plane and Mulligan (1997) introduced the methods based on the Gini coefficient in order to gauge the degree of spatial inequality that exists in the relative volumes of a set of origin-destination-specific flows in the US interstate migration system. The Gini coefficient[2] is one of the most common indices to measure income distribution in economics. Using the Gini index measures, they compared the degree to which the sources of in-migration *versus* the destinations of out-migration are spatially focused for the US migration movements in the 1980s. This study replicates their application of Gini indices to explore overall shifts in the geographical patterns of flows in terms of "spatial concentration" or "spatial dispersion" in the US interstate trade system for 1993–2007.[3] Several sets of the Gini index are calculated in this section to show the spatial concentration of importing or exporting states in the US interstate commodity flow movements.

A total Gini coefficient for a commodity $m$, ${}^{T}G(m)$, is first calculated based on gross commodity flows among 48 states ($n = 48$) excluding intrastate movements (flows within a state) as

---

[2]For a set of $n$ numbers of observations, a general formula of a Gini index is defined as:

$$G = \frac{\left[\sum_{a=1}^{n} \sum_{b=1}^{n} |y_a - y_b|\right]}{2n^2\mu},$$

where $y_a, y_b$ represent two of different observations, and $\mu$ is the mean of all $n$ numbers of observations.

[3]For the detailed method explanation, see Plane and Mulligan (1997).

Equation (5.1):

$$
{}^{T}G(m) = \frac{\sum_{i=1}^{n}\sum_{\substack{j=1\\ j\neq i}}^{n}\sum_{g=1}^{n}\sum_{\substack{h=1\\ h\neq g}}^{n}|f_{ij}-f_{gh}|}{2[n(n-1)]^{2}\left[\sum_{i=1}^{n}\sum_{\substack{j=1\\ j\neq i}}^{n} f_{ij}\right]T/[n(n-1)]}
= \frac{\sum_{i=1}^{n}\sum_{\substack{j=1\\ j\neq i}}^{n}\sum_{g=1}^{n}\sum_{\substack{h=1\\ h\neq g}}^{n}|f_{ij}-f_{gh}|}{2[n(n-1)]T}, \tag{5.1}
$$

where $f_{ij}$ = commodity flows from state $i$ to state $j(i, j = 1, \ldots, 48)$,

$$
T = \sum_{i=1}^{n}\sum_{\substack{j=1\\ j\neq i}}^{n} f_{ij}\text{: total interstate commodity flows between two different states.}
$$

The second three sets of interstate trade Gini index measure the spatial equality of the total commodity flows divided into three components: gross outflows, gross inflows, and net trade exchanged among states. The gross outflow Gini index for commodity $m$, ${}^{T}G_{R\bullet}(m)$, is calculated as the difference between interstate commodity flows leaving a same origin state (by row in a state-to-state commodity flow matrix) so as to show the relative extent to which the destination selections of commodity outflows of each state are spatially focused in the entire trade system as Equation (5.2):

$$
{}^{T}G_{R\bullet}(m) = \frac{\sum_{i=1}^{n}\sum_{\substack{j=1\\ j\neq i}}^{n}\sum_{\substack{h=1\\ h\neq i,j}}^{n}|f_{ij}-f_{ih}|}{2[n(n-1)]T}. \tag{5.2}
$$

The Gini index of gross inflows for commodity $m$, ${}^{T}G_{\bullet C}(m)$, is also calculated in a similar way as above, but based on the differences between interstate commodity inflows to a same destination state from various origin states (by column in a state-to-state commodity flow matrix). The gross inflows Gini index is calculated based on Equation (5.3) and represents the degree of spatial concentration of commodity flows from all the various origins.

$$ {}^{T}G_{\bullet C}(m) = \frac{\sum_{j=1}^{n}\sum_{\substack{i=1\\ i\neq j}}^{n}\sum_{\substack{g=1\\ g\neq j,i}}^{n}|f_{ij}-f_{gj}|}{2[n(n-1)]T}. \tag{5.3} $$

The exchange Gini index, ${}^{T}G_{RC,CR}(m)$, is calculated based on the difference between each commodity flow ($f_{ij}$) and its counterpart's flow ($f_{ji}$) following the formula in Equation (5.4):

$$ {}^{T}G_{RC,CR}(m) = \frac{\sum_{i=1}^{n}\sum_{\substack{j=1\\ j\neq i}}^{n}|f_{ij}-f_{ji}|}{2[n(n-1)]T} \tag{5.4} $$

The index varies from 0 to 1. The Gini index is equal to 0 when all commodity movements are evenly distributed among all possible origins and destinations. An index of 1 indicates that all movements are concentrated in a single interstate trade flow, which means that there is only one dominant origin producing all outflows or there exists only one destination absorbing all inflow shipments. When a comparison among indices over time is needed, using $t$ to denote the time period, standardization is possible by dividing each Gini index value by the total flow Gini index value to facilitate comparison among indices over time. The relative values obtained through Equation (5.5) reveal whether outflow or inflow or net exchange is more spatially focused in an entire interstate trade system over different time periods.

$$ \begin{aligned} &{}^{T}G^{*}_{R\bullet}(m)_t = 100 \times {}^{T}G_{R\bullet}(m)_t / {}^{T}G(m)_t \\ &{}^{T}G^{*}_{\bullet C}(m)_t = 100 \times {}^{T}G_{\bullet C}(m)_t / {}^{T}G(m)_t \\ &{}^{T}G^{*}_{RC,CR}(m)_t = 100 \times {}^{T}G_{RC,CR}(m)_t / {}^{T}G(m)_t \\ &{}^{T}G^{*}_{R\bullet}(m)_t + {}^{T}G^{*}_{\bullet C}(m)_t + {}^{T}G^{*}_{RC,CR}(m)_t + {}^{T}G^{*}_{Other}(m)_t = 100, \end{aligned} \tag{5.5} $$

where

$$ \begin{aligned} &{}^{T}G_{Other}(m)_t = {}^{T}G(m)_t - [{}^{T}G_{R\bullet}(m)_t + {}^{T}G_{\bullet C}(m)_t + {}^{T}G_{RC,CR}(m)_t] \\ &{}^{T}G^{*}_{Other}(m)_t = 100 \times {}^{T}G_{Other}(m)_t / {}^{T}G(m)_t. \end{aligned} $$

The last two sets of Gini indices introduced by Plane and Mulligan (1997) are more relevant since they decompose the gross outflow and inflow Gini indices further, so as to facilitate the examination of the contributions of each state to the entire system. The two additional more disaggregated indices are defined as the outflow field Gini index, ${}^{O}G_{k\bullet}(m)$ and the inflow field Gini index, ${}^{I}G_{\bullet k}(m)$ for commodity $m$, respectively. Each field Gini index can be computed employing the expression in Equation (5.6):

$$
\begin{aligned}
{}^{O}G_{k\bullet}(m) &= \frac{\sum_{\substack{j=1\\ j\neq k}}^{n} \sum_{\substack{h=1\\ h\neq k}}^{n} |f_{kj} - f_{kh}|}{2(n-1)^2 \sum_{\substack{j=1\\ j\neq k}}^{n} f_{kj}/(n-1)} \\
&= \frac{\sum_{\substack{j=1\\ j\neq k}}^{n} \sum_{\substack{h=1\\ h\neq k}}^{n} |f_{kj} - f_{kh}|}{2(n-1)O_k} \\
{}^{I}G_{\bullet k}(m) &= \frac{\sum_{\substack{i=1\\ i\neq k}}^{n} \sum_{\substack{g=1\\ g\neq k}}^{n} |f_{ik} - f_{gk}|}{2(n-1)^2 \sum_{\substack{i=1\\ i\neq k}}^{n} f_{ik}/(n-1)} \\
&= \frac{\sum_{\substack{i=1\\ i\neq k}}^{n} \sum_{\substack{g=1\\ g\neq k}}^{n} |f_{ik} - f_{gk}|}{2(n-1)I_k},
\end{aligned}
\tag{5.6}
$$

$$O_k = \sum_{\substack{j=1\\ j\neq k}}^{n} f_{kj}\text{: total outflows from the origin state } k$$

where

$$I_k = \sum_{\substack{i=1\\ i\neq k}}^{n} f_{ik}\text{: total inflows to the destination state } k$$

These outflow and inflow field Gini indices also vary between 0 and 1. This study considers the $z$-scores[4] for each field Gini index for a clearer comparison. Table 5.7 summarizes the actual formulas

[4] $z$-scores can be calculated by subtracting the averages across all states in the interstate trade system and dividing by their standard deviation. The scores are computed using the SPSS software (SPSS Statistics version 17.0).

**Table 5.7.** Calculation equations of Gini indices for the US interstate CFS data for 1993, 1997, 2002 and 2007.

| Gini index | Equation | Gini index | Equation |
|---|---|---|---|
| Total flows | ${}^{T}G^{m,t} = \frac{\sum_{i=1}^{48}\sum_{j=1, j\neq i}^{48}\sum_{g=1}^{48}\sum_{h=1, h\neq g}^{48} \lvert f_{ij}^{m,t} - f_{gh}^{m,t}\rvert}{2[48(48-1)]T^{m,t}}$ | Outflow field | ${}^{O}G_{k\bullet}^{m,t} = \frac{\sum_{j=1, j\neq k}^{48}\sum_{h=1, h\neq k}^{48} \lvert f_{kj}^{m,t} - f_{kh}^{m,t}\rvert}{2(48-1)O_k^{m,t}}$ |
| Outflows | ${}^{T}G_{R\bullet}^{m,t} = \frac{\sum_{i=1}^{48}\sum_{j=1, j\neq i}^{48}\sum_{h=1, h\neq i,j}^{48} \lvert f_{ij}^{m,t} - f_{ih}^{m,t}\rvert}{2[48(48-1)]T^{m,t}}$ | Inflow field | ${}^{I}G_{\bullet k}^{m,t} = \frac{\sum_{i=1, i\neq k}^{48}\sum_{g=1, g\neq k}^{48} \lvert f_{ik}^{m,t} - f_{gk}^{m,t}\rvert}{2(48-1)I_k^{m,t}}$ |
| Inflows | ${}^{T}G_{\bullet C}^{m,t} = \frac{\sum_{j=1}^{48}\sum_{i=1, i\neq j}^{48}\sum_{g=1, g\neq j,i}^{48} \lvert f_{ij}^{m,t} - f_{gj}^{m,t}\rvert}{2[48(48-1)]T^{m,t}}$ | | $f_{ij}^{m,t}$: Commodity flows from state $i$ to $j$ for commodity $m$ at time $t$<br>$T^{m,t} = \sum_{i=1}^{48}\sum_{j=1, j\neq i}^{48} f_{ij}^{m,t}$: Total gross flows from $i$ to $j$ for commodity $m$ at time $t$ |
| Exchanges | ${}^{T}G_{RC,CR}^{m,t}(m) = \frac{\sum_{i=1}^{48}\sum_{j=1, j\neq i}^{48} \lvert f_{ij}^{m,t} - f_{ji}^{m,t}\rvert}{2[48(48-1)]T^{m,t}}$ | | $O_k^{m,t} = \sum_{j=1, j\neq k}^{48} f_{kj}^{m,t}$: Total outflows from origin $k$ for commodity $m$ at time $t$<br>$I_k^{m,t} = \sum_{i=1, i\neq k}^{48} f_{ik}^{m,t}$: Total inflows to destination $k$ for commodity $m$ at time $t$ |

*Source*: Lee, JS (2010).

applied to compute the Gini indices from the 48 by 48 interstate trade matrices for each commodity group ($m$) at time $t$ in the Section 5.3.

#### 5.3.2.2. *Flow matrix factor analysis: Identification of trade regions of interstate trade*

In the next phase, factor analysis was employed in order to extract an underlying structure of flows from such a large and complex origin-to-destination interaction matrix by reducing the sets of flows into basic flow components. A principal component analysis (PCA) procedure is used as an extraction method for flow matrix factor analysis.

##### 5.3.2.2.1. Dyadic factor analysis of commodity flow

The basic purpose of flow matrix factor analysis is the derivation of clusters of areas with a similar spatial structure of interstate trade in terms of the geographic origins and destinations of the flows (Berry, 1971). Trading areas (or trading zones) are identified and categorized based on relative similarity of their flows, displaying a particular combination of source or destination locations of commodity flows among the states.

In undertaking a PCA with commodity flow data, two matrices are examined closely: the origin-to-destination commodity flow matrix and the connection matrix. According to Berry (1966), the $R$-mode and the $Q$-mode factor analyses need to be carried out for columns and rows of the original flow matrix separately, to identify the factors (or components) explaining the spatial structure of commodity flows. This is necessary because while the origin-to-destination flow matrices are square, they are not usually symmetric. Therefore, a separate analysis should be conducted for columns and rows, and different factors are likely to be obtained. The first step is to compute the correlations between patterns of individual state's inflows ($R$-mode) or outflows ($Q$-mode). For the $R$-mode PCA, a set of 48 by 48 matrices of correlation coefficients between 48 columns representing 48 origin states is produced, while the $Q$-mode PCA requires a set of 48 by 48 matrices of correlation coefficients between 48 rows indicating destination states. These correlation matrices are considered as connection matrices required for flow matrix factor analysis. Two states whose rows have a correlation coefficient of 1 are believed to have *proportionally* identical amount of outflows to every other state. When the coefficient for two states is less than 1, it indicates the extent to which the destinations of two state's outflows differ. A parallel explanation can be made for the correlation between two state's inflows.

The next step is to extract principal components for grouping states with similar commodity flow patterns based on the correlation matrices produced in the first step. The $Q$-mode PCA extracts a set of components based on the similarities in the way origins ship their products to destination so as to yield groups of origin or producing regions, while the $R$-mode PCA accomplishes something of a similar nature, based on the similarities in the way destinations assemble their needs, so as to identify the selection of destination states. States with high component loadings indicate that they are sharing *proportionally* similar destinations in the former analysis. In the latter analysis, states with high component loadings are interpreted that they have *proportionally* similar origins in common for their inflows. To simplify the structure of component loadings, a rotation technique is often used. In conjunction with loadings on components, the standardized component scores (usually called 'factor scores') on the components for the each state's outflow and inflow, assist in understanding the characteristics of the commodity flows. They measure the significance of a destination or an origin for the group of states that have similar outflow or inflow patterns, respectively. When looking into the outflow shipments, a large positive score indicates an especially strong destination of the outflows for those states that load highly on the component. A large negative score, conversely, indicates an extremely weak destination for the outflows from these states that have high component loadings. The interpretation for the inflow shipments can be made in a similar manner. For the states that have high loadings on the component, a large positive score indicates a particularly strong source of inflows, whereas a large negative score represents an extremely weak origin for the inflow shipment into these states.

The dyadic factor analysis was conducted on state-to-state commodity flow matrices over the periods 1993, 1997, 2002, and 2007 using the SPSS software. The analyses are executed with the aggregated shipments of all the commodities in terms of value of shipments. These dyadic factor analyses will portray the structure of commodity flows in the US in an expression of "trade regions (or trade zones)" based on the spatially similar trading patterns in terms of sharing origins and destinations in an interstate trade system.

## 5.4. Analysis Results: Spatial Patterns of US Interstate Commodity Flows

### 5.4.1. *"Spatial focusing" in interstate trade system*

First, four components of the Gini index for the total flows of US interstate trade for 1993, 1997, 2002, and 2007 were calculated and summarized as the raw coefficients as well as the standardized values, as shown in Table 5.8.

The values of the overall total flows Gini index for all the four years are greater than 0.7 in terms of the value of shipments and 0.8 in terms of tons shipped. Although overall fluctuations have been observed, a relatively slight decrease in 2007 is noticed compared to the overall total flow Gini index of 1993, which would suggest the overall extent of trade system is becoming a little less spatially focused. In a comparison of the total flows index values between those for flows in value terms and in weight of shipments, those for tons appear to be greater indicating that they are more spatially focused. The result reflects that the volume of commodities shipped might be influenced by distance factors, so that the movement appears more spatially focused, or more localized; further, the sources of many of these flows are not ubiquitous. However, the *spatially focused* basis of the Gini index value does not necessarily mean the pairs of trading state are located close to each other in terms of distance. With the exception of 2002, the column Gini index values for the origin selections of inflows are higher than the row Gini index values

**Table 5.8.** Total flows Gini index values for the US interstate trade for 1993, 1997, 2002, and 2007.

| | 1993 | | 1997 | | 2002 | | 2007 | |
|---|---|---|---|---|---|---|---|---|
| | Index | % | Index | % | Index | % | Index | % |
| In terms of value component | | | | | | | | |
| Rows (outflows) | 0.012638 | 1.724 | 0.012393 | 1.714 | 0.012758 | 1.737 | 0.012384 | 1.703 |
| Columns (inflows) | 0.012721 | 1.735 | 0.012438 | 1.721 | 0.012735 | 1.733 | 0.012842 | 1.766 |
| Exchanges | 0.000089 | 0.012 | 0.000087 | 0.012 | 0.000102 | 0.014 | 0.000091 | 0.012 |
| Other flows* | 0.707601 | 96.529 | 0.697942 | 96.553 | 0.709061 | 96.516 | 0.701919 | 96.519 |
| Overall total flows | 0.733049 | — | 0.722860 | — | 0.734656 | — | 0.727236 | — |
| In terms of ton component | | | | | | | | |
| Rows (outflows) | 0.015581 | 1.890 | 0.015518 | 1.886 | 0.015680 | 1.892 | 0.015428 | 1.875 |
| Columns (inflows) | 0.015640 | 1.897 | 0.015545 | 1.889 | 0.015562 | 1.878 | 0.015629 | 1.900 |
| Exchanges | 0.000178 | 0.022 | 0.000186 | 0.023 | 0.000187 | 0.023 | 0.000186 | 0.023 |
| Other flows* | 0.793002 | 96.191 | 0.791456 | 96.202 | 0.797228 | 96.207 | 0.791438 | 96.202 |
| Overall total flows | 0.824401 | — | 0.822705 | — | 0.828657 | — | 0.822682 | — |

*Source*: Lee, JS (2010).
*Other flows includes all other non-trivial flows except outflows, inflows and bilateral exchange flows.
Since the number of pairs is relatively large, their indices are marked as high values.
*Data source*: BTS, CFS.

for the destination selections of outflows, even though the differences between the row and column indices are quite small.

Tables 5.9 and 5.10 summarize the results (for values and tons respectively) based on the CFS movements of all the comprehensive commodities; it would be expected that the general interstate trade flows would tend to show similar counter-stream in two opposite flow directions of outflow and inflow. In essence, the flows in both directions between large states generally will be larger than those between smaller states, and this structural property would result in fairly similar row and column indices. When looking into these index values for mining and manufacturing commodities shipped separately, mining products shipped appear to have a more spatially focused movement over the interstate trade system compared to other manufactured goods. As for the row and column Gini indices, the mining products tend to have higher column Gini index values for all four years, whereas manufactured goods are no different from the general trends of the aggregated commodities shipped. These differences stem from the fact that mining products, as natural resources, are much more dependent on specific sources.

Next, the outflow and inflow field Gini indices for each state are computed and their standardized index values in a form of $z$-score are plotted in Figure 5.3 (for values; Figure 5.5 presents data based on tonnage). A positive $z$-score means that a state's trade field is more spatially focused than average, indicating its strong role in the interstate trade system. Negative $z$-scores indicate that a state's field is broader, or less focused. Negative $z$-scores for inflows indicate that commodities are shipped from diverse origin states, whereas negative $z$-scores for the outflow field Gini index suggest that commodities are shipped to widely dispersed destinations. When a 45° line is drawn on the scatter plots in Figure 5.3, the relative magnitudes of the standardized outflow and inflow field indices can be compared easily. States with larger $z$-score of inflow field index than that of outflow are plotted above the 45° line. The corresponding state is one where outflow is relatively uniform across all destinations, whereas inflow is more highly focused and comes from selective origins. States plotted below the 45° line represent to have a larger outflow field

**Table 5.9.** Total flows Gini indices for the values of shipment in 1993, 1997, 2002 and 2007.

| | | 1993 | | 1997 | | 2002 | | 2007 | |
|---|---|---|---|---|---|---|---|---|---|
| Sector | Components | Index | % | Index | % | Index | % | Index | % |
| Mining | Overall total flows | 0.96829 | — | 0.95896 | — | 0.97451 | — | 0.95353 | — |
| | Rows (outflows) | 0.01831 | 1.89 | 0.01793 | 1.87 | 0.01834 | 1.89 | 0.01822 | 1.91 |
| | Columns (inflows) | 0.01949 | 2.01 | 0.01909 | 1.99 | 0.01955 | 2.01 | 0.01904 | 2.00 |
| | Exchanges | 0.00040 | 0.04 | 0.00038 | 0.04 | 0.00042 | 0.04 | 0.00038 | 0.04 |
| | Other flows* | 0.93010 | 96.05 | 0.92157 | 96.10 | 0.93620 | 96.07 | 0.91589 | 96.05 |
| Manufacturing | Overall total flows | 0.77213 | — | 0.78054 | — | 0.80476 | — | 0.77950 | — |
| | Rows (outflows) | 0.01333 | 1.73 | 0.01342 | 1.72 | 0.01428 | 1.77 | 0.01335 | 1.71 |
| | Columns (inflows) | 0.01346 | 1.74 | 0.01342 | 1.72 | 0.01369 | 1.70 | 0.01362 | 1.75 |
| | Exchanges | 0.00009 | 0.01 | 0.00009 | 0.01 | 0.00012 | 0.02 | 0.00009 | 0.01 |
| | Other flows* | 0.74525 | 96.52 | 0.75360 | 96.55 | 0.77668 | 96.51 | 0.75242 | 96.53 |
| (1) Non-durable | Overall total flows | 0.78375 | — | 0.79378 | — | 0.82275 | — | 0.79553 | — |
| | Rows (outflows) | 0.01386 | 1.77 | 0.01395 | 1.76 | 0.01493 | 1.82 | 0.01406 | 1.77 |
| | Columns (inflows) | 0.01393 | 1.78 | 0.01386 | 1.75 | 0.01438 | 1.75 | 0.01411 | 1.77 |
| | Exchanges | 0.00011 | 0.01 | 0.00009 | 0.01 | 0.00014 | 0.02 | 0.00012 | 0.02 |
| | Other flows* | 0.75585 | 96.44 | 0.76588 | 96.49 | 0.79330 | 96.42 | 0.76724 | 96.44 |
| (2) Durable | Overall total flows | 0.78363 | — | 0.79069 | — | 0.81704 | — | 0.78828 | — |
| | Rows (outflows) | 0.01318 | 1.68 | 0.01337 | 1.69 | 0.01425 | 1.74 | 0.01316 | 1.67 |
| | Columns (inflows) | 0.01368 | 1.75 | 0.01370 | 1.73 | 0.01402 | 1.72 | 0.01387 | 1.76 |
| | Exchanges | 0.00011 | 0.02 | 0.00012 | 0.02 | 0.00014 | 0.02 | 0.00012 | 0.02 |
| | Other flows* | 0.75666 | 96.56 | 0.76350 | 96.56 | 0.78864 | 96.52 | 0.76113 | 96.56 |

*Source*: Lee, JS (2010).
*Other flows includes all other non-trivial flows except outflows, inflows and bilateral exchange flows.
Since the number of pairs is relatively large, their indices are marked as high values.
*Data source*: BTS, CFS.

**Table 5.10.** Total flows Gini indices for tons shipped in 1993, 1997, 2002 and 2007.

| | | 1993 | | 1997 | | 2002 | | 2007 | |
|---|---|---|---|---|---|---|---|---|---|
| Sector | Components | Index | % | Index | % | Index | % | Index | % |
| Mining | Overall total flows | 0.97499 | — | 0.97400 | — | 0.97962 | — | 0.97312 | — |
| | Rows (outflows) | 0.01781 | 1.83 | 0.01814 | 1.86 | 0.01803 | 1.84 | 0.01754 | 1.80 |
| | Columns (inflows) | 0.01969 | 2.02 | 0.01968 | 2.02 | 0.01983 | 2.02 | 0.01978 | 2.03 |
| | Exchanges | 0.00040 | 0.04 | 0.00040 | 0.04 | 0.00042 | 0.04 | 0.00040 | 0.04 |
| | Other flows* | 0.93709 | 96.11 | 0.93578 | 96.08 | 0.94134 | 96.09 | 0.93539 | 96.12 |
| Manufacturing | Overall total flows | 0.81932 | — | 0.82702 | — | 0.85068 | — | 0.82251 | — |
| | Rows (outflows) | 0.01530 | 1.87 | 0.01526 | 1.85 | 0.01604 | 1.89 | 0.01530 | 1.86 |
| | Columns (inflows) | 0.01527 | 1.86 | 0.01523 | 1.84 | 0.01572 | 1.85 | 0.01521 | 1.85 |
| | Exchanges | 0.00012 | 0.02 | 0.00012 | 0.01 | 0.00016 | 0.02 | 0.00012 | 0.02 |
| | Other flows* | 0.78862 | 96.25 | 0.79642 | 96.30 | 0.81876 | 96.25 | 0.79188 | 96.28 |
| (1) Nondurable | Overall total flows | 0.82824 | — | 0.84151 | — | 0.86519 | — | 0.83274 | — |
| | Rows (outflows) | 0.01545 | 1.87 | 0.01564 | 1.86 | 0.01633 | 1.89 | 0.01552 | 1.86 |
| | Columns (inflows) | 0.01554 | 1.88 | 0.01564 | 1.86 | 0.01621 | 1.87 | 0.01546 | 1.86 |
| | Exchanges | 0.00014 | 0.02 | 0.00014 | 0.02 | 0.00019 | 0.02 | 0.00015 | 0.02 |
| | Other flows* | 0.79710 | 96.24 | 0.81009 | 96.27 | 0.83246 | 96.22 | 0.80161 | 96.26 |
| (2) Durable | Overall total flows | 0.83984 | — | 0.83757 | — | 0.86877 | — | 0.84064 | — |
| | Rows (outflows) | 0.01540 | 1.83 | 0.01505 | 1.80 | 0.01614 | 1.86 | 0.01533 | 1.82 |
| | Columns (inflows) | 0.01575 | 1.88 | 0.01551 | 1.85 | 0.01613 | 1.86 | 0.01576 | 1.88 |
| | Exchanges | 0.00015 | 0.02 | 0.00016 | 0.02 | 0.00019 | 0.02 | 0.00014 | 0.02 |
| | Other flows* | 0.80854 | 96.27 | 0.80685 | 96.33 | 0.83632 | 96.27 | 0.80940 | 96.28 |

*Source*: Lee, JS (2010).
*Other flows includes all other non-trivial flows except outflows, inflows and bilateral exchange flows. Since the number of pairs is relatively large, their indices are marked as high values.
*Data source*: BTS, CFS.

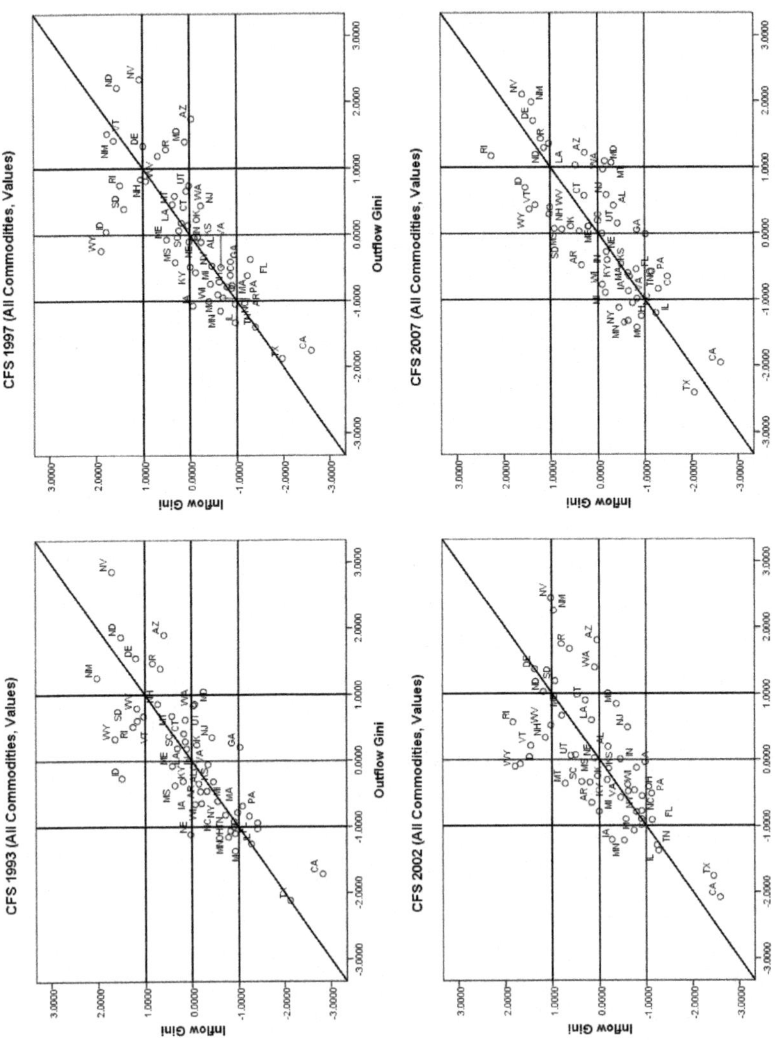


**Figure 5.3.** Scatter plots of field Gini index values for US interstate commodity flows, 1993–2007.

*Note*: Calculated on the basis of the value of shipment for all commodities.
*Source*: Lee, JS (2010).

index values than inflow field index values. The state that falls into the latter category is one where inflow is relatively uniform across all origins while outflow goes to selective destinations wherever they might be.

However, states with index values greater than one standard deviation above or below the mean would be of special interest when examining the scatter plots shown in Figure 5.3. The state with a $z$-score of the row field index value greater than 1 implies that the state has spatially focused destinations for its outflows, whereas the state whose $z$-score of the column field index is greater than 1 means that the source states of its inflows are spatially focused. The state that has the $z$-score of each field indices' values of less than $-1$ represents to have distinctively broad or spatially extensive trade fields with substantially below-average spatial focusing. The former cases are defined as "states with focused trade fields", while the latter ones are as "states with broad trade fields". Table 5.11 summarizes the typology of spatial focusing of interstate outflows and inflows fields in the interstate trade system for all the aggregate commodities across the four time periods. First, there is no state that has a focused trade field of origins but a broad trade field of destinations, or *vice versa.* Secondly, no state switches between the list of focused fields and the list of broad fields. Thirdly, the high positive correlation between the outflow and inflow trade field measures is confirmed. In most cases, outflow and inflow fields for particular states are similar, and the corresponding states are indicated in a bold letter in Table 5.11 and displayed on the maps in Figures 5.4 (values) and 5.6 (tons).

When looking into the spatially focused trade fields, there appear to be three potential clusters: one each in the West, Central and East. As for the spatially broad trade fields, California, Texas, and Illinois or Tennessee are detected as dominant node states for both their outflows and inflows. These states interact with others in the context of the total US trade system compared to the states that have focused trade fields. In particular, California is identified as the strongest trade consuming state that attracts outflows from various states over the four time periods. At the same time, California has

**Table 5.11.** Typology of focusing of interstate inflow and outflow fields for 1993, 1997, 2002, and 2007.

| | Destinations | | | | Origins | | | |
|---|---|---|---|---|---|---|---|---|
| Year | 1993 | 1997 | 2002 | 2007 | 1993 | 1997 | 2002 | 2007 |
| States with focused trade fields of | **NV** | **NV** | **NV** | **NV** | **NM** | WY | RI | **RI** |
| | AZ | **ND** | NM | **NM** | **NV** | ID | WY | **NV** |
| | **ND** | AZ | AZ | **DE** | WY | **VT** | ID | ID |
| | **DE** | **VT** | OR | **OR** | **ND** | **NM** | VT | WY |
| | OR | **NM** | WA | **ND** | ID | **ND** | **DE** | **NM** |
| | **NM** | MD | **DE** | AZ | RI | RI | **ND** | **DE** |
| | (6) | DE | SD | **RI** | **DE** | SD | NH | VT |
| | | OR | **ND** | MD | WV | **NV** | WV | **ND** |
| | | (8) | (8) | MT | SD | WV | **NV** | **OR** |
| | | | | LA | VT | (9) | (9) | NH |
| | | | | (10) | (10) | | | WV |
| | | | | | | | | (11) |
| States with broad trade fields of | **TX** | **TX** | **CA** | **TX** | **CA** | **CA** | **CA** | **CA** |
| | **CA** | **CA** | **TX** | **CA** | **TX** | **TX** | **TX** | **TX** |
| | **IL** | **TN** | **IL** | MN | **IL** | **TN** | **IL** | CO |
| | MN | IL | **TN** | MD | CO | GA | **TN** | **IL** |
| | NE | MN | MN | **IL** | PA | FL | FL | PA |
| | MO | IA | IA | NY | GA | (5) | (5) | TN |
| | OH | NC | MO | OH | (6) | | | GA |
| | (7) | (7) | (7) | (7) | | | | (7) |

*Notes*: Based on the values of shipment.
States listed in each grouping are ranked in descending order of the size of the larger of their two *Gini* indices.
*Source*: Lee, JS (2010).
*Data source*: CFS.

a dominant role in distributing commodities to other states over the entire US during all four periods. As a distributor to other states, Texas is identified as a state that is more significant compared to California, except in 2002.

These simple Gini measures are useful measures to examine system-wide properties of the interstate commodity flows and simply compare the degree to which the sources of inflows *versus* the

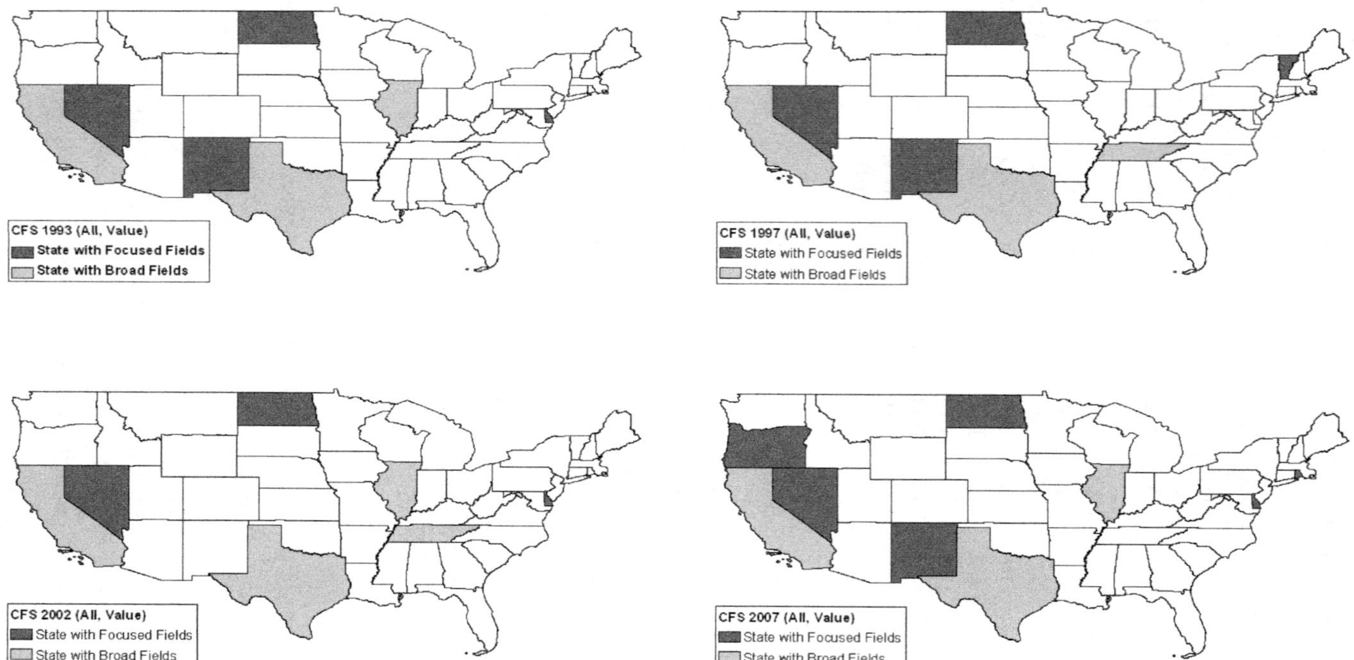


**Figure 5.4.** States with highly focused or especially broad interstate trade fields, 1993–1997–2002–2007.

*Source*: Lee, JS (2010).
*Data source*: CFS (all commodities, value).

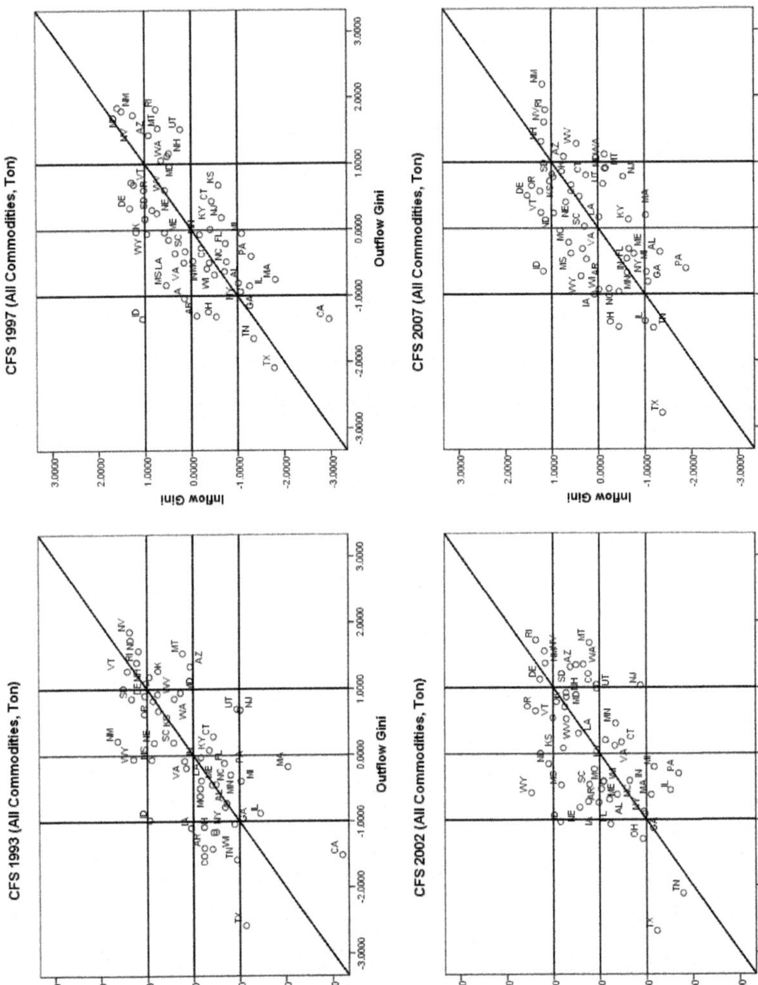


**Figure 5.5.** Scatter plots of field Gini index values for US interstate commodity flows, 1993–2007.

*Note*: Calculated on the basis of the tonnage of shipment for all commodities.
*Source*: Lee, JS (2010).

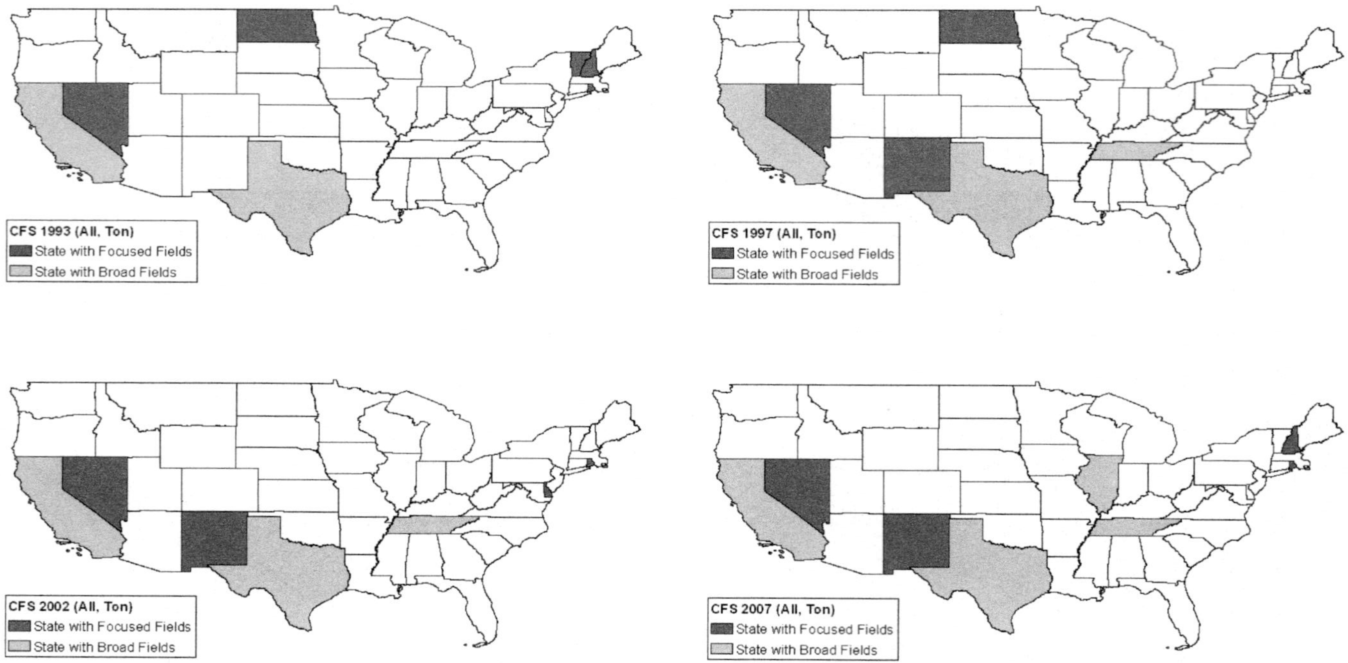


**Figure 5.6.** States with highly focused or especially borad interstate trade fields, 1993–1997–2002–2007.

*Source*: Lee, JS (2010).

*Data source*: CFS (all commodities, ton).

destinations of outflows for each state are spatially focused. For instance, the simple Gini measures in this study reveal that Illinois has played a significant role as a major trade distributor for both outflows and inflows in the US interstate trade system, even though its Gini field index values fluctuate over the four time periods. Tennessee has been another emerging important trade distributor; the pattern of spatial focusing of interstate trade fields based on the tonnage of shipment appears very similar to the pattern based on the value of shipment over the four time periods.

However, the Gini measures neither identify the location of the dominant source/origin or market/destination nor sort out effects that make trade system a spatially focused phenomenon. For example, the Gini measures tell us Nevada has the highest level in terms of a focused trade field for its outflows, but this value does not reveal where the major destinations trading with Nevada are located and why it has such a focused outflow trade field. For this reason, in the next section, the focus will be oriented more on identifying the trading partners of each state in the whole US interstate trade system.

### 5.4.2. *Identification of US interstate trade regions*

The simple Gini measures examined the degree of spatial focusing in an interstate trade system in the previous section. This section places more attention on the spatial extent of shipments of commodities based on the similarity of spatial structure of their trade flows so as to group the entire Unites States into a typology of regional trade regions.

#### 5.4.2.1. *Regional stability of commodity flow patterns*

This section presents the results obtained from the dyadic factor analysis on commodity flow matrix. The PCA procedures produce trade regions as typologies by identifying clusters of areas with a similar spatial structure of commodity trade flow as given by the geographic origin of their inflows or the geographic destination of their outflows. Essentially, the crucial criterion for regional grouping is the relative similarity of their flows with other trading states. Hence, the trade regions here can be defined as typologies, each representing a particular combination of source or destination states in the whole interstate trade system. The states categorized as one trade region based on commodity inflows represent consuming (or importing) regions (see Figure 5.7), while the states grouped as one trade region based on commodity outflows stand for producing (or exporting) regions (see Figure 5.8).

The results are summarized based on the most prominent features of interstate trade patterns. First of all, the regional groupings of states having similar trade outflow patterns and the locations of those having similar inflow patterns are not similar. The areas of a trade-producing region are, on an average, larger than those of a trade-consuming region. The number of regional groupings based on inflow movements is a little larger than that of regional groupings based on outflow movements. It might imply the geographical patterns of inflows are more spatially concentrated, which is consistent with the results based on the Gini measures in the previous section. When comparing the rows and columns indices, the column Gini index values demonstrated that the spatial focusing of inflows were larger than row Gini index values, measured based on outflows. Secondly, a tight geographic pattern of commodity flows is noted for each year. This means that members in a trading zone (or region) are geographically adjacent states based on either common destinations or origins for their commodity flows. Thirdly, greater stability is observed when examining the trend for the overall patterns of trade-producing regions, notwithstanding some local variations across the four time periods. From 1997, the trade outflow system with seven trade regions seems to have been established even though a small number of disturbances are observed. In 1993, 47 US states are grouped into eight trade producing regions: West, South Central, Middle Central, East North Central, West North Central, South Atlantic, Middle Atlantic and New England. In 1997, New England and Middle Atlantic regions appear to have three trade producing sub-regions. However, a more remarkable finding is that states in the Middle Central region were included into either the

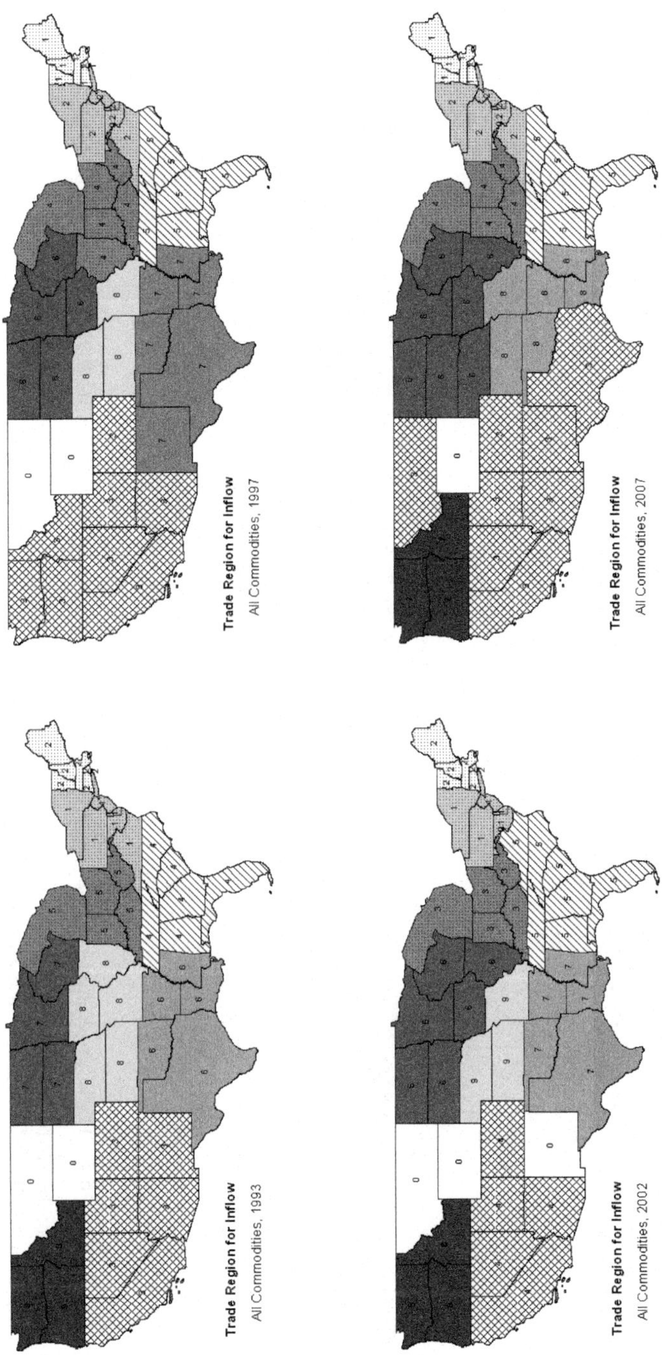


**Figure 5.7.** Trade consuming regions based on the inflows in the United States in 1993, 1997, 2002, and 2007.

*Source*: Lee, JS (2010).
*Data source*: CFS 1993–2007 (all commodities, value).

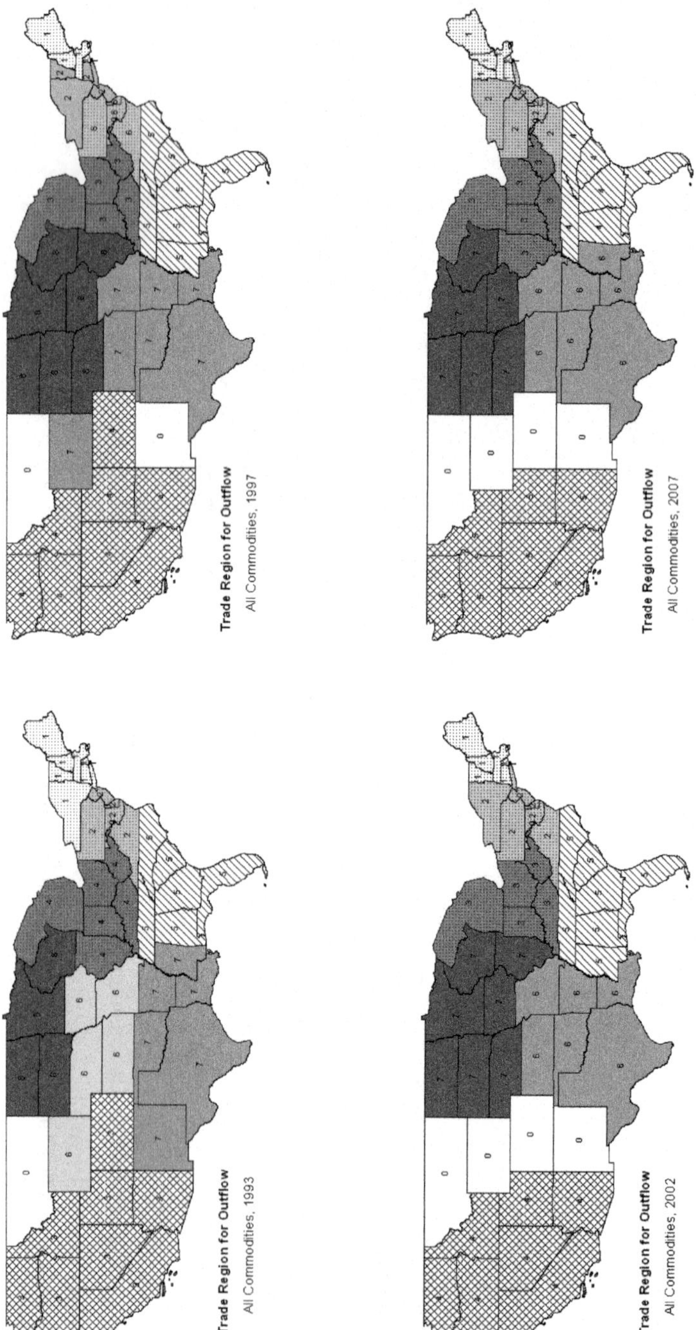


**Figure 5.8.** Trade producing regions based on the outflows in the United States in 1993, 1997, 2002, and 2007.

*Source*: Lee, JS (2010).
*Data source*: CFS 1993–2007 (all commodities, value).

West North Central or South Central regions. In particular, a seven-region structure based on the trade outflows has been in place since 2002, although some shifts are observed in Illinois and Mississippi between 2002 and 2007.

Finally, a less stable trend over time is observed in the overall patterns of trade consuming regions. Even though there is a variation in Virginia from 1993 to the later years, the trade consuming regions in the East coast are strongly stable across four different time periods. For the western part of the US, two major trade consuming regions, North West trade consuming region that covers Washington, Oregon and Idaho and the South West trade consuming region that includes California, Nevada, Arizona, Utah, Colorado and Kansas, are identified. However, this general pattern shows remarkable changes in 1997 and 2007, respectively. The South West trade consuming region is extended to embrace Texas and Montana in 1997. In 2007, the two trade consuming regions, the North West and South West, amalgamated into one large West trade consuming region. Along with these shifts in the western area, some turbulence is also observed in the Mountain region, including Montana, Wyoming and New Mexico, over the time periods. In particular, Texas makes several shifts in affiliation across the four time periods. Texas is one major member of the trade consuming region in the South Central area in 1993, 2002 and 2007. However, it is found as one constituent of the South West trade consuming region that encompasses California, Arizona, Nevada, Utah, Colorado, New Mexico and Montana instead of the usual South Central trade consuming region in 1997. With this variation of Texas, the Central trade consuming regions are newly arranged and defined in 1997 as well. For the central area, only two trade consuming regions can be defined: South Central and West North Central regions. Along with this turbulence in the Central regions, the changes in the spatial roles or effects of Illinois and Iowa as trade consuming states are also notable. However, all these detected shifts are interpreted in relative terms to the stability of trade producing regions. Although the trade consuming regions seem to have more dynamically variegated geographical arrangements compared to the geographical association patterns that the trade producing regions revel since 1993, one still can conclude that trade consuming regions also show a marked degree of regional stability for the period of analysis with the number of regional groupings remaining between eight and nine over the study years.

The maps visualizing each trade region with states either having common dominant destination states or common dominant origin states in Figures 5.7 and 5.8, do not provide the detailed information on the locations of the destinations or origins. Based on the standardized component scores, the dominant destinations of outflows (based on $Q$-mode PCA) and the dominant origins of inflows (based on $R$-mode PCA) for each trade producing region and trade consuming region are detected and presented on the checkerboards in the Tables 5.12 and 5.13, respectively. The destinations or the origins that have the component scores greater than 1.0 are considered dominant ones in this study.

When examining the dominant destination states for the corresponding trade producing regions, the pairs of origin-destination states are roughly consistent (Table 5.12). As for the selection of origins of trading consuming regions, the pairs of destination-origin states seem more variable (Table 5.13). However, they are not really dramatically different from each other. A cell which is lightly shaded and contains an asterisk in tables indicates that the state is one of the members comprising the corresponding trade region, at the same time, it is one of the dominant destination (or origin) states that imports (or exports) more commodities from (or to) the trade region compared to others. Overall, the trade system based on the spatial structure of outflows show a more stable structure by region and over time. In particular, the correspondence between origins and destination is prominent in 2007. If a cell is found shaded but not to have an asterisk, the corresponding state is a weak destination (or origin) for the corresponding trade producing region (or trade consuming region). More attention should be directed to the cell that has an asterisk but not shaded, since the cell represents one of the very influential destinations (or origins) in the whole US interstate trade system. For the outflows, California, Texas, Illinois, New York, Virginia, Tennessee, Alabama, Iowa and West Virginia are

**Table 5.12.** Checkerboard identifying the dominant destination states for each trade producing regions, 1993–2007.

| Q | TR | MA | NY | NH | CT | CA | RI | PA | NJ | MD | VA | UT | WA | NV | OR | AZ | ID | OH | MI | IN | IL | KY | NC | GA | SC | FL | TN | AL | MO | KS | TX | IA | NE | OK | LA | MS | AR | MN | ND | SD | WI | ME | CO | DE | MT | NM | VT | WV | WY |
|---|---|---|---|---|---|---|---|---|---|---|---|---|---|---|---|---|---|---|---|---|---|---|---|---|---|---|---|---|---|---|---|---|---|---|---|---|---|---|---|---|---|---|---|---|---|---|---|---|---|
| 1993 | 1 | * | * | * | * | * | * | | | | | | | | | | | | | | | | | | | | | | | | | | | | | | | | | | | | | | | | | | |
| | 2 | | * | | | | | * | * | * | * | | | | | | | | | | | | | | | | | | | | | | | | | | | | | | | | | | | | | | |
| | 3 | | | | | * | | | | | | * | * | * | * | * | * | | | | | | | | | | | | | | | | | | | | | | | | | | | | | | | | |
| | 4 | | | | | | | | | | | | | | | | | * | * | * | * | * | | | | | | | | | | | | | | | | | | | | | | | | | | | |
| | 5 | | | | | | | | | | * | | | | | | | | | | | | * | * | * | * | * | * | | | | | | | | | | | | | | | | | | | | | |
| | 6 | | | | | | | | | | | | | | | | | | | | * | | | | | | | | * | * | * | * | * | * | | | | | | | | | | | | | | | |
| | 7 | | | | | | | | | | | | | | | | | | | | | | | | | | * | * | | | * | | | * | * | * | * | | | | | | | | | | | | |
| | 8 | | | | | | | | | | | | | | | | | | | | | | | | | | | | | | | * | | | | | | * | * | * | * | | | | | | | | |
| 1997 | 1 | * | | | | * | * | | | | | | | | | | | | | | | | | | | | | | | | | | | | | | | | | | | * | | | | | | | |
| | 2 | | * | | * | | | * | * | | | | | | | | | | | | | | | | | | | | | | | | | | | | | | | | | | | | | | * | | |
| | 3 | | | | | | | | | | | | | | | | | * | * | * | * | * | | | | | | | | | | | | | | | | | | | | | | | | | | | |
| | 4 | | | | | * | | | | | | * | * | * | * | * | * | | | | | | | | | | | | | | | | | | | | | | | | | | | | | | | | |
| | 5 | | | | | | | | | | | | | | | | | | | | | | * | * | * | * | * | * | | | | | | | | | | | | | | | | | | | | | |
| | 6 | | | | | | | * | | * | * | | | | | | | | | | | | * | | | | | | | | | | | | | | | | | | | | | * | | | | * | |
| | 7 | | | | | * | | | | | | | | | | | | | | | | | | | | | | | * | * | * | | | * | * | | * | | | | | | | | | | | | |
| | 8 | | | | | * | | | | | | | | | | | | | | | * | | | | | | | | | | | * | * | | | | | * | * | * | * | | | | | | | | |
| 2002 | 1 | * | * | * | * | | | | | | | | | | | | | | | | | | | | | | | | | | | | | | | | | | | | | * | | | | | | | |
| | 2 | | * | | | | | * | * | * | * | | | | | | | | | | | | | | | | | | | | | | | | | | | | | | | | | * | | | | | |
| | 3 | | | | | | | | | | | | | | | | | * | * | * | * | * | | | | | * | | | | | | | | | | | | | | | | | | | | | | |
| | 4 | | | | | * | | | | | | * | * | * | * | * | * | | | | | | | | | | | | | | | | | | | | | | | | | | | | | | | | |
| | 5 | | | | | * | | | | | | | | | | | | | | | | | * | * | * | * | * | * | | | | | | | | * | | | | | | | | | | | | | |
| | 6 | | | | | | | | | | | | | | | | | | | | * | | | | | | | | * | * | * | | | * | | | * | | | | | | | | | | | | |
| | 7 | | | | | * | | | | | | | | | | | | | | | * | | | | | | | | | | | * | * | | | | | * | * | * | * | | | | | | | | |
| 2007 | 1 | * | * | * | * | | * | | | | | | | | | | | | | | | | | | | | | | | | | | | | | | | | | | | | | | | | | | |
| | 2 | | * | | | | | * | * | * | * | | | | | | | | | | | | | | | | | | | | | | | | | | | | | | | | | * | | | | | |
| | 3 | | | | | | | | | | | | | | | | | * | * | * | * | * | | | | | | | | | | | | | | | | | | | | | | | | | | * | |
| | 4 | | | | | | | | | | | | | | | | | | | | | | * | * | * | * | * | * | | | | | | | | | | | | | | | | | | | | | |
| | 5 | | | | | * | | | | | | * | * | * | * | * | * | | | | | | | | | | | | | | | | | | | | | | | | | | | | | | | | |
| | 6 | | | | | | | | | | | | | | | | | | | | | | | | | | | | * | * | * | | | * | * | * | * | | | | | | | | | | | | |
| | 7 | | | | | | | | | | | | | | | | | | | | * | | | | | | | | | | | * | * | | | | | * | * | * | * | | | | | | | | |

*Notes* 1. The authors summarized the results of $Q$-mode PCA with the value of shipment for each state's outflow.
2. The cell with an asterisk indicates one of dominant destination states of the corresponding trade producing region (by row). The member states of the trade producing region are identified by shading the cell representing the corresponding state in light gray.
3. The order of columns is determined by following the descending order of the component scores for each trade regions for the year of 1993.

*Source*: Lee, JS (2010).
*Data source*: BTS, CFS 1993, 1997, 2002, and 2007.

detected as such influential destinations. Here, several features should be noted. First, California, Texas, Illinois and New York play a significant role as one of the dominant destinations in the West, South, Central and East, respectively. Secondly, Mid-western states such as

**Table 5.13.** Checkerboard identifying the dominant origin states for each trade consuming regions, 1993–2007.

| R | 1993 | | | | | | | | | 1997 | | | | | | | | 2002 | | | | | | | | | 2007 | | | | | | | |
|---|---|---|---|---|---|---|---|---|---|---|---|---|---|---|---|---|---|---|---|---|---|---|---|---|---|---|---|---|---|---|---|---|---|
| TR | 1 | 2 | 3 | 4 | 5 | 6 | 7 | 8 | 9 | 1 | 2 | 2 | 3 | 4 | 5 | 6 | 7 | 1 | 2 | 3 | 4 | 5 | 6 | 7 | 8 | 9 | 1 | 2 | 3 | 4 | 5 | 6 | 7 | 8 |
| MA | | * | | | | | | | | * | | | | | | | | | * | | | | | | | | * | | | | | | | |
| NY | * | * | | | | | | | | * | * | | | | | | | * | * | | | | | | | | * | * | | | | | | |
| NH | | * | | | | | | | | * | | | | | | | | | * | | | | | | | | * | | | | | | | |
| CT | | * | | | | | | | | * | | | | | | | | | * | | | | | | | | * | | | | | | | |
| CA | | | * | | | | | | * | | | * | | | | | | | | | * | | | | * | | | | * | | * | | * | |
| RI | | * | | | | | | | | | | | | | | | | | * | | | | | | | | * | | | | | | | |
| PA | * | | | | | | | | | | * | | | | | | | * | | | | | | | | | | * | | | | | | |
| NJ | * | | | | | | | | | | * | | | | | | | * | | | | | | | | | | * | | | | | | |
| MD | * | | | | | | | | | | * | | | | | | | * | | | | | | | | | | * | | | | | | |
| VA | * | | | | | | | | | | * | | | | | | | * | | | | * | | | | | | * | | | | | | |
| UT | | | * | | | | | | | | | * | | | | | | | | | * | | | | | | | | | | | | * | |
| WA | | | | | | | | | * | | | * | | | | | | | | | | | | | * | | | | | | | | * | |
| NV | | | | | | | | | | | | * | | | | | | | | | * | | | | | | | | * | | | | | |
| OR | | | | | | | | | * | | | * | | | | | | | | | | | | | * | | | | | | | | * | |
| AZ | | | * | | | | | | | | | * | | | | | | | | | * | | | | | | | | * | | | | | |
| ID | | | | | | | | | * | | | | | | | | | | | | | | | | * | | | | | | | | * | |
| OH | | | | | * | | | | | | | | * | | | | | | | * | | | | | | | | | | * | | | | |
| MI | | | | | * | | | | | | | | * | | | | | | | * | | | | | | | | | | * | | | | |
| IN | | | | | * | | | | | | | | * | | | | | | | * | | | | | | | | | | * | | | | |
| IL | | | | | * | | * | * | | | | | * | | * | | * | | | * | | | * | | | * | | | | * | | * | | |
| KY | | | | | * | | | | | | | | * | | | | | | | * | | | | | | | | | | * | | | | |
| NC | | | | * | | | | | | | | | | * | | | | | | | | * | | | | | | | | | * | | | |
| GA | | | | * | | | | | | | | | | * | | | | | | | | * | | | | | | | | | * | | | |
| SC | | | | * | | | | | | | | | | * | | | | | | | | * | | | | | | | | | * | | | |
| FL | | | | * | | | | | | | | | | * | | | | | | | | | | | | | | | | | * | | | |
| TN | | | | * | | * | | | | | | | | * | | | | | | * | | * | | * | | | | | | | * | | | * |
| AL | | | | * | | | | | | | | | | * | | | | | | | | * | | * | | | | | | | * | | | |
| MO | | | | | | | | * | | | | | | | | | * | | | | | | | | | * | | | | | | * | | * |
| KS | | | | | | | | * | | | | | | | | | * | | | | | | | | | * | | | | | | | | * |
| TX | | | * | | | * | | | | | | * | | | | * | | | | | | | | * | | * | | | * | | | | | * |
| IA | | | | | | | * | * | | | | | | | * | | * | | | | | | * | | | * | | | | | | * | | |
| NE | | | | | | | | * | | | | | | | | | * | | | | | | | | | * | | | | | | * | | |
| OK | | | | | | * | | | | | | | | | | * | | | | | | | | * | | * | | | | | | | | |
| LA | | | | | | * | | | | | | | | | | * | | | | | | | | * | | | | | | | | | | * |
| MS | | | | | | * | | | | | | | | | | * | | | | | | | | * | | | | | | | | | | * |
| AR | | | | | | * | | | | | | | | | | * | | | | | | | | * | | | | | | | | | | * |
| MN | | | | | | | * | | | | | | | | * | | | | | | | | * | | | | | | | | | * | | |
| ND | | | | | | | * | | | | | | | | * | | | | | | | | * | | | | | | | | | * | | |
| SD | | | | | | | * | | | | | | | | * | | | | | | | | * | | | | | | | | | * | | |
| WI | | | | | | | * | | | | | | | | * | | | | | | | | * | | | | | | | | | * | | |
| ME | | * | | | | | | | | | | | | | | | | | * | | | | | | | | * | | | | | | | |
| CO | | | | | | | | | | | | | | | | | | | | | * | | | | | | | | * | | | | | |
| DE | | | | | | | | | | | | | | | | | | * | | | | | | | | | | * | | | | | | |
| MT | | | | | | | | | | | | | | | | | | | | | | | | | | | | | | | | | | |
| NM | | | | | | | | | | | | | | | | * | | | | | | | | | | | | | * | | | | | |
| VT | | | | | | | | | | | | | | | | | | | | | | | | | | | | | | | | | | |
| WV | | | | | * | | | | | | | | | | | | | | | | | | | | | | | | | * | | | | |
| WY | | | | | | | | | | | | | | | | | | | | | | | | | | | | | | | | | | |

*Notes* 1. The authors summarized the results of $R$-mode PCA with the value of shipment for each state's inflow.
2. The cell with an asterisk indicates one of dominant origin states of the corresponding trade consuming region (by column). The member states of the trade consuming region are identified by shading the cell representing the corresponding state in light gray.
3. The order of rows is just following the defined order of columns in Table 5.12.

*Source*: Lee, JS (2010).
*Data source*: BTS, CFS 1993, 1997, 2002, and 2007.

Illinois and Iowa or southeastern states such as Alabama, Tennessee and West Virginia might have a more significant influence on the local outflow trade system in the Mid-west and South areas, respectively. Thirdly, most states with the exception of California are usually importing more from the close states based on their geographic contiguity; California acts as a dominant destination for its close states as well as for distant states across all the four time periods.

This finding is consistent with the negative trade Gini field index for outflows from California. Comparable patterns are detected in Table 5.13, presenting the selection of dominant origin states of inflows moving into the trade consuming regions. A more varied trend in the selections of origins over time is observed for inflows compared to the selections of destinations for outflows. However, these variations might be negligible in contributing to the total understanding of the overall US interstate trade system. In both cases, the observed fluctuations are smoothed out if a broader range of geographical configuration is considered. When comparing the boundaries of the regional groups in both cases described above, to the boundaries of eight economic regions designated by the US Bureau of Economic Analysis (BEA) based on economic similarities among contiguous states, they are roughly parallel, even though not identical. This obviously reflects the fact that trade is just one component of regional economic activities, one product of regional economies as well as one stimulus of regional economies. To what degree the spatial pattern of interstate trade might reflect regional economic structure for each state in a multi-state economy such as the US, remains to be explored. It is also shown from the observation that the overall trade regions in the US interstate trade system based on major origin–destination pairs are ultimately mapped into four large regions: West, Mid-west, South, and North East, that are consistent with the four US Census regions.

## 5.5. Conclusion

This study explores the spatial pattern of US interstate trade among 48 states for four different time periods of 1993, 1997, 2002, and 2007 in order to understand the shifts observed in the US trade system during the last 15 years. Two main methods are employed: trade Gini measures and dyadic factor analysis on commodity flow. Using the simple trade Gini indices, the analysis presents the spatial association in the distribution of interstate trade. In particular, trade field Gini indices help examine whether a state has a spatially focused or a broad trade field in the US interstate commodity flow system. Dyadic factor analyses defined the trade regions on the basis of the outflows as well as inflows of the individual states.

The main results are summarized as follows. The global spatial pattern or structure of the US interstate commodity flows has been relatively stable during the years of analysis. However, some variations or disturbances at a more detailed or local level are noted although they are quite subtle. Since 1993, the entire interstate commodity flow system seems to have become less spatially focused based on the total trade flows Gini measure. In addition to the decreased total flows Gini measure, trade regions defined by flow factor analysis display more expanded areas of trading regions with fewer numbers of trade regions over time, even though the degrees of changes are relatively small. These findings should not be surprising as they reflect the impacts of removal of trade regulations in the 1980s that began with the Staggers' Act in 1980 deregulating the US railroads. The provisions were eventually extended to highway transportation and resulted in significant decreases in the real costs of transportation over the next two decades. These legislative changes facilitated the changing spatial structure of production through both hollowing-out effect and the fragmentation of production (see Parr *et al.*, 2002; Hewings and Parr, 2009 for a focus on the Mid-west of the US). Each region has experienced a shift in its industrial production structures, so that it has extended or reorganized its trading extent by opening up its new markets or finding it new sources. With the availability of more detailed or micro-level spatial scale-based trade data, more attention could be directed to the degree to which changes in structure and trade involved broader or more narrowly defined spatial regimes. In addition, the analysis needs to be complemented by an exploration of the kind conducted for the Mid-west by Munroe *et al.* (2007) which explored the role of intra-industry trade and trade overlap in accounting for the increases in interstate trade.

Another finding is that the general spatial pattern of interstate trade still reflects a geographical structure based on contiguity, except in the case of California. California is observed as the most significant and influential trading actor in the US interstate trade system across all the years of analysis. Not only the geography, but also the influence of increased energy cost might explain the geographical contiguity observed in inter-regional trade partnership, offering scope for additional research to explore the role of energy prices in the production fragmentation process and regional trade patterns. Generally speaking, similar and correspondent counter-stream flow patterns exist in the trade flows between origin states and destination states even though the selection of origins of the inflows appear more spatially focused and more variable over time than the selection of destinations of the outflows. In essence, the commodity flows provide confirmation of one of Ravenstein's (1885) migration laws — namely that every flow generates a counter flow. However, all these patterns are mainly based on the analyses with the whole aggregate commodity groups. If commodity-specific flows would be examined, more diverse and interesting results could be obtained.

In conclusion, the regional stability of US interstate trade system in terms of the general spatial focusing, trade zoning and trade partnership was detected through the analyses in this study. This stabilized spatial pattern of US interstate commodity flows are summarized into several major geographical clusters centered on: (1) California serving the West as well as the entire US, (2) Texas mainly serving the South West, (3) the Mid-west represented by Illinois, Indiana, Michigan, and Ohio, (4) the Middle Atlantic represented by New York, New Jersey and Pennsylvania, mainly serving the East and the Mid-west, and (5) Georgia and Florida serving the South East.

In spite of imperfect dataset with its own intrinsic problems (only commodity flows are identified, ignoring service activities), this study has significance since it explores the spatial patterns and changes in the patterns of flows in the entire US, based on the recent flow data set over time. Even though there is a great deal of theory about the role of trade, very little of the theory has been applied to intra-country flows. Concomitantly, there has been surprisingly little analysis of the patterns of trade. This study deals with these issues by exploring the ways of visualizing and interpreting the spatial patterns of the US interstate commodity flows across all four different time periods. The interpretation of the general patterns of the US interstate trade system in the geographical and spatial context provided in this study would provide the basis for further analyses in the field of US interstate trade study. Regionalizing the individual states into trade zones based on the interconnectivity among them instead of a simple spatial similarity of trade flow, conducting more commodity-specific analysis, and sorting out the distance effects in terms of transportation cost could be further developed and researched so as to refine or validate existing inter-regional trade theory.

## References

Berry, B (1962) *Structural Components of Changing Transportation Flow Networks.* Fort Eustis, VA: U.S. Army Transportation Research Command.

Berry, B (1966) Essays on commodity flows and the spatial structure of the Indian economy. *Department of Geography Research Paper No.* 111, Chicago, IL: University of Chicago.

Berry, B (1971) Introduction: the logic and limitations of comparative factorial ecology, *Economic Geography* 47, 209–218.

Black, W (1973) Toward a factorial ecology of flow, *Economic Geography* 48, 59–67.

Bureau of Economic Analysis (1990–2008) Real Gross Domestic Product (chained dollars), Survey of Current Business, http://bea.gov/scb/index.htm#chartsandtables.

Bureau of Transportation Statistics (1993, 1997, 2002 and 2007) Commodity Flow Survey, http://www.rita.dot.gov/bts/sites/ria.dot.gov.bts/files/publications/commodity_flow_survey/index.html.

Cox, KR (1965) The application of linear programming to geographic problems, *Tijdschrift voor Economische enSsociale Geografie* 56, 228–236.

Ellis, M, R Barff and B Renard (1993) Migration regions and interstate labor flows by occupation in the United States, *Growth and Change* 24, 166–190.

Frankel, JA (Ed.) (1998) *The Regionalization of the World Economy.* Chicago: University of Chicago Press.

Hewings, GJD, M Sonis, J Guo, PR Israilevich and GR Schindler (1998) The hollowing-out process in the Chicago economy, 1975–2015, *Geographical Analysis*, 30, 217–233.

Hewings, GJD and JB Parr (2009) The changing structure of trade and interdependence in a mature economy: The US Mid-west. In *Technological Change and Mature Industrial Regions: Firms, Knowledge, and Policy.* P McCann (Ed.). Cheltenham, UK: Edward Elgar, 64–84.

Hewings, GJD and J Oosterhaven (2013) Interregional trade models. In *Handbook of Regional Science.* MM Fischer and P Nijkamp (Eds.). Heidelberg: Springer-Verlag, 903–925.

Israilevich, P and R Mahidhara (1991) Hog butchers no longer: Twenty years of employment change in metropolitan Chicago, *Economic Perspectives* (Federal Reserve Bank of Chicago) 15, 2–13.

Knudsen, DC (1988) On the stability of trade partnerships, *Environment and Planning A* 20, 1335–1343.

Krugman, P and AJ Venables (1990) Integration and the competitiveness of peripheral industry. In *Unity with Diversity in the European Economy.* C Bliss and JB de Macedo (Eds.). Cambridge, UK: Cambridge University Press, 56–75.

Krguman, P (1979) Increasing returns, monopolistic competition, and international trade, *Journal of International Economics* 9, 469–479.

Krugman, P. (1980) Scale economics, product differentiation, and the pattern of trade, *American Economic Review* 70, 950–959.

Krugman, P (1989) Space: The final frontier, *Journal of Economic Perspectives* 12, 161–174.

Lee, JS (2010) Trade and spatial economic interdependence: U.S. inter-regional trade and regional economic structure. *Unpublished doctoral dissertation,* Urbana–Champaign, IL: University of Illinois.

Munroe, DK, GJD Hewings and D Guo (2007) The role of intra-industry trade in inter-regional trade in the Mid-west of the US. In *Globalization and Regional Economic Modeling.* RJ Cooper, KP Donaghy and GJD Hewings (Eds.). Heidelberg: Springer-Verlag, 87–106.

Okazaki, F (1989) The 'hollowing out' phenomenon in economic development. Paper presented at the Pacific Regional Science Conference. July 3–7, 1989, Singapore.

Pandit, K (1994) Differentiating between subsystems and typologies in the analysis of migration regions: A U.S. example, *Professional Geographer* 46, 331–345.

Parr, JB, GJD Hewings, J Sohn and S Nazara (2002) Agglomeration and trade: Some additional perspectives, *Regional Studies* 36, 675–684.

Perobelli, F and E Haddad (2003) Interdependence among the Brazilian states: An input–output approach. *Discussion Paper* 03-T-18, University of Illinois, Urbana: Regional Economics Applications Laboratory.

Plane, D and A Isserman (1983) U.S. interstate labor force migration: An analysis of trends, net exchanges, and migration subsystems, *Socioeconomic Planning Science* 17, 251–266.

Plane, D and G Mulligan (1997) Measuring spatial focusing in a migration system, *Demography* 34, 251–262.

Ravenstein, EG (1885) The laws of migration, *Journal of the Statistical Society of London* 48, 167–235.

Rodgers, JM (1971) *State Estimates of Inter-regional Commodity Trade* 1963. New York: Lexington-Heath Books.

Rogers, A, F Willenkens, J Little and J Reymer (2002) Describing migration spatial structure, *Papers in Regional Science* 81, 29–48.

Smith, RHT (1964) Toward a measure of complementarity, *Economic Geography* 40, 1–8.

Tobler, W (1975) A preliminary analysis of the spread of the depression, *Geographical Analysis* 7, 427–434.

Tobler, W (1981) A model of geographic movement, *Geographical Analysis* 13, 1–20.

Tobler, W (1987) Alternatives in movement mapping. *Proceedings, 13th International Cartographical Conference.* Morelia, Mexico, 345–350.

Ullman, EL (1957) *American Commodity Flow.* Seattle: University of Washington Press.

# Chapter 6

## Manufacturing Fetishism: The Neo-Mercantilist Preoccupation with Protecting Manufacturing*

*Alecia Waite Cassidy*[†], *Edward Tower*[‡] *and Xiaolu Wang*[§]
[†]*University of Michigan*
[‡]*Duke University*
[§]*Cornell University*

Two common views are that a country cannot develop without a strong manufacturing base and that trade restrictions are essential to facilitate the development of that strong manufacturing base and thus spur economic growth. We ask:

- Does a strong manufacturing share of GDP facilitate economic growth?
- Do trade restrictions ensure the development of a strong manufacturing base?
- How can governance affect manufacturing share?
- And are the relationships we find robust across regions?

We find the manufacturing share is not significantly correlated with a higher standard of living. Nor it is related significantly and consistently to economic growth. We also find that trade restrictions both at home and abroad shrink the manufacturing base and smother

*Thanks to Omer Gokcekus, May (Zhimeng) Li, Mia Mikic, Lincoln Richards, Steve Rosefielde, Kevin Torck, Tom Willett and participants at the 2014 meeting of the Asia Pacific Economic Association for constructive comments. Their approval is not implied. For supplementary materials such as the datasets, code and other specifications, please contact Xiaolu Wang. This paper continues the investigation started in Tower and Waite (2011). Tower is also a visiting professor at Chulalongkorn University and Nanyang Technological University.

economic growth. A better way than protectionism and subsidies, specific to industry to enhance economic growth, is to improve governance effectiveness and the quality of regulation.

## 6.1. Manufacturing Fetishism Thrives

"Emotional arguments over protectionism today harken back to the second half of the 18th century, when Physiocracy, the philosophy that 'only the farmer really made something out of more or less nothing' was popular. The Physiocrats thus reasoned that manufacturing was unlikely to benefit an economy. Similarly, today, our gut reaction to the closing down of a factory is that we are allowing a central part of our economy to perish" (Gopnik, 2010). Like the farms of the Physiocrats, factories for the manufacturing fetishists are tangible symbols of a country's prosperity. We show in this paper that all of us need to be careful not to overstate its importance.

"Manufacturing fetishism — the idea that manufacturing is the central economic activity and everything else is somehow subordinate — is deeply ingrained in human thinking. The perception that only tangible objects represent real wealth and only physical labour real work was probably formed in the days when economic activity was the constant search for food, fuel and shelter" (Kay, 2012).

Kay continues: "When you look at the value chain of manufactured goods we consume today, you quickly appreciate how small a proportion of the value of output is represented by the processes of manufacturing and assembly. Most of what you pay reflects the style of the suit, the design of the iPhone, the precision of the assembly of the aircraft engine, the painstaking pharmaceutical research, the quality assurance that tells you products really are what they claim to be."

Yet, in spite of Kay's argument, manufacturing fetishism thrives. Ian Fletcher, in his *Free Trade Doesn't Work: What Should Replace it and Why*, argues that a strong manufacturing sector is crucial for providing jobs (Fletcher, 2009, p. 196). He equates services with haircuts and notes "the more of a nation's economy is in good industries, the stronger its economy will be today and the better its growth prospects will be tomorrow" (Fletcher, 2009, p. 197). He advocates a uniform import tariff of 25% to bring industries home to the US (Fletcher, 2009, p. 236) combined with an export subsidy (Fletcher, 2009, p. 248). However, he ignores the circular flow of income. Chinese sales of goods to the US finance degrees for Chinese students, a service provided at Duke University, making possible more research, more scholarships and better education for American students. He ignores the possibility that import restrictions perpetuate monopoly power which may incentivize American firms to take advantage of the ability to sell a smaller quantity at a higher price, thereby reducing employment. (Kaempfer *et al.*, 2004). In his discussion of how a value-added export tax rebate subsidizes exporters, he seems to be unaware of the Lerner neutrality theorem which states that an across-the-board import tariff combined with an across-the-board export subsidy has no general equilibrium effect (Kaempfer and Tower, 1982).

Paul Craig Roberts (2013), a former Reagan administration Assistant secretary of the Treasury, supports manufacturing fetishism. In the preface to Roberts's *The Failure of Laissez Faire Capitalism*, Johannes Maruschzik writes "The change towards a service society that has been promoted by apologists for globalization has proved to be a fatal delusion" (Roberts, 2013, p. 15).

Maruschzik goes on to write: "Nations are able to create wealth only with products and services they are able to sell in global markets" (Roberts, 2013, p. 15). He ignores the obvious point that if exports were truly the only path to wealth, the world would never create wealth, for the world is a closed economy. Maruschzik writes "Germany with 30% of the working population in industry is better off than the US where only some 11% of the population still works in the manufacturing sector of the economy" (Roberts, 2013, p. 18). The fact that in 2012, US gross domestic product (GDP) per capita was 23.5% higher than Germany's, is one data point that casts doubt on his argument. Maruschzik also ignores Paul Krugman's (1993b) point that what creates wealth is the productivity of a country's factors of production.

Roberts follows up this introduction by arguing that "millions of jobs have been moved offshore" (Roberts, 2013, p. 33). This perpetuates the erroneous view that there are a fixed number of jobs in the world economy (Mussa, 1993). Roberts continues "Monetary and fiscal policy cannot help when the problem is that American jobs have been relocated offshore" (Roberts, 2013, p. 43). This ignores the mechanism that a trade deficit permits a fall in the interest rate, without igniting inflation which stimulates investment and job growth (Krugman, 1993b, pp. 157–158).

### 6.2. *The Economist* Debate

*The Economist* (2010) considered the belief in the importance of manufacturing, what some have named "manufacturing fetishism", to be so important that it hosted an online debate on the proposition: "This House Believes that an Economy cannot Succeed without a Big Manufacturing Base." Cambridge University's Ha-Joon Chang argued in favor of the proposition against Columbia's Jagdish Bhagwati. Chang won the debate 76% to 24% according to the readers' vote. In the process of the debate, the share of manufacturing fetishists fell from 80% to 76%. So while Bhagwati did not win the debate, he shrank the proportion of manufacturing fetishists. These numbers illustrate the sway of manufacturing fetishists.

There is an alternative way to pick the winner. 95 comments were submitted from the floor by readers after introductory remarks by the chief protagonists. 53 comments were submitted after the debate was over. We counted the votes implied in the comments. We dropped all but one comment, when multiple comments were submitted by the same contributor, and we dropped comments that did not take a side. After the opening remarks, the vote was 44 for Chang and 35 for Bhagwati, with Chang winning by 66% to 44%. The comments submitted after the closing statements voted 13 for Chang and 16 for Bhagwati with Chang collecting 44% to Bhagwati's 55%. Our assessment of these comments is admittedly subjective, but free of intentional bias. Sometimes a decision was hard to call, for example when a commenter remarked that for most countries manufacturing is essential, but for some it is not. The discrepancy between the two ways of measuring who won lead us to conclude that the folks who evaluated the debate carefully enough to comment were less pro manufacturing than those voters who just reflexively clicked the "vote yes" or "vote no" buttons on their computer screens.

Chang (2014) reiterates the importance of manufacturing, and, in particular, advocates infant industry trade protectionism. Lin and Chang (2009) debate how much a developing nation's incentives should cause it to deviate from comparative advantage. Lin recommends interventions to correct externalities, a position close to Bhagwati's, while Chang (2009, p. 502) recommends interventions, even when a favored industry fails to be profitable for four decades "for example Japanese and Korean cars". He suggests these interventions should include trade barriers.

At its simplest level, the modern-day protectionist argument assumes that manufacturing is central to an economy. Hence, the logic goes, capital goods and knowledge accumulation in manufacturing is a tried-and-true recipe for growth. Moreover, concerns over structural unemployment and national security are used to argue that countries must keep manufacturing within their borders, and prevent offshoring.

## 6.3. Our Study

*The Economist* debate along with the Fletcher and Roberts' books made us eager to find out what determines the share of manufacturing in GDP, what the relationship is between manufacturing share and prosperity as measured by per capita GDP, and what the relationship is between manufacturing share and economic growth.

We would like to make strong statements about whether a high manufacturing share causes prosperity and growth, but proving a causal relationship is harder than showing an association, so we content ourselves with exploring the association in the presence of various controls. In the paper, when we say $X$ positively affects $Y$

holding $Z$ constant, we just mean that a regression of $Y$ on $X$ and $Z$ yields a positive coefficient for $X$.

## 6.4. Data

The five major public datasets relevant to this topic are: (1) The World Development Indicators (WDIs)[2] dataset by the World Bank; (2) The World Governance Indicators (WGIs)[3] dataset by the World Bank; (3) The National Accounts Main Aggregates Dataset (NAMAD)[4] by the United Nations; (4) The Manufacturing Industry Database by the National Bureau of Economic Research (NBER)[5]; and (5) The Trade Restriction Indices 2009 dataset[6] by the World Bank. We summarize the characteristics of these datasets. Then we describe the datasets we constructed for our analysis.

### 6.4.1. *World Bank: WDIs*

WDIs are "the primary World Bank collection of development indicators, compiled from officially-recognized international resources". This dataset is the collection of the "most current and accurate global development data available, and includes national, regional and global estimates". The coverage is long: from 1960–2013, but is problematically replete with missing values in the earliest decades. The dataset includes six indicators. From this dataset, we draw manufacturing share of GDP and per capita GDP.

---

[2]Data source: http://data.worldbank.org/data-catalog/world-development-indicators.
[3]Data source: http://info.worldbank.org/governance/wgi/index.aspx#home.
[4]Data source: http://unstats.un.org/unsd/snaama/Introduction.asp.
[5]Data source: http://www.nber.org/nberces/.
[6]Data source: http://econ.worldbank.org/WBSITE/EXTERNAL/EXTDEC/EXTRESEARCH/0,,contentMDK:22574446~pagePK:64214825~piPK:64214943~theSitePK:469382,00.html.

### 6.4.2. *World Bank: WGIs*

WGIs are indicators of six key dimensions of governance. These estimates are "constructed based on 30 underlying data sources reporting the perception of governance by a large number of survey respondents and expert assessments worldwide". The estimates range from −2.5 to 2.5. For each of the six indicators, we convert the estimates to a percentile rank as our explanatory variable, so these variables can be intuitively understood, as the strength of each governance characteristic relative to all the countries in the dataset. These are described in Table 6.2. We combine the WDIs and WGIs (see below) to form our main dataset. For discussion on the WGIs, see Kaufmann *et al.* (2007a, 2007b, 2009, 2010a, 2010b) and The International Bank for Reconstruction and Development (IBRD, 2007).

### 6.4.3. *World Bank: Trade restriction indices 2009*

This dataset "summarizes the trade policy stance of a country by calculating the uniform tariff that will keep its overall imports at the current level when the country in fact has different tariffs for different goods". It is one of the most recent and well-developed dataset measuring trade restrictions. Kee *et al.* (2008, 2009) developed the empirical methodology, by calculating the weighted average tariff for many countries, where the weights are combinations of import volume and import demand elasticity for each imported product.[7]

The manufacturing share of GDP recorded in the WDI dataset is typically larger than that recorded in the NAMAD dataset.[8] We constructed a dataset by merging the WDI and WGI datasets. After some data manipulation, we generated five datasets for our

[7]There are two intermediate datasets in the construction of the Trade Restriction Indices 2009 dataset: (1) Import Demand Elasticities; (2) Ad-Valorem Equivalents of Non-Tariff Measures. They are all included in the same page.

[8]There are two manufacturing shares recorded in the United Nations NAMAD dataset: Mining, Manufacturing, Utilities (ISIC C-E) and Manufacturing (ISIC D). We use the latter, because it is more like those defined in the WDIs data.

**Table 6.1.** Summary of our datasets.[9]

| Analysis | Information |
|---|---|
| Section 6.5. Manufacturing share | Merged from selected information in WDI and WGI datasets. Data for 205 countries at country–year level, in 1996–2011. |
| Table 6.8a. Long-term growth | 15-year annual continuously compounded growth rate[10] calculated. Average level of WGIs over 1996–2011. Initial GDP, manufacturing share, and WGIs recorded in 1996. |
| Table 6.8b. Short-term growth[11] | Five-year annual continuously compounded growth rate. Average level of WGIs over 2006–2011. Initial GDP, manufacturing share, and WGIs recorded in 2006. |
| Table 6.10. Trade restrictions affect manufacturing share | Trade Restriction Indices 2009 dataset merged with manufacturing dataset 1996–2011. Based on trade restrictiveness indices estimates in 2009, for all trade and for manufacturing trade; measured for both tariff barriers and the combination of tariff and non-tariff barriers (NTBs). |
| Table 6.11. Trade restrictions affect short-term growth | Trade Restriction Indices 2009 dataset merged with short-term growth dataset. Aggregate dataset with five-year continuously compounded growth rate, initial GDP and manufacturing share in 2006, average level WGI variables 2006–2009, and trade restriction indices in 2009. |

manufacturing share analysis and growth analysis. The merged dataset contains panel data from 1996–2011, where the years are restricted because the WGI dataset begins in 1996 (with some gaps afterwards). Table 6.1 tells the names and basic information from these datasets. Table 6.2 defines the WGIs. Table 6.3 defines the trade restrictiveness indices.

[9]We also added a regional indicator to all these datasets. We separate the regions by continent. Check http://en.wikipedia.org/wiki/List_of_intergovernmental_organizations for details.

[10]We focus on long-term growth, since annual growth is strongly affected by random shocks and business cycles.

[11]We define short-term growth rate as the most recent five-year growth rate.

**Table 6.2.** Definitions of WGI.

| Symbol | Indicators | Meaning |
|---|---|---|
| Voice | Voice and accountability (va) | Citizens' participation in government selection; freedom of expression, of association and of media. |
| Stability | Political stability and absence of violence (pv) | Governments' stability facing unconstitutional or violent means (e.g., politically-motivated violence and terrorism). |
| Effectiveness | Government effectiveness (ge) | Quality of public and civil service; policy and government commitment. |
| Regulation | Regulatory quality (rq) | Quality of policy and government regulations that permit and promote private sector development. |
| Law | Rule of law (rl) | Quality of contract enforcement, property rights, courts. |
| Honesty | Control of corruption (cc) | Extent to which public power is used for private gain; control of both petty and grand forms of corruption. |

**Table 6.3.** Definitions of trade restriction indicators.

| Indicators | Meaning |
|---|---|
| ***Import Barriers*:**<br>**otri:** *Overall Trade Restrictiveness Index*;<br>**otrit:** *Tariff-only Overall Trade Restrictiveness Index.* | **otri** captures "the trade policy distortions that each country imposes on its import bundle". It measures the uniform tariff equivalence of the country tariff and NTBs that generates the same level of import value for the country in a given year. For tariff measures **otrit**, we picked the series for Applied Tariffs (which takes into account the bilateral trade preferences and patterns). |
| ***Export Barriers*:**<br>**maotri:** *Market Access Overall Trade Restrictiveness Index*;<br>**maotrit:** *Tariff-only MAOTRI.* | **maotri** captures "the trade policy distortions imposed by the trading partners of each country on its export bundle". Similarly, it measures the uniform tariff equivalent of both tariff and NTBs that would generate the same export level in a given year. Again, we picked the measures for Applied Tariffs. In both **maaotri** and **maotrit**, the *ad-valorem* equivalent of NTBs are used (Kee *et al.*, 2009). |

We use WGIs. These indicators are based on various surveys and official data.

## 6.5. Manufacturing Analysis

### 6.5.1. *Is a higher manufacturing share a marker for a higher living standard?*

What is the statistical relationship between living standards and manufacturing share? The variables are described in Table 6.4. We regress per capita GDP on manufacturing share and other controls. As shown in Table 6.5, the signs of coefficient estimates for manufacturing share are quite different across different regions, and the sign can flip after adding governance as extra controls.

What does Table 6.5a say? For the world, each one-percent increase in the manufacturing share is associated with an insignificant increase in per capita income. The point estimate is that

**Table 6.4.** Notation.

| Symbol | Meaning |
|---|---|
| *manushare* | Manufacturing share, i.e., manufacturing value added (% of GDP) |
| *WGIs* | The six-dimension governance indicators (va, pv, ge, rq, rl, cc as in Table 6.2) |
| log(*pcGDP*) | Log(per capita GDP, measured in inflation adjusted US \$). |
| *period*(*dummies*) | Separate 1996–2011 into three periods: 1996–2000, 2001–2005, 2006–2011 |
| *regions*(*dummies*) | Separate 205 countries into six regions, by continents (dummy variables) |
| *region* × *period* | Region–period interactions (assuming different time trends across regions). |
| AF | Africa |
| AS | Asia |
| EU | Europe |
| NA | North America |
| OC | Oceania |
| SA | South America |

**Table 6.5.** How manufacturing share affects per capita GDP.[12]

| | (a) | (b) | (c) | (d) | (e) | (f) | (g) |
|---|---|---|---|---|---|---|---|
| | World | AF | AS | EU | NA | OC | SA |
| Variables | Dependent variable is log of per capita GPD (inflation adjusted $) | | | | | | |
| ***Panel a: Simple regression (only controls are regional and period dummies)*** | | | | | | | |
| Manushare | 0.00253 | **0.0419**$^{***}$ | −0.0122 | **−0.0283**$^{**}$ | **−0.0181**$^{**}$ | **0.0654**$^{***}$ | **0.0637**$^{***}$ |
| | (0.00376) | (0.00541) | (0.00807) | (0.0115) | (0.00785) | (0.0193) | (0.00731) |
| Period | Yes | Yes | Yes | Yes | Yes | Yes | Yes |
| Region | Yes | No | No | No | No | No | No |
| Observations | 2,089 | 571 | 501 | 439 | 296 | 127 | 155 |
| R-squared | 0.435 | 0.114 | 0.054 | 0.073 | 0.097 | 0.120 | 0.394 |
| ***Panel b: Adding WGIs (Governance Indicators) as extra controls*** | | | | | | | |
| Manushare | **−0.00504**$^{**}$ | **0.0121**$^{**}$ | **−0.0229**$^{***}$ | −0.00506 | **0.00643**$^{**}$ | 0.00474 | **0.0589**$^{***}$ |
| | (0.00253) | (0.00540) | (0.00453) | (0.00488) | (0.00305) | (0.0172) | (0.00642) |
| WGIs | Yes | Yes | Yes | Yes | Yes | Yes | Yes |
| Period | Yes | Yes | Yes | Yes | Yes | Yes | Yes |
| Region | Yes | No | No | No | No | No | No |
| Observations | 2,051 | 570 | 500 | 432 | 290 | 104 | 155 |
| R-squared | 0.779 | 0.414 | 0.761 | 0.867 | 0.821 | 0.815 | 0.609 |

*Note*: Robust standard errors[13] in parentheses.
$^{***}p < 0.01$, $^{**}p < 0.05$, $^{*}p < 0.1$, where *ps* are for two tailed tests.

[12]For all the worldwide analyses, we included regional dummies as controls for heterogeneous regional characteristics. This inclusion significantly increased the adjusted R-square and estimation significance.

[13]Robust standard errors: "In regression and time-series modelling, basic forms of models make use of the assumption that the errors or disturbances $u_i$ have the same variance across all observations. When this is not the case, the errors are said to have heteroscedasticity, and this behavior will be reflected in the residuals $\hat{u}_i$ estimated from a fitted model. Robust standard errors are used to allow the fitting of a model that does contain heteroscedastic residuals" (refer to: http://en.wikipedia.org/wiki/Heteroscedasticity-consistent_standard_errors).

a one-percentage-point increase in the manufacturing share is associated with a 0.253% increase in the per capita real income. When this is broken down into regions, three show a positive relationship, and three show a negative relationship. For three regions: Asia, Europe, and North America, the relationship is negative. There is no robust positive relationship between manufacturing share and per capita GDP.

What does Table 6.5b say? When governance indicators are introduced as controls, a higher manufacturing share is associated with a smaller per capita GDP. For the world, each one-percent increase in manufacturing share, holding governance indicators constant, reduces per capita income by 0.504%, and this is significant at the 5% level on a two-tailed test. This indicates that increases in manufacturing shares induced by influences other than favorable governance indicators lowers per capita income. This might be taxation of agriculture, sector- and firm-specific subsidies to manufacturing or occupational licensing that holds back the service sector. The regional sign patterns are a negative influence for Asia and Europe and a positive one for the others.

### 6.5.2. *What determines manufacturing share?*

Assuming the manufacturing share each year is exogenously affected by governance-related factors, we seek to analyze the determination of manufacturing share using linear regression models. A pooled cross-sectional specification performs better than an unbalanced panel specification.

If manufacturing share is solely determined by WGIs and affected by non-linear time trend, then:

$$manushare = \beta_0 + \beta_1 \cdot WGIs + \beta_2 \cdot period\ (dummies) + \varepsilon \quad (6.1)$$

Manufacturing share should depend on income level. Adding the log of per capita GDP to control for living standards yields

$$\begin{aligned} manushare = \beta_0 + \beta_1 \cdot WGIs + \beta_2 \cdot period\ (dummies) \\ + \beta_3 \cdot \log(GDP) + \varepsilon \end{aligned} \quad (6.2)$$

Adding regional dummies to capture continent-specific effects gives

$$manushare = \beta_0 + \beta_1 \cdot WGIs + \beta_3 \cdot \log(GDP) + \beta_4 \cdot regions(dummies) + \varepsilon \quad (6.3)$$

Finally, including all the dummies and their interactions gives

$$manushare = \beta_0 + \beta_1 \cdot WGIs + \beta_2 \cdot period(dummies) + \beta_3 \cdot \log(GDP) + \beta_4 \cdot regions\ (dummies) + \beta_5 \cdot region \times period(dummies) + \varepsilon \quad (6.4)$$

Table 6.6 presents the estimates of these four equations for the world. IpcGDP in the tables denotes Ln(per capita GDP).

**Table 6.6.** How governance indicators affect manufacturing share.

| Variables | (1) | (2) | (3) | (4) |
|---|---|---|---|---|
| | Dependent variable is manufacturing share (% value added in GDP) | | | |
| IpcGDP | | 0.473** | −0.716*** | −0.399** |
| | | (0.192) | (0.192) | (0.202) |
| Voice and accountability | −0.0132 | −0.0142 | −0.0497*** | −0.0485*** |
| | (0.0115) | (0.0116) | (0.0135) | (0.0136) |
| Political stability | −0.0363*** | −0.0423*** | −0.0337*** | −0.0391*** |
| | (0.00999) | (0.00982) | (0.00946) | (0.00949) |
| **Government effectiveness** | **0.183***** | **0.171***** | **0.161***** | **0.155***** |
| | (0.0209) | (0.0226) | (0.0218) | (0.0221) |
| Regulatory quality | 0.0480*** | 0.0393*** | 0.0262* | 0.0217 |
| | (0.0142) | (0.0140) | (0.0147) | (0.0146) |
| Rule of law | −0.0892*** | −0.0852*** | −0.0640*** | −0.0607*** |
| | (0.0167) | (0.0166) | (0.0177) | (0.0182) |
| Control of corruption | −0.0464*** | −0.0476*** | −0.0137 | −0.0174 |
| | (0.0172) | (0.0172) | (0.0169) | (0.0168) |
| Observations | 2,060 | 2,051 | 2,051 | 2,051 |
| Adjusted R^2 | 0.126 | 0.126 | 0.194 | 0.201 |
| R-squared | 0.129 | 0.130 | 0.199 | 0.210 |

*Note*: Robust standard errors in parentheses.
***$p$ <0.01, **$p$ <0.05, *$p$ <0.1.

In Table 6.6, progressing from specification (1) to (4), we observe increases in R square, as must be the case when more explanatory variables are introduced, and adjusted R square never falls. We see that government effectiveness positively influences manufacturing share. This is true in all four specifications, and government effectiveness has the largest influence of the six GPIs. The same is true of regulatory quality, except the effect is always less than 27% as strong. All of the government effectiveness coefficients are significant at the 1% level. The impacts of government effectiveness are similar whether we include as controls, the per capita income, regional dummies, regional dummies interacted with time dummies, or none of them. **Taking the median value of 0.166, we see that improving the government effectiveness rank by 10 percentiles, increases manufacturing share by 1.66%.** The median value for regulatory quality is 0.030. Thus increasing both ranks by 10 percentiles raises manufacturing share by 1.96%. So a disturbance that reduces manufacturing share by that amount could be offset by a 10-percentile improvement in government effectiveness plus regulatory quality.

Manufacturing share is reduced by increases in voice and accountability. Perhaps that is associated with a less docile labor force. Surprisingly, improvements in political stability, rule of law, and control of corruption have negative effects on manufacturing share and in most cases these effects are significant. The regressions indicate that these improvements have a larger favorable impact on the rest of the economy than on manufacturing. A rationale for why rule of law and control of corruption might have negative signs is that if laws are inefficient ways to preserve rents for an elete, corruption and other ways around the law might make the economy work better. See Bhagwati (1974) and Gokcekus and Bengyak (2014).

Based on Equation (6.4), Table 6.7 separates the dataset into subsamples and allows heterogeneous effects of governance performance across continents. Table 6.7 reproduces Table 6.6, column 4, for individual regions. The signs for effectiveness and regulation are the same as before, except that the sign for effectiveness in North America and regulation in South America changes. The median value

**Table 6.7.** Regional effects on manufacturing share: Sub-sample analysis.

| | (1) | (2) | (3) | (4) | (5) | (6) | (7) |
|---|---|---|---|---|---|---|---|
| | AF | AS | EU | NA | OC | SA | World |
| Variables | Dependent variable is manufacturing share (% value added in GDP) | | | | | | |
| IpcGDP | 0.586* | −1.932*** | −0.544 | 2.415* | 0.168 | 4.103*** | −0.399** |
| | (0.299) | (0.399) | (0.529) | (1.352) | (0.607) | (0.652) | (0.202) |
| Voice | **−0.0885*** | **−0.0558** | **−0.204*** | **0.125** | **−0.152*** | **0.106*** | **−0.0485*** |
| | (0.0253) | (0.0229) | (0.0432) | (0.0637) | (0.0319) | (0.0593) | (0.0136) |
| Stability | −0.0159 | **−0.107*** | **0.129*** | **−0.193*** | 0.00860 | −0.0144 | **−0.0391*** |
| | (0.0179) | (0.0155) | (0.0152) | (0.0429) | (0.0381) | (0.0374) | (0.00949) |
| Effectiveness | 0.0519 | **0.370*** | **0.0776*** | **−0.198** | **0.152*** | **0.0748*** | **0.155*** |
| | (0.0385) | (0.0419) | (0.0457) | (0.0819) | (0.0417) | (0.0429) | (0.0221) |
| Regulation | **0.0666** | 0.00741 | 0.00943 | **0.114*** | 0.0443 | −0.0381 | 0.0217 |
| | (0.0326) | (0.0259) | (0.0425) | (0.0494) | (0.0365) | (0.0350) | (0.0146) |
| Law | −0.0267 | 0.0414 | **−0.0976** | **−0.203*** | −0.0197 | **−0.0939*** | **−0.0607*** |
| | (0.0325) | (0.0436) | (0.0408) | (0.0780) | (0.0445) | (0.0503) | (0.0182) |
| Honesty | **0.108*** | **−0.172*** | **0.0838** | **0.121*** | −0.0142 | −0.0377 | −0.0174 |
| | (0.0315) | (0.0349) | (0.0372) | (0.0698) | (0.0265) | (0.0375) | (0.0168) |
| Observations | 570 | 500 | 432 | 290 | 104 | 155 | 2,051 |
| Adjusted R^2 | 0.193 | 0.240 | 0.257 | 0.218 | 0.634 | 0.252 | 0.201 |
| R-squared | 0.206 | 0.254 | 0.273 | 0.242 | 0.666 | 0.296 | 0.210 |

*Note*: Robust standard errors in parentheses.
$^{***}p < 0.01$, $^{**}p < 0.05$, $^{*}p < 0.1$.

for government effectiveness in the six regions is 0.0762, and for regulatory quality 0.0580 for a sum of 0.134, so increasing both by 10 percentiles, should increase manufacturing share by 1.34%.

A comparison of Table 6.6 and Table 6.7 suggests that: (1) Sub-sample analysis supports our hypothesis of heterogeneous government behavior and government effect in manufacturing share determination, as the coefficients on WGIs are quite different (both in sign and in magnitude) across regions; (2) The coefficient of determination also increases in all specifications, even after we adjust the potential over-fitting (the $R^2$ and adjusted-$R^2$ give us basically the same information); (3) The six governance indicators are most significant in the sub-sample of Europe and North America, with most indicators significant — even though they tell us different stories in these two continents. This suggests that observed differences in multi-dimensional government performance might have stronger effects for countries in Europe and North America; (4) Stronger voice and accountability correlates with higher manufacturing share in North America and South America (coefficient estimates of Voice); a more effective government increases manufacturing share in every region except in North America.

Figure 6.1 graphs the portion of manufacturing share unexplained after controlling all other explanatory variables, except government effectiveness *versus* government effectiveness, by region. In each case, except for North America, the relationship is positive. For example in Asia according to the regression line, improving government effectiveness from worst to best raises the manufacturing share by around 38 percentage points. To sum up, our graphical results indicate that: (1) The linear fittings for the scatter plot work well for almost all regions (except Africa), which is good evidence that government effectiveness is an important attribute in the determination of manufacturing share; (2) The magnitude of the slope (the effect of government effectiveness) is different across regions, with positively significant slopes for Asia, Europe, and Oceania, while these effects in Africa, North America and South America are somewhat ambiguous; (3) The unexplained manufacturing share is best explained by

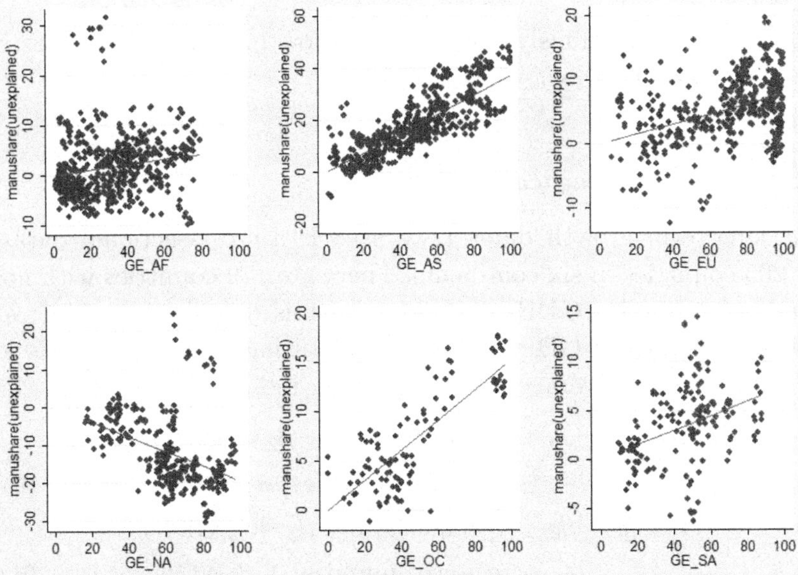


**Figure 6.1.** Manufacturing share and government effectiveness, by region.

government effectiveness in Asia. The fact that the percentile ranks vary from close to zero to close to 100 corroborates our hunch that in some Asian countries, governments play a strong role in resource allocation and make relevant policy efficiently, while in others they play a strong role and do a remarkably bad job.

## 6.6. Explaining Growth

### 6.6.1. *Measures of growth*

We label the annual continuously compounded growth rate over 15 years (1996–2011) and that over five years (2006–2011) as long-term and short-term growth rates, respectively. Denote the annual continuously compound growth rate as $r$. Then the per capita GDP after $N$ years, starting in year 0, is given by $\mathrm{GDP}_{0+N} = \mathrm{GDP}_0 \cdot e^{rN}$.

Thus, we have

$$\text{annual continuously compounded growth rate over } N \text{ years} = \frac{\ln(\text{GDP}_{0+N}) - \ln(\text{GDP}_0)}{N}.$$

### 6.6.2. *Model specifications*

The long-term growth dataset we used is a cross-sectional dataset for 205 countries in six continents. There are 179 countries with non-missing per capita GDPs. The base year is defaulted as 1996. We use initial levels of GDP, while manufacturing share and WGIs are calculated as the average values of the six indicators over 1996–2011

$$\begin{aligned} \text{growth} = \beta_0 + \beta_1 \cdot \text{manushare} + \beta_2 \cdot \log(\text{GDP}) \\ + \beta_3 \cdot \text{regions(dummies)} + \varepsilon \end{aligned} \tag{6.5}$$

$$\begin{aligned} \text{growth} = \beta_0 + \beta_1 \text{manushare} + \beta_2 \cdot \log(\text{GDP}) \\ + \beta_3 \text{ regions(dummies)} + \beta_4 \text{WGIs} + \varepsilon \end{aligned} \tag{6.6}$$

### 6.6.3. *Results comparison and discussion*

Table 6.8 presents the effects of manufacturing share on growth rate. We only report the regressions with relatively high prediction power (R square higher than 0.25) and relatively reliable inferences (coefficients of variables cannot be all insignificant). Note that columns (1)–(3) and (6)–(8) are sub-sample analysis for Equation (6.5), with regional dummies excluded; column (4) and (9) are worldwide analysis using all countries and controlling for regional fixed effects; column (5) and (10) are estimations based on Equation (6.6), which includes WGIs.

Table 6.8a column 4 shows that a 10% increase in manufacturing share increases the fifteen-year growth rate of the economy by 0.117% per year without governance indicators as controls. Table 6.8a column 5 shows that the same increase in manufacturing share increases fifteen-year growth by 0.08% per year, holding WGIs constant. So about a third of the effect of manufacturing share on growth is due to good WGIs. The manufacturing share coefficients for five-year growth rates are slightly higher for the world but not in all regions.

**Table 6.8.** Regional effects of manufacturing share on growth.

| | (1) | (2) | (3) | (4) | (5) |
|---|---|---|---|---|---|
| | AS | EU | SA | World | World |
| Variables | (a) Dependent variable: 15-year continuously compound growth rate | | | | |
| manu96 | −0.0165 | −0.0593 | **−0.379**$^{***}$ | 0.0117 | 0.00760 |
| | (0.0708) | (0.0555) | (0.0946) | (0.0303) | (0.0319) |
| lpcGDP96 | −1.255$^{***}$ | −2.031$^{***}$ | −0.351 | −1.045$^{***}$ | −1.359$^{***}$ |
| | (0.288) | (0.235) | (0.600) | (0.164) | (0.279) |
| Observations | 39 | 33 | 12 | 161 | 161 |
| R-squared | 0.298 | 0.745 | 0.565 | 0.312 | 0.359 |
| | (6) | (7) | (8) | (9) | (10) |
| | AS | EU | NA | World | World |
| Variables | (b) Dependent variable: Five-year continuously compound growth rate | | | | |
| manu06 | −0.0375 | 0.0415 | **0.107**$^{*}$ | 0.0260 | 0.0162 |
| | (0.0953) | (0.0695) | (0.0597) | (0.0377) | (0.0365) |
| lpcGDP06 | −1.955$^{***}$ | −2.556$^{***}$ | −1.310$^{**}$ | −1.642$^{***}$ | −1.532$^{***}$ |
| | (0.472) | (0.390) | (0.467) | (0.257) | (0.390) |
| Observations | 38 | 37 | 22 | 163 | 163 |
| R-squared | 0.358 | 0.616 | 0.337 | 0.524 | 0.543 |

*Note*: Robust standard errors in parentheses.
$^{***}p < 0.01$, $^{**}p < 0.05$, $^{*}p < 0.1$.

The coefficients for the first three regions on manufacturing share are negative. They are presented as examples of regressions without WGIs as controls.

Results for both long-term and short-term growth rates are: (1) Manufacturing share didn't always contribute to economic growth, with most coefficients of manufacturing share being insignificant; (2) In the long-term: base level manufacturing share in 1996 has a significantly negative effect on economic growth in South America; (3) In the short-term: base level manufacturing share in 2006 has a positive effect on economic growth in North America; (4) The estimates in columns (3) and (8) are partially restricted by the small sample size (12 and 22 respectively).

Table 6.9 provides sub-sample analysis with WGIs as extra control variables, measured in average values over the growth period.[14] Again we selectively report the regression results as for Table 6.8. Here are some conclusions:

(1) Log per capita GDP is always significantly negative: poorer countries grow faster.
(2) For long-term growth: political stability and absence of violence have highly significant positive impacts on long-term economic growth, especially for Europe.
(3) For short-term growth: voice and accountability decreases growth in Europe but raises growth in North America. This can be a result of different levels of democracy in the two continents. Barro (1999) concludes that there is a growth-maximizing level of democracy.
(4) Higher control of corruption raises long-term growth in Europe but reduces growth in the most recent five years; while higher control of corruption leads to decreased short-term growth rate in North America.
(5) Europe is best predicted.

The EU manufacturing share has a negative, but insignificant, coefficient. For the world, an autonomous decrease in the manufacturing share by 10% could be counter-balanced by an increase in effectiveness and regulation by $0.0760/(0.0197 + 0.0330) = 0.0760/0.0527 = 1.44$ percentiles. So there are ways to get growth up, besides directly increasing manufacturing share (the coefficient of which is insignificant). For the world regressions, stability enhances growth. The other WGIs are insignificant.

Figure 6.2 reports the scatter plots of long-term growth rate (unexplained by manufacturing share) *versus* base level

[14]We compared the estimation results using both WGIs in 1996 (2006) and average WGI over 1996–2011 (2006–2011), and the latter performs much better in both prediction power and estimation inferences.

**Table 6.9.** Regional effects of WGIs on growth (sub-sample analysis).

| | (1) | (2) | (3) | (4) | (5) |
|---|---|---|---|---|---|
| | AS | EU | World | EU | NA |
| Variables | Dependent variable is growth rate | | | | |
| Span | Long | Long | Long | Short | Short |
| manu_t0 | 0.0222 | −0.0994 | 0.00760 | −0.0172 | 0.0100 |
| | (0.0818) | (0.0656) | (0.0319) | (0.0936) | (0.0785) |
| lpcGDP_t0 | $-1.289^{***}$ | $-2.878^{***}$ | $-1.359^{***}$ | $-2.138^{**}$ | $-2.892^{**}$ |
| | (0.471) | (0.451) | (0.279) | (0.816) | (1.007) |
| Voice_avg | −0.0423 | −0.0691 | −0.0310 | **−0.131**$^{**}$ | **0.205**$^{**}$ |
| | (0.0334) | (0.0651) | (0.0190) | (0.0478) | (0.0925) |
| Stability_avg | **0.0576**$^{**}$ | **0.0805**$^{***}$ | **0.0436**$^{***}$ | 0.0321 | −0.00976 |
| | (0.0239) | (0.0274) | (0.0162) | (0.0341) | (0.0440) |
| Effectiveness_avg | −0.0582 | −0.0439 | 0.0197 | 0.0533 | **−0.210**$^{*}$ |
| | (0.0811) | (0.0587) | (0.0295) | (0.0827) | (0.112) |
| Regulation_avg | 0.0325 | **0.122**$^{*}$ | 0.0330 | −0.0118 | **0.381**$^{***}$ |
| | (0.0505) | (0.0711) | (0.0243) | (0.0919) | (0.0973) |
| Law_avg | 0.0746 | −0.121 | −0.0121 | $0.150^{*}$ | 0.0254 |
| | (0.0940) | (0.0867) | (0.0369) | (0.0758) | (0.0694) |
| Honesty_avg | −0.0706 | **0.117**$^{*}$ | −0.0297 | **−0.125**$^{**}$ | **−0.177**$^{**}$ |
| | (0.0836) | (0.0631) | (0.0305) | (0.0610) | (0.0786) |
| Observations | 39 | 33 | 161 | 37 | 22 |
| R-squared | 0.444 | 0.862 | 0.359 | 0.697 | 0.688 |

*Note*: Robust standard errors in parentheses.
$^{***}p<0.01$, $^{**}p<0.05$, $^{*}p<0.1$

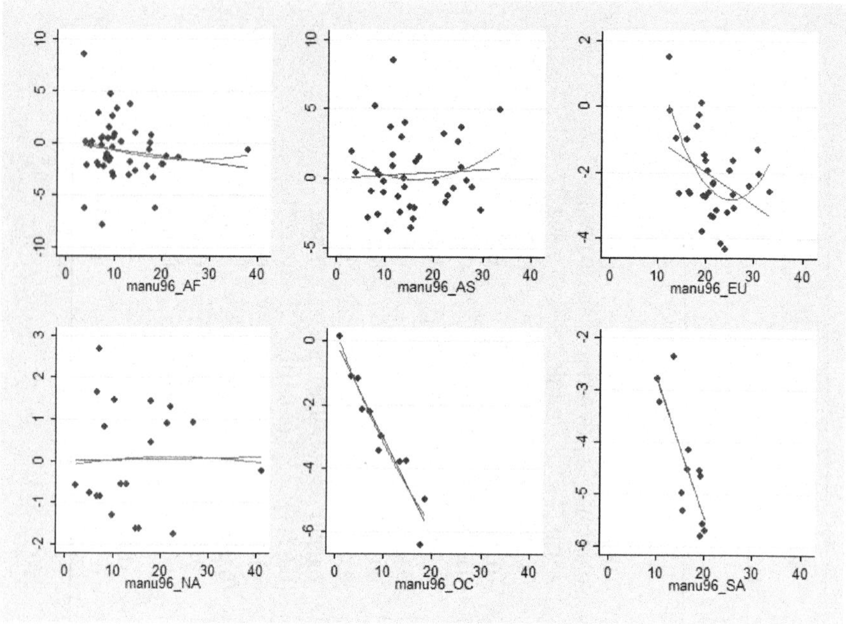


**Figure 6.2.** Long-term growth explained by base level manufacturing share, by region.

manufacturing share in 1996, as described in Equation (6.6), except that the regional dummies are excluded. They show that for four regions, the effect of manufacturing share on growth is negative when WGIs are included as controls. For one it is very close to zero, and for one it is positive. However, most of the points are quite scattered, which also mirrors the insignificant estimates in Table 6.8.

## 6.7. Trade Restriction Analysis

### 6.7.1. *Assumptions and model specifications*

Do trade restriction determine manufacturing share and economic growth? A newly constructed dataset developed by Kee *et al.* (2008, 2009) enables us to explore this issue. The specifications used here are similar to Equations (6.4) and (6.6). We added a pair of indices (for export and import barriers) and got rid of period–region interactions to avoid over fitting.

$$\begin{aligned}\text{manushare} &= \beta_0 + \beta_1 \cdot \text{WGIs} + \beta_2 \cdot \text{period(dummies)} \\ &\quad \cdot 1(\text{worldwide}) + \beta_3 \cdot \log(\text{GDP}) \\ &\quad + \beta_4 \cdot \text{trade\_barriers} + \varepsilon \qquad (6.7) \\ \text{growth} &= \beta_0 + \beta_1 \text{manushare} + \beta_2 \cdot \log(\text{GDP}) \\ &\quad + \beta_3 \text{regions} \cdot 1(\text{worldwide}) \\ &\quad + \beta_4 \text{WGIs} + \beta_5 \cdot \text{trade\_barriers} + \varepsilon \qquad (6.8)\end{aligned}$$

where worldwide is an indicator that is 1 for worldwide analysis and 0 for regional analysis.

The definitions of trade barriers in specifications (6.7) and (6.8) are different. Equation (6.7) predicts resource allocation, so relative trade barriers in manufacturing sector is the relevant indicator of trade barriers in this case. Equation (6.8) uses the indicator of all trade barriers to predict growth.[15] The trade restriction indicators are treated as exogenous and holding constant over years at the reference level in 2009. This assumption is too strong, but we suffer from this curse since the data series has not been updated.

Specifically, the relative barrier in the manufacturing sector, is: $rt\text{manu}$ or $r\text{manu} = \frac{(1+T_{\text{manu}})}{(1+T_{\text{overall}})}$, where $T$ denotes the tariff equivalent of trade barriers expressed as a proportion (either pure-tariff barriers or the combination of both tariff and NTBs).

### 6.7.2. *Do trade restrictions raise manufacturing share?*

The time period ranges from 1996–2011 in this updated manufacturing analysis with trade restrictions, to keep it in line with the previous manufacturing analysis. Import and export combined restrictions in the manufacturing sector relative to all trade restrictiveness are denoted as $r$manu_im and $r$manu_ex, respectively; the corresponding

[15] Recall that we did both cross-sectional and unbalanced panel analysis in the original manufacturing share analysis without trade restriction, and the results showed that cross-sectional outputs are better than the panel analysis: Higher adjusted $R^2$, more significant estimates.

import and export pure-tariff restrictions in the manufacturing sector relative to overall trade restrictiveness are denoted as *rt*manu_im and *rt*manu_ex, respectively. "im" refers to the country's barriers and "ex" to the barriers of its trading partners.

Table 6.10a says that for the world, protecting manufacturing with tariffs and NTBs lowers the manufacturing shares. Starting from free trade, the −87.97 is Δ[Manufacturing share]/Δ[relative manufacturing tariff equivalent]. Thus if a country's imports are 50% manufactured goods, raising the manufacturing tariff from 0 to 1%, raises the relative manufacturing tariff equivalent by 0.5%, so the $x$ variable takes on a value of 0.005, and the manufacturing share falls by $0.8797/2 = 0.44$ percentage points. Assuming a 50% manufacturing share of a country's exports, an increase in the foreign tariff on manufacturing from 0 to 1% cuts the manufacturing share by (an insignificant) 0.017 percentage points.

Table 6.10b gives similar results for just import tariff barriers. It gives much stronger results for foreign tariff barriers than for foreign tariffs and NTBs in Table 6.10a. We are not sure why. It may be that some of the NTBs are voluntary export restraints which if set low enough may facilitate monopoly power and profits on the part of the exporter. In both cases WGIs are in place.

The negative coefficients on the relative import tariff and relative import tariff and NTB may be due to import tariffs or anti-dumping restrictions on intermediate inputs into manufacturing, which make manufacturing less competitive. It may also be that countries with high degrees of protection, on an average are likely to vary their levels of protection more frequently, and this creates uncertainty for manufacturing, thereby shrinking that sector.

### 6.7.3. *Do trade restrictions smother growth?*

We focus on short-term growth with trade restrictions, since the trade restriction indices with 2009 as reference year are a better proxy for short-term trade restrictiveness. We selectively report results in Table 6.11. We see (1) even after adding trade barriers, the coefficient estimates of base year manufacturing shares are still insignificant;

**Table 6.10.** Manufacturing analysis with trade restrictions [specification (6.7)].

| | (1) | (2) | (3) | (4) | (5) | (6) | (7) |
|---|---|---|---|---|---|---|---|
| | AF | AS | EU | NA | OC | SA | World |
| Variables | Dependent variable: Manufacturing share (% value added in GDP) | | | | | | |
| ***Panel a: Manufacturing analysis with relative barriers(tariff + NTB)*** | | | | | | | |
| *r*manu_im | **−58.96**$^{***}$ | **−421.8**$^{***}$ | **296.7**$^{***}$ | **−89.28**$^{***}$ | **−653.1**$^{***}$ | 7.375 | **−87.97**$^{***}$ |
| | (14.84) | (41.79) | (38.04) | (33.41) | (162.6) | (20.61) | (13.14) |
| *r*manu_ex | **−41.39**$^{***}$ | 8.033 | **69.74**$^{***}$ | **−176.6**$^{***}$ | −7.595 | −0.898 | −3.411 |
| | (7.583) | (5.837) | (13.54) | (18.14) | (7.743) | (8.742) | (4.626) |
| lpcGDP | 2.388$^{***}$ | −2.292$^{***}$ | 3.675$^{***}$ | −2.418$^{**}$ | 1.131 | 1.465$^{***}$ | −0.0942 |
| | (0.517) | (0.371) | (1.068) | (1.093) | (1.057) | (0.356) | (0.335) |
| Observations | 389 | 319 | 114 | 150 | 54 | 129 | 1,155 |
| R-squared | 0.289 | 0.631 | 0.781 | 0.603 | 0.874 | 0.543 | 0.186 |
| ***Panel b: Manufacturing analysis with relative tariff barriers*** | | | | | | | |
| *rt*manu_im | **−147.1**$^{***}$ | **−525.5**$^{***}$ | **84.69**$^{*}$ | **302.4**$^{**}$ | **1,848**$^{***}$ | **127.0**$^{*}$ | **−64.66**$^{***}$ |
| | (35.01) | (41.21) | (47.70) | (120.9) | (141.2) | (74.94) | (24.72) |
| *rt*manu_ex | **−68.39**$^{***}$ | **−128.9**$^{***}$ | **−553.7**$^{***}$ | **−598.3**$^{***}$ | **−97.83**$^{***}$ | 20.74 | **−69.88**$^{***}$ |
| | (19.75) | (25.49) | (194.6) | (51.59) | (4.785) | (21.20) | (15.70) |
| lpcGDP | 2.396$^{***}$ | −2.256$^{***}$ | 0.584 | −2.533$^{***}$ | −3.122$^{***}$ | 1.358$^{***}$ | 0.348 |
| | (0.538) | (0.399) | (0.987) | (0.945) | (0.509) | (0.323) | (0.331) |
| Observations | 389 | 319 | 114 | 150 | 54 | 129 | 1,155 |
| R-squared | 0.242 | 0.604 | 0.749 | 0.710 | 0.972 | 0.555 | 0.188 |
| ***Other controls variables for both:*** | | | | | | | |
| WGIs | Yes | Yes | Yes | Yes | Yes | Yes | Yes |
| period | Yes | Yes | Yes | Yes | Yes | Yes | Yes |
| region | No | No | No | No | No | No | Yes |

*Note*: Robust standard errors in parentheses.
$^{***}p < 0.01$, $^{**}p < 0.05$, $^{*}p < 0.1$

**Table 6.11.** Short-term analysis with trade restrictions [specification (6.8)].

| | (1) | (2) | (3) | (4) | (5) | (6) |
|---|---|---|---|---|---|---|
| | otri | otrit | tri_manu | trit_manu | otrit_AF | otrit_AS |
| Variables | Dependent variable: Five-year continuously compound growth rate (% per year) | | | | | |
| barrier_im | −0.0351 | −0.149 | −0.0200 | −0.146 | −0.0690 | **−0.660**$^{***}$ |
| | (0.0339) | (0.116) | (0.0357) | (0.105) | (0.155) | (0.211) |
| barrier_ex | **−0.152**$^{***}$ | **−0.542**$^{***}$ | −0.0758 | **−0.540**$^{***}$ | **−0.374**$^{*}$ | **−0.967**$^{**}$ |
| | **(0.0549)** | **(0.162)** | (0.0685) | **(0.239)** | (0.188) | (0.411) |
| manu06 | 0.0609 | 0.0567 | 0.0415 | 0.0241 | −0.0611 | −0.0333 |
| | (0.0651) | (0.0761) | (0.0661) | (0.0695) | (0.0875) | (0.142) |
| lpcGDP_06 | −1.851$^{***}$ | −1.636$^{***}$ | −1.624$^{***}$ | −1.482$^{***}$ | −0.0789 | −2.289 |
| | (0.607) | (0.527) | (0.605) | (0.555) | (0.430) | (1.295) |
| WGI_avg | Yes | Yes | Yes | Yes | Yes | Yes |
| Regiondum | Yes | Yes | Yes | Yes | No | No |
| Observations | 90 | 90 | 90 | 90 | 30 | 24 |
| R-squared | 0.458 | 0.491 | 0.415 | 0.457 | 0.558 | 0.711 |

*Note*: Robust standard errors in parentheses.
$^{***}p < 0.01$, $^{**}p < 0.05$, $^{*}p < 0.1$.
otri is overall trade restrictiveness index (tariffs + NTBs);
otrit is overall trade restrictiveness index (tariffs only);
tri_manu is trade restrictiveness index for manufacturing (tariffs + NTBs);
trit_manu is trade restrictiveness index for manufacturing (tariffs only).

(2) Export trade barriers, no matter whether measured as pure tariff barriers or overall trade barriers including tariff and NTBs, negatively impact the growth rate across regions and worldwide; (3) Import trade barriers also have negative coefficient estimates, but most of them are insignificant, except for tariff import trade barriers in Asia; (4) Africa and Asia are the two regions that have relatively largest negative impact from export barriers to short-term growth. We find Asia is the largest victim of both import and export tariff trade barriers compared to other continents. This might be due to the international trading structure across countries: some Asian countries embraced tremendous economic growth at least, partially thanks to the increasing smoothly and well-developed international trade in manufacturing goods, and African countries have a high variance of trade restrictions. More open economies and economies with higher variance of trade restrictions typically exhibit more significance.

What is interesting in Table 6.11? All the coefficients of home and foreign barriers to imports have negative effects on economic growth. Columns (1)–(4) are the world trade barriers, either just tariffs or tariffs plus NTBs, lower growth; tariff barriers at home and abroad, lower growth; and manufacturing trade barriers at home and abroad, lower growth. That also happens for Africa and Asia. Let us take the most significant estimates in column (6) for Asia. A 10-percentage-point increase in the tariff lowers the growth rate by 6.6% per year. For column (2), a 10% point increase lowers the growth rate by 1.49% per year. Foreign trade barriers are typically worse, i.e., they decrease economic growth with larger magnitude. For column 2, a 10-percentage-point increase in foreign trade barriers reduces the five-year growth rate by 5.4% per year, while a rise in the manufacturing share by 10% raises the growth rate by 0.567% per year. Foreign protection worsens the terms of trade; domestic protection does not always do so. Hence, foreign protection is more damaging than domestic protection to economic growth.

Figure 6.3 plots the part of unexplained growth *versus* different measures of export barriers. The graphical results match our regression estimates, with the linear fitting and quadratic fitting lines, all downward sloping.

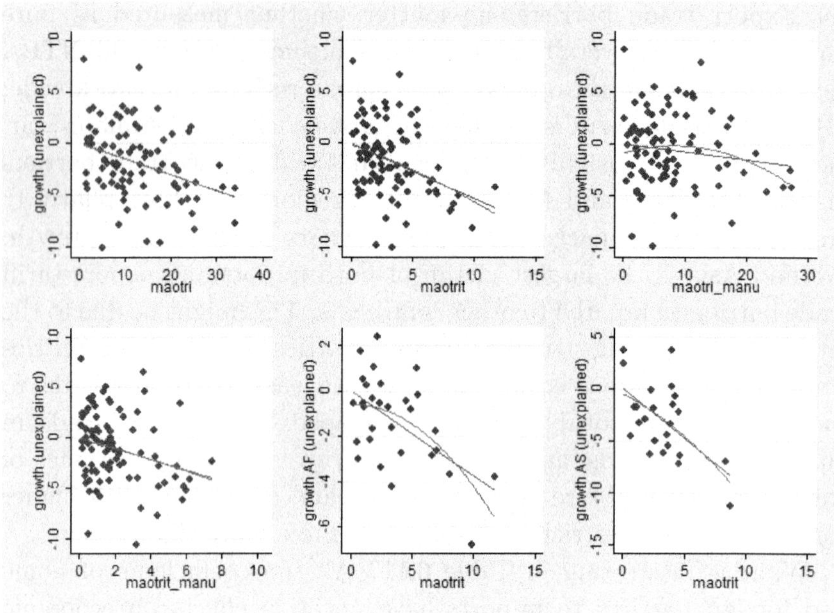


**Figure 6.3.** Short-term growth (unexplained part) *versus* export trade restrictions.

*Note*: The six sub-plots are corresponding to the six specifications in Table 6.11; order: first by row, then by column. "ma" refers to market access for exports.

## 6.8. What Should We All Take Away from These Tables and Graphs?

Our findings are based on examining the relationship between manufacturing share, protection, per capita GDP, and economic growth over a wide range of countries over a fifteen year period.

Our main findings are:

(1) An increase in the manufacturing share of GDP increases per capita income insignificantly, and the point estimate is that a 10% increase in manufacturing share increases per capita GDP by only 2.5%. (Table 6.5a)
(2) When governance indicators are held constant the manufacturing share of GDP decreases per capita income significantly. (Table 6.5b)

(3) One representative calculation shows that an autonomous decrease in manufacturing share of GDP by 1.96 percentage points, could be counter-balanced by a simultaneous increase of 10 percentiles in government effectiveness and regulatory quality to leave manufacturing share unchanged. Thus, domestic reforms are effective in increasing the manufacturing share. (Table 6.6)
(4) One representative calculation shows that an autonomous decrease in the manufacturing share by 10% would cut growth by an insignificant, but not economically unimportant, 0.076% per year over the next 15-year period. However, this effect on growth could be counter-balanced by an increase in government effectiveness and the quality of regulation by 1.44 percentiles. (The column 'World' in Table 6.9)
(5) An increase in the protection of the manufacturing sector relative to the rest of the economy actually reduces the manufacturing share. Similarly, an increase in an exporter's trading partners' barriers to its exports of manufactures relative to its other exports reduces the exporter's manufacturing share. (Table 6.10)
(6) Trade barriers at home and abroad significantly reduce economic growth. (Table 6.11). Thus, domestic protection diminishes both the manufacturing sector and economic growth to the extent that it precipitates a trade war.

Our primary conclusion is that while a larger manufacturing share may have a salutatory effect on economic growth, an autonomous drop in the manufacturing share can be balanced by a small improvement in governance effectiveness and regulatory quality. Our secondary conclusion is that trade restrictions hamper economic growth and manufacturing share, so it makes no sense to use trade restrictions to improve economic growth *via* the impact of trade restrictions on manufacturing share.

## 6.9. Reflections

Our paper provides support for remarks by Corden, Mussa, Mill, and Irwin.

Is it wise to use trade policy to achieve domestic objectives such as a high manufacturing share? Corden (1998, p. 284) closes his book *Trade Policy and Economic Welfare* with the statement "Complex interventions pursued by well informed, analytically well-trained and high-minded officials or politicians might well be optimal, but information and understanding are often limited, and policymakers are rarely immune from various sectional pressures."

Mussa (1993, p. 374) makes a similar argument "When the political power of special interests combines with the pernicious effects of the fixed-number-of-jobs fallacy, the result will almost inevitably be some divergence from the free-trade policies that would probably best serve the broad public interest. Realizing that the battle will be unending and that the contest will be somewhat uneven, the practical question for economists working on trade policy is how to keep the damage to a minimum."

Another aspect of freer trade is explored by Liu and Ornelas (2014). They find that free trade agreements (FTAs) "can critically reduce the incentive of authoritarian groups to seek power by destroying protectionist rents, thus making democracies last longer. This gives governments in unstable democracies, an extra motive to form FTAs". They "find robust support for these predictions".

Irwin (1991, p. 203) notes "[John Stewart] Mill condemned any general policy of protection — 'an organized system of pillage of the many by the few', he called it — but reiterated that, in principle, the infant industry claim to protection was valid" (Elliot, 1910, p. 295). Irwin (1991, p. 207) continues,

> Theories emerge periodically suggesting how tariffs can be beneficial, under certain and particular circumstances and these theories struggle to gain acceptance into the main body of economic theory. When legitimate exceptions to free trade are accepted into economic theory, there may come a period of diminished confidence among economists in free trade as a policy. Yet repetition of this pattern over the decades has not ultimately led to uneasiness among economists in their belief that the gains from international trade are substantial and that a free trade policy is difficult to improve upon. Identification of possible exceptions to free trade by economic theorists means neither that such circumstances can be isolated and identified in practice nor that such exceptions would

> constitute sound economic policy. If the past is any guide, new theories related to strategic trade policy will indeed provide important economic insights, but will not fundamentally challenge the belief of economists in free trade.

As Copeland *et al.* (1989) reiterate, the optimum tariff is not the best way to transfer resources between countries. A preferable alternative is an explicit transfer.

Popkin and Kobe (2010, pp. i–ii) make recommendations which are consistent with our findings.

- Emphasize ... worker training and early education that nurtures math and science proficiency.
- Reduce the corporate income tax rate on profits earned from production in the United States to match those of our major trading partners.
- Eliminate one important uncertainty in private decisions to undertake R&D by making the R&D tax credit permanent.
- Governments at all levels should make investments in infrastructure.

Nowhere in the report is protectionism recommended in service of jobs, productivity, or competitiveness.

Baily and Bosworth (2014) write,

> We agree with those who think manufacturing is important, but we do not agree that this justifies special treatment for the sector, such as special tax rates or other subsidies. Such policies are hard to enforce and an invitation to arbitrageurs who seek ways to capture the gains from such subsidies with little or no actual change in real behavior. However, certain policy decisions have had a particularly large adverse impact on manufacturing because it is so exposed to global competition (Baily and Bosworth, 2014, p. 19). While we do not support special subsidies, it is important to ensure that existing policies are supportive of manufacturing — or at least do not discriminate against it. (Baily and Bosworth, 2014, p. 22).

They suggest (Baily and Bosworth, 2014, pp. 23–24) "trade negotiations that help to pry open foreign markets, [and] negotiations with countries that manage their exchange rates about the appropriate level of their exchange rates", and write "The marginal rate of corporate taxation in the United States is too high, particularly in relationship to the tax rates of other countries.... The United States has the highest corporate tax rate within the OECD, and, at a combined 39 percent, it exceeds the average by 14 percentage points. The United States needs to follow the lead of other countries in shifting toward greater reliance on consumption-based taxation.... "US 15-year-olds rank 25th in math and 17th in science.... among OECD nations.... Greater attention needs to be paid to reversing the deterioration in US workforce skills." ... "[T]he United States suffers from a deteriorating physical infrastructure that raises the costs of production and limits the location of export activities". "The key to expanding US exports and reaching manufacturing's employment potential is to have companies, domestic and foreign, judge it is profitable to manufacture here." Nowhere do they suggest protection against foreign competition.

It seems to us that the best way to keep manufacturing high and income distribution decent is to eliminate the corporation income tax, allow everybody to accumulate income in a tax deferred account and then to levy a progressive income tax on assets withdrawn from those accounts, using the proceeds for an earned income tax credit to benefit the relatively unskilled.

Two foci of the American trade policy debate also deserve contemplation. Boldrin and Levine (2013) notes,

> Current international trade negotiations that affect patents, often occur as part of either the Agreement on Trade-Related Aspects of Intellectual Property Rights (TRIPS), which was signed in 1995 as part of the World Trade Organization negotiations, or as part of the World Intellectual Property Organization, an agency of the United Nations. The nature of these agreements and organizations is well indicated by the use of the propaganda term "intellectual property" in their titles. In both cases, these talks are often focused on how to prevent ideas from high-income countries from being used in low-income countries — what we would characterize as essentially a neo-mercantilist approach toward free trade in goods and ideas. We should be highly cautious about this agenda. Within a couple of decades, the "balance of trade in ideas" between the US and European economies and emerging economies in Asia might easily equalize or reverse. Engaging in "mercantilism of ideas" may seem favorable to certain large US firms now, but such rules

may become costly to the US economy if they are applied to protect patents held in the future by producers in the now-developing Asian economies.

This conjecture is supported by Kerr (2013). He finds (2013, p. 14) "The contribution of Chinese and Indian ethnic inventors [in the US] displays exceptional growth [over the last 30 years], increasing from under 2% each to 9% and 6% respectively". He goes on to say "[his] work quantifies how a larger ethnic community in the United States aids the transfer of new technologies to the home country. This transfer is strong enough to show up in manufacturing output and productivity data for the home country, and it is even evident in trade patterns".

On the issue of intellectual property, Boldrin and Levine (2013, p. 3) write "The case against patents can be summarized briefly: There is no empirical evidence that they serve to increase innovation and productivity, unless productivity is identified with the number of patents awarded — which, as evidence shows, has no correlation with measured productivity.... Our preferred policy solution is to abolish patents entirely and to find other legislative instruments, less open to lobbying and rent seeking, to foster innovation when there is clear evidence that laissez-faire undersupplies it."

A second issue is raised by Roberts' (2013, p. 76) comment "The excess supply of labor in China and India today exceeds the total of the employed labor forces of the US and Europe. How far will US and European wages have to fall in order to become equalized with Chinese and Indian wages?" This argument ignores that China is adding to its physical capital at an amazing rate. It is even conceivable that China could ultimately become a capital intensive country given its saving rate and the US saving rate, and the US could be importing capital intensive goods and exporting labor intensive goods. China is also augmenting its human capital rapidly. For example, in Fall 2013, of the 29 junior students in the Duke economics department with the top grades, 22 have Chinese or Korean family names; and of Duke's MA entering class of 2013, 64% are Chinese or Korean.

Moreover, offshoring and immigration need not cost American jobs. Ottaviano *et al.* (2013) write: "When immigrant and offshore workers become increasingly employable, efficiency gains can be reaped by hiring them to perform tasks in which they have a comparative advantage, giving native workers the opportunity to specialize in the tasks in which they exhibit their own comparative advantage. If strong enough, the productivity effect associated with this improved task assignment may offset the displacement effect of immigration and offshoring on native workers' employment.

Despite the widely held belief that immigration and offshoring are reducing the job opportunities of US natives, we have found instead that, during our period of observation, manufacturing industries with a larger increase in global exposure (through offshoring and immigration) fared better than those with lagging exposure in terms of native employment growth."

## 6.10. Some Reflections on *The Economist*'s Bhagwati–Chang Debate

In closing, we return to some of the issues raised in the Bhagwati–Chang debate on the importance of manufacturing. We looked for a plea for subsidies to manufacturing or for manufacturing protectionism through all 103 pages of the debate. No one made such a plea explicitly. However, we are not clear whether the pro forces are justifying subsidizing manufacturing through explicit subsidies or through trade policy or by eliminating distortions that frustrate manufacturing. Moreover, Bhagwati refers to "the revival in the public domain of the view that therefore manufactures must be supported".

He also makes the classic point: "if the returns to better technology accrue to the firm, there is no reason to subsidize: one needs to establish an externality to advocate a subsidy" (*The Economist*, 2010).

We argue, furthermore, that even if subsidies are desirable to correct externality nothing should be subsidized until there is a consensus methodology of how to determine optimal subsidies. And the objective should be global welfare, not national welfare, with transfer payments handling the distribution of welfare between countries. All this is a preposterously tall order, especially since we can think of many interventions that do not even serve national welfare.

However, there is much to be said for leveling incentives by eliminating subsides elsewhere, such as in agriculture, both to re-allocate resources directly and to free up funds for efficiency-enhancing government spending and distortion-removing tax shrinkage as discussed in Stoeckel *et al.* (1989).

Sir Geoffrey Owen, of the London School of Economics and previously editor of the *Financial Times*, in his comment on the debate (as part of the interchange hosted by *The Economist*) writes:

> There are plenty of things the government can do to improve the supply side of the economy, but trying to alter the balance between manufacturing and services is not one of them.

He adds:

> Past experience in Europe suggests that attempts by governments to alter the structure of their economies by favouring one sector over another generally cause more problems, than they solve. The effect in many cases has been to preserve uncompetitive businesses, often at great cost to the tax-payer, and to slow down the re-deployment of resources into areas where they can be put to better use....
>
> Countries should specialize in what they are best at. One of the weaknesses in British industrial policy in the 1960s and 1970s was the reluctance to accept that Britain could not expect to compete against America in all the major high-technology industries; for example, a great deal of effort was wasted in trying to create a national champion in computers that could hold its own against IBM. Similarly, today many people envy Germany's manufacturing strength and look for ways of emulating it. But for a mixture of historical and institutional reasons Britain's competitive advantage lies in different areas, some of which are outside manufacturing — financial services, business and professional services, creative industries and the like.

Returning to one of our favorite articles, Paul Krugman (1993a, p. 26) writes:

> Now there are reasons, such as external economies, why a preference for some industries over others may be justified. But this would be true in

a closed economy, too. Students need to understand that the growth of world trade provides no additional support for the proposition that our government should become an active friend to domestic industry.

Finally, to the extent that a small share of manufacturing in an economy is a marker for business-hostile economic policies, we agree that a larger share of manufacturing predicts economic success. So in that sense one can vote for the proposition without being a manufacturing fetishist, just an efficiency fetishist.

## 6.11. The Red Threads

The red threads running through the fabric of our analysis are:

- Effective governance is positively related to a high manufacturing share. We interpret this as supporting the idea that effective governance creates an economy in which firms feel safe to build up their capital stocks, and this stimulates manufacturing, relative to less capital-intensive services.
- The manufacturing share is not significantly correlated with a higher standard of living measured by per capita GDP. Nor it is related significantly and consistently to economic growth.
- Trade restrictions both at home and abroad shrink the manufacturing base and smother economic growth.
- A better way than protectionism and subsidies, specific to industry to enhance economic growth is to improve governance effectiveness and the quality of regulation and taxation.

## 6.12. Some Reactions to This Chapter

One reader suggested that technological advance cannot occur without a strong manufacturing sector. We believe that open borders to migration are an even more important channel of technological advancement. Another cited the "the beggar thy neighbor" Chinese policy of maintaining a trade surplus. We see no reason why that need cause unemployment. In fact to eliminate the trade surplus might even cause more employment. Suppose China expanded absorption and the US raised taxes to reduce absorption; if the US tax takes the form of a value added tax, part of the incidence of that tax will be borne by labor, thereby reducing the demand for labor and if real wages are inflexible downward, causing unemployment. Thus, perhaps we should thank the Chinese for helping with our unemployment problem.

A similar argument is made by Pettis (2013) who argues that Greece's unemployment can be blamed in part on the German export surplus. He ignores that any country with a surplus of saving drives down world interest rates. This encourages its trade partners to invest, which shifts outward their demand for labor, and either raises employment or wages.

One reader noted the rampant agricultural fetishism in the US and Europe and in some less developed countries, leading to policies that reduce manufacturing share.

## References

Baily, MN and BP Bosworth (2014) U.S. manufacturing: Understanding its past and its potential future, *Journal of Economic Perspectives* 28, 3–26.

Barro, RJ (1999) *Determinants of Economic Growth: A Cross-Country Empirical Study*, 2nd edition. Cambridge: MIT Press.

Bhagwati, JN (Ed.) (1974) *Illegal transactions in International Trade:Theory and Measurement*. Amsterdam: North Holland.

Boldrin, M and DK Levine (2013) The case against patents, *The Journal of Economic Perspectives* 27, 3–22.

Chang, H-J (2014) *Economics:The User's Guide*. London: Penguin.

Copeland, B, E Tower and M Webb (1989) On negotiated quotas, tariffs and transfers, *Oxford Economic Papers* 41, 774–788.

Corden, WM (1998) *Trade Policy and Economic Welfare*, 2nd Edition. Oxford: Oxford University Press.

Elliot, HSR (Ed.) (1910) *The Letters of John Stuart Mill*, 2 volumes. New York: Longmans Green.

Fletcher, I (2009) *Free Trade Doesn't Work: What Should Replace it and Why?* Washington DC: U.S. Business and Industry Council.

Irwin, D (1991) Retrospectives: Challenges to free trade, *Journal of Economic Perspectives* 5, 201–208.

Gokcekus, O and K Bengyak (2014) *Peculiar Dynamics of Corruption*. Singapore: World Scientific.

Gopnik, A (2010) Market man; what did Adam Smith really believe? *The New Yorker* 86, 32–82. http://www.newyorker.com/magazine/2010/10/18/market-man.

Kaempfer, WH and E Tower (1982) The balance-of-payments approach to trade tax symmetry theorems, *Weltwirtschaftliches Archiv* 118, 148–165.

Kaempfer, WH, E Tower and TD Willett (2004) The employment maximizing import quota under domestic monopoly, *Journal of International Logistics and Trade* 1, 71–83.

Kaufmann, D, A Kraay and M Mastruzzi (2007a) Growth and governance: A reply, *Journal of Politics* 69, 555–562.

Kaufmann, D, A Kraay and M Mastruzzi (2007b) The worldwide governance indicators project: Answering the critics, World Bank Policy Working Paper No. 4149. World Bank. http://info.worldbank.org/governance/wgi/pdf/critics.pdf.

Kaufmann, D, A Kraay and M Mastruzzi (2009) Governance matters 2009: Learning from over a decade of the worldwide governance indicators. Washington DC: The Brookings Institution. http://www.brookings.edu/research/opinions/2009/06/29-governance-indicators-kaufmann.

Kaufmann, D, A Kraay and M Mastruzzi (2010a) Response to 'the worldwide governance indicators: six, one, or none'. http://info.worldbank.org/governance/wgi/pdf/ResponseKL.pdf.

Kaufmann, D, A Kraay and M Mastruzzi (2010b) Response to 'what do the worldwide governance indicators measure? *European Journal of Development Research* 22, 55–58.

Kay, J (2012) Fetish for making things ignores real work, *Financial Times*. November 14, 2012, p. 9. http://www.johnkay.com/2012/11/14/fetish-for-making-things-ignores-real-work.

Kee, HL, A Nicita and M Olarreaga (2008) Import demand elasticities and trade distortions, *Review of Economics and Statistics* 90, 666–682.

Kee, HL, A Nicita and M Olarreaga (2009) Estimating trade restrictiveness indices, *Economic Journal* 119, 172–199.

Kerr, W (2013) High-skilled immigration, domestic innovation, and global exchanges, *NBER Reporter* 4, 13–19. http://www.nber.org/reporter/2013number4/kerr.html.

Krugman, P (1993a) What do undergrads need to know about trade? *American Economic Association Papers and Proceedings* 83, 23–26. Reprinted as Chapter 8 of Krugman (1996).

Krugman, P (1993b) The uncomfortable truth about NAFTA, *Foreign Affairs* 72, 13–19. Reprinted as Chapter 10 of Krugman (1996).

Krugman, P (1996) *Pop Internationalism.* Cambridge: MIT Press.

Lin, J and H-J Chang (2009) DPR debate: Should industrial policy in developing countries conform to comparative advantage or defy it? a debate between Justin Lin and Ha-Joon Chang, *Development Policy Review* 27, 483–502.

Liu, X and E Ornelas (2014) Free trade agreements and the consolidation of democracy, *American Economic Journal: Macroeconomics* 6, 29–70.

Mussa, M (1993) Making the practical case for freer trade, *The American Economic Association Papers and Proceedings* 83, 372–376.

Ottaviano, GIP, P Giovanni and GC Wright (2013) Immigration, offshoring, and American jobs, *American Economic Review* 103, 1925–1959.

Pettis, M (2013) *The Great Rebalancing: Trade, Conflict and the Perilous Road Ahead for the World Economy.* Princeton, NJ: Princeton University Press. See also the review of this book by Victor (Yifan) Yi (2014) in the United Nations ESCAP ArtNet collection. http://www.unescap.org/sites/default/files/Book-Review-12-July-2014.pdf.

Popkin, J and K Kobe (2010) Manufacturing resurgence: A must for US prosperity. *National Association of Manufacturers and the NAM Council of Manufacturing Associations*, 8. Prepared by Joel Popkin and Company for the NAM and the NAM Council of Manufacturing Associations, Washington, DC. http://www.nam.org/Data-and-Reports/Facts-About-Manufacturing/Popkin-Report–Manufacturing-Resurgence—A-Must-for-U_S_-Prosperity/.

Roberts, PC (2013) *The Failure of Laissez Faire Capitalism.* Atlanta: Clarity Press.

Stoeckel, AB, D Vincent and S Cuthbertson (Eds.) (1989) *Macroeconomic Consequences of Farm Support Policies.* Durham: Duke University Press.

*The Economist* (2010) This house believes that an economy cannot succeed without a big manufacturing base. *The Economist* online debate between Jagdish Bhagwati and Ha-Joon Chang. June 28–July 8. http://www.economist.com/debate/debates/overview/207.

The International Bank for Reconstruction and Development (IBRD), The World Bank (2007) A decade of measuring the quality of governance: Governance matters 2007, *Worldwide Governance Indicators, 1996–2006.* http://siteresources.worldbank.org/NEWS/Resources/wbi2007-report.pdf.

Tower, E and A Waite [Cassidy] (2011) Does the data support the neo-mercantilist preoccupation with protecting manufacturing? Asia–Pacific Research and Training Network on Trade Working Paper Series No. 106. Presented at *the ARTNeT Symposium: "Towards a Return of Industrial Policy"*? 25–26 July, UNCC, Bangkok.

# Chapter 7

# The Evolution of Freight Movement and Associated Non-Point-Source Emissions in the Midwest–Northeast Transportation Corridor of the United States, 1977–2007*

*Benjamin Brown-Steiner*[†], *Jialie Chen*[‡] *and Kieran Donaghy*[§1]

[†]*Department of Biological and Environmental Engineering, Cornell University*

[‡]*Johnson School of Management, Cornell University*

[§]*Department of City and Regional Planning, Cornell University*

## 7.1. Introduction[2]

Perhaps the most significant change in the global economy over the past several decades has been the extent to which globalization, or the integration of economies at all scales, has proceeded (Castells, 2000). This progressive integration is reflected in increased movements of people, goods, material, money and information. One of the most striking aspects of this development is the explosive growth in the movement of freight in the forms of intermediate and final goods (Levinson, 2008).[3] According to the US Bureau of Transportation

*The research reported in this chapter has been supported by grant RD-8342831 from the US Environmental Protection Agency STAR program, "Regional Infrastructure/Air Quality Planning and Global Change".

[1]The authors would like to express their deep gratitude to Randall Jackson, Gianfranco Piras, and Geoffrey Hewings, without whose invaluable assistance this chapter could not have been written.

[2]Several sentences in this introduction are taken from Donaghy (2009).

[3]The New York State Energy Research and Development Authority (NYSERDA) observes that the amount of weight shipped by trucks through New York State alone has doubled in the past thirty years, as has associated greenhouse gas emissions (NYSERDA, 2014).

Statistics (US BTS), the volume of freight movement (in value terms) for all distances in the United States has been growing at an annual rate of 6.6%, which is several times faster than the rate of growth of the country's gross national product (GNP) (US BTS, 2014).

The acceleration of flows of intermediate and final goods through space can be accounted for largely by technological advances in communications and transportation and the emergence of far-flung value chains, which are driven by economizing behavior and abetted by increasingly liberal trade agreements and industrial deregulation. These developments have enabled firms to exploit *economies of scale* and *scope* by fragmenting production processes and dispersing activities to least-cost locations (Feenstra, 1998; Jones and Kierzkowski, 2001).

Consequently, the production of most goods worldwide now takes place in a distributed pattern over many locations in which semi-finished goods are shipped from one *specialized* establishment to another. *What* activities are carried out and *where* they agglomerate appear to be *path dependent* — initial advantages are reinforced due to scale effects (Krugman and Venables, 1995; Venables, 2006). And with the increased use of just-in-time inventory management methods, production has become more *transport intensive.* The increasing transport intensity of economic activity imposes significant externalities on areas that are transport network hubs or multi-modal gateways to regional markets.

One effect related to this development is that much trade is now between establishments operating in the *same* industry. As a consequence, the industrial cores of many regional economies, formerly characterized by *inter*-industry trade, have become '*hollowed out*' and regional economies world-wide have become increasingly interdependent through their reliance on global supply chains (Munroe *et al.*, 2007).

A broad-based community of stakeholders is concerned about these developments, in large part because they lack a clear sense of how these developments are related and what they portend. Moreover, the design of effective policies to accommodate further anticipated increases in freight movement and to promote public/private partnerships that can abate and mitigate deleterious externalities — including greenhouse gas emissions and stress upon transportation infrastructure systems — requires a better understanding of how cost and incentive structures affect the form and functioning of supply chains.

While some empirically supported theoretical explanations of fragmentation at the firm and industry levels, spatial agglomerations of industrial activity, public/private partnerships at urban and regional levels, and network externalities at the systems level are available, we still lack theories and models that *explicitly link decision-making of producers (or shippers) and carriers with impacts on nodes as well as links in transportation networks.* And while work is proceeding in developing further the theories and models that may deliver the desired explicit linkages and which will support empirically based forecasting of future developments and analysis of appropriate policy responses (Donaghy, 2009), a more fundamental need is time-series data on inter-regional inter- and intra-industry trade and freight movements, without which much of our theorizing will be ineffective, if not pointless.

This chapter presents a methodology, discussed in greater detail in Donaghy and Chen (2011), for generating such data and a demonstration of its application in producing annual time series on interstate inter-industry freight flows in the Midwest–Northeast transportation corridor of the United States and associated non-point source emissions. The methodology for generating the data involves several steps. We first specify a dynamic multi-regional econometric input–output model (or REIM) for 13 Midwestern, New England, and North Atlantic states and the rest of the United States (RUS) and 13 industries. To benchmark the REIM's interstate inter-industry sales coefficients, we exploit an approach Jackson *et al.* (2006) have taken to construct commodity-by-industry flow matrices. We estimate the REIM econometrically using published time-series data from the US Bureau of Economic Analysis (US BEA) and the US Bureau of Labor Statistics US BLS) and then, following Israilevich *et al.* (1997), we back out of the estimated REIM, the annual inter-regional inter-industry sales coefficients, from which data on interstate inter-industry sales can be generated and freight flows derived using conversion factors.

In the remaining parts of this chapter, we discuss our approach to overcoming the lack of spatial time series (in Section 7.2), provide a cursory analysis of some of the derived time-series data on freight flows we have generated (in Section 7.3), discuss imputed estimates of non-point source emissions associated with freight movement through the Midwest–Northeast transportation corridor of the United States (in Section 7.4), and conclude briefly with summary remarks and discussion of continuing research (in Section 7.5).

The research reported in this paper is part of a larger project to develop coupled economic, chemistry, and climate models to simulate the linkages between local air quality, the meteorological system, the global economy and economic activities in the Northeastern region of the United States.[4] In this larger project, we will contrast emissions projections obtained from our coupled models with those projected by the Intergovernmental Panel on Climate Change (IPCC) on the basis of global integrated assessment models. We will also examine how apparent synergies between climate and air quality change when regional/local planning considerations are included.

## 7.2. Overcoming the Lack of Spatial Time Series

Ideally, one would like to have annual observations on, or projections of, interstate (or inter-regional) commodity flows or inter-industry

[4]The principal objective of this research is to develop modeling capability to investigate questions of interest to air quality planners. Questions of interest we are addressing in our research include: (1) How will emerging technologies, infrastructure changes (including transportation), global climate and air pollution policies impact regional air quality by 2050? (2) How will urban and regional landscapes evolve in response to changes in production and distribution at regional and global scales? How will associated changes in land use affect emissions and air quality? (3) How will regional and national policy decisions affect the urban landscape and what are the implications for air quality under a future climate scenario? (4) What are the synergies between climate and air quality regulation? How can the results of these studies be best used to inform present and future policy decisions?

sales. The BTS publishes estimates of state-to-state commodity flows, obtained from their Commodity Flow Survey (CFS), over multiple-year periods. These estimates are not as useful as one would wish for several reasons. One is the fact that all the data of CFS are collected from the origin and destination of shipment instead of the manufacturing location. The desired data, collected on the basis of manufacturing location, would correspond to interstate (inter-regional) inter-industry sales coefficients updated on an annual basis. Unfortunately, such sales coefficients, when available, are not updated annually. It is for this reason, among others, that the REIM approach to modeling time-varying inter-regional inter-industry sales was developed (Conway, 1990; Israilevich *et al.*, 1997).

The REIM approach does require matrices of coefficients on inter-regional inter-industry sales and sales to final demand for a benchmark year, however such coefficients are usually obtained from a national or multi-regional social accounting matrix (SAM), whose construction is infrequently attempted because of the difficulty in estimating export distribution (Jackson *et al.*, 2006). The REIM model in this study has been benchmarked with data extracted from a SAM model developed by Jackson *et al.* (2006), to be discussed in the next sub-section.

### 7.2.1. *Jackson et al.'s (2006) approach to constructing commodity-by-industry flow matrices*

On the basis of national data, Jackson *et al.* (2006) have estimated inter-regional commodity flow distributions and modified the trade portion of each regional SAM to retain consistency.[5] Following Miller and Blair (1985), we have derived inter-regional inter-industry sales coefficient matrices from the SAMs produced by Jackson *et al.* (2006).

In discussing this derivation procedure, it is helpful to recall the structure of a SAM. While we are concerned in the present case

[5]It is important to note that the commodity flow data Jackson *et al.* (2006) have developed at the national level differ from those prepared for the US DOT CFS.

with *inter-regional* commodity flow characterizations, we reproduce in Table 7.1, for purposes of review, one of the most widely-used conventional frameworks for constructing a SAM for a *single* region (Jackson and Schwarm, 2011). In this table, domestic final demand includes consumption, investment and government spending, the sum of which is denoted by $F$, and exports ($X$) net of imports ($M$). The Matrices $U$, $V$, $W$, and $E$ are, respectively, the 'Use, Make, Value added and Final demand' matrices, while $Q$ and $X$ correspond to commodity production and total industrial output. The 'Use' matrix represents the industry purchase of each row commodity and the 'Make' matrix represents the commodity output of each row industry. Value added includes all payments sectors, whereas final demand represents row commodity final demand by column final demand activity.

From Table 7.1, it can be seen that elements of a column vector of commodity production, $Q$, can be computed by adding the row sums of 'Use' and 'Final demand' matrices, $U$ and $E$, whereas the elements of a column vector of industrial outputs, $X$, can be computed by taking the row sums of the 'Make' matrix, $V$. The corresponding commodity production and industry output identities can be stated as

$$X_i = V_{i1} + V_{i2} + \cdots + V_{im}, \tag{7.1}$$

$$Q_i = U_{i1} + U_{i2} + \cdots + U_{im} + E_i. \tag{7.2}$$

Recall that the definition of a technical coefficient in the general input–output model is

$$a_{ij} = \frac{Z_{ij}}{X_j}, \tag{7.3}$$

**Table 7.1.** Conventional commodity-by-industry framework for a single region.

| | Commodity | Industry | Final demand | Total |
|---|---|---|---|---|
| Commodity | — | $U$ | $E = F + X(M)$ | $Q$ |
| Industry | $V$ | — | — | $X$ |
| Value added | — | $W$ | — | — |
| Total | $Q'$ | $X'$ | — | — |

where, $a_{ij}$ defines the total value of output from industry $i$ flowing to industry $j$, $Z_{ij}$, for each additional dollar value of industry $j$'s output, $X_j$. The matrix form of this relationship is

$$A = Z(X^{\wedge})^{-1}, \tag{7.4}$$

where $X^{\wedge}$ denotes a *diagonalized vector* of total output. Similarly, we can write the matrix form of an analogous relationship in commodity-by-industry terms as

$$B = U(X^{\wedge})^{-1}. \tag{7.5}$$

Given Equation (7.5), Equation (7.2) can be rewritten as

$$Q = BX + E. \tag{7.6}$$

Upon obtaining the total outputs of commodities and industries, one has two options to choose between in obtaining the inter-industry sales coefficient matrix — the commodity-based approach and the industry-based approach. According to the former approach, which we shall follow, one assumes that an industry's total output is made up of commodities in fixed proportions and thus one can obtain the industry-output proportion as

$$C = V'(X^{\wedge})^{-1}. \tag{7.7}$$

Under the direct definition of technology assumptions, one can define the commodity-by-commodity direct requirements matrices under the commodity-based technology assumption, $A_c$, as

$$A_c = BC^{-1}. \tag{7.8}$$

According to Equations (7.5) and (7.7), one could also rewrite Equation (7.8) as:

$$A_c = U(V')^{-1}. \tag{7.9}$$

Hence, one can define the commodity-by-commodity direct requirements matrix under the commodity-based technology assumption directly in terms of the original Make and Use matrices.

We have employed interstate inter-industry sales matrices so obtained to benchmark a four-region (Midwest, Northeast, Atlantic, and rest of the US) regional econometric input–output (or REIM) model comprising 13 industries and 13 states and the rest of the U.S.[6] Important characteristics of the four-region REIM and its sectoral scheme are summarized in Tables 7.2 and 7.3, below. We have estimated the equations of the model with a non-linear generalized least-squares (NLGLS) estimator implemented in the statistical package R.

Among the blocs of equations that make up a typical REIM are stochastic equations of productivity and wages. Productivity equations characterize the relationship between an industry's total shipments, $X_{it}$, and total employment, $N_{it}$, which is defined as:

$$\log(X_{it}/N_{it}) = \alpha_0 + \alpha_z(N_{it-1}/X_{it-1}) + \alpha_g G_{it} + \xi_{it} \tag{7.10}$$

for all $i = 1, \ldots, n$ and for all $t = 1, \ldots, T$, where $G_{it}$ is a set of exogenous variables selected by the modeler. Wage equations combine the total earnings in an industry, $Y_{it}$, with the total industry employment, $N_{it}$, to obtain the estimates of

**Table 7.2.** Characteristics of the three-region model.

| Project horizon | 1977–2007 (31 years) |
|---|---|
| Model size | 182 equation blocs |
| Industry detail | 13 industries with projections of output and inter-industry/regional commodity flow |
| Selected exogenous variables | Gross regional products<br>Personal consumptions<br>Residential and non-residential investment<br>Federal government expenditures<br>State and local government expenditures<br>Population<br>Unemployment rate<br>Personal income<br>Consumer price index (CPI) |

[6]For key references on the construction and estimation of REIMS, see Conway (1990) and Israelevich *et al.* (1997).

**Table 7.3.** Three-region input–output table sector definitions.

| Sector | Description | NAICS code |
|---|---|---|
| 1 | Agriculture, forestry, fishing, and hunting | 11 |
| 2 | Mining | 21 |
| 3 | Construction | 23 |
| 4 | Food product manufacturing | 311 |
| 5 | Chemical manufacturing | 325 |
| 6 | Primary metal manufacturing | 331 |
| 7 | Fabricated metal product manufacturing | 332 |
| 8 | Machinery manufacturing | 333 |
| 9 | Computer and electronic product manufacturing | 334, 335 |
| 10 | Transportation equipment | 336 |
| 11 | Other non-durable manufacturing | 312–316, 322–324, 326 |
| 12 | Other durable manufacturing | 321, 327, 337, 339 |
| 13 | TCU, Services and Government enterprises | 42, 44, 45, 48, 49, 51–56, 61, 62, 71, 72, 81 |

personal income,

$$\log(Y_{it}/N_{it}) = \alpha_0 + \alpha_z(N_{it-1}/Y_{it-1}) + \alpha_g G_{it} + \xi_{it}. \tag{7.11}$$

for all $i = 1, \ldots, n$ and for all $t = 1, \ldots, T$.

Equations (7.10) and (7.11) imply a direct relationship between income, output, and final demand. With that relationship in mind, it is straightforward to determine the relationship between income, or final demand, and output. This relationship can then be used to compute the so-called *inter-industry gross output correlation matrix*, which can be regarded as the Leontief inverse, and from which the inter-regional inter-industry sales coefficient matrix can then be easily obtained.[7]

[7]We acknowledge that this approach will yield at best an approximation of interstate inter-industry sales coefficient matrix $A$ for a given time period and corresponding trade flows. Given the quality of the data on which this work is based, it is unlikely that the imputed inter-regional inter-industry sales coefficient matrix and Leontief inverse matrix will ever be identical to the true but unknown

From Equations (7.10) and (7.11), the following relationships can be derived:

$$\gamma_{it} \equiv X_{it}/N_{it} = \exp(\alpha_0 + \alpha_z(N_{it-1}/X_{it-1}) + \alpha_g G_{it}), \text{ and} \quad (7.12)$$

$$\mu_{it} \equiv Y_{it}/N_{it} = \exp(\alpha_0 + \alpha_z(N_{it-1}/Y_{it-1}) + \alpha_g G_{it}), \quad (7.13)$$

which imply two further relationships,

$$N = (\gamma^\wedge)^{-1}X, \quad (7.14)$$

and

$$Y = (\mu^\wedge)N. \quad (7.15)$$

Substituting (7.14) into (7.15) gives the following explicit relationship between final demand and total output.

$$Y = (\mu^\wedge)(\gamma^\wedge)^{-1}X. \quad (7.16)$$

With (7.16) in hand, the Leontief inverse matrix of output multipliers can be written in the following form.

$$B = [(I - \beta^\wedge A)^{-1}\beta^\wedge](\mu^\wedge)(\gamma^\wedge). \quad (7.17)$$

Given annual estimates of the Leontief inverse matrix, $B_t$, annual estimates of the inter-regional inter-industry sales coefficients matrix $A_t$ can be derived as

$$A_t = I - B_t^{-1}, \quad (7.18)$$

and annual inter-regional inter-industry trade flows can be computed from annual regional (or state) aggregate output levels as

$$x_{ijt}^{lm} = a_{ijt}^{lm} X_{jt}^{m}, \quad \forall i, j, l, m, \quad (7.19)$$

where $x_{ijt}^{lm}$ denotes the sales of industry $i$ in region (state) $l$ to industry $j$ in region (state) $m$ in year $t, X_{jt}^{m}$ denotes aggregate output of sector $j$ in region (state) $m$ in year $t$, and $a_{ijt}^{lm}$ is the corresponding inter-regional (interstate) inter-industry sales coefficient for year $t$. Physical characteristics of the shipments — volume and

matrices and, unfortunately, there are no effective approaches to assess the accuracy of the computations based on Israilevich *et al.* (1997), described above.

weight — can be estimated from sales figures in the usual manner from industry coefficients (Boyce, 2002; Ham *et al.*, 2005).[8]

## 7.3. Data Analysis

Solution of the model for annual interstate inter-industry trade flows over the period of the sample by the approach of Israilevich *et al.* (1997) yields 2,366 time series — 13 sectors × 13 sectors × 13 states plus the rest of the United States. We will therefore not attempt to offer here a comprehensive characterization of either the evolution of the commodity or freight flows or a commentary on regions that have come to specialize in activities involving various trade activities. We will, however, comment on aggregate changes in volumes of shipments, intra-industry shipments, and associated black-carbon emissions that result from the movement of goods.

### 7.3.1. *Changes in volumes of shipments*

Presented below in Tables 7.4a–7.4b and 7.5a–7.5b are five-year averages of volumes of freight shipments (in kilotons) as inputs and outputs by industries within the 13 states under consideration and by these states and the rest of the US. Emerging from the data are trends indicating that there are cycles around trends and differential changes — both positive and negative — in the amounts of freight being shipped to firms in industries in different states. States shipping more freight over time include Connecticut, Illinois, New Jersey, New York, Wisconsin, and the rest of the US. States; states shipping less freight include Maine, Massachusetts, Michigan, Ohio, and Pennsylvania. Clearly there is a mix of Mid-western and Northeastern/Mid-Atlantic states in both groups. From Tables 7.4a and 7.4b, one can see that there is about a five-fold increase in inputs

[8]Conversion factors in millions of constant year-2001 US dollars per kiloton for the 13 sectors are respectively 0.888524, 0.262133, 0.181015, 1.403953, 2.012055, 1.180493, 0.061437, 9.415343, 22.01849, 7.725906, 1.560004, 1.631441, and 3.103150 (USDOT CFS for 2007).

**Table 7.4a.** Interstate input shipments by sector (in kilotons).

| Sector | Five-year averages, Input | | | | | |
|---|---|---|---|---|---|---|
| | 1997–1982 | 1983–1987 | 1988–1992 | 1993–1997 | 1998–2002 | 2003–2007 |
| 1 | 156,894.619 | 211,203 | 189,299.508 | 216,616.613 | 262,408.292 | 336,512.415 |
| 2 | 281,401.586 | 579,733.373 | 388,537.932 | 390,155.424 | 540,563.975 | 941,356.298 |
| 3 | 318,702.205 | 468,246.616 | 617,106 | 685,157.445 | 992,065.1 | 1,469,286.38 |
| 4 | 62,453.89 | 84,227.7851 | 108,276.937 | 138,679.389 | 154,302.386 | 183,309.218 |
| 5 | 117,139.044 | 161,338.439 | 202,729.28 | 263,658.059 | 337,059.336 | 409,305.751 |
| 6 | 150,870.383 | 155,495.221 | 201,458.958 | 247,011.548 | 285,832.205 | 311,288.595 |
| 7 | 412,121.495 | 496,212.301 | 614,526.343 | 834,323.093 | 1,117,692.12 | 1,106,692.62 |
| 8 | 18,781.0408 | 24,046.9963 | 27,348.3745 | 38,101.77 | 62,688.14 | 75,538.104 |
| 9 | 339.6206 | 633.3861 | 863.5891 | 1,515.889 | 3,793.921 | 3,277.22 |
| 10 | 1,620.2772 | 2,012.3913 | 3,348.0436 | 4,679.373 | 7,084.076 | 8,341.005 |
| 11 | 303,272.107 | 428,800.19 | 536,271.157 | 735,668.786 | 1,016,411.78 | 1,140,333.38 |
| 12 | 25,143.492 | 33,915.2023 | 44,514.9534 | 65,122.443 | 105,494.548 | 139,021.107 |
| 13 | 2,304,594.43 | 3,387,510.06 | 4,388,639.4 | 5,036,037.13 | 4,674,053.47 | 6,234,255.57 |
| **Total** | **4.15E + 06** | **6.03E + 06** | **7.32E + 06** | **8.66E + 06** | **9.56E + 06** | **1.24E + 07** |

*Note*: 1 — Agriculture, forestry, fishing, and hunting; 2 — Mining; 3 — Construction; 4 — Food product manufacturing; 5 — Chemical manufacturing; 6 — Primary metal manufacturing; 7 — Fabricated metal product manufacturing; 8 — Machinery manufacturing; 9 — Computer and electronic product manufacturing; 10 — Transportation equipment; 11 — Other non-durable manufacturing; 12 — Other durable manufacturing; 13 — TCU, Services and Government enterprises.

**Table 7.4b.** Interstate output shipments by sector (in kilotons).

| Sector | Five-year averages, Output | | | | | |
|---|---|---|---|---|---|---|
| | 1997–1982 | 1983–1987 | 1988–1992 | 1993–1997 | 1998–2002 | 2003–2007 |
| 1 | 164,660.894 | 208,487.95 | 240,578.35 | 272,523.92 | 236,766.48 | 260,166.92 |
| 2 | 552,091.647 | 957,604.88 | 649,053.08 | 612,929.47 | 678,288.66 | 1,281,683.48 |
| 3 | 1,055,728.62 | 1,687,541.52 | 2,251,582.71 | 2,489,337 | 2,796,446.08 | 4,094,909.19 |
| 4 | 193,628.551 | 268,083.3 | 356,178.58 | 426,909.04 | 402,963.55 | 479,720.11 |
| 5 | 68,246.369 | 99,402.39 | 140,789.19 | 177,392.28 | 195,020.75 | 255,588.58 |
| 6 | 108,934.912 | 94,978.02 | 130,738.67 | 147,626.48 | 127,824.3 | 165,033.45 |
| 7 | 1,541,435.72 | 1,990,602.91 | 2,558,613.42 | 3,300,281.45 | 3,812,386.46 | 4,161,612.53 |
| 8 | 16,880.826 | 18,851.13 | 22,198.57 | 27,859.33 | 30,822.15 | 31,940.12 |
| 9 | 5,787.784 | 10,323.1 | 13,912.97 | 18,627.95 | 21,006.22 | 19,398.97 |
| 10 | 13,177.999 | 22,146.79 | 31,924.16 | 43,683.8 | 57,349.16 | 69,606.83 |
| 11 | 239,424.114 | 365,293.19 | 482,734.27 | 588,346.59 | 650,075.64 | 822,580.63 |
| 12 | 48,434.42 | 68,487.84 | 98,905.78 | 125,649.87 | 128,189.77 | 156,267.08 |
| 13 | 144,902.339 | 241,571.94 | 345,710.71 | 425,559.75 | 422,310.11 | 560,009.77 |
| **Total** | **4.15E + 06** | **6.03E + 06** | **7.32E + 06** | **8.66E + 06** | **9.56E + 06** | **1.24E + 07** |

*Note*: 1 — Agriculture, forestry, fishing, and hunting; 2 — Mining; 3 — Construction; 4 — Food product manufacturing; 5 — Chemical manufacturing; 6 — Primary metal manufacturing; 7 — Fabricated metal product manufacturing; 8 — Machinery manufacturing; 9 — Computer and electronic product manufacturing; 10 — Transportation equipment; 11 — Other non-durable manufacturing; 12 — Other durable manufacturing; 13 — TCU, Services and Government enterprises.

**Table 7.5a.** Freight shipments received by state and rest of the US (in kilotons).

| | Sector Five-year averages, Input | | | | | |
|---|---|---|---|---|---|---|
| | 1997–1982 | 1983–1987 | 1988–1992 | 1993–1997 | 1998–2002 | 2003–2007 |
| **CT** | 51,086.71 | 63,233.03 | 86,089.75 | 128,793.7 | 162,496.3 | 215,596.5 |
| **IL** | 527,04.74 | 68,328.05 | 94,231.03 | 138,167.8 | 176,577.3 | 237,779.6 |
| **IN** | 54,573.53 | 69,877.52 | 95,695.79 | 139,385.3 | 177,856.8 | 229,036.5 |
| **ME** | 51,360.58 | 63,871.27 | 86,314.23 | 127,359 | 159,098.7 | 204,762.2 |
| **MA** | 50,479.46 | 61,992.48 | 84,615.57 | 126,714.6 | 160,436.6 | 215,646.6 |
| **MI** | 44,228.41 | 57,047.69 | 78,827.06 | 118,009.3 | 153,240.7 | 201,819.5 |
| **NJ** | 49,074.75 | 61,768.4 | 84,282.74 | 126,241.6 | 162,575.2 | 224,852.1 |
| **NY** | 41,691.6 | 53,896.5 | 76,288.29 | 116,186.1 | 154,928.5 | 219,920.9 |
| **OH** | 48,755.48 | 63,169.18 | 87,323.54 | 130,847.9 | 167,597.5 | 220,501 |
| **PA** | 45,523.56 | 58,853.39 | 81,759.86 | 122,600.9 | 162,200 | 219,224.3 |
| **RI** | 55,042.04 | 68,089.53 | 92,489.24 | 134,506.5 | 164,376.4 | 214,076.4 |
| **VT** | 53,184.17 | 66,456.44 | 90,146.82 | 131,553 | 162,704.4 | 210,817.7 |
| **WI** | 48,777.33 | 62,159.57 | 85,370.68 | 124,987 | 160,132.2 | 209,189.5 |
| **US** | 3,506,851.84 | 5,214,631.91 | 6,199,485.87 | 6,991,374.4 | 7,435,228.8 | 9,535,294.9 |
| **Total** | **4.15E + 06** | **6.03E + 06** | **7.32E + 06** | **8.66E + 06** | **9.56E + 06** | **1.24E + 07** |

*Note*: CT — Connecticut; IL — Illinois; ME — Maine; MA — Massachusetts; MI — Michigan; NJ — New Jersey; NY — New York; OH — Ohio; PA — Pennsylvania; RI — Rhode Island; VT — Vermont; WI — Wisconsin; US — Rest of the United States.

**Table 7.5b.** Freight shipments shipped by state and rest of the US (in kilotons).

| | Sector Five-year averages, Output | | | | | |
|---|---|---|---|---|---|---|
| | 1997–1982 | 1983–1987 | 1988–1992 | 1993–1997 | 1998–2002 | 2003–2007 |
| **CT** | 26,940.41 | 34,844.39 | 47,241.43 | 72,078.95 | 101,769.51 | 148,415.11 |
| **IL** | 82,483.86 | 126,347.82 | 167,726.36 | 241,036.33 | 362,108.79 | 542,696.68 |
| **IN** | 101,792.7 | 144,218.61 | 194,108.25 | 277,195.82 | 397,832.32 | 522,450.62 |
| **ME** | 16,786.19 | 22,108.23 | 29,380.24 | 42,514.47 | 58,247.4 | 84,621.35 |
| **MA** | 24,494.29 | 32,337.08 | 45,227.36 | 69,212.26 | 101,770.54 | 158,529.02 |
| **MI** | 232,275.39 | 303,275.53 | 407,351.11 | 597,092.24 | 814,823.27 | 1,000,041.76 |
| **NJ** | 44,514.04 | 60,809.83 | 81,457.62 | 126,534.31 | 195,665.96 | 305,502.05 |
| **NY** | 37,280.56 | 55,830.44 | 82,982.04 | 129,510.42 | 207,004.97 | 333,876.1 |
| **OH** | 107,949.09 | 152,551.83 | 209,143.19 | 318,866.28 | 455,034.02 | 582,048.17 |
| **PA** | 42,342.32 | 66,209.24 | 92,832.65 | 136,290.39 | 207,074.37 | 322,861.02 |
| **RI** | 16,988.04 | 21,507.97 | 29,320.31 | 41,277.18 | 54,442.06 | 79,289.49 |
| **VT** | 17,652.71 | 22,587.94 | 29,671.6 | 41,200.99 | 54,787.88 | 75,197.15 |
| **WI** | 58,282.03 | 78,568.12 | 104,653.53 | 146,616.34 | 207,987.7 | 292,692.82 |
| **US** | 3,343,552.57 | 4,912,177.94 | 5,801,824.79 | 6,417,300.99 | 6,340,900.54 | 7,910,296.33 |
| **Total** | **4.15E+06** | **6.03E+06** | **7.32E+06** | **8.66E+06** | **9.56E+06** | **1.24E+07** |

*Note*: CT — Connecticut; IL — Illinois; ME — Maine; MA — Massachusetts; MI — Michigan; NJ — New Jersey; NY — New York; OH — Ohio; PA — Pennsylvania; RI — Rhode Island; VT — Vermont; WI — Wisconsin; US — Rest of the United States.

by weight and about a halving of outputs by weight, indicative of production processes that are increasingly weight-losing or substitution of foreign or extra-regionally produced inputs for regional inputs. While agriculture appears to be the only sector in which both input and output shipments by weight increased over the sample period, sectors 8 through 13 (in the aggregated scheme employed) experienced significant increases in input volumes from other states while reducing output volumes, also indicative of the growing importance of supply chains. Even as markers of globalization appear in the data, it is interesting to observe that the rate of growth in freight movement between firms in sectors in the 13 states considered in this study is smaller than the national trend. This observation suggests that much freight movement through the Midwest–Northeast corridor must constitute pass-through shipments.

### 7.3.2. *Intra-industry trade*

As discussed thoroughly and insightfully in Munroe *et al.* (2007), much regional and inter-regional trade is now intra-industrial in nature because of the amount of fragmentation occurring. The importance of intra-industrial trade (IIT) to a sector is often characterized by computing the associated Grubel—Lloyd index (Grubel and Lloyd, 1975). (Please see the appendix.). One would expect to find clustering of activities in sectors in which there is much IIT as economies of scale and scope are exploited by firms, even as we are unable to detect such phenomena at the level of sectoral and spatial aggregation at which we are working and by the descriptive approach we are taking. (But see Chen and Donaghy (2012) for an analysis that does find significant scale economies.)

Figure 7.1 provides a map of US states in the Midwest–Northeast transportation corridor (with their largest cities located within them) onto which bidirectional trade flows will be gridded.

In Figures 7.2a– f, we provide spatial plots of sectoral IIT (in both directions) and the plots over time of the Grubel–Lloyd indices for six of the 13 industries studied, which illustrate a number of salient points about interstate IIT.

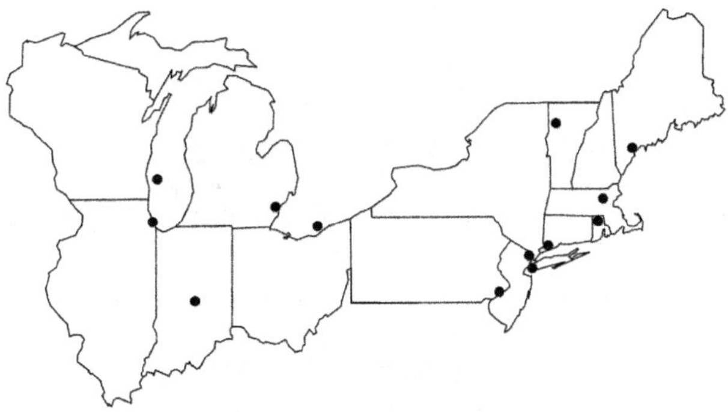

**Figure 7.1.** US states in the Midwest–Northeast transportation corridor.

- For some sectors and between some states there is considerable variation in IIT.
- IIT is very limited across all sates in some industries in which there is specialization — e.g., transportation equipment — but also fairly high across many states in other industries — e.g., other non-durable manufacturing.
- There have not been dramatic changes in IIT patterns over the 31-year period of the sample, certainly less so than we may have expected; but it may be the case that IIT increased significantly in the late 1960s and 1970s before it was closely studied.
- Some regional trade patterns in the Midwest–Northeast corridor have emerged as Munroe *et al.* (2007) observed more narrowly within the Midwest — in the cases of agriculture, food product manufacturing, and TCU, Services, and Government Enterprises — while corridor-wide patterns have emerged in others — in the case of other non-durable manufacturing — and virtually not at all in others — e.g., in the case of transportation equipment.

## 7.4. Non-Point Source Emissions Associated with Freight Movement

As noted above, a major concern raised by the exponential increase in freight movement is that it will, if it has not already done so, have a deleterious effect on air quality in major transportation corridors.

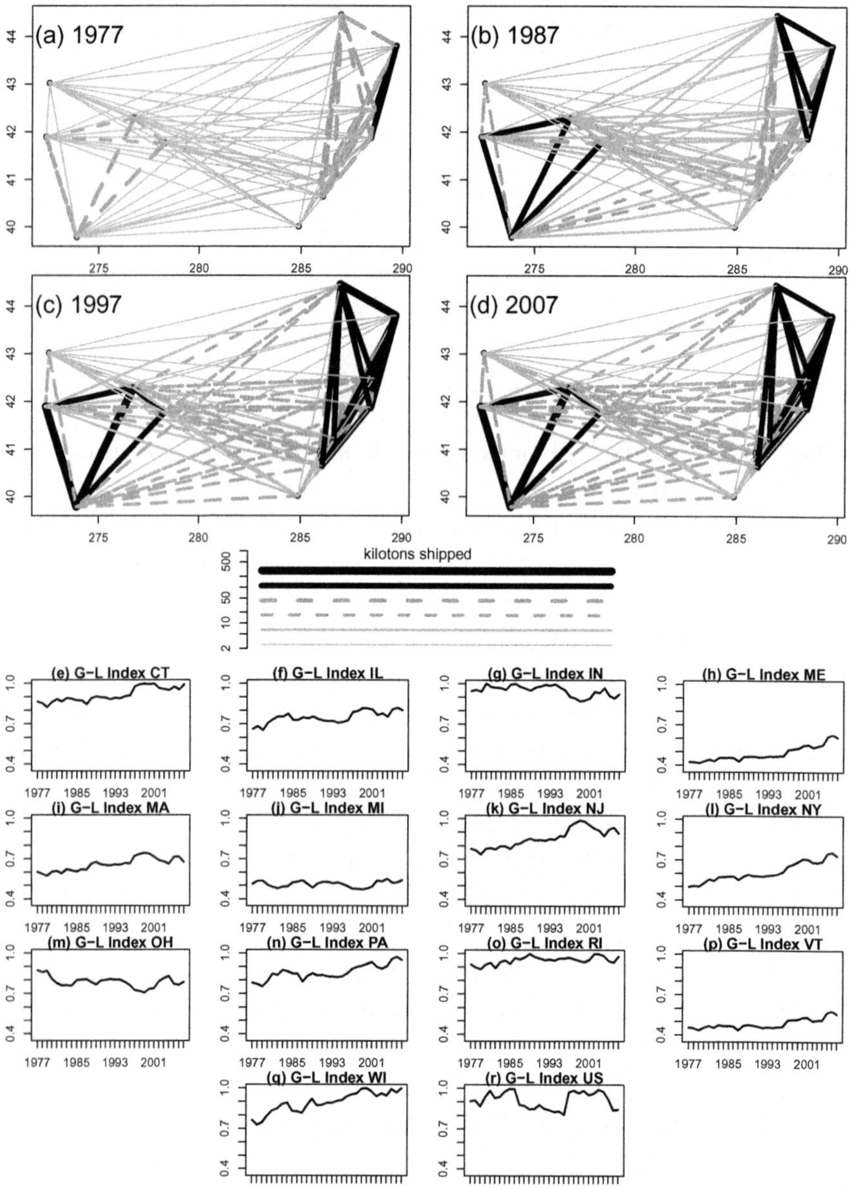


**Figure 7.2a.** Intra-industry shipments for agriculture and state Grubel–Lloyd indices.

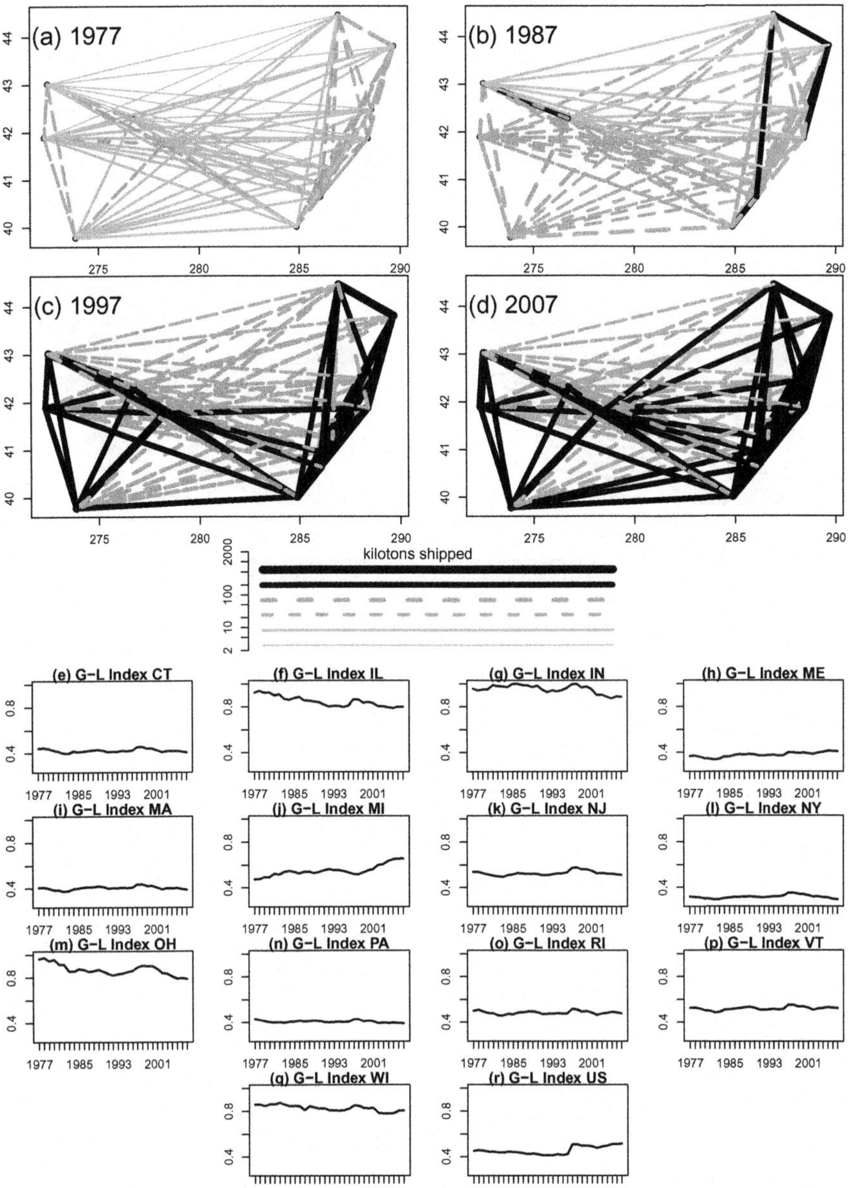


**Figure 7.2b.** Intra-industry shipments for food product manufacturing and state Grubel–Lloyd indices.

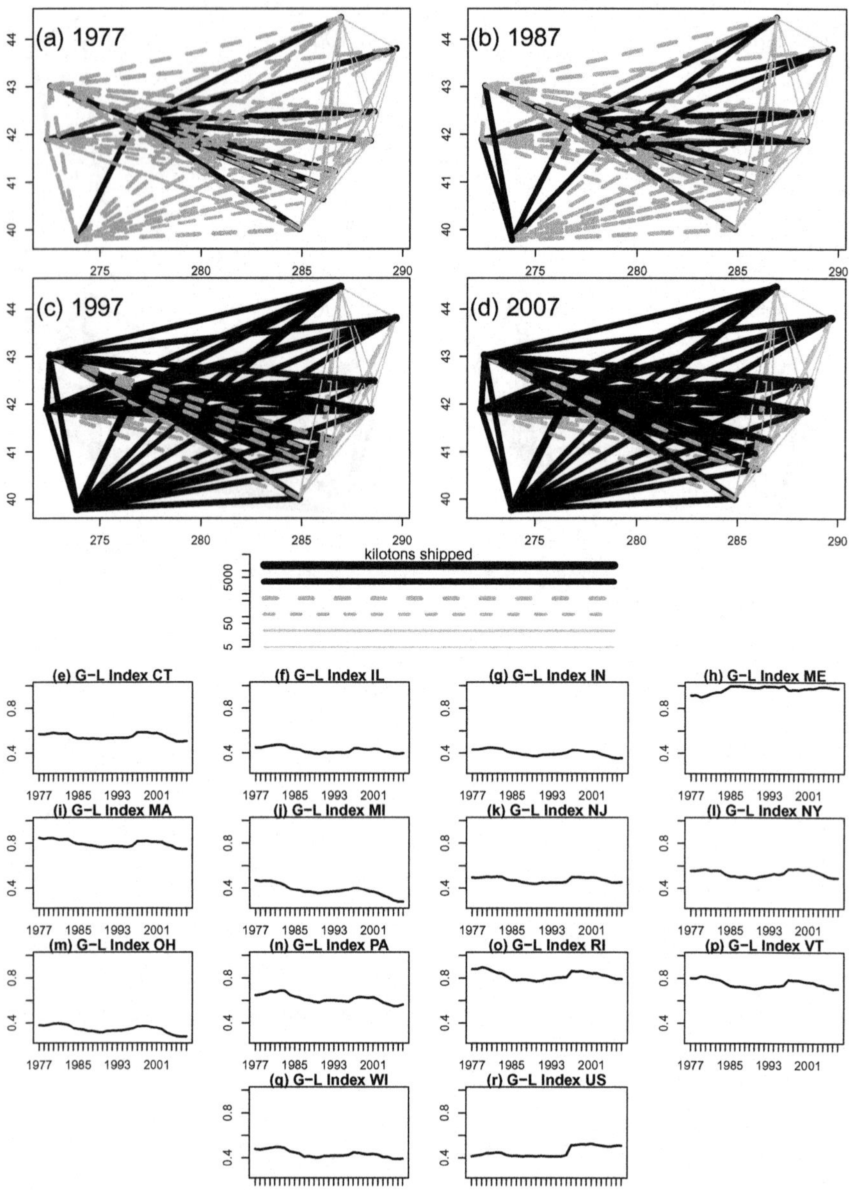


**Figure 7.2c.** Intra-industry shipments for fabricated metal product manufacturing and state Grubel–Lloyd indices.

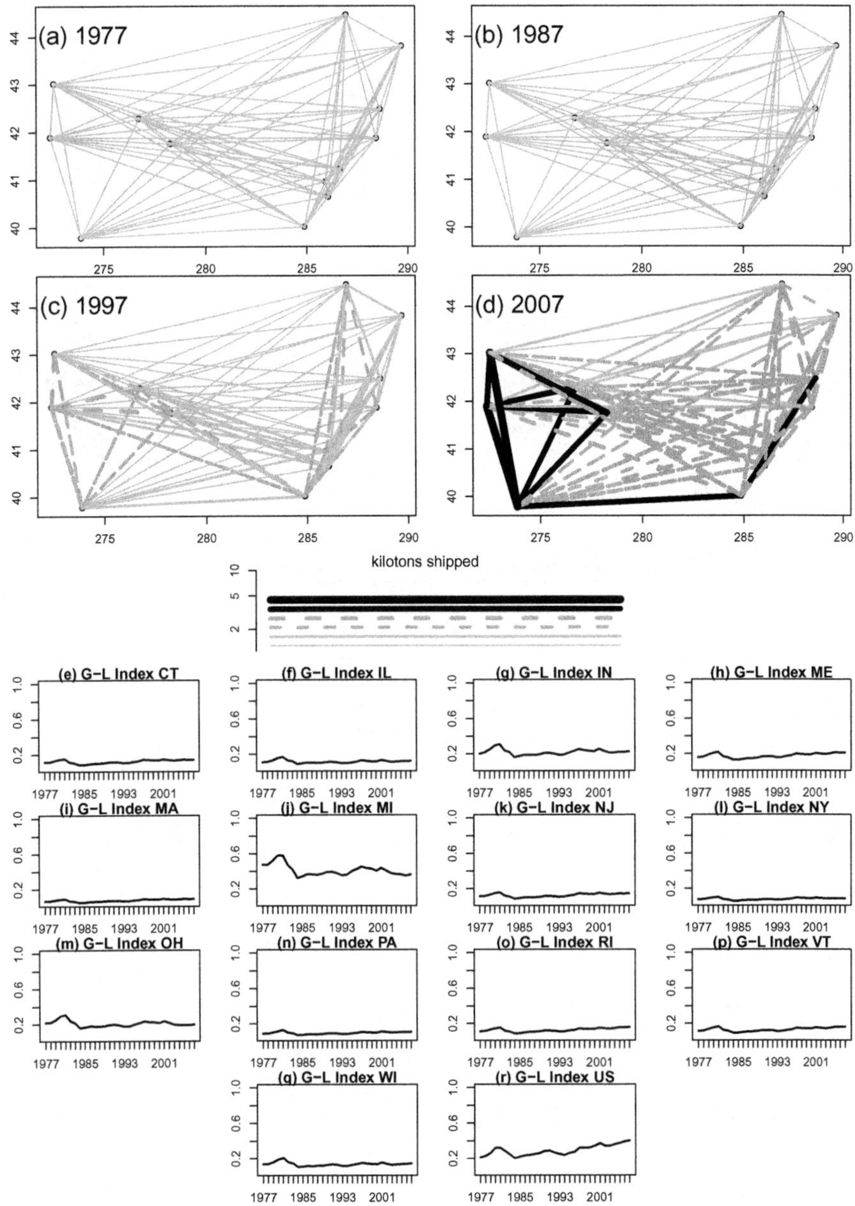


**Figure 7.2d.** Intra-industry shipments of transportation equipment and state Grubel–Lloyd indices.

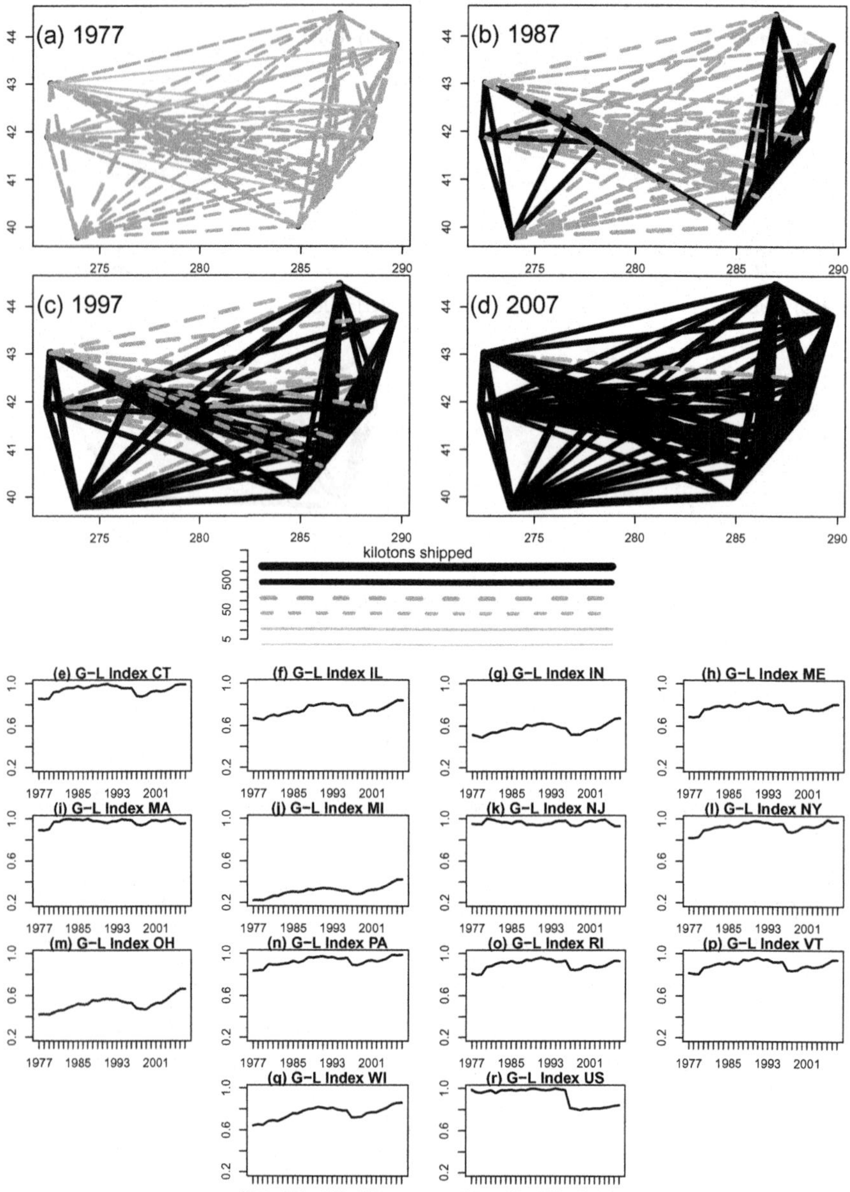


**Figure 7.2e.** Intra-industry shipments of other non-durable manufacturing and state Grubel–Lloyd indices.

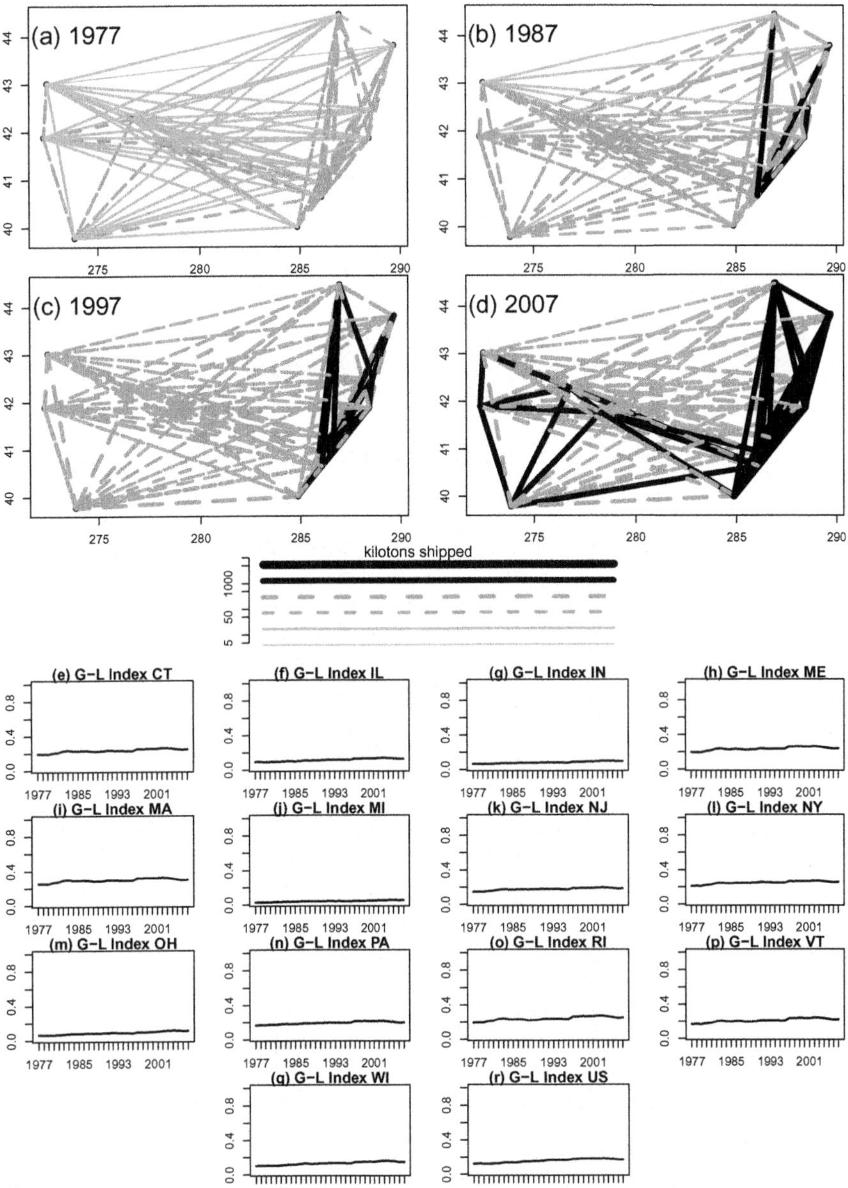


**Figure 7.2f.** Shipments of TCU, services, and government enterprises and state Grubel–Lloyd indices.

**Table 7.6.** Five-year averages of cross-section freight-movement-related BC emissions from latitudes 40 N to 44 N.

| | | 1977–1982 | 1983–1987 | 1988–1992 | 1993–1997 | 1998–2002 | 2003–2007 |
|---|---|---|---|---|---|---|---|
| Latitude (degrees N) | 44 | 1.2E + 09 | 1.6E + 09 | 1.9E + 09 | 2.4E + 09 | 2.5E + 09 | 2.3E + 09 |
| | 43 | 4.9E + 09 | 6.4E + 09 | 7.6E + 09 | 9.4E + 09 | 9.8E + 09 | 9.2E + 09 |
| | 42 | 6.5E + 09 | 8.6E + 09 | 1.0E + 10 | 1.3E + 10 | 1.3E + 10 | 1.2E + 10 |
| | 41 | 3.3E + 09 | 4.3E + 09 | 5.2E + 09 | 6.4E + 09 | 6.7E + 09 | 6.4E + 09 |
| | 40 | 1.4E + 09 | 1.9E + 09 | 2.2E + 09 | 2.7E + 09 | 2.8E + 09 | 2.7E + 09 |

Units: molecules/$cm^2$/second

Table 7.6 summarizes preliminary estimates of black carbon (BC) emissions associated with commodity shipping from all sectors in the 13 states and rest of the US here studied by heavy-duty diesel trucks (HDDV) and railroads across a latitudinal band crossing some east-west shipping lanes (see Figure 7.1). This particular latitudinal band is meant to represent the shipment trends observed in the rest of the domain. These emission estimates, obtained by employing coefficients from the EPA MOVES (Motor Vehicle Emissions Simulator) software with data generated in this study, are stated in units of molecules of BC per centimeter squared per second, as required by the Community Earth System Global Climate Model (CESM).

These emission estimates were created by dividing the domain (see Figure 7.1) into $0.5 \times 0.5$ degree latitude and longitude grid cells and summing the emissions along each link (for interstate shipping) and for each state (for intrastate emissions) distributed by county population.

Note that the northernmost and southernmost grid cells have comparable emissions, since both are outside of, or on the outskirts of, the transportation corridor. In contrast, the innermost grid cell has the peak emissions, which are roughly three to four times as high as the northernmost and southernmost grid cells. The innermost grid cells have multiple transportation corridors within their boundary. This spatial distribution remains consistent throughout the time series.

Also note that every grid cell has a minimum value at the beginning of the time series (1977–1982). These values roughly double by the 1993–1997 timeframe, after which they plateau, rising much more gradually and eventually decreasing by the end of the time series (2003–2007). This plateau is a combination of: (1) increasing transportation throughout the time series; and (2) rapid and widespread emission regulations and technological advancements in the 1990s and 2000s leading to emissions reductions, as one might expect from US DOT (2003) and Tao *et al.* (2007).

## 7.5. Conclusions and Continuations

In this chapter we have argued for the need to produce time-series data on inter-regional/interstate inter-industry sales and their associated freight movements and non-point source emissions; we need to do so to understand better developments in a globalizing world, to improve our theorizing and forecasting abilities regarding these developments, and to support planning for further changes in economic geography and air quality, *inter alia.* We have presented a methodology for generating inter-regional/interstate inter-industry sales, demonstrated an application of this methodology in producing annual time series on interstate inter-industry freight flows in the Midwest–Northeast transportation corridor of the United States, and illustrated how these data can be used to produce estimates of associated non-point source emissions. In continuing the ongoing study from which this chapter represents an interim report, we will complete the estimation of a structural-equation model of shippers and carriers and associated emissions, discussed in Chen and Donaghy (2012), and conduct simulations of potential effects of continued growth in trade and transportation infrastructure changes, and continue to pursue the research agenda discussed in the introduction and set out in footnote 4.

## References

Boyce, D (2002) Combined model of interregional commodity flows on a transportation network. In *Trade, Networks, and Hierarchies: Modeling Regional and Interregional Economies.* GJD Hewings, M Sonis, and D Boyce (Eds.). Berlin: Springer, 29–40.

Castells, M (2000) *The Rise of the Network Society,* 2nd edition. Oxford: Blackwell.

Conway, RS (1990) The Washington projection and simulation model: Ten years of experience with a regional inter-industry econometric model, *International Regional Science Review* 13, 141–165.

Chen, J and KP Donaghy (2012) Econometric estimation and qualitative analysis of a dynamic commodity-flow model for studying impacts of globalization and infrastructure system changes on regional air quality. Paper presented at *the North American Meetings of the Regional Science Association International,* 8 November, Ottawa, Canada.

Donaghy, KP (2009) Modeling the economy as an evolving space of flows: Methodological challenges. In *Complexity and Spatial Networks.* A Reggiani and P Nijkamp (Eds.). Berlin: Springer, 151–164.

Donaghy, KP and J Chen (2011) Generating spastial time series on interstate inter-industry freight flows. Paper presented at *the National Urban Freight Conference*, 12–14 October, Long Beach, California.

Feenstra, RC (1998) Integration of trade and disintegration of production in the global economy, *Journal of Economic Perspectives* 12, 31–50.

Grubel, HG and PJ Lloyd (1975) *Intra-industry Trade.* London: Macmillen.

Ham, H, TJ Kim and D Boyce (2005) Implementation and estimation of a combined model of inter-regional multimodal commodity shipments and transportation network flows, *Transportation Research B* 39, 65–79.

Israilevich, P, GJD Hewings, M Sonis and GR Schindler (1997) Forecasting structural change with a regional econometric input–output model, *Journal of Regional Science* 37, 565–590.

Jackson, RW and WR Schwarm (2011) Accounting foundations for inter-regional commodity-by-industry input–output models. *Letters in Spatial and Resource Sciences* 4, 187–196.

Jackson, RW, WR Schwarm, Y Okuyama and S Islam (2006) A method for constructing commodity by industry flow matrices, *Annals of Regional Science* 40, 909–920.

Jones, RW and H Kierzkowski (2001) A framework for fragmentation. In *Fragmentation: New Production Patterns in the World Economy.* SW Arndt and H Kierzkowski (Eds.). New York: Oxford University Press, 17–34.

Krugman, P and AJ Venables (1995) Globalization and the inequality of nations, *Quarterly Journal of Economics* 110, 857–880.

Levinson, M (2008) *The Box: How the Shipping Container Made the World Smaller and the World Economy Bigger.* Princeton, NJ: Princeton University Press.

Miller, R and P Blair (1985) *Input–Output Analysis: Foundations and Extensions.* Englewood Cliffs, NJ: Prentice-Hall.

Munroe, D, GJD Hewings and D Guo (2007) The role of intra-industry trade in inter-regional trade in the Mid-West of the US. In *Globalization and Regional Economic Modeling.* RJ Cooper, KP Donaghy and GJD Hewings (Eds.). Heidelberg: Springer-Verlag, 87–105.

New York State Energy Research and Development Administration (NYSERDA) (2014) Institutionalizing integrated solutions supporting accessible multimodal transportation networks, *Program Opportunity Notice* No. 2881.

Tao, Z, A Williams, K Donaghy and G Hewings (2007) A socio-economic method for estimating future air pollution emissions — A Chicago case study, *Atmospheric Environment* 41, 5398–5409.

United States Bureau of Transportation Statistics (US BTS) (2014) *Freight Facts and Figures 2013.* http://www.rita.dot.gov/bts/programs/freight_transportation/.Accessed June 2, 2014.

United States Department of Transportation (US DOT) (2003) *Modeling of Advanced Technology Vehicles.* Washington DC: US DOT.

Venables, AJ (2006) Shifts in economic geography and their causes. *Federal Reserve Bank of Kansas City Economic Review, Fourth Quarter*, 61–85.

## Appendix

Following Munroe *et al.* (2007), for a single industry, $i$, in some state, $s$, the Grubel–Lloyd index of intra-industry trade is computed as follows:

$$SIIT_{si} = 1 - \{|X_{si}^e - M_{si}^e| \div (X_{si}^e + M_{si}^e)\},$$

where

$$\begin{aligned}
X_{si}^e &= X_{si}\{(X_s + M_s)/2X_s\},\\
M_{si}^e &= M_{si}\{(X_s + M_s)/2M_s\},\\
X_{si} &= \text{exports of industry } i \text{ in state } s,\\
M_{si} &= \text{imports of industry } i \text{ in state } s,\\
X_s &= \text{total exports by all industries in state } s,\\
M_s &= \text{total imports by all industries in state } s.
\end{aligned}$$

For the aggregate economy (all industries) of a state, the index would be computed as follows:

$$SIIT_s = 1 - \left\{\left[\sum_i |X_{si}^e - M_{si}^e|\right] \div \left[\sum_i (X_{si}^e + M_{si}^e)\right]\right\}.$$

A value of 1.0 indicates perfect trade overlap, whereas a value of zero indicates perfect specialization.

# Chapter 8

## Multipliers in an Island Economy: The Case of the Azores

*Eduardo Haddad*[*], *Vasco Silva*[†], *Alexandre Porsse*[‡] *and Tomaz Dentinho*[§]

[*]*Universidade de São Paulo, São Paulo, Brasil*
[†]*Universidade dos Açores, Angra do Heroísmo, Portugal*
[‡]*Universidade Federal do Paraná, Curitiba, Brasil*
[§]*Universidade dos Açores, Angra do Heroísmo, Portugal*

*In this chapter, we present the inter-island input–output system for the Azores. It includes the economy of the nine islands of the archipelago, considering 25 different economic activities. The chapter also analyzes the impacts of the main drivers of the islands' economy, incorporating both spillover and feedback effects in the evaluation of the multipliers: (i) dairy and beef exports; (ii) external public support; and (iii) tourism, both from the rest of the country and from abroad. It is shown that: (i) the economic structure of the islands is quite different from each other; (ii) the specific economic base of the islands are also different and, as expected, the biggest islands not only capture an important part of the impact of external pushes done in smaller islands, but also they constitute important drivers of smaller islands.*

### 8.1. Introduction

Insularity results from the combination of smallness, associated with limiting factors, and remoteness, linked to the distant location of its final demand. Smallness can be viewed as land insufficiency, lack of specialized labor or shortage of venture capital, reduced markets and scale diseconomies, also in standardized public services. Insularity is then a technological specificity, where some resources are available but bounded, that shapes the social structures and geographical identities. The combination of smallness with remoteness explains the occurrence of export monocultures because the whole island stays within the same Von Thünen ring influenced by local capabilities and by distant external markets. Being so, small changes in market conditions or in external accessibilities can produce great modifications in the export base generating economic cycles with strong effects in the islands' livelihoods. Finally the overwhelming pressure for monoculture creates rents over the scarce economic resources whose spatial allocation depends on the control over transport value chains and on the structure of ownership. Being so, the regional coefficients of the input–output (IO) matrix of each island can be quite different from the one observed in another island or in the mainland, either because there is some limiting factor or because the income generated migrates elsewhere.

The challenge of this chapter is to analyze the effects of insularity in the economy looking into the IO multiplier effects in archipelagic economies for the case of the nine islands of the Azores.

The Azores are nine small islands (Figure 8.1) spread across 600 km — East–West — in the North Atlantic, half way between Portugal and Newfound Land. The islands are wet and green, warm but windy, with average temperatures between 16°C in January and 22°C in August and with rainfall ranging between 762 and 1,525 mm. Less than a quarter of a million Portuguese people live in the islands, quite different in size and population and with very different distances from each other. The economy of the Azores, like any other place, rests on its human, social and productive capital moulded by four main natural features: good conditions for agriculture, strategic location, unique beauty, and a large Exclusive Economic Zone (EEZ). The use of these potentialities, driven by outside markets and by outward strategic equilibria, evolved through time determining the performance of the economy, its crises and recoveries (Dentinho, 1995).

The economic base of the Azores has evolved throughout time. Based on their agricultural capabilities, the islands exported wheat since the 16th century until the middle of the 20th century, ink

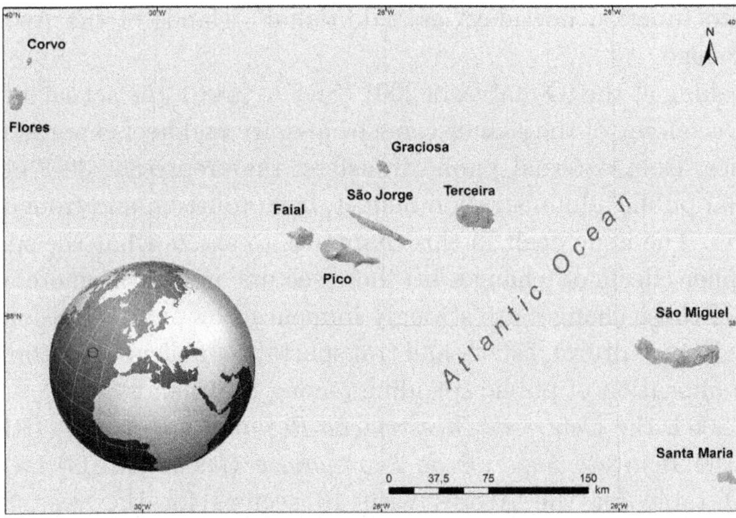


**Figure 8.1.** The Azores archipelago.

plants in the 17th and 18th century, oranges in the 19th century, and dairy products since the 1960s. Grounded on its strategic location, the Azores islands were essential for sail navigation from the 16th to the 19th century for the return trips to Europe, from America, from Africa and from Asia through the Cape of Good Hope. Steam engines and railways created a backlash on that relative centrality, but transcontinental flights find some utility in the islands for civil and military purposes after the Second World War (Monjardino, 1989). The large EEZ is gaining its importance, and the unilateral public transfers from mainland Portugal and from the European Union, that took place in the last decades, are the counterpart of securing some ownership over these ocean resources. The unique beauty of the landscape is also providing some benefits from the increasing touristic flows, although never reaching the importance of the other natural capital. Finally, the islands also export human resources that, for some time, generate unilateral transfers to the households and to the economy; the South of Brazil was populated by Azoreans in the 18th century, and the Azorean communities in Bermuda, New England, California and

Toronto function nowadays as "additional" islands of the Azorean archipelago.

Looking at the IO matrix of 2001 (SREA, 2006), the actual inflows to the economy of the islands come from dairy and beef exports, from fisheries, from external public transfers, that represent 30% of the regional public administration budget, from tourism, and from other exports. The issue dealt in this chapter is to assess what the spatial multiplier effects of (changes in) those sectors are; furthermore when most of those changes are strongly influenced by public decisions — through agricultural, fishery and transportation policies, and through direct allocation of public spending among the islands.

In 2004, the *Centro de Investigação Regional e Urbana* (CIRIUS) from the *Instituto Superior de Economia e Gestão* (ISEG) created an IO table for the Azores with 16 sectors for the year 1998. Alves *et al.* (2004) tried to use statistical data on maritime transportation to estimate the flows between the Azores and mainland Portugal. Ramos and Sargento (2003) disaggregated the IO matrix for 1995 for seven Portuguese regions, including the Azores. The *Serviço Regional de Estatística dos Açores* (SREA) published in 2006, an enlarged table of employment for the Azores in 2001, with 25 sectors. Ferreira (2006) built up the regional IO table for the Azores with 45 sectors, using information on the employment and production, according to the method described in Almond (2000). Then, based on disaggregation methods (Flegg, 1994) and bi-proportional techniques (Jackson, 2004), in the particular form of crossed entropy methods (Robinson and Cattaneo, 2001), Ferreira (2006) was able to disaggregate that table for the Azores into three regional IO tables: São Miguel, Terceira and the Rest of the Azores, nevertheless without looking into the inter-island flows.

The aim now is to generate an inter-regional IO system, including all the islands of the Azores, through the estimation of the inter-industry and inter-island economic flows and their association with the existing structure of the transport and communication system. There has been many approaches to merge IO models with transportation network analysis (Boyce, 2002) along the models reviewed by Batten and Boyce (1986) and following the initial work by Wilson (1970) on inter-regional commodity flows. Other contributors include Polenske (1980), Hewings (1985) and, more recently, Haddad *et al.* (2011).

Summing up: first, the application of IO models to archipelagos cannot be done assuming that the productive system is totally explained by the technological coefficients of the whole archipelago without considering the decisive role of transportation networks and bounded resources; second, it is advisable to create spatially disaggregate models for archipelagos because policies and their effects are necessarily spatially disaggregated; and, finally, recent techniques and improved data allow the development of operational models suitable to support decision makers. In this context, the aim of this chapter is to analyze the effects of insularity in the economy looking at the IO multiplier effects of the economic base in archipelagic economies for the case of the nine islands of the Azores. More specifically, the aim is to provide insights and support for the analysis of the impacts of the main basic activities in the archipelagos, namely agricultural and dairy, fishery, external public transfers, and tourism.

To address these issues, the study is divided in four distinct parts beyond the introduction. Section 8.2 describes the methodological framework to be used in the analysis, describing the inter-island IO model for the archipelago. Section 8.3 briefly discusses the main aspects related to the estimation of the inter-island IO system, which serves as the basis for the application that is carried out in Section 8.4 to analyze differential multiplier effects of the main components of the economic bases of the island economies, followed by final remarks.

## 8.2. Methodology

The conventional IO model is given by the system of matrix equations (Miller and Blair, 2009):

$$x = Ax + f, \tag{8.1}$$

$$x = (I - A)^{-1} f = Bf, \tag{8.2}$$

where $x$ and $f$ are the vectors of gross output and final demand, respectively; $A$ consists of input coefficients $a_{ij}$ defined as the amount of product $i$ required per unit of product $j$ (in monetary terms), for $i, j = 1, \ldots, n$; and $B$ is known as the Leontief inverse.

Let us consider Equations (8.1) and (8.2) in an inter-regional context, with $R$ different regions, so that:

$$x = \begin{bmatrix} x^1 \\ \vdots \\ x^R \end{bmatrix}; \quad A = \begin{bmatrix} A^{11} & \cdots & A^{1R} \\ \vdots & \ddots & \vdots \\ A^{R1} & \cdots & A^{RR} \end{bmatrix};$$

$$f = \begin{bmatrix} f^1 \\ \vdots \\ f^R \end{bmatrix}; \quad \text{and} \quad B = \begin{bmatrix} B^{11} & \cdots & B^{1R} \\ \vdots & \ddots & \vdots \\ B^{R1} & \cdots & B^{RR} \end{bmatrix} \tag{8.3}$$

and

$$\begin{aligned} x^1 &= B^{11} f^1 + \cdots + B^{1R} f^R \\ &\vdots \\ x^R &= B^{R1} f^1 + \cdots + B^{RR} f^R. \end{aligned} \tag{8.4}$$

Focusing on the elements directly related to the economic base, let us also consider the different components of $f$, which include tourists expenditures in the islands, both from the rest of Portugal, $t$, and from abroad, $i$, exports of goods and services to mainland Portugal, $p$, and to foreign markets, $s$, government expenditures financed by external unilateral transfers,[1] $c$, and other final demand

[1]Regarding public transfers, there would be a need to include the discrimination of public expenditures supported by external unilateral transfers to the islands, both from the rest of Portugal and from abroad. Even though this information can be obtained from the regional accounts, which provide the monetary values of supports coming mostly from mainland Portugal and from the European Union, we did not make this distinction. The reason is that we have assumed the same structure of public expenditures in the islands regardless the source of financing. Thus, the $p$ vector was estimated as a share of government expenditures.

expenditures, $e$.

$$t = \begin{bmatrix} t^1 \\ \vdots \\ t^R \end{bmatrix}; \quad i = \begin{bmatrix} i^1 \\ \vdots \\ i^R \end{bmatrix}; \quad p = \begin{bmatrix} p^1 \\ \vdots \\ p^R \end{bmatrix}; \quad e = \begin{bmatrix} s^1 \\ \vdots \\ s^R \end{bmatrix}$$

$$c = \begin{bmatrix} c^1 \\ \vdots \\ c^R \end{bmatrix}; e = \begin{bmatrix} e^1 \\ \vdots \\ e^R \end{bmatrix}.$$

Thus, we can re-write Equation (8.4) as:

$$\begin{aligned} x^1 &= B^{11}(t^1 + i^1 + p^1 + s^1 + c^1 + e^1) \\ &\quad + \cdots + B^{1R}(t^R + i^R + p^R + s^R + c^R + e^R) \\ &\vdots \\ x^R &= B^{R1}(t^1 + i^1 + p^1 + s^1 + c^1 + e^1) \\ &\quad + \cdots + B^{RR}(t^R + i^R + p^R + s^R + c^R + e^R). \end{aligned} \tag{8.5}$$

With Equation (8.5), we can then compute the contribution of the components of the economic base to the islands' output. It is clear from Equation (8.5) that an island's output depends, among others, on direct money injections in the island itself, depending on the degree of inter-regional integration among the islands in the Azores, and also on injections in other islands.

## 8.3. The Inter-island IO Model for the Azores

This section provides an overview of the process through which the inter-island IO model for the Azores (IIOMA) was constructed, based on the available data. The departure point was IO table for the Azores (2001) which includes 25 sectors.

The first step was to disaggregate the Azorean data into the nine islands, using information provided by the SREA on employment by sector and by island, average wages per island and average wages per sector in the whole of Portugal, the balance of supply and demand per sector in each one of the islands, and on the distances between the islands, corrected for the cost of embark and disembark.[2]

Table 8.1 presents the shares of each of the islands in the various components of the final demand in the archipelago. We have highlighted the exports of agricultural and dairy products (agro), as well as the exports fishery products. A general result is the spatial concentration of aggregate final demand in São Miguel (53.4%) and Terceira (22.7%), which is very likely influenced by the distribution of economic activity and population of the islands.

The economic base of the archipelago is just 25.1% of the final demand[3] and mainly constituted by (Table 8.2) dairy and beef exports (32.5%), unilateral transfers (28.1%), other exports — mainly from transport, financial services and other agricultural products (24.4%), tourism (10.4%), and fishery (4.6%). Concerning exports, 98.4% of dairy and beef, 64.7% of fishery, 42.5% of tourism, and 76.3% of other exports go to mainland Portugal.

There are specificities in the economic base of the islands: dairy and beef is more relevant for Graciosa and São Jorge; unilateral transfers are more important for Corvo and Terceira, due respectively to the smallness of Corvo and the existence of an American military base in Terceira; fishery plays an important relative role in Faial and Pico; tourism is relatively more relevant for São Miguel, Pico, Faial and Flores; and other exports are more significant for the more diversified island of São Miguel and for the special case of Santa Maria, where the Air Control of the North Atlantic is located.

The second step was to disaggregate the Azorean IO matrix into the nine islands of the archipelago. Following Chenery (1956) and Moses (1955), we assumed, for each island, the same commodity mixes for different users (producers, investors, households and government) as those presented in the regional IO tables for the Azores. For sectoral cost structures, value added generation may be different across regions. Trade matrices for each commodity were used to disaggregate the origin of each commodity in order to capture the

[2]Details on the methodology can be found in Haddad et al. (2011).
[3]This is equivalent to 43.1% of the archipelago GRP.

**Table 8.1.** Shares of the islands in the components of final demand in the Azores.

| | Santa Maria (%) | São Miguel (%) | Terceira (%) | Graciosa (%) | São Jorge (%) | Pico (%) | Faial (%) | Flores (%) | Corvo (%) | Total (%) | Structure of Final Demand (%) |
|---|---|---|---|---|---|---|---|---|---|---|---|
| Investment | 1.8 | 54.3 | 21.4 | 1.9 | 3.2 | 7.6 | 7.7 | 1.9 | 0.2 | 100.0 | 21.9 |
| Consumption | 2.3 | 53.5 | 23.5 | 1.8 | 4.0 | 6.0 | 7.0 | 1.7 | 0.2 | 100.0 | 33.7 |
| Exports agro Portugal | 1.5 | 54.7 | 20.3 | 2.9 | 4.6 | 6.0 | 8.3 | 1.6 | 0.1 | 100.0 | 8.0 |
| Exports agro other | 1.3 | 49.4 | 17.8 | 5.7 | 2.7 | 3.6 | 18.5 | 1.1 | 0.0 | 100.0 | 0.1 |
| Exports fishery Portugal | 2.2 | 46.4 | 11.6 | 1.0 | 4.6 | 23.8 | 9.6 | 0.6 | 0.1 | 100.0 | 0.8 |
| Exports fishery other | 2.1 | 45.0 | 10.5 | 0.7 | 4.9 | 26.1 | 10.2 | 0.4 | 0.1 | 100.0 | 0.4 |
| Exports other Portugal | 8.5 | 67.2 | 9.9 | 0.5 | 2.4 | 1.7 | 7.9 | 1.8 | 0.0 | 100.0 | 4.7 |
| Exports other other | 8.9 | 64.0 | 12.0 | 0.7 | 1.5 | 2.3 | 8.5 | 2.0 | 0.1 | 100.0 | 1.4 |
| Tourism Portugal | 2.3 | 49.6 | 20.1 | 1.9 | 2.6 | 6.7 | 14.4 | 2.4 | 0.0 | 100.0 | 1.1 |
| Tourism other | 1.7 | 65.0 | 12.4 | 0.7 | 1.9 | 6.2 | 10.1 | 2.0 | 0.0 | 100.0 | 1.5 |
| Government | 2.3 | 48.3 | 28.3 | 1.9 | 3.8 | 5.2 | 7.8 | 1.9 | 0.3 | 100.0 | 23.5 |
| Stocks | 1.5 | 52.1 | 20.6 | 2.8 | 8.3 | 9.2 | 3.3 | 1.6 | 0.5 | 100.0 | 2.9 |
| Final demand | 2.5 | 53.4 | 22.7 | 1.9 | 3.8 | 6.2 | 7.6 | 1.8 | 0.2 | 100.0 | 100.0 |

**Table 8.2.** Structure of the economic base of the islands.

| | Santa Maria (%) | São Miguel (%) | Terceira (%) | Graciosa (%) | São Jorge (%) | Pico (%) | Faial (%) | Flores (%) | Corvo (%) | Total (%) |
|---|---|---|---|---|---|---|---|---|---|---|
| Exports agro Portugal | 13.8 | 31.4 | 33.7 | 51.1 | 41.5 | 33.9 | 30.8 | 29.6 | 21.8 | 32.0 |
| Exports agro other | 0.2 | 0.4 | 0.5 | 1.6 | 0.4 | 0.3 | 1.1 | 0.3 | 0.1 | 0.5 |
| Exports fishery Portugal | 1.8 | 2.5 | 1.8 | 1.7 | 3.9 | 12.6 | 3.4 | 1.0 | 3.1 | 3.0 |
| Exports fishery other | 1.0 | 1.3 | 0.9 | 0.6 | 2.3 | 7.5 | 1.9 | 0.4 | 1.2 | 1.6 |
| Exports other Portugal | 44.6 | 22.5 | 9.6 | 5.5 | 12.8 | 5.4 | 17.1 | 18.9 | 4.9 | 18.6 |
| Exports other other | 14.5 | 6.6 | 3.6 | 2.2 | 2.5 | 2.3 | 5.7 | 6.5 | 2.6 | 5.8 |
| Tourism Portugal | 2.8 | 3.9 | 4.6 | 4.7 | 3.3 | 5.2 | 7.4 | 6.0 | 1.5 | 4.4 |
| Tourism other | 2.8 | 7.0 | 3.9 | 2.3 | 3.2 | 6.5 | 7.1 | 6.9 | 1.0 | 6.0 |
| Government (dependent)* | 18.5 | 24.3 | 41.4 | 30.4 | 30.2 | 26.0 | 25.6 | 30.4 | 64.0 | 28.1 |
| Economic base | 100.0 | 100.0 | 100.0 | 100.0 | 100.0 | 100.0 | 100.0 | 100.0 | 100.0 | 100.0 |

*Note*: *Government expenditures financed by external transfers.

structure of the spatial interaction in the Azorean economy. In other words, for a given user, say agriculture sector, the mix of intermediate inputs will be the same in terms of its composition, but it will differ from the sources of supply.

The strategy for estimating the 25 trade matrices (one for each commodity in the system) included the following steps:

1. We have initially estimated total supply (output) of each commodity by island, excluding exports to other countries. Thus, for each island, we obtained information for the total sales of each commodity for the domestic markets.

$$\text{Supply}(c, s) = \text{supply for the domestic markets of commodity } c \text{ by island } s.$$

2. Following that, we have estimated total demand, in each island, for the aforementioned 25 commodities. To do that, we have assumed the respective users' structure of demand followed the Azorean pattern. With the island levels of sectoral production, investment demand, household demand and government demand, we have estimated the initial values of total demand for each commodity in each island, from which the demand for imported commodities were deducted. The resulting estimates, which represent the island total demand for Azorean goods, were then adjusted so that, for each commodity, demand across islands equals supply across islands.

$$\text{Demand}(c, d) = \text{demand of commodity } c \text{ by island } d.$$

3. With the information for *Supply*$(c, s)$ and *Demand*$(c, d)$, the next step was to estimate, for each commodity $c$, matrices of trade $(9 \times 9)$ representing the transactions of each commodity among Azorean islands. We have fully relied on the methodology described in Dixon and Rimmer (2004), based on the so called Horridge formulae. The procedure considered the following steps:
   (a) For the diagonal cells, Equation (8.6) was implemented, while for the off-diagonal elements, Equation (8.7) is the

relevant one:

$$\mathrm{SHIN}(c,d,d) = Min\left\{\frac{\mathrm{Supply}(c,d)}{\mathrm{Demand}(c,d)}, 1\right\} * F(c), \tag{8.6}$$

$$\mathrm{SHIN}(c,o,d) = \left\{\frac{1}{Dist(o,d)} \cdot \frac{\mathrm{Supply}(c,o)}{\sum_{k=1}^{22}\mathrm{Supply}(c,k)}\right\} * \left\{\frac{1-\mathrm{SHIN}(c,d,d)}{\sum_{j=1,j\neq d}^{22}\left[\frac{1}{Dist(j,d)} \cdot \frac{Supply(c,j)}{\sum_{k=1}^{22} Supply(c,k)}\right]}\right\}. \tag{8.7}$$

where $c$ refers to a given commodity, and $o$ and $d$ represent, respectively, origin and destination regions.

The variable *Dist* $(o,d)$ refers to the distance between two trading islands. The factor $F(c)$ gives the extent of tradability of a given commodity. For non-tradable (usually services), typically assumed to be locally provided goods, we have used the value of 0.9 for $F(c)$, adopting a usual assumption, while for tradable, the value of $F(c)$ was set to 0.5. It can be shown that the column sums in the resulting matrices add to one. What these matrices show are the supply-adjusted shares of each island in the specific commodity demand by each island of destination.

Once these share coefficients are calculated, we then distribute the demand of commodity $c$ by region $d$ [*Demand* $(c,d)$] across the corresponding columns of the SHIN matrices. Once we adopt this procedure, we have to further adjust the matrices to make sure that supply and demand balance. This is done through a RAS procedure.

Tables 8.3 and 8.4 show the resulting structure of trade among the Azores islands, (aggregated across commodities) respectively, excluding and including the inter-island flows for consumption and investment goods. We have also included island demand for imported commodities (last row), estimated considering the structure of demand according to the Azorean pattern. It is clear that the sources of supply for the archipelago are mainland Portugal, São Miguel and Terceira — regarding intermediary flows —, and São

**Table 8.3.** Structure of inter-island trade flows of intermediary goods and services.

| | Santa Maria (%) | São Miguel (%) | Terceira (%) | Graciosa (%) | São Jorge (%) | Pico (%) | Faial (%) | Flores (%) | Corvo (%) | Total (%) |
|---|---|---|---|---|---|---|---|---|---|---|
| Santa Maria | 25 | 2 | 0 | 1 | 1 | 1 | 1 | 0 | 1 | 1 |
| São Miguel | 13 | 41 | 17 | 20 | 19 | 17 | 16 | 13 | 24 | 31 |
| Terceira | 2 | 8 | 29 | 9 | 7 | 7 | 7 | 4 | 9 | 13 |
| Graciosa | 0 | 0 | 0 | 31 | 0 | 0 | 1 | 0 | 0 | 1 |
| São Jorge | 0 | 1 | 1 | 2 | 29 | 2 | 2 | 1 | 2 | 2 |
| Pico | 0 | 2 | 1 | 2 | 3 | 28 | 3 | 2 | 3 | 3 |
| Faial | 0 | 1 | 1 | 2 | 2 | 3 | 34 | 2 | 3 | 3 |
| Flores | 0 | 0 | 0 | 0 | 0 | 0 | 0 | 32 | 3 | 1 |
| Corvo | 0 | 0 | 0 | 0 | 0 | 0 | 0 | 0 | 37 | 0 |
| Imports | 60 | 45 | 49 | 33 | 39 | 42 | 37 | 45 | 18 | 45 |
| Total | 100 | 100 | 98 | 100 | 100 | 100 | 101 | 99 | 100 | 100 |

**Table 8.4.** Structure of inter-island trade flows of intermediary and final goods and services.

| | Santa Maria (%) | São Miguel (%) | Terceira (%) | Graciosa (%) | São Jorge (%) | Pico (%) | Faial (%) | Flores (%) | Corvo (%) | Total (%) |
|---|---|---|---|---|---|---|---|---|---|---|
| Santa Maria | 32 | 2 | 1 | 1 | 1 | 1 | 1 | 1 | 1 | 3 |
| São Miguel | 20 | 55 | 23 | 24 | 22 | 21 | 20 | 17 | 29 | 39 |
| Terceira | 3 | 10 | 42 | 12 | 9 | 9 | 9 | 6 | 12 | 17 |
| Graciosa | 0 | 0 | 0 | 37 | 1 | 1 | 1 | 0 | 1 | 1 |
| São Jorge | 0 | 1 | 1 | 2 | 38 | 2 | 2 | 1 | 2 | 3 |
| Pico | 0 | 2 | 2 | 3 | 3 | 38 | 3 | 2 | 3 | 4 |
| Faial | 1 | 1 | 1 | 3 | 3 | 4 | 43 | 2 | 4 | 4 |
| Flores | 0 | 0 | 0 | 1 | 0 | 1 | 1 | 45 | 4 | 1 |
| Corvo | 0 | 0 | 0 | 0 | 0 | 0 | 0 | 0 | 36 | 0 |
| Imports | 44 | 29 | 31 | 18 | 23 | 24 | 21 | 26 | 8 | 28 |
| Total | 100 | 100 | 100 | 100 | 100 | 100 | 100 | 100 | 100 | 100 |

Miguel, mainland Portugal and Terceira — for flows of intermediary and final goods and services.

In the next section, we continue to evaluate the general structure of the IO matrix for the archipelago of the Azores focusing on the multiplier effects of the economic base.

## 8.4. Inter-island Multiplier Effects of the Economic Base

This section presents the results of the economic base multiplier effects derived from the IIOMA. We first look at the aggregate output multipliers for the main components of the archipelago's economic base (Table 8.5), identifying the main drivers of the Azorean economy.

We then consider, for each island, the ratio of the total effects generated in the local economy by the whole Azorean economic base to the island economic base itself. This indicator gives the extent to which the island is capable of internalizing a bigger share of the multiplier benefits of the archipelago's economic base. Whenever this indicator is greater than the average multiplier for the whole archipelago, the island is shown to have a greater capability of benefiting from the structural interdependence in the system (Table 8.6).

**Table 8.5.** Economic-base total output multipliers in the Azores, by component.

| | |
|---|---|
| Exports agro Portugal | 1.96 |
| Exports agro Other | 2.12 |
| Exports fishery Portugal | 1.61 |
| Exports fishery other | 1.66 |
| Exports other Portugal | 1.57 |
| Exports other other | 1.48 |
| Tourism Portugal | 1.83 |
| Tourism other | 1.83 |
| Government (dependent) | 1.31 |
| **Economic base** | **1.65** |

**Table 8.6.** Island-economic-base output multipliers in the Azores.

| | |
|---|---|
| Santa Maria | 1.78 |
| São Miguel | 1.65 |
| Terceira | 1.69 |
| Graciosa | 1.57 |
| São Jorge | 1.83 |
| Pico | 1.68 |
| Faial | 1.49 |
| Flores | 1.56 |
| Corvo | 1.53 |
| **Total** | **1.65** |

Finally we perform a spatial decomposition of the archipelago's output by taking into account not only the multiplier structure embedded in the IIOAM, but also the structure of the economic-base components of final demand in the nine islands (Sonis *et al.*, 1996). According to Equation (8.5), the Azorean output multiplier was decomposed, and the contributions of the (aggregated) components of the economic bases from different islands were calculated. Differently from the previous exercise, which considers the combined effect of the archipelago's economic base, we consider here the standard definition of the output multiplier for each island economic base separately. The results are presented in Table 8.7.

Looking at the main drivers of the Azorean economy it is quite clear that, although agricultural-related (agro) exports and external public transfers (government-dependent) are the main components of the economic base of the islands (Table 8.2), their multiplier effects are quite different. The higher multipliers are associated with agro exports to Portugal and to other countries, highlighting the importance of the cluster associated with dairy exports. This suggests a major challenge to expand agro exports to other countries since they have an output multiplier of 2.12 (Table 8.5), although representing only 0.5% of the economic base (Table 8.2). It is also revealing that the multiplier effect of external transfers is just 1.31 indicating that the leakages associated with most of public spending, driven by self-financed government spending or by external transfers,

**Table 8.7.** Spatial decomposition of the multipliers of the islands' economic bases.

| | Origin of the economic base | | | | | | | | | |
|---|---|---|---|---|---|---|---|---|---|---|
| | Santa Maria (%) | São Miguel (%) | Terceira (%) | Graciosa (%) | São Jorge (%) | Pico (%) | Faial (%) | Flores (%) | Corvo (%) | Total (%) |
| Santa Maria | 84.1 | 1.4 | 0.5 | 0.5 | 0.4 | 0.5 | 0.6 | 0.6 | 0.4 | 3.8 |
| São Miguel | 12.1 | 87.6 | 15.4 | 15.4 | 13.8 | 14.3 | 13.3 | 10.5 | 10.7 | 55.5 |
| Terceira | 2.2 | 6.4 | 79.8 | 6.2 | 5.1 | 5.4 | 5.3 | 3.8 | 3.9 | 19.7 |
| Graciosa | 0.1 | 0.4 | 0.3 | 72.2 | 0.4 | 0.5 | 0.5 | 0.3 | 0.2 | 1.7 |
| São Jorge | 0.4 | 1.3 | 1.2 | 1.8 | 76.2 | 1.9 | 1.7 | 1.1 | 1.1 | 3.9 |
| Pico | 0.5 | 1.6 | 1.4 | 2.0 | 2.1 | 74.8 | 2.6 | 1.3 | 1.3 | 5.7 |
| Faial | 0.4 | 1.1 | 1.1 | 1.6 | 1.7 | 2.3 | 75.5 | 1.2 | 1.3 | 7.7 |
| Flores | 0.1 | 0.3 | 0.3 | 0.4 | 0.3 | 0.4 | 0.4 | 80.9 | 1.2 | 1.7 |
| Corvo | 0.0 | 0.0 | 0.0 | 0.0 | 0.0 | 0.0 | 0.0 | 0.1 | 80.1 | 0.1 |
| **Multiplier** | **1.57** | **1.67** | **1.61** | **1.72** | **1.63** | **1.65** | **1.69** | **1.59** | **1.40** | **1.65** |
| ***Intra-regional*** | ***1.32*** | ***1.46*** | ***1.28*** | ***1.24*** | ***1.24*** | ***1.23*** | ***1.28*** | ***1.29*** | ***1.12*** | — |
| ***Interregional*** | ***0.25*** | ***0.21*** | ***0.32*** | ***0.48*** | ***0.39*** | ***0.41*** | ***0.41*** | ***0.30*** | ***0.28*** | — |

is very high. This somehow reinforces the idea that the combination of smallness with remoteness explains the occurrence of export monocultures in the islands (see Section 8.1) and it should be through the improvement of the competitiveness of those monocultures that it would be possible to promote growth.

The results of Table 8.6 can be explained by the smallness and remoteness of the different islands that compose the Azorean archipelago, as well as the spatial hierarchy within the Azores. As expected, the economic base of São Miguel, representing more than half of the islands' economy, presents a multiplier effect of its economic base very close to the multiplier effect of the economic base of the archipelago. With exception of Santa Maria, very much closed and linked to São Miguel, all the other smaller and more remote islands — Graciosa, Faial, Flores and Corvo — have stronger leakages associated with their economic base multiplier effects when compared to the average economic base multiplier effect of the Azores. Furthermore, the islands that present relatively lower leakages than the average are relatively larger and are also closer to each other — Terceira, Pico and São Jorge.

Table 8.7 decomposes the multiplier effect of the economic base of each island on the island itself and on the different islands. There are many issues that arise. First, looking at the information on the magnitudes of the multipliers, it is clear that islands like Graciosa, more specialized in agro exports (Table 8.2) — that has higher multiplier effects (Table 8.5) — have higher multiplier effects associated with their economic base than islands, such as the case of Corvo, more dependent on external public transfers (Table 8.2). Second, and as expected, the bigger island, São Miguel, internalizes a major share of the multiplier effect, presenting the highest intra-regional multiplier. Nevertheless, showing the protection created by distance, more remote islands, like Santa Maria, Flores and Corvo, are also able to integrate more than 80% of the multiplier effect. Third, islands of the central group that are closer to each other (Terceira, Graciosa, São Jorge, Pico and Faial) share the multiplier effects with the neighbor islands. Fourth, the bigger island of São Miguel and also, to some extent, the second biggest island (Terceira) are able to capture some of the multiplier effects of the economic base of the other islands revealing the centralities of the archipelago. Finally, there are clear signs of spatial spillovers between Faial and Pico made possible by the short distance (five kilometer) and interconnection (frequent ferryboat) between those two islands.

## 8.5. Concluding Remarks

The argument of this chapter is that economic models for archipelagic regions should be disaggregated into different islands in order to understand the functioning of the economy and to evaluate policy impacts more accurately. With the data available and using IO disaggregation methodology, we show that: (i) the economic structure of the islands is quite different from each other; (ii) the specific economic base of the islands are also different and, as expected, the biggest islands not only capture an important part of the impact of external pushes done in smaller islands, but they also constitute important drivers of smaller islands.

## References

Almond, C (2000) Product-to-product tables via product-technology with no negative flows, *Economic Systems Research* 12(1), 27–43.

Alves, M *et al.* (2004) Sistemas de matrizes regionais de input–output para a região autónoma dos Açores 1998. *Relatório Metodológico e Resultados. Subsecretário Regional do Planeamento e Assuntos Europeus.* Direcção Regional de Estudos e Planeamento, Abril.

Batten, DF and DE Boyce (1986) Spatial interaction, transportation and inter-regional commodity flow models. In *Handbook of Regional and Urban Economics, Volume I.* P Nijkamp (Ed.). Amsterdam: North-Holland, pp. 357–406.

Boyce, D (2002) Combined model of inter-regional commodity flows on a transportation network. In *Trade, Networks and Hierachies, Modelling Regional and Inter-regional Economies.* JD Hewings, M Sonis and D Boyce (Eds.). Heidelberg: Springer-Verlag.

Chenery, HB (1956) Inter-regional and international input–output analysis. In *The Structure Interdependence of the Economy*, 29–40. T Barna (Ed.). New York: Wiley, 341–356.

Dentinho, TP (1995) Information and communication technologies and regional development. *The case of the Azores dairy value chain. PhD Thesis.* United Kingdom: University of Newcastle.

Dixon, PB and MT Rimmer (2004) Disaggregation of results from a detailed general equilibrium model of the US to the state level. *General Working Paper No.* 145, Centre of Policy Studies, April.

Ferreira, P (2006) Projecção espacial da tabela input–output dos Açores. *Tese de Mestrado.* Departamento de Economia e Gestão, Universidade dos Açores.

Flegg, AT (1994) On the appropriate use of location quotients in generating regional input–output tables, *Regional Studies* 29(6), 547–561.

Haddad, EH, JMG Samaniego, AA Porsse, DAO Jimenez, WSO Moreno and LGA Souza (2011) Inter-regional input–output system for Equador, 2007: Methodology and results. *TD Nereus* 03. São Paulo.

Hewings, GJD (1985) *Regional Input–Output Analysis.* Beverly Hills: Sage Publications Inc.

Jackson, R (2004) Alternative input–output matrix updating formulations, *Economic Systems Research* 16(2), 135–148.

Miller, R and P Blair (2009) *Input–Output Analysis — Foundations and Extensions*, 2nd Edition. Cambridge, UK: Cambridge University Press.

Monjardino, A (1989) Os Açores no contexto do Atlântico. *Relações Transatlânticas No Limiar Do Século XXI.* Universidade dos Açores, 205–212.

Moses, LN (1955) The stability of inter-regional trading patterns and input–output analysis, *American Economic Review* 45(5), 803–832.

Polenske, KR (1980) The *U.S. Multiregional Input–Output Accounts and Model.* Lexington, MA: Lexington Books (D.C. Heath and Co.).

Ramos, P and A Sargento (2003) Estimating trade flows between Portuguese regions using an input–output approach. *43th Congress of the European Regional Science Association.* Jywaskyla (Finland), August 27–30.

Robinson, S and ME-S Cattaneo (2001) Updating and estimating a social accounting matrix using cross entropy methods, *Economic Systems Research* 13(1), 47–64.

Sonis, M, GJD Hewings and J Guo (1996) Sources of structural change in input–output systems: A field of influence approach, *Economics Systems Research,* 8(1), 15–32.

SREA (2006) Matrizes intersectoriais dos Açores, 2001. *Serviço Regional de Estatística dos Açores.*

Wilson, AG (1970) Inter-regional commodity flows: Entropy maximizing procedures, *Geographical Analysis* 2, 255–282.

# Annexure

## A.1. Distances in the Azores

### A.1.1. *Direct distance*

| | Santa Maria | São Miguel | Terceira | Graciosa | São Jorge | Pico | Faial | Flores | Corvo |
|---|---|---|---|---|---|---|---|---|---|
| Santa Maria | 0 | 100 | 265 | 345 | 330 | 340 | 360 | 575 | 585 |
| São Miguel | 100 | 0 | 170 | 250 | 250 | 260 | 280 | 500 | 510 |
| Terceira | 265 | 170 | 0 | 95 | 120 | 125 | 145 | 360 | 370 |
| Graciosa | 345 | 250 | 95 | 0 | 75 | 80 | 85 | 270 | 280 |
| São Jorge | 330 | 250 | 120 | 75 | 0 | 20 | 40 | 250 | 260 |
| Pico | 340 | 260 | 125 | 80 | 20 | 0 | 25 | 240 | 250 |
| Faial | 360 | 280 | 145 | 85 | 40 | 25 | 0 | 235 | 245 |
| Flores | 575 | 500 | 360 | 270 | 250 | 240 | 235 | 0 | 15 |
| Corvo | 585 | 510 | 370 | 280 | 260 | 250 | 245 | 15 | 0 |

### A.1.2. *Frequency of transport*

| | Santa Maria | São Miguel | Terceira | Graciosa | São Jorge | Pico | Faial | Flores | Corvo |
|---|---|---|---|---|---|---|---|---|---|
| Santa Maria | 0 | 2 | 2 | 2 | 2 | 2 | 2 | 2 | 3 |
| São Miguel | 2 | 0 | 1 | 2 | 2 | 2 | 1 | 2 | 3 |
| Terceira | 2 | 1 | 0 | 2 | 2 | 2 | 1 | 2 | 3 |
| Graciosa | 2 | 2 | 2 | 0 | 2 | 2 | 2 | 2 | 3 |
| São Jorge | 2 | 2 | 2 | 2 | 0 | 2 | 2 | 2 | 3 |
| Pico | 2 | 2 | 2 | 2 | 2 | 0 | 1 | 2 | 3 |
| Faial | 1 | 1 | 1 | 2 | 2 | 1 | 0 | 2 | 3 |
| Flores | 2 | 1 | 1 | 2 | 2 | 2 | 2 | 0 | 1 |
| Corvo | 3 | 2 | 2 | 3 | 3 | 3 | 3 | 1 | 0 |

## A.1.3. *Formula* (*distance of the model* = 150 + 0.5* *direct distance* +10* *frequency*)

| | Santa Maria | São Miguel | Terceira | Graciosa | São Jorge | Pico | Faial | Flores | Corvo |
|---|---|---|---|---|---|---|---|---|---|
| Santa Maria | 150 | 220 | 302.5 | 342.5 | 335 | 340 | 350 | 457.5 | 472.5 |
| São Miguel | 220 | 150 | 245 | 295 | 295 | 300 | 300 | 420 | 435 |
| Terceira | 302.5 | 245 | 150 | 217.5 | 230 | 232.5 | 232.5 | 350 | 365 |
| Graciosa | 342.5 | 295 | 217.5 | 150 | 207.5 | 210 | 212.5 | 305 | 320 |
| São Jorge | 335 | 295 | 230 | 207.5 | 150 | 180 | 190 | 295 | 310 |
| Pico | 340 | 300 | 232.5 | 210 | 180 | 150 | 172.5 | 290 | 305 |
| Faial | 340 | 300 | 232.5 | 212.5 | 190 | 172.5 | 150 | 287.5 | 302.5 |
| Flores | 457.5 | 410 | 340 | 305 | 295 | 290 | 287.5 | 150 | 167.5 |
| Corvo | 472.5 | 425 | 355 | 320 | 310 | 305 | 302.5 | 167.5 | 150 |

# Chapter 9

## Inter-Regional Trade in Research-Based Knowledge: The Case of the EISCAT Radar System

*Folke Snickars and Simon Falck*
*Royal Institute of Technology (KTH), Department of Urban Planning and Environment, SE-100 44 Stockholm*

*This study makes use of a unique micro-database on research performed at the European Incoherent Scatter Scientific Association (EISCAT) radar system to provide some new perspectives on inter-regional and international knowledge trade as regards theory, empirics and practice. More broadly, the study examines the economic and societal importance of EISCAT in a spatial context from the perspective of inter-regional trade of knowledge. The fundamental research question is whether the establishment of such scientific infrastructure leads to clustering of related activities in proximity to its location or whether they are spread world-wide independently of the location. We aim to illustrate this question with regard to how inter-regional trade in a research-based knowledge system is fashioned. This is also relevant considering the projected investment in a novel EISCAT system, and prior studies emphasizing that highly-skilled professionals are vital in the knowledge-driven economy, influencing the global dynamics of science-based industries and regions.*

## 9.1. Background

Research is by definition a global sector of the knowledge economy in which inter-regional and international cooperation abounds. Fundamental research in the natural sciences involves networks across all continents. The experimental work relies on research infrastructures placed in optimal locations for the benefit of the research field. Conceptually one might imagine that system is a knowledge production network of value added chains. It is competitive, dynamic and resource-demanding. It should be fruitful to analyze the functioning of this system through the lens of inter-regional and international trade. This chapter analyzes the role of a research infrastructure for this system. The novel perspective is to pitch a knowledge trading system against a classical trading system such as mining. A case in point is found in the Kiruna region in northern Sweden where iron ore mining and space research coexist.

Over the last three decades, the European Incoherent Scatter Scientific Association (EISCAT) has provided the scientific community with outstanding high-latitude data for research on the atmosphere and ionosphere using the incoherent scatter radar technique. The research facilities are located north of the Arctic Circle in Finland, Norway, Sweden, and in Svalbard, with a concentration on Kiruna. EISCAT was first taken into operation in 1981 and has since then contributed to a remarkable scientific output. This research has contributed to enhance the understanding of different space and atmospheric phenomena and opened up several new fields of research. EISCAT is currently planning the next generation research facility, EISCAT_3D, which is a projected investment of more than 1.1 billion SEK (135 million €) with planned start of construction in 2016, first operations in 2018, and to be in full operation in 2021. EISCAT_3D is anticipated to provide researchers with opportunities to conduct novel scientific experiments that may shift the frontiers in several scientific disciplines. It may also be utilized to develop services with specific societal values such as monitoring climate change and identifying orbital debris (Kero *et al.*, 2013).

Kiruna is also the home to one of the world's richest iron ore mines, which has been in production for more than one hundred years. The mining enterprise LKAB supplies highly processed iron ore products for blast furnaces and direct reduction, services to the steel industry, customized minerals for other industries and mining products and technologies. In addition, LKAB also provides an analysis laboratory, and a centre for rock mechanics and technical development. New finds have been made which indicate that another hundred year perspective lies ahead for the mining operations. In this process, the downtown area has to be relocated since the mine is expanding to lower areas below the city centre. LKAB, the municipality of Kiruna, and the Swedish government are financing the relocation. This means that the northernmost part of Sweden is currently one of the most dynamic and globalised industrial operations in the world with competitors in all continents. There is a logistic system of supreme efficiency to bring the ore up and shipping it to ports, mainly the Norwegian port of Narvik, and to steel works, mainly in the Swedish city of Luleå. The Technical University of Luleå has one of its research and education sites in the Kiruna environment.

The implication of this is that there are two subsystems of international and inter-regional trade operating in the region. The mining trade system is highly competitive with long delivery contracts in a market with volatile prices. The research system is highly competitive as well, with long contracts among researchers in different countries to perform experiments in a market where societal demand for results are increasing rapidly.

The mining system is seen to be at the core of the classical trade theory with transport cost playing an important role for the competitive edge. Kiruna has to compensate for its remote location in relation to markets with competitive products, high technology in extraction, and efficient logistics. The knowledge system is at the core of modern space physics with the Kiruna region serving as a hub in the European system of research infrastructures. In fact, the EISCAT radar system was the first investment in all, undertaken by the EU in its road map to European research infrastructures.

While the theory and practice of inter-regional and international trade is well-known in the field of manufacturing (Cerina *et al.*, 2014), the corresponding theory and practice of knowledge trade is much less known. There is also relatively little empirical knowledge about the patterns of knowledge trade. Seen from this perspective, we can understand the role of the research facilities in Kiruna in two complementary ways in comparison to the iron ore case. In the iron ore context, it is evident that the regional resource is at the heart of a long and complex global-value-chain. In the research case, we can see the EISCAT system as a basic infrastructure located in the region because of its high latitude, climatic conditions, and other related space activities including the Swedish Institute of Space Physics (IRF), and Esrange, as well as a node of inter-regional and international accessibility in both rail and air systems. These connections for the use of the research based infrastructure are of course a side-effect of the mining operations. Hence, while mining serves as a traditional example of international trade, EISCAT can be viewed as a modern case of how new knowledge arises through value-added activities in global chains. This has implications on how to interpret regional competitiveness in the contemporary era of globalization.

This study makes use of a unique micro-database on research performed at the EISCAT radar system to provide some new perspectives on knowledge trade as regards to theory, empirics and practice. More broadly, the study examines the economic and societal importance of EISCAT in a spatial context from the perspective of inter-regional trade of knowledge. There is no intention to be explicit about the scientific value of EISCAT. The fundamental research question is whether the establishment of such scientific infrastructure leads to clustering of related activities in proximity to its location or whether they are spread world-wide independently of the location. We aim to illustrate this question with regard to how inter-regional trade in a research-based knowledge system is fashioned. However, this is also relevant considering the projected investment in EISCAT_3D and prior studies emphasizing that highly-skilled professionals are vital in the knowledge-driven economy, influencing the rise and dynamic evolution of science-based industries and regions (Thorn and Holm-Nielsen, 2008; Trippl and Maier, 2011a).

In terms of results, the study shows that EISCAT contributes to new and diverse technology including how it arises and is traded through network collaborations. Hence, EISCAT provides an example of how inter-regional trade in research-based knowledge is played out. In the case of Kiruna, EISCAT contributes to strengthening the regional competitiveness, mainly through scientific output and inter-regional linkages. New and diverse knowledge enables continual renewal and dynamism of regional competitiveness. EISCAT has also implied a large injection of research funding to the region. However, results also indicate that EISCAT generates minor economic effects in the region. It is argued that ESICAT should not only be considered as a research facility with great scientific value but also as an interconnecting organization in value creating knowledge networks. The study predicts the anticipated development of EISCAT_3D as an investment with many potential implications. Yet, related development work needs to carefully consider how to promote a high level of absorptive capacity among organizations with related activities.

The study is organized as follows. Next section reviews related literature. Section 9.3 presents the development and organization of EISCAT including related research. Section 9.4 examines the economic and societal importance of EISCAT with a specific focus on the scientific outcome and the importance of EISCAT in Kiruna. Concluding remarks, including comparative reflections between space research and mining are found in the end.

## 9.2. Research Infrastructures and Knowledge Trade

Modern economic analysis emphasizes the importance of agglomeration, i.e., the benefits from location-specific external economies of scale, which arise from spatial proximity through the availability of market information, local networking, skilled labor pools, and technology transfers.[1] Hence, producers may enjoy increased productivity by sharing information, common resources and fixed costs, suggesting agents will co-locate and contribute to a dynamic process of increasing returns. However, the evidence of agglomerative effects arising from investments in scientific research infrastructures appears scarce, especially for highly specialized facilities. Horlings *et al.* (2012) argue that the existing literature provides no direct empirical evidence demonstrating that impacts actually occur around scientific research facilities and that there is insufficient evidence to support the claim that such investments will, for instance, attract and retain talent, and promote innovation.

Helmers and Overman (2013) is perhaps the first study to provide empirical evidence on the relationship between agglomeration and a large-scale scientific research infrastructure. Their study considers agglomerative effects of investments in a so-called synchrotron light source in the United Kingdom, and found that the establishment of the Diamond Light Source in Didcot induced clustering of related research activities and increased the research output of nearby organizations, also of organizations that did not utilize the facility. Rekers (2012) has theoretically portrayed the European Spallation Source (ESS) as an enormous injection in the (innovation-based) economy of the Öresund region, and argues that the anticipated benefits associated with ESS are tied to the degree of embeddedness of the facility in regional knowledge networks that facilitate localized learning. However, it is also emphasized that innovation is uncertain, unanticipated and non-linear, where investments do not predictably lead to successful outputs. The argument is rather that impacts can be proactively created.

Although there are theoretical arguments and some empirical evidence in favour of a positive relationship between investments in scientific research infrastructures and agglomeration, at least

[1]Related work has largely been focused on externalities between firms, alternatively university–industry linkages, emphasizing localized knowledge spillover effects and functional regions as arenas for knowledge flows (see for instance: Jaffe, 1989; Jaffe *et al.*, 1993; Saxenian, 1996; Audretsch and Feldman, 1996; Furman *et al.*, 2005).

regarding investments in larger research facilities, there is an alternative approach to understand the locational benefits of research infrastructures. Indeed, there seems to be a general agreement that research infrastructures forge networks and scientific alliances. While David *et al.* (1992) consider this as a potential by-product from establishing new research facilities. Agglomeration and networks are in fact two complementary ways of solving problems of market exchange. This since networks may provide some or all of the external utility gains derived from agglomeration, and precisely for the same reasons (Johansson and Quigley, 2004). For instance, knowledge networks in the global scientific community enlarging the pool of specialized workers can be considered as inter-regional sources of new and diverse knowledge. Owen-Smith and Powell (2004) argue that global networks that consist of nodes of excellence function as pipelines of formal (explicit) and informal (tacit) knowledge. In turn, networks and scientific alliances may have important implications for regional competitiveness.

The importance of networks is further accentuated by the fact that world-class researchers are strongly concentrated in a few major places and tend to embed themselves in these regions by creating multiple knowledge linkages to actors from the academic, industrial and policy sphere. This makes them vital for economic development and growth (Trippl and Maier, 2011b). In general, highly-skilled professionals tend to co-locate and seek places where the most interesting work is being done (Florida, 2002). This increases the importance of being part of networks that include nodes of excellence, which applies to regions with relatively few star scientists and highly skilled professionals. However, as emphasized by Rekers (2012), knowledge does not simply spillover between agents who happen to be located in the same area, and is often not the result of active and intended interaction. Instead, spillovers resulting from alliances seem to be closely related to the institutional commitments and practices of members of the network (Owen-Smith and Powell, 2004). This suggests that in today's globalized knowledge-based economy, where researchers and knowledge work are networked engines of growth and development, it is vital to consider how to promote trade of research knowledge and how to interpret spatially relevant configurations for knowledge accumulation.

Research on highly specialized research facilities appears very limited. Falck *et al.* (2011) have made an attempt to demonstrate how the MAX synchrotron facility in Lund is utilized by researchers across the world and whether there is scope to consider MAX Lab as a research infrastructure with implications in the Baltic Sea region. The main result from this study is that it is not possible to consider MAX as a regional research facility without taking into account the importance of its Nordic, European, and global linkages. This type of empirical study is crucial to understand the locational benefits associated to research facilities, perhaps especially in remote regions with specific environmental conditions.

The study should be conceived in the framework of current attempts to provide a comprehensive map of the pathways to impact of scientific research (see Snickars *et al.*, 2013, for a review). Academic impacts have several interconnecting dimensions. A research project, or a research program, or a research infrastructure, can also generate a wide variety of social and economic impacts, see for instance the analysis in Barber *et al.* (2011) and LeSage *et al.* (2008) for European research network applications.

These impacts occur in different time scales but also in different spatial scales. Since EISCAT has been for a long time identified as a research infrastructure of international importance, its impacts surely have occurred in the global environment. It has constantly produced impact for at least 30 years. It thus seems natural that a proposal like the one presented in Kero *et al.* (2013) would be a prime candidate for continued high priorities. The EISCAT_3D case is further strengthened by its impacts in the region up to now and the impacts created by giving proactive attention to the role of space research in the region.

EISCAT is a research infrastructure for researchers housed in universities at various distances. The research performed is mainly in the area of space physics meaning that such departments around the world are prepared to perform experiments. Even though EISCAT is not a university department, some researchers work in-house in cooperation with researchers in collaborating universities. Seen in the context of inter-regional trade, EISCAT serves as a producer of intermediary inputs for the production of scientific papers. The universities involved have long-term contracts of use. There is a user community which has priority to the use of the facilities.

Other users can also use the facilities but with a lower level of priority. Seen in another perspective of inter-regional trade, the EISCAT research infrastructure provides outputs of experimental results which are shipped to the universities where the scientists are located. The model assumption is that the access to the infrastructure both in activity space and in geographical space determines the level and quality of output. Some papers are co-authored but all have made use of EISCAT. The commonly used assumption in inter-regional trade modeling is whether there is distance decay in knowledge trade, and whether there are economies of scale in scientific production based on experiments.

Krugman (1991) set the stage for a succinct theory of the interplay between geography and trade. He argues that increasing returns to scale have a fundamental role in the economy and that these returns give a decisive role to the historical paths in determining the geography of production and trade. His analysis puts the emphasis on the interplay between increasing returns to scale and geographical accessibility. Harrington *et al.* (1991) review studies of producer or intermediate-services exports from local regions. They structure the studies according to the three basic methodologies: surveys, location quotients, and input–output models. The activities have as their major function inter-regional or international transfer or trade. The distributive services have widespread clients, and benefit from locations with substantial physical and communications infrastructure. Among business and financial services, most establishments serve a local region. The exceptions are particularly specialized, as large firms, or parts of multiregional enterprises. Such firms tend to locate in larger or more specialized urban places. Research itself is not explicitly included in this survey.

Rossi-Hansberg (2005) has developed a spatial theory of trade in which the equilibrium relationship between trade and the spatial distribution of economic activity, as well as the effect of trade frictions exist. In the study a trade model was used with a continuum of regions, transport costs, and agglomeration effects caused by production externalities. In this fashion equilibrium specialization and trade patterns for different levels of transport costs and externality parameters could be derived. Understanding trade *via* the distribution of economic activity in space clarifies the trade-off between border effects and the gravity model assumptions. For the former, the effect of trade barriers is amplified by the formation of new industrial clusters, which affects total factor productivity in some regions. The latter is an immediate implication of spatial agglomeration and congestion forces. We will attempt to apply the theory to knowledge trade in the context of the EISCAT research infrastructure. Agglomeration is fundamental in the global research system. Border effects are created through memberships in the EISCAT organization which impact on the role of distance costs.

Much theoretical and empirical work has been put into the construction of inter-regional input–output tables. An early example of this is the work by Snickars (1979) where a complete system of such tables was estimated for the Swedish economy. The work of Oosterhaven (1988) for the Dutch economy is a seminal contribution to the field. Later research has built operational computable general equilibrium models for regional economies with such tables as fundamental building blocks; see for instance Cascetta *et al.* (2009) for a freight sector application. Recent reviews have been provided by Oosterhaven and Hewings (2014) and Polenske and Nockler (2014) in which benefits and drawbacks of different approaches have been discussed. A common element of most of these approaches is the approach chosen to model the inter-regional flows among sectors and regions. The Leontief–Strout scheme and the Chenery–Moses method are the most commonly used in situations where survey methods are combined with non-survey methods. Even with the advent of so-called big data analysis we are still far away from being able to build the ideal inter-regional and inter-sectoral input model according to the specifications of Leontief and Isard.

The current chapter has used the Chenery–Moses specification as a starting point for the modeling work. To provide an introduction to the approach, let us introduce $X(i, j, r, s)$ as the notation for the flow of intermediate commodities, goods or services, between sector $i$ in region $r$ and sector $j$ in region $s$. The approach in the Chenery–Moses model is the model which flows as a composition of a transport component and a production technology component. Thus $X(i, j, r, s) = T(i, r, s)*A(i, j, s)$ where $A(i, j, s)$ is the input pattern among sectors, $i$, for sector $j$ in region $s$. At the same time $T(i, r, s)$ represents the commodity flows of outputs from sector $i$ in region $r$ among destination region $s$. The assumption is that those flows arrive in regions and are then distributed amongst using sectors $j$. The normal assumption is that $T(i, r, s)$ sums to one when integrating across sending regions, $r$.

In the current application we have information for a single region, Kiruna. Having the pattern of authorships among researchers in various university regions as micro-data we can investigate both the forward and the backward linkages. Looking at the forward linkages, we can see how the flow of knowledge runs from the EISCAT experiments to researchers in different universities. Looking at the backward linkages, we can see how the researchers at EISCAT co-operate across their inter-regional and international networks. Since we have micro-data for a long time series we can perform different explorative analyses of the flow patterns using joint publications as the major indicators of knowledge flows.

At the same time we can illustrate the question of economies of scale by looking at the benefits accruing to different sectors of the Kiruna economy through the specific composition of the economy, the competence of the labor force, and the efficiency of the local and regional economic policies. An interesting question is to what extent the high technology production of the Kiruna mining sector manages to create economies of scale and scope with the space industry. Another interesting question is whether local and regional policy is effective in creating a common business environment. Since the Kiruna region is a very isolated region geographically, one should be able to draw more precise conclusions in this direction than if we were analyzing production externalities in a metropolitan region.

## 9.3. EISCAT

It was the access to the auroral region that was the main reason for the European Space Research Organization (ESRO) to locate the European sounding rocket range (Esrange) to the Kiruna area in the 1960s (taken over by Sweden in 1973) and the same arguments were behind the decision by France, Germany and Great Britain to be part of the first incoherent scatter radar in the auroral zone, scientifically and economically, which led to the establishment in the 1970s of the EISCAT. It is the first, and still the only, international research facility with its seat in Sweden, operating in accordance with Swedish laws.[2]

In the mid-1970s academies and research councils in Finland, France, Germany, Norway, Sweden, and United Kingdom decided to make a joint effort to exploit the incoherent scatter radar technique in order to study the aurora and high altitude ionosphere. This effort resulted in the establishment of the EISCAT and the art radar systems located north of the Arctic Circle in Sodankylä, Tromsø, and Kiruna, and later also on Spitsbergen, near Longyearbyen, at Svalbard. Japan joined EISCAT in 1996 and the People's Republic of China in 2007, while France left the association in 2006 and Germany in 2011. The exit of France and Germany was partly caused by changes in scientific direction and the lack of long term support for research involving EISCAT. The present member states of the association are, China Research Institute of Radiowave Propagation (CRIRP), Academy of Finland (SA), National Institute of Polar Research (NIPR) and Solar-Terrestrial Environment Laboratory of Nagoya University (STEL) from Japan, The Research Council of Norway (RCN), Swedish Research Council (VR), and Natural Environment Research Council (NERC) of the United Kingdom.

[2]For a detailed background to the history and development of EISCAT, see e.g., Hultqvist (2011), Oksman (2011) and Holt (2012).

EISCAT's facilities represent the state of the art in global incoherent scatter radars, operating three radar systems: one 224 MHz tri-static radar system with transmitter in Tromsø and receivers in Sodankylä and Kiruna, one 931 MHz UHF radar in Tromsø and two 500 MHz UHF radars in Svalbard. In addition, EISCAT operates an ionosphere modification heating facility situated nearby Tromsø. In total, there are ten incoherent scatter radars in the world. The most recent of the world's incoherent scatter radars are EISCAT's Svalbard Radar and the Resolute Bay Incoherent Scatter Radars (RISR) in North America.[3]

There are two main operation modes for experimental work at EISCAT. Common programs are designed to the requests of the members and include internationally and often globally coordinated observations of the ionosphere and magnetosphere, as well as long term observations. Special programs cover most user requests and include, for instance, observations of the dynamics and structure of the ionosphere and magnetosphere, and coordinated projects involving several instruments, satellite overpasses, and rocket launches. There is also an additional mode with other programs covering all other requests.

In terms of accessibility to the research facilities, the member states nominate a contact point for observation time. A limited amount of observation time is available for researchers from third party users, i.e., non-member states. Third party time is distributed through international competition by peer-review. Research projects using data from EISCAT are expected to acknowledge the provided support in published research work, such as journal articles and PhD theses. Over the period 2005–2013, nearly 700 researchers have contributed with scientific publications with a link to EISCAT. Three out of four of these researchers were affiliated to institutes in the member states. Scientific publications are the most important outcome from research work linked to EISCAT and most publications are the result of joint efforts.

---

[3] http://amisr.com/amisr/about/resolute-bay-isrs/.

The research usually takes place within a granted research project and comprises several participating researchers from different institutes and countries. Larger projects typically involve 10–15 researchers (for instance, Havnes *et al.*, 2006; Blagoveshchenskaya *et al.*, 2011), while smaller projects often consisted of only a single researcher and his advisor or a few experienced researchers (for instance, Grydeland *et al.*, 2005; Baddeley *et al.*, 2011). There are also non-experimental projects that seek to describe or anticipate some methodological, technical or organizational developments of EISCAT (see for instance, Virtanen *et al.*, 2008; Wannberg *et al.*, 2010).

Collaboration between the research team and EISCAT staff is central in most projects. For instance, the research team defines an experiment to which EISCAT staff contributes with specific technological knowledge and experience, and assists in project implementation. It is not unusual that EISCAT staff is also actively involved as researchers in the projects, including authoring journal articles. The specific technological knowledge and experience of EISCAT staff makes them a central ingredient in many research projects. This implies that EISCAT staff is fundamental for the research output and, more generally, in generating new scientific knowledge.

EISCAT_3D is the next generation international atmosphere and geospace research radar with planned start of construction in 2016, first operations in 2018, and to be in full operation in 2021. For a full EISCAT_3D system, the required investments are estimated to more than 1.1 billion SEK (135 million €), including 105 million SEK (12 million €) contingency. The operating budget will amount to approximately 65–70 MSEK per year including 30 employees. EISCAT_3D is still a projected joint-investment by the EISCAT member states. Third party usage will be possible.

Fully developed, EISCAT_3D is planned to be composed of five radar stations spread out over a distance of several hundred kilometres comprising large fields of antennas. One of the stations will be equipped with a powerful (10 MW) transmitter. This will facilitate combined radar observations in magnetic zenith with *in-situ* measurement payloads onboard rockets launched from the Esrange Space Centre in Kiruna.

Observations using EISCAT_3D will contribute substantially to enhancing climate models and thus give more accurate information in the climate change field. Furthermore, EISCAT_3D will be used to measure the inflow of meteoric material toward the Earth and thus enable a deeper understanding of the mechanisms of cloud formation. This form of cloud computing will also be of use to assess the dangers of these fast-flying objects for satellites and human space excursions. Further areas of societal relevance where EISCAT_3D can be useful are in the mapping space debris and to understand the effects of space weather. This will contribute to guarantee that infrastructures of vital importance to society continue to function, e.g., satellite communication and navigation, and power grids.

## 9.4. Data and Methods

Annual micro-data on scientific publications (journal articles and PhD theses) are utilized to examine research processes linked to EISCAT. All known published journal articles that appeared in adequately refereed scientific journals with an obvious link to EISCAT are included. The link to EISCAT is identified either through the inclusion of an acknowledgment to EISCAT in each journal article, the use of EISCAT observations, or through some obvious and adequate contents that may take the form of anecdotal evidences and prospect papers linked to the EISCAT facilities. Theoretical papers are included if the reported work arises directly from EISCAT research. PhD theses are considered as an additional indication of research processes linked to EISCAT.

All reported publications are unique, i.e., a publication may only appear once over the specified time period. Other types of research outcomes are excluded, including conference papers, technical reports, and student reports. Furthermore, conference papers sometimes may be considered as an early form of journal articles, at least usually aiming at being published in academic journals. Hence, omitting this form of papers should also reduce the risk of the same work being counted more than once. The quality of the assembled publication database is estimated to be high.

The included publication data are divided into two time periods. The first time period comprises general information on all publications (journal articles and PhD theses) since EISCAT was first taken into operation until the last known publication in the present year, i.e., from 1982–2013, implying all available observations are included. The second time period comprises detailed information on each publication over the period 2005–2013. This information includes annual metadata on the affiliation of each author, collected publication-by-publication from the journal websites. When an author has multiple affiliations, only the first listed affiliation as given on each specific publication is considered. We also use journal impact factor (JIF) information from Thomas Reuters to derive a quality measure of the scientific publications linked to EISCAT. The resulting micro-database is used to analyze and explore the scientific work related to EISCAT and discuss the importance of scientific networks for the inter-regional trade of research knowledge.

The methodological approach is to utilize bibliometric information to explore and analyze the above mentioned research questions. The results are used to indicate where research processes take place and how these processes are inter-related, rather than how these processes arise and their implications. The preparatory data manipulation rests upon a set of specific routines developed and implemented in 'Stata' to collect the geographical location of the affiliated institutes of all researchers listed as authors in publications linked to ESICAT. The information on latitudes and longitudes of each affiliation is collected for each city *via* Google maps through an application programming interface (API) coding (for a description, see Ozimek and Miles, 2011). A geographical information system (GIS) is used to map these results.

Furthermore, since the bibliometric information is authorship-specific, we are able to derive a matrix with detailed information of how all authors are inter-related including how many co-authorships each relationship rests upon. From the perspective of network theory (Johansson and Quigley, 2004, among others), researchers' affiliations (research institutes) are network nodes and co-authorships establishes edges between the nodes. As a result, nodes and edges form pairwise linkages including link-weights for each publication, where linkages indicate joint-publications and link-weights indicate the number of joint-publications between a specific pair. Double back relationships between nodes are controlled so that each pairwise linkage is unique. It is within the presented networks that transactions of knowledge trade can be expected to take place. The visual exploration of the networks is made using 'Gephi' (for a description, see Bastian *et al.*, 2008, among others). In addition to the pairwise information, we use the number of authorships by each research institute to indicate the scientific productivity in EISCAT related research.

## 9.5. Results

After the facilities were taken into operation in 1981, there has been a remarkable scientific output in terms of publications. The first journal articles were published in 1982 and the first PhD theses in 1984. Subsequently, more than 1,600 journal articles and almost 100 PhD theses have been completed. Figure 9.1 illustrates the annual number of published journal articles and PhD theses over the period 1982–2013.

Overall, the figure signals a strong development and regeneration of researchers using incoherent scatter radar techniques including EISCAT. Access to research funds, trends and regeneration in research and education are presumable factors that can be expected to impact the yearly development of scientific output in terms of journal articles and PhD theses. Notably, the publication rate appears to have declined during the 2000s.

Citation analysis (White and McCain, 1989), considers counts of citations to a given work to acknowledge the influence, value and usefulness of that specific piece of work. It has not been possible in this context to collect micro information to follow scientometric principles to measure and analyze the influence of scientific publications linked to EISCAT. Instead, we use JIFs to arrive at an

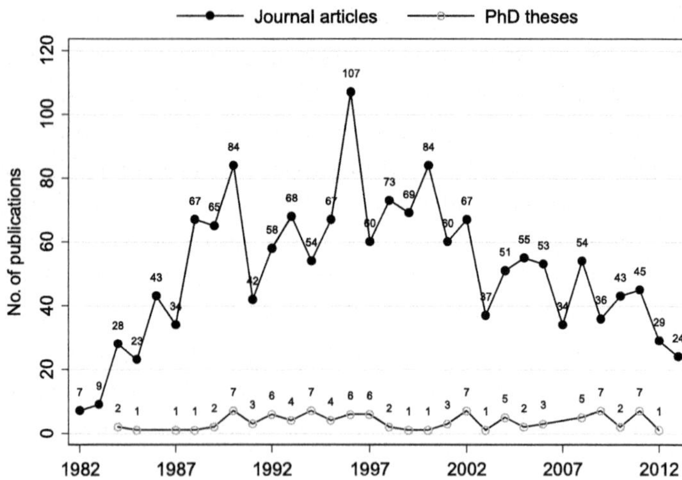


**Figure 9.1.** Published journal articles and PhD theses, 1982–2013.

*Sources*: Own computation of publication data from EISCAT.

applicable quality measure of each publication: <1 Low impact, 1–3 Medium impact, 3–10 High impact, >10 Very high impact. The impact factor is a measure of the frequency with which the average article in a specific journal has been cited in a particular year or period. The classification is founded upon JIF-information for 2012 from Thomas Reuters and seeks to separate related journals by importance. The impact factors range from 0.17 to 38.6 with a mean of 2.2 and standard deviation of 3.2. Journals without impact factor are omitted. Figure 9.2 illustrates the annual number of published journal articles by impact factor category. Notably, the publication impact rate seems to have declined during the 2000s.

Most articles are published in journals with a medium or high impact factor, suggesting between 1 and 10 expected citations per article. Relatively few articles are published in journals with low or very high impact factor. In total, 14 articles have been published in top ranked journals (very high impact factor): '*Nature*', '*Physics Reports*', and '*Reviews of Geophysics*', which all had a journal impact factor above 10 in 2012. However, only one of those articles has been published in top ranked journals since 1996. Nearly 80% of all

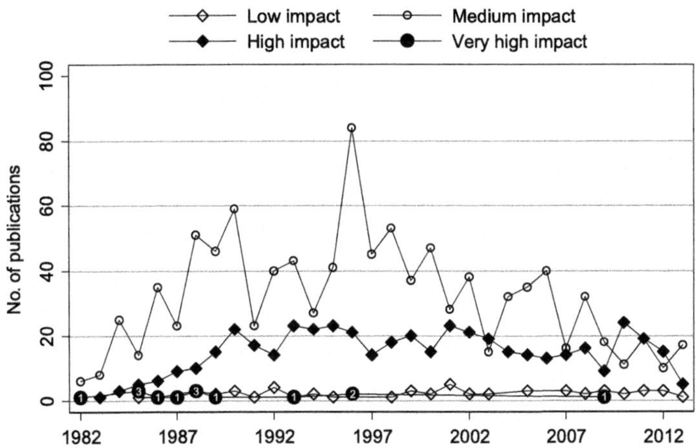


**Figure 9.2.** Published journal articles by impact factor category, 1982–2013.

*Note*: JIFs: <1 Low impact, 1–3 Medium impact, 3–10 High impact, >10 Very high impact. The number of publications with very high impact factor is labelled within the points of the corresponding slope.

*Sources*: Own computation of publication data from EISCAT, and information on JIFs in 2012 from Thomas Reuters.

articles have been published in five different scientific journals, which are classified as medium or high impact journals, with *Geophysical Research Letters* and *Journal of Geophysical Research: Space Physics*, belonging to the top range.

The most obvious approach to examine the spatial configuration of scientific work is to consider the spatial dimension of the affiliation(s) of each researcher participating in research projects. One could also examine career dynamics among researchers, and study how researchers from different institutes collaborate to achieve new results. In the present context, spatial information is useful to enhance the understanding of the importance of EISCAT to researchers in different parts of the world and how a research infrastructure contributes to promote inter-regional trade of knowledge through global pipelines among knowledge agents.

We continue by examining each researcher's spatial affiliation as listed in each published journal article and completed PhD thesis between 2005 and 2013. Spatial affiliation is the location of each affiliated institute by city. If a researcher has registered multiple affiliations on a published article, only the first listed affiliation is considered. This reduces complexity but also implies that some links may be omitted. Since researchers may have contributed to several publications and also have had multiple (first listed) affiliations over the period, we let the scientific production be denoted by academic authorship. Authorship is claimed by individuals who made an intellectual contribution to the completion of the research described in the published journal article. This approach implies that when a journal article has more than one author, there is as much authorship as there are authors. Using authorships should ease the interpretation of the spatial configuration of scientific work linked to EISCAT.PhD theses are treated as individual works.

Before the spatial configuration of scientific work linked to EISCAT is presented, it is necessary to first review the data for the examined period 2005–2013. In total, the data comprises 373 published journal articles, including 2,060 authorships, made by 678 researchers affiliated to 196 institutes across 31 different countries. In addition, 27 PhD theses were completed by doctoral candidates from seven different countries, all members of EISCAT. Figure 9.3 illustrates the spatial configuration of scientific work linked to EISCAT over the period 2005–2013. The figure also specifies which countries are members, prior members, and non-members of the association, and the locations of existing incoherent scatter radars in the world, showing the EISCAT facilities are the only incoherent scatter radars in the European Union.

Even if the researchers that utilize the facilities are widely spread across the world and EISCAT appears as a global research infrastructure, there is a large concentration of authorship claimed by researchers affiliated to institutes in the member states of EISCAT and in the United States. Out of the totally 2,060 authorship, 20% are linked to institutes in the United Kingdom, 13% to institutes in Norway, 11% to institutes in Sweden and the United States, and 9% to institutes in Finland and Japan. This implies that totally approximately 75% of the scientific production is linked to institutes in the member states or in the United States.

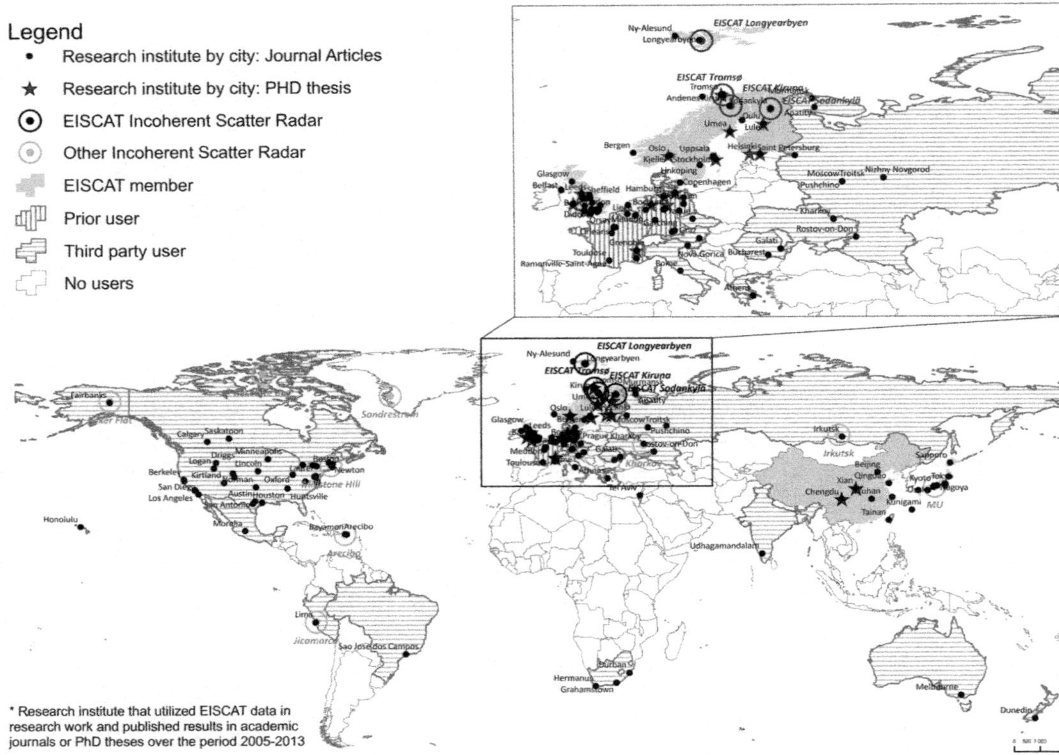


**Figure 9.3.** Spatial configuration of scientific work linked to EISCAT 2005–2013.

*Sources*: Own computation of publication data from EISCAT and journal websites, and locational information on latitudes and longitudes of affiliations by city *via* Google maps through API coding.

If we decompose these results by institute, the 10 most productive institutes make up almost 44% of all authorships. These institutes are situated in Sweden, Norway, Finland, United Kingdom, and Japan. The three institutes with most authorships are the Swedish Institute of Space Physics (IRF), EISCAT Scientific Association,[4] and the University of Tromsø. Nearly every fifth of the authorships is linked to these institutes. The Arctic and Antarctic Research Institute (AANII), which is a Russian research institute situated in St. Petersburg, has most authorships among institutes in non-member states.

EISCAT should not solely be considered as a scientific research facility, it is also to be seen as an interconnecting infrastructure and organization in value, creating knowledge networks with global reach. The value of these networks cannot be ignored since most of the scientific outputs linked to EISCAT are the results of joint efforts, i.e., most journal articles have multiple authors that are often affiliated to different institutes and frequently also to different countries. Research projects linked to EISCAT should therefore enable global transactions of formal (explicit) and informal (tacit) knowledge between researchers.

In general, this suggests that collaboration between researchers is not only crucial for the scientific results; it is also an important outcome, at least when knowledge transactions and other effects arise through network alliances. Hence, there are potentials for knowledge trade and spillovers between researchers participating in joint-projects, which would be worthy of further empirical study, for instance through interviews (see also Owen-Smith and Powell, 2004). A researcher that is member of a relatively productive researcher network may benefit from his membership by improved scientific productivity and excellence. Other potential benefits may take the

[4]As a single transnational organization, EISCAT Scientific Association is the second most productive institute. However, if we decompose authorships by subunit, EISCAT in Kiruna and Tromsø would be the seventh and ninth most productive institutes with 60 and 55 authorships, respectively, while EISCAT in Longyearbyen and Sodankylä would only have a few authorships.

form of demonstration effects such as insights on alternative working procedures and ways to organize research, and network linkages that imply access to additional networks, funds, and research facilities. There may also be benefits in the form of new career opportunities and hence that knowledge can be more easily transferred across institutions. These are unprized advantages that can be denoted technological spillovers to which EISCAT contributes as an interconnecting infrastructure and organization by motivating collaboration between researchers.

The following graphs are based on micro-data analysis using graph theoretic models (described by Bastian *et al.*, 2008, among others). The analyses are performed with the help of the software package 'Gephi' in which the strength of interaction links are formally analyzed. The data used consist of collaboration in article production across the indicated time period. Figure 9.4 demonstrates collaborations (internal and external) between institutes[5] that resulted in published journal articles associated with EISCAT over the period 2005–2013. The figure is founded upon the earlier presented data for the period 2005–2013, comprising 373 published journal articles including 2,060 authorships, made by 678 researchers affiliated to 196 institutes across 31 different countries. The figure also specifies whether an institute is situated in a member state (nodes are blue), prior member state (nodes are red) or third party state (nodes are green). Institutes are nodes proportional to the (log) number of authorships. Linkages are coloured by the main source node and widths are proportional to the (log) number of pairwise joint-publications.

The main result is that scientific work linked to EISCAT is largely the outcome of research collaborations, and not by individual organizations or researchers. The strongest linkages appear to be between a few institutes in the member states, which have many joint publications and also a relatively large scientific output in terms of authorships. These nodes and links appear as the main research

[5]Research institutes are used as arbiters to researchers in order to reduce complexity in the resulting network plot.

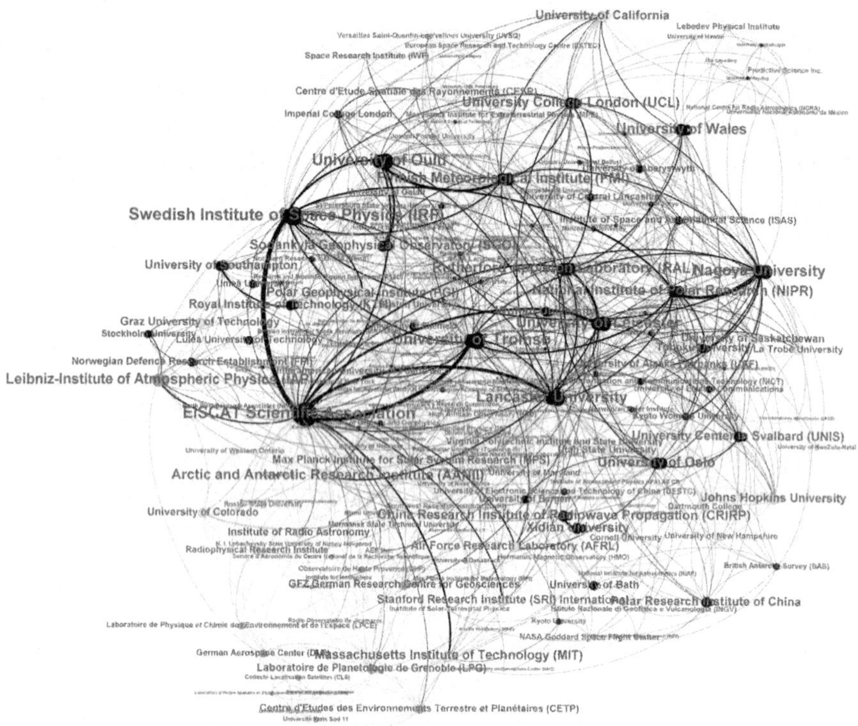


**Figure 9.4.** Scientific collaborations (research projects) that resulted in published articles, 2005–2013.

*Notes*: Nodes are black when an institute is situated in a member state, grey signifies prior member states (France and Germany), and light grey signifies third party user, i.e., institute from a non-member state that is not a prior member. Institutes are nodes proportional to the (log) number of authorships. Linkages are coloured by the source node and are proportional to the (log) number of pairwise joint-publications.

structure associated with EISCAT. The links between institutes in old member states of EISCAT and Chinese institutes are relatively weak. China is the most recent member state and only joined in 2007. The figure also demonstrates the importance of the relatively small EISCAT staff which is linked to a remarkable number of joint publications. Overall, this is a relatively strong indication that EISCAT promotes inter-regional trade of research knowledge across the globe.

The answer to the question of EISCAT's regional implications has several distinct features to it. While one feature relates to purely economic effects, another feature is how EISCAT contributes to strengthen the regional competitiveness. The overall assessment is that EISCAT contributes to strengthen the regional competitiveness but generates only minor purely economic effects, such as consumption of local goods and facilities including hotels, airports, energy, tourist attractions, and so on.[6]

Indeed, though we do not make a thorough examination of economic effects, the magnitude of the latter type of effects is reflected by the nature and scale of activities related to EISCAT at each site. The activities in Sodankylä, Tromsø and Svalbard are mainly operational, including radar work and assisting researchers to conduct experiments at site or remotely. Only few employees are located at these sites. Operational work is also made in Kiruna, where EISCAT headquarters are based and most non-operational activities take place, including administration, project management, and development work. In 2012, EISCAT had 22 employees in total of which 11 were situated in Kiruna, seven in Tromsø, three in Svalbard, and one in Sodankylä.[7] In addition, a large number of researchers

[6]For instance, there is an indirect link between EISCAT and northern lights tourism. Kiruna is located at the aurora belt and statistically offers relatively many occasions for observing northern lights (Aurora Borealis). Mainly because Kiruna and particularly the nearby mountain lodge Abisko are located in one of the darkest areas in Europe with little artificial lights from nearby cities, which also enjoys rain shadow from the Atlantic Ocean, implying relatively good conditions for observing northern lights. There are about half million tourists visiting Kiruna every year, of which about 30% are foreigners that mainly make visits between September and March, i.e., the months when conditions are particularly good for northern lights observations. The turnover of the tourist industry in Kiruna is estimated to about 600 million SEK (65 million €), of which perhaps about a third, associates to a combination of winter tourist attractions including northern lights and the Ice Hotel. There are special Aurora seminars given by the Swedish Institute of Space Physics (IRF), which partly is founded on research derived from EISCAT. A particularity for this tourism is that there is a direct air link (nine hour flight) between Tokyo and Kiruna, which is exclusive in Sweden.

[7]Personnel costs account for about half of EISCATs total budget which in 2012 amounted to nearly 30 million SEK.

who conduct experiments with EISCAT usually make visits during the project work.

The amount of visiting researchers varies from year to year but usually amounts to at least 100 persons every year. In general, this indicates that it is unlikely to expect major economic effects from EISCAT in terms of consumption and employment.[8] Indeed, EISCAT is a relatively small entity at the regional scale, even in Kiruna where a range of space-related activities have been in operation since the end of the 1950s. That period started with the establishment of what today is known as the Swedish Institute of Space Physics (IRF) and the Esrange Space Centre (rockets and balloons).

EISCAT has been used by both researchers from member countries and by researchers from third party countries. Is there reason to believe that the academic impacts of the publications differ and to what extent do these patterns differ geographically? In the first instance, member countries would have a higher priority to funding research using EISCAT which would imply, *ceteris paribus*, higher academic impacts. We have not tested the hypothesis statistically but from a first analysis there is no distinct pattern. The second hypothesis would be that membership acts like a global selection mechanism and shield. Thus distance would not be as important among researchers from member countries as from third party countries. Analysing distance decay would also have a connection to the hypothesis of the Chenery–Moses model in which trade flows go from EISCAT to different countries and are then providing input into their production sectors. Figure 9.5 shows the number of publications among researchers in different cities and regions worldwide using EISCAT facilities. The left part shows the pattern for researchers in current or former member countries. The right part shows the corresponding pattern for researchers in third party countries.

We observe that research production is higher among researchers in current or former member countries. Membership clearly boosts the number of publications. There is one pattern for European

[8]In comparison, there were about 13,000 employees in Kiruna municipality in 2011, of which space-related work amounted, in total, to about 1%.

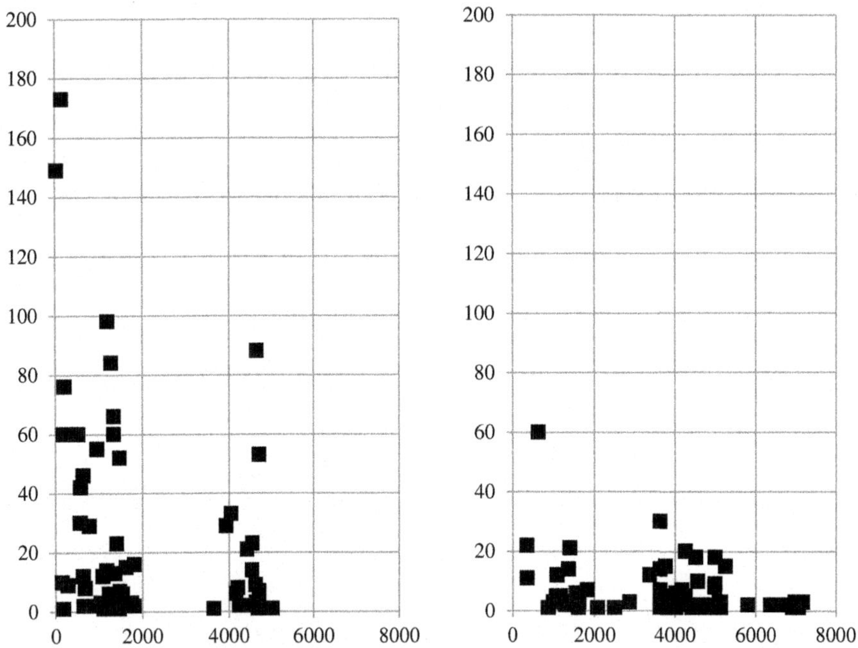


**Figure 9.5.** Number of publications 2005–2013 by air distance from EISCAT for members or former members (left) and third party users (right).

linkages and one for intercontinental linkages. A weak element of distance decay can be observed which is also corroborated through a set of regressions. There is a two-tier structure of the results; some publications seem to originate within the European research networks while others are generated in intercontinental networks. The third party distance pattern seems to follow the gravity assumption, somewhat more clearly than the membership one. A deeper analysis of the data strengthens the idea that there are research hubs in the space physics field in different countries in which researchers work on similar problems and engage in collaboration using the EISCAT radar systems.

Several space-related educational activities were established during the 1990s (see Hultqvist, 2011). The number of employees in space-related activities in Kiruna is illustrated in Figure 9.6, demonstrating a strong development especially during 1990s, including

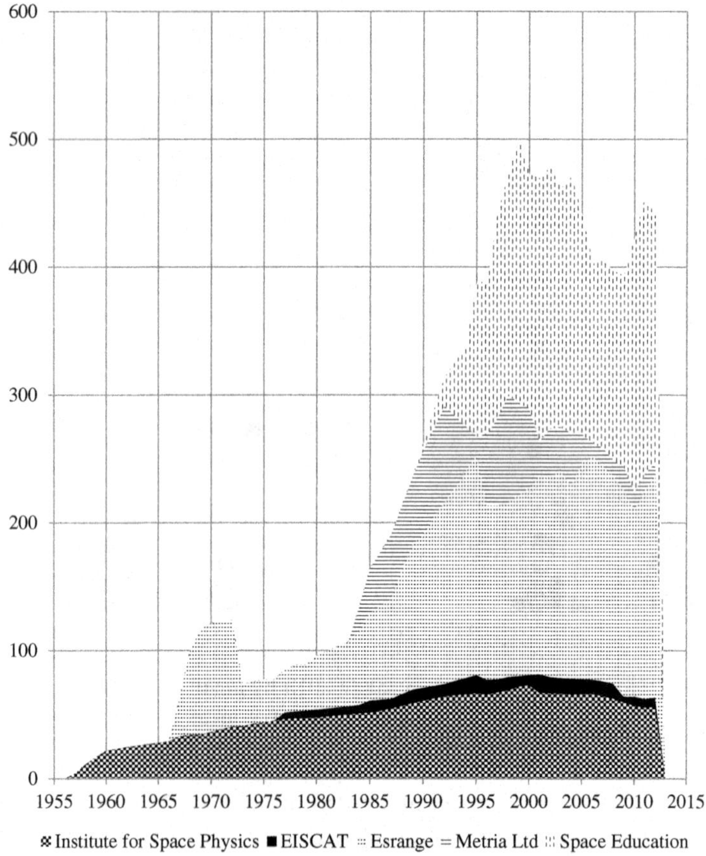


**Figure 9.6.** Number of employees (and students) in space-related activities including EISCAT in Kiruna, 1957–2012.

*Sources*: Swedish Institute of Space Physics (IRF).

the relative importance and development of EISCAT in terms of employment. The figure also illustrates the well-known relationship between basic research and commercial applications. It took a few decades of basic research, including the very early activities at Esrange, until commercial services related to various kinds of space activities were established and they then grew much faster than the basic research activities in terms of number of employees.

Several local and regional organizations collaborate with EISCAT. For instance, there is a continuous collaboration with Luleå University of Technology (LTU) where EISCAT staff participates as lecturers in a course on optical and radar based observations. This course also enables students to actively use EISCAT's facilities. EISCAT staff also participates in giving advice on how to develop the course and provides opportunities for students to use EISCAT in thesis work. Approximately 50 students participate in this course every year. There are also some associated educational activities at the University Centre in Svalbard (UNIS), which in turn is closely related to the University of Tromsø. There is no specific link between EISCAT and the Space gymnasium (upper secondary school) in Kiruna.

In addition, researchers use EISCAT as a complementary research facility to Esrange, which is a state owned non-defence related facility mainly used for launching rockets, balloons, and testing technologies such as high-velocity vehicles. Approximately 20 launches take place at Esrange Space Centre every year, which usually are made within the framework of five or six campaigns.[9] Some experiments within these campaigns are linked to EISCAT, which typically is used for measurements on the space environment that may influence the course of rockets.

There have traditionally been few commercial interests even in very advanced special elements used in the EISCAT equipment because the market is very small. Currently, there appears no particular economic relationship between EISCAT and private firms. If we consider the overall space industry in Sweden, there are only few commercial organizations with space industry applications, which totally amount to less than 40 organizations and around 1,200 employees. Nearly all of these employees (about 95% in 2010) are located in greater Stockholm and greater Gothenburg. They are oriented toward applications not directly related to EISCAT, and thus it is challenging to consider agglomerative effects at least in terms of corporate entrepreneurship arising from EISCAT.

[9]A rocket campaign costs about 5–10 million SEK.

Furthermore, the engineering and development work associated with the current facilities has largely been made in-house by EISCAT staff in cooperation with universities. However, the implementation of EISCAT_3D will be made through procurements of equipment and construction work from different organizations.

Another observation to be made is that EISCAT is a high-technology organization with activities in relatively small remote regional economies that interconnects many scientific organizations and communities across the world. EISCAT is a visitor-intensive activity, albeit at a small scale of operation. These network linkages may imply the same type of external utility gains derived from agglomeration of similar or dissimilar activities (see also Gunasekara, 2006). They are expected to arise by connecting the region to extra-regional sources of new and diverse knowledge.

The strategic context of EISCAT may also be extended to regional development work in northern Sweden. EISCAT and in particular EISCAT_3D relates to several of the flagship incentives and investments priorities in the EU Horizon 2020 framework, for instance, promoting technology transfers and smart specialization. In addition, EISCAT_3D was included as a Swedish initiative to the EU research infrastructure roadmap in 2008 as one of the 44 largest research infrastructures in Europe within the environmental sciences. Investments in research infrastructure facilities through structural funds are pointed out as vital to increase the overall competitiveness of the European Union. A specific target is to achieve linkages between regions with little competitive advantages in other fields of activity. Hence, EISCAT can be considered as a prioritized infrastructure also in a strategic context, which may have important implications in several small remote European regions.

An example to increase the understanding for the regional importance of EISCAT in a strategic context is that EISCAT has brought into the region more financial resources than Sweden has paid in fees to EISCAT. The research funding in EISCAT related projects from the Swedish Research Council (VR) alone is significant and has over the last 12 years amounted to approximately 32 million

SEK (~3.6 million €) across 20 different projects. More than a third has directly been allocated to EISCAT and the Swedish Institute of Space Physics (IRF) in Kiruna. All in all, this indicates that EISCAT is not only a strategic infrastructure for scientific research; it also represents a large regional injection in terms of research funding.

## 9.6. Concluding Analysis

While the scientific value of EISCAT is widely accepted, the knowledge on its economic and societal importance is scarce. This question is the focal point in this study and arises when one considers the present work with the next generation of such research facilities. Thus, EISCAT_3D is anticipated to provide researchers with opportunities to conduct novel scientific experiments that may shift the frontiers in several scientific disciplines and could also be used to develop services with specific societal values. Can there also be innovative ways of boosting the role of the new installation for science? Can we learn from an analysis of the international and inter-regional knowledge trade patterns? Is there reason to alter the role of the EISCAT organization to open the infrastructure for more fundamental free-rider research?

We have examined the economic and societal importance of EISCAT, including the nature, scale, and spatial configuration of related scientific work and other activities. It has been demonstrated that ESICAT will give rise to slightly more diversified local labor market, positively affect the human capital level and consumption of local goods and facilities, and perhaps also function as a magnet for highly-skilled professionals. However, it appears that EISCAT neither resulted in any substantial clustering of related activities nor had any significant agglomerative economic effects in the short and medium term. Instead, EISCAT seems to contribute to strengthen regional competitiveness and attractiveness in a more general sense, suggesting the economic and societal importance of EISCAT as a knowledge infrastructure is long term and should be interpreted in a strategic context. There are several aspects to this, of which, one aspect is that EISCAT is an important node in the space cluster in northern Scandinavia, which includes several complementary organizations such as the Swedish Institute of Space Physics, the Esrange Space Centre and Luleå University of Technology. EISCAT has also implied an additional injection of research funding in the region to the benefit of Swedish, and European, space research.

Another important aspect of impact is that EISCAT is an interconnecting infrastructure in knowledge networks with global reach. The gains from these network linkages or global knowledge pipelines relate to transactions of formal and informal knowledge and other advantages including memberships in scientific communities that contribute to renewal and dynamism of local knowledge. These network linkages may imply the same type of external utility gains derived from any agglomeration of similar or dissimilar activities, and can be expected to arise from extra-regional sources of new and diverse knowledge. An example of a spillover channel through which this knowledge may percolate is, for example, educational contributions that EISCAT staff is engaged in at Luleå University of Technology, and in doctoral works related to EISCAT.

The study concludes that among the important potential implications of EISCAT, perhaps the main advantage of hosting EISCAT_3D in Kiruna and Northern Scandinavia is that it will be the world's best research facility of its kind, which will significantly strengthen the international status of Kiruna as a centre of space-related physics research. If conceived in a proactive mode it will make a significant contribution to the regional competitiveness and attractiveness. However, the related development work needs to carefully consider how to promote a high level of absorptive capacity among organizations with related activities, i.e., the mining industry. This is in order to maximize the potential benefits of hosting one of the world's most advanced scientific research infrastructures and to facilitate localized learning and thus contribute to strengthen the nation and region as well as the city of Kiruna. In terms of the classification of impacts presented in the chapter introduction several observations can be made.

First of all, the main impacts of EISCAT stay within the academic system. It creates worldwide academic advancement through the use of innovative equipments, techniques and technologies in a cross-disciplinary setting. The existence of the infrastructure in northern Sweden has a positive side-effect for training and teaching of students at several academic levels and in several Swedish universities engaged in space-related research and education.

EISCAT has played a role in creating social and economic impacts but there is no distinct profile. It is clear that EISCAT's activities increase public engagement and interest in research on space. The fact that this research is effectively performed in Kiruna clearly adds to the role of northern Sweden as a space cluster. This aspect of EISCAT could be further promoted through linking with other infrastructures in Kiruna, such as Esrange. It might also be remarked that the LKAB mining activities are also research-intensive, adding to the role of Kiruna as a northern research-specialized region.

EISCAT enhances cultural enrichment and quality of life in view of its attractiveness for cultural tourism. In summary, it might be said that there is a considerable potential to promote social and economic impacts of the space sector in Kiruna, especially if one considers the sector in broad terms. The space sector is also a good example of how organizations can work together in the regions above the Arctic Circle. In this context it is interesting to observe that EISCAT has had a very strong role in the national research infrastructure system in Sweden, and at the European level. It is still the only research infrastructure at the European level for which Sweden has been the host for the longest period. This international visibility, however, does not seem to fully penetrate to the level of regional and local decision making. There is room for action, for instance in relation to the new policy round within the structural funds.

The final issue to consider is the empirical EISCAT study's contribution to the theory and practice of inter-regional and international trade, and the theory of agglomeration and spillovers. We will do this in the context of the Krugman and Rossi-Hansberg arguments of geography and trade, in which competitiveness arises and regional development occurs though the interplay between economies of scale and scope and inter-regional and international accessibility. First, it is obvious from the analysis that there are no direct linkages between space research and research in mining. The two production systems simply coexist in the region without explicit mediation of contacts *via* the university system and the public sector. There is also very little spillover of competence within the labor force. The space research networks do not seem to coincide with the mining research networks. The most important factors producing scale and scope economies seems to be trough education, and through inter-regional and international accessibility created through the air transport system. Second, geography plays a role further to the one related to accessibility, simply in view of the climatic conditions in northern Sweden and its desolate nature. Resources opened up for global use by the mining sectors have created an opportunity for Kiruna to compete also in the specialized field of experimental space physics. In the future, there should be vast opportunities to develop the Kiruna science cluster making use of such synergies.

The study has not included a balanced treatment of the space research and mining industries. It would be interesting to perform such a study in which the two global sectors would be treated on an equal empirical basis. There is some reason to believe that the knowledge trade in technological development in mining should have characteristics similar to the ones in space research. Long term user contracts in space research would then correspond to long-term delivery contracts in the value-added chains of mining. Such a comparative approach could also be used to more formally test the classical theories and models of inter-regional and international trade.

The main assumption of the Chenery–Moses model in this context is the separation of input technology in different sectors from the transport component. Also in this context the current analysis is exploratory. The novelty comes from the systematic publication data on research cooperation as a way of testing the functional characteristics of the $T(i, r, s)$-component in the Chenery–Moses model. We have shown the global nature of these networks and discussed the importance of those networks for science itself, and for the status of the EISCAT radar system and the Kiruna region.

We have shown that the research system seems to have a two-tier structure with intercontinental knowledge flows complemented by flows within the space physics research agglomerations within continents. More research should be fruitful in this field.

## Acknowledgments

We would like to express our highest appreciation to the EISCAT staff and all other participators for their willingness to enable this project and for providing access to the sources of information not earlier made available for evaluation research. Particular thanks go to Dr Anders Tjulin, Dr Assar Westman, Dr Craig Heinselman, Dr Ingemar Häggström, Dr Ingrid Mann, Dr Mike Rietveld, and Mr Henrik Andersson, all at EISCAT, who have contributed with valuable information, insights, and support. The project has also benefited from important insights from Dr Johan Kero at the Swedish Institute of Space Physics (IRF) that also contributed with the text in box 3.1, Nicola Manuel Schlatter at the Royal Institute of Technology (KTH) that provided inputs on the text describing the research process, Dr Lars Eliasson, Director at IRF, Mattias Abrahamsson at SSCSPACE, and Mattias Mannberg from the tourist section of Kiruna in Swedish Lapland. The project is also grateful to Dr Magnus Friberg at EISCAT and the Swedish Research Council (VR) who initiated the project, and for general support from Professor Göran Cars, Professor Ulf Karlsson, Dr Nickolay Ivchenko, all at KTH, Dr Johan Holmberg at VR, Governor Sven-Erik Österberg at the County Administrative Board of Norrbotten, and Municipal Director Peter Niemi and Anders Lundgren at Kiruna municipality. Last, we are highly grateful for valuable comments on a draft version of the study from Professor Bengt Hultqvist that also contributed with several detailed insights and suggestions as well as clarifying texts which are included in the report. The project has been financed by EISCAT Scientific Association. The authors are fully responsible for the content, conclusions and possible mistakes.

## References

Audretsch, DB and MA Feldman (1996) R&D spillovers and the geography of innovation and production, *The American Economic Review* 86(3), 630–640.

Baddeley, LJ, I Häggström, TK Yeoman and MT Rietveld (2011) First observations of SPEAR-induced top- and bottom-side sporadic E-layer heating observed using the EISCAT Svalbard and SuperDARN radars, *Journal of Geophysical Research* 117, 401307.

Barber, MJ, MM Fischer and T Scherngell (2011) The community structure of R&D cooperation in Europe: Evidence from a social network perspective, *Geographical Analysis* 43(4), 415–432.

Bastian, M, S Heymann and M Jacomy (2008) Gephi: An open source software for exploring and manipulating networks. *Proceedings of the Third International ICWSM Conference 2009*, 361–362.

Blagoveshchenskaya, NF, TD Borisova,VA Kornienko, MT Rietveld, TK Yeoman, DM Wright, M Rother, HL Luhr, EV Mishin, C Roth, VL Frolov, M Parrot and JL Rauch (2011) Modification of the high-latitude ionosphere by high-power hf radio waves. Results of coordinated satellite and ground-based observations. *Radiophysics and Quantum Electronics* 54(2), 89–101.

Cascetta, E, V Marzana and A Papola (2009) Multi-regional input models for freight demand simulation at the national level. In *Recent Developments in Transport Modeling: Lessons for the Freight Sector*. M Ben-Akiva, H Meersman and E Voorde (Eds.). United Kingdom: Emerald Group Publishing, 93–116.

Cerina, F, Z Zhu, A Cessa and M Riccaboni (2014) World input–output network. *6 IMT Institute for Advanced Studies Lucca*, ISSN 2279–6894.

David, P, D Mowery and WE Steinmueller (1992) Analysing the economic payoffs from basic research, *Economics of Innovation and New Technology* 2, 73–90.

Falck, S, F Snickars and H Westlund (2011) Research hubs in the Baltic Sea region: An explorative study about research cooperation and the usage of research facilities in Physics and Life Sciences. KTH Royal Institute of Technology.

Florida, R (2002) The economic geography of talent, *Annals of the Association of American Geographers* 92(4), 743–755.

Furman, JL, MK Kyle, IM Cockburn and R Henderson (2005) Public and private spillovers, location and the productivity of pharmaceutical research. *Annales d'Economie et de Statistique* 79/80, 167–190.

Grydeland, T, C La Hoz, V Belyey and A Westman (2005) A procedure to correct the effects of a relative delay between the quadrature components of radar signals at base band, *Annals of Geophysics* 23, 39–46.

Gunasekara, C (2006) Reframing the role of universities in the development of regional innovation systems, *The Journal of Technology Transfer* 31(1), 101–113.

Harrington, JW, AD MacPhersin and JR Lombard (1991) Inter-regional trade in producer services: Review and synthesis, *Growth and Change* 22(4), 75–94.

Havnes, I,C La Hoz, A Aylward, E Belova, TW Hartquist, MJ Kosch, G Morfill, GOL Jones, LI Næsheim, MT Rietveld, M Rubin-Zuzic and F Sigernes (2006) Observations of the overshoot effect during the 2004 EISCAT PMSE campaign, *Advances in Space Research* 38, 2344–2352.

Holt, O (2012) History of EISCAT — part 3: The early history of EISCAT in Norway, *History of Geo- and Space-Sciences* 3, 47–52.

Horlings, E, T Gurney, A Somers and P van den Besselaar (2012) The societal footprint of big science: A literature review in support of evidence-based decision making. *Working paper* 1206, Den Haag: Rathenau Instituut.

Hultqvist, B (2011) History of EISCAT — part 1: On the early history of EISCAT with special reference to the Swedish part of it, *History of Geo- and Space Sciences* 2, 115–121.

Jaffe, A (1989) Real effects of academic research, *American Economic Review* 9(5), 957–970.

Jaffe, A, M Trajtenberg and R Henderson (1993) Geographic localization of knowledge spillovers as evidenced by patent citations, *The Quarterly Journal of Economics* 108(3), 577–598.

Johansson, B and JM Quigley (2004) Agglomeration and networks in spatial economies, *Papers in Regional Science* 83, 1–13.

Kero, J (2008) High resolution meteor exploration with tristatic radar methods. *PhD thesis.* Umeå University, Faculty of Science and Technology, Physics. IRF Scientific Report 293, ISSN 0284-1703.

Kero, J, S Kirkwood, N Ivchenko, L Magner and T Carozzi (2013) EISCAT_3D: The next generation international atmosphere and geospace research radar. Application of the National Research Council (VR) No. 2013-36344-101447-34.

Krugman, P (1991) *Geography and Trade.* Cambridge: MIT Press.

LeSage, JP, MM Fischer and T Scherngell (2008) *Knowledge spillovers across Europe. Evidence from a Poisson spatial interaction model with spatial effects.* WU Vienna: University of Economics and Business.

Oksman, J (2011) History of EISCAT — part 2: The early history of EISCAT in Finland, *History of Geo- and Space-Sciences* 2, 123–128.

Oosterhaven, J (1988) On the plausibility of the supply-driven input–output model, *Journal of Regional Science* 28(2), 203–217.

Oosterhaven, J and G Hewings (2014) Inter-regional input–output models. In *Handbook of Regional Science.* MM Fischer and P Nijkamp (Eds.). Heidelberg: Springer-Verlag, 875–901.

Overman, H and C Helmers (2013) My precious! The location and diffusion of scientific research: Evidence from the Synchrotron Diamond Light Source, *ERSA conference papers ersa13p654*, European Regional Science Association.

Owen-Smith, J and WW Powell (2004) Knowledge networks as channels and conduits: The effects of spillovers in the Boston biotechnology community, *Organization Science* 15(1), 5–21.

Ozimek, A and D Miles (2011) Stata utilities for geocoding and generating travel time and travel distance information, *The Stata Journal* 11(1), 106–119.

Polenske, KR and NO Nockler (2014) Ideal or not ideal inter-regional accounts and models, *International Regional Science Review* 37(1), 66–77.

Rekers, JV (2013) The ESS and the geography of innovation. In *Legitimizing ESS: Big Science as Collaboration across Boundaries*. T Kaiserfeldt and T O'Dell (Eds.). Lund: Nordic Academic Press, 105–122.

Rossi-Hansberg, E (2005) A spatial theory of trade, *American Economic Review* 95(5), 1464–1491.

Saxenian, AL (1996) Inside-out-regional networks and industrial adaptation in Silicon Valley and route 128, *Cityscape: A Journal of Policy Development and Research* 2(2), 41–60.

Snickars, F (1979) Construction of inter-regional input–output tables by efficient information adding. In *Exploratory and Explanatory Statistical Analysis of Spatial Data*. CPA Bartels and RH Ketellapper (Eds.). Boston, MA: Martinus Nijhoff Publishers, 73–112.

Snickars, F, J Blaus, T Eriksson and G Reitberger (2013) Economic and social impacts of KTH research: A follow-up study of the research assessment exercise 2012. In *New Perspectives on Internationalization and Competitiveness: Integrating Economics, Innovation and Higher Education*. E Ullberg (Ed.). Heidelberg: Springer-Verlag, forthcoming.

Thorn, K and L Holm-Nielsen (2008) International mobility of researchers and scientists: Policy options for turning a drain into a gain. In *The International Mobility of Talent*. A Solimano (Ed.). Oxford, UK: Oxford University Press, 145–167.

Trippl, M and G Maier (2011a) Knowledge spillover agents and regional development. In *Innovation, Growth and Competitiveness. Advances in Spatial Science*. P Nijkamp and I Siedschlag (Eds.). Heidelberg: Springer-Verlag, 91–111.

Trippl, M and G Maier (2011b) Star scientists as drivers of the development of regions. In *Innovation, Growth and Competitiveness. Advances in Spatial Science*. P Nijkamp and I Siedschlag (Eds.). Heidelberg: Springer-Verlag, 113–134.

Virtanen, II, MS Lehtinen, T Nygren, M Orispää and J Vierinen (2008) Lag profile inversion method for EISCAT data analysis, *Annals of Geophysics* 26, 571–581.

Wannberg, G, H Andersson, R Behlke, V Belyey, P Bergqvist, J Borg, A Brekke, J Delsing, L Eliasson, I Finch, T Grydeland, B Gustavsson, I Häggström, RA Harrison, T Linatti, G Johansson, J Johansson, C La Hoz, T Laakso, R Larsen, M Larsmark, T Lindgren, L Lundberg, M Nordenvaad, J Markkanen, I Marttala, I McCrea, D McKay, M Postila, W Puccio, T Renkwitz, E Turunen, A van Eyken, LG Vanhainen, A Westman and I Wolf (2010) EISCAT_3D: A next-generation European radar system for upper atmosphere and geospace research, *Radio Science Bulletin* 332, 75–88.

White, H and K McCain (1989) Bibliometrics, *Annual Review of Information Science and Technology* 24, 119–186.

# Part IV

# Theory and Empirics

# Chapter 10

# Trade Openness and City Interaction

*Mauricio Ramírez Grajeda* and Ian M. Sheldon†*
**Universidad de Guadalajara, Centro Universitario de Ciencias Económico Administrativas, Departamento de Métodos Cuantitativos*
*†The Ohio State University Department of Agricultural, Environmental, and Development Economics*

The New Economic Geography framework supports the idea that international economic integration plays an important role in second nature geography such as the size of cities. By using Fujita *et al.* (1999) as a theoretical motivation, information on the most important cities of 84 countries from 1970 to 2000, and spatial econometric specifications, we find that the size of main cities decline and the size of secondary cities increase, as a result of more exposure to external trade. Similar outcomes are observed for cities with a population over a million. However, cities that represent a large fraction of the urban population grow independently of their position in the urban ranking. Such results are in general consistent for different definitions of trade openness. Furthermore, an implication of international trade openness is higher levels of internal trade among secondary cities.

"Trade is spatial by nature"
Rossi-Hansberg (2006).

*Mauricio Ramírez Grajeda acknowledges Conacyt for partial support for this research. We also thank Paulina Brambila Trejo and José María González for their research assistance.

## 10.1. Introduction

During the 1950s, 1960s and 1970s the "import substitution" paradigm dominated within policy circles in many countries of the developing world such as Brazil, India and Mexico among others (see Edwards, 1993; Krueger, 1997). In addition, metropolises also emerged in those countries: Sao Paulo, Bombay and Mexico City. In this regard, this chapter deals with the impact of foreign trade on internal geography under the New Economic Geography (NEG) paradigm. In particular, it focuses on the distribution of economic activity across space. It is worth mentioning that according to Fujita and Thisse (1996), there are two other major approaches that can also be used to address this issue. One takes informational spillovers under perfect competition as a centripetal force (see Henderson, 1974; Rauch, 1991), while the other considers spatial competition under strategic interaction (see Hotelling, 1929).

By assuming spatial dependence, the aim in this chapter is to disentangle the effects of trade openness on the size of the most important cities for 84 countries after controlling for political, geographic and economic factors over the period 1970–2000. In our analysis we specify spatial econometric models. The key conclusions are that main cities reduce in size and secondary cities (ranked from two to five) grow when trade openness is increased. Similar results arise for a sample consisting of cities with a population over a million. In both cases our results are consistent over time and for different trade openness definitions related to trade volumes. With respect to the sample of cities whose population represents five percent or more of the urban population little can be said though, even for different definitions of trade openness. We also show that the size of the secondary cities depend upon the size of the other cities. Therefore under our theoretical framework we can conjecture that international trade increases internal trade among secondary cities.

In this context, neoclassical trade theory neither provides a sound explanation for intra-industry trade and its spatial implications nor an explicit model with inter-metropolitan implications (Ionnides, 2004). The theoretical basis for this chapter, therefore, includes the previous contributions of Krugman and Livas (1996) and Fujita *et al.* (1999), which frame old ideas on space, intra-industry trade and city interaction by embedding trade costs, increasing returns to scale and love for variety within a general equilibrium setting. The former authors claim that "restrictive trade policies of the developing countries and their tendency to develop huge metropolitan cities are closely linked". The latter authors claim that trade openness undermines the advantages of urban concentration, which arises from proximity to industrial suppliers and consumers. In the urban economics literature, concentration implies three types of advantages (see Puga, 2010). First, there is a more efficient use of local infrastructure and amenities. Second, there is a better matching among agents within both the product market and the labor market. Third, there are positive spillovers in terms of knowledge between firms. The market structure associated with Krugman and Livas (1996), and Fujita *et al.* (1999) is one of monopolistic competition following Dixit and Stiglitz (1977). Given three local cities and high international trade costs, the larger a city is, in terms of population, the higher its real wage is with respect to the secondary cities (centripetal force). Therefore, consumers/workers migrate from the secondary cities to the main city. Although more concentration negatively affects real wages due to congestion or higher land prices (centrifugal forces), workers keep flowing to the main city up to the point where real wages are equalized across cities because both opposite forces cancel each other out. This self-reinforcing dynamic is interrupted when international trade costs fall below a threshold, where agglomeration does not sustain differentials in real wages for further population growth. In sum, concentration of production activities arises from the interplay of centripetal and centrifugal agglomeration forces. These models work for any level of urban population and suggest that city interaction arises as a consequence of trade openness because it enhances competition among secondary cities to attract workers that have moved out from the main city. Agglomeration of consumers/workers reduces both average cost and trade costs, and increases competition within the market for factors of production. The net result is high real wages in large cities *versus* low real wages in small cities. On the empirical side, this chapter is partially inspired by Nitsch (2006) because it also covers secondary cities, as well as by Ades and Glaeser (1995).

The contribution of this chapter consists of testing the outcomes of an extended version of Fujita *et al.* (1999), where a third secondary city is incorporated into the home country. In theory, given a group of cities in a specific country, by lowering international trade costs, the population of the main city would flow to secondary cities. Therefore, the internal urban structure changes: secondary cities have more population, trade more and increase their real wages (welfare). Furthermore, under this extension, the size of secondary cities also would depend upon the size of the other cities including the main one. Our empirical results are consistent with this theoretical prediction. We test both the direct effect of international trade openness on the size of cities and the indirect effect of the size of cities on the population of a particular city. Our methodology is based upon different reduced form spatial econometric specifications, where we estimate the parameters under the maximum likelihood criterion. Another contribution of this chapter is that we consider different definitions of trade openness, in terms of both trade volumes and tariffs, and we incorporate time as an explanatory variable. A shortcoming that we find within the NEG paradigm is that the size of cities is a vague variable: the size of a city can be understood either as an absolute number or as relative number. Therefore, we construct data sets of city size under several criteria. Finally, it is worth noting that our theoretical model is highly stylized, which is extremely sensitive to the value of the parameters.

Regarding the stylized facts, trade openness and urbanization have steadily grown since 1970. In Figure 10.1, we observe a positive correlation between exports of goods and services as a percentage of gross domestic product (GDP) and urban population as a percentage of the total population at the global level. From 1970 to 2000, the former variable changed from 13 to 42%, the latter from 23 to 47%. Nowadays, most people around the world live in urban areas.

The remainder of the chapter is divided up as follows. Section 10.2 reviews the literature related to trade and second nature geography,

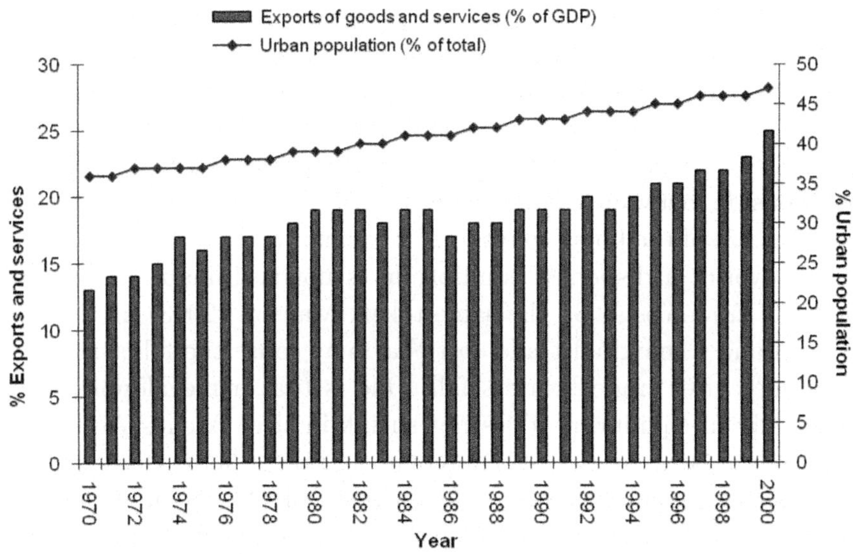


**Figure 10.1.** International trade *versus* urbanization in the world.

*Sources*: World Bank Indicators.

in particular, the size of cities. Section 10.3 contains the theoretical framework and presents the hypotheses on trade openness and city size that are tested. Section 10.4 is focused on the model specification and the estimation strategy. Definitions of trade openness are provided in Section 10.5. In Section 10.6, the construction of the data set is explained, while in Section 10.7, the basic results are shown. Finally, some implications of the results are presented.

## 10.2. Literature Review

The NEG paradigm reintroduces old ideas on space from Von Thünen (1826), Weber (1909), Christaller (1933) and Lösch (1940). In this vein, other economists have given a prominent role to the effects of international trade on the size of the world's main cities. For example, Venables (1998) investigates the effects of external trade costs on the share of manufacturing employment. A single city will have a high amount of employment when the economy of a country is closed to external trade. However, when the economy has access to imports due to lower trade costs the amount of industrial employment goes down. The economy develops a duo-centric structure if it is open to external trade. Following Krugman and Livas (1996), Alonso-Villar (2001) adds a new foreign country and suggests that the negative relationship between trade openness and city size depends on the relative size of the home country. If it is small with regard to the rest of the world, a dispersed equilibrium is not sustainable given low levels of trade costs. By the same token, Mansori (2003) introduces a fixed and a marginal trade cost that may cause the following two outcomes after trade barriers fall. One is that a megalopolis that is already in equilibrium does not shrink in size: Buenos Aires and Bangkok are examples of this outcome; and the other is that cities in the dispersed equilibrium become a megalopolis like Seoul. Contrary to what Mansori claims, Henderson *et al.* (2001) find that Korea has experienced a process of de-concentration of manufacturing due to infrastructure improvements. Behrens *et al.* (2007) present similar outcomes to Krugman and Livas (1996) but they assume an immobile rural centripetal force as in Krugman (1991).

In the NEG literature, there are different explanations of urban concentration. For example, Puga (1998) explains the urbanization differences between Europe and developing countries. He finds that European countries developed a balanced urban system in the 19th century due to high trade costs, weak economies of scale and a relatively low supply of labor from rural areas. On the contrary, during the same period in developing countries trade costs were low, economies of scale at the firm level were strong and there was an abundant pool of peasants available to migrate into their cities.

On the empirical side, Rosen and Resnick (1980) show that countries that export a small fraction of their gross national product (GNP) tend to have a larger degree of urban primacy. Ades and Glaeser (1995) examine the forces that cause concentration of population in a single city. They define three types of agglomeration force: political, economic and geographic. They use a sample of 85 countries and information on their prime cities. Their basic results related to political forces are that main cities are 42% larger if they are also capitals; they are 45% larger in countries with dictatorial regimes. Furthermore, political factors affect urban concentration but not the other way round. The results related to economic forces are the following: first, a one standard-deviation increase in the share of trade in GDP reduces the size of the main city by 13%; second, a one percent increase in the ratio of import duties increases size by three percent; and finally, a one percent increase in the share of government transportation expenditure in GDP reduces the size by 10%. Regarding geographic forces, a 10% increase in the area of the country increases population in the main city by about 1.2%. They also provide political and historical factors that explain urban concentration such as in London, Buenos Aires, Mexico City or Tokyo.

Hanson (1998) summarizes the literature on changes in spatial organization among North American countries since the North American Free Trade Agreement (NAFTA) was implemented in 1994. More precisely, he focuses on the case of Mexico City to demonstrate that its population decreased due to a process of trade liberalization that started in the mid-1980s. After forty years of industrialization based on the "import substitution" paradigm, Mexico opened its economy to international trade by becoming a member of the General Agreement on Tariffs and Trade (GATT). Hanson (1996, 1997) finds that trade liberalization has contributed toward the break-up of the traditional manufacturing belt around Mexico City and the formation of export-oriented centers along the US–Mexican border for trade and investment reasons.

Gaviria and Stein (2000) find that the impact of international trade on cities depends on geography. Population growth does not change in cities located at ports whereas landlocked cities exhibit slower growth. Nitsch (2006) tests the effects of trade volumes on the main cities for 111 countries. His most important result is that both main and secondary cities (from two to five) reduce their size with higher trade flows.

It is worth mentioning that the relationship between external trade and city size does have a different explanation outside of the NEG theory. For example, Ades and Glaeser (1995), explain that the current size of Buenos Aires is the result of two factors that arose in the late 19th century: first, international migration mainly from Italy and Spain; and second, the concentration of rent-seeking activities around international trade activities at this port. Another case is the primacy of Mexico City due to the strong incentives created by the political system to migrate from rural areas. Related references are Richardson and Bae (2005); Kresl and Fry (2005), who give an overview of the relationship between urbanization and globalization. In particular, the latter study analyses the cases of Mexico City, Sao Paulo, Tijuana and Bogota.

## 10.3. Theory and Hypotheses

To motivate the hypotheses to be tested in this chapter, this section outlines Fujita *et al.*'s (1999) outcomes for four locations, which draws heavily on Krugman and Livas (1996). The model embeds imperfect competition in a dynamic general equilibrium setting, and assumes an exogenous congestion cost that directly affects real wages. Specific assumptions are set in order to analyze the way cities interact within an international context for different levels of trade openness. The economy consists of one sector, which is monopolistically competitive.

There are $j = 1, \ldots, J$ locations, each one is endowed with $L_j$ agents (consumers/workers). It is assumed that

$$\sum_{j=1}^{J} L_j = L = 1. \tag{10.1}$$

Therefore, $L_j$ denotes the fraction of the population that lives in location $j$.

Trade costs are of the Samuelson (1952) type: $T_{jj} \geq 0$ denotes the amount of any variety dispatched per unit received. For Limão and Venables (2001) the cost of doing business across countries depends on geography, infrastructure, administrative barriers, e.g., tariffs, and the structure of the shipping industry, e.g., carriage, freight and insurance. It is assumed that if $j = j'$ then $T_{jj'} = 1$; and $T_{jj'} = T_{j'j}$. It is worth mentioning four implications of assuming this type of trade costs. First, it avoids the introduction of a transportation industry, which might complicate the model when solving for the equilibrium. Second, it is a necessary condition for preserving a constant elasticity of aggregate demand. This feature simplifies the conditions of profit maximization. A constant elasticity of aggregate demand means that firms maximize profits by setting a price that is a constant mark-up over marginal cost. A specific level of production satisfies this condition. Third, $T_{jj'}$ may represent an explicit *ad valorem* tariff whose revenues are redistributed among economic agents but dissipated as a consequence of rent-seeking. Agents devote resources, lobbying expenses, lawyer's fees and public relations costs, to obtain these tariff revenues. And fourth, trade costs are not related to the variety or distance between locations.

The representative agent in location $j$ derives their utility from consumption represented by

$$U_j = \left( \sum_{n=1}^{N} c_{nj}^{\frac{\sigma-1}{\sigma}} \right)^{\frac{\sigma}{\sigma-1}}, \tag{10.2}$$

where $\sigma$ is the elasticity of substitution between any pair of varieties and $c_{nj}$ is the consumption of each available variety, $n$, in location $j$. Under these preferences, desire for variety is measured by $(\sigma - 1)/\sigma$. If it is close to 1, for example, varieties are nearly perfect substitutes.

At the level of the firm, technology exhibits increasing return to scale. Increasing returns to scale are essential in explaining the distribution of economic activities across space. This is known as the "Folk Theorem of Spatial Economics". The quantity of labor required to produce $q$ units of variety $n$ in region $j$ is

$$l_{jn} = F + vq_{jn}, \tag{10.3}$$

where $F$ and $v$ are fixed and marginal costs, respectively. The firm that produces variety $n$ in region $j$ pays nominal wage, $w_{jn}$, for one unit of labor. In order to characterize the equilibrium, $F = 1/\sigma$ and $\nu = (\sigma - 1)/\sigma$. To assume a particular value of $F$ means to choose units of production such that solving for the equilibrium is easier. The number of firms in location $j$, $n_j$, is endogenous. $N = n_1 + \cdots + n_J$ is the total number of available varieties.

There are two types of prices: mill (or free on board) and delivered (carriage, insurance and freight). Firms charge the former. The latter, paid by consumers, are defined as

$$p_{jj'}^{n} = p_{j}^{n} T_{jj'}, \tag{10.4}$$

where $p_j^n$ denotes the mill price of a good of variety $n$ produced in location $j$. $p_{jj'}^n$ is the delivered price in location $j'$. By the assumptions on trade costs, both prices are equal when $j = j'$.

Real wages in location $j$ are defined as

$$\omega_j = w_j G_j^{-1}, \tag{10.5}$$

where $G_j$ is a price index, which is the minimum cost of achieving one unit of utility given $N$ varieties and $N$ prices associated with them. $G$ is defined in Equation (10.6).

The economy reaches its short-run equilibrium when agents and firms optimize their utility and profit functions respectively, such that the market clearing conditions in both the labor and product markets are satisfied.

Assumptions on agent's tastes, trade costs, technology parameters, free entry and exit of firms and a potentially unlimited value of $N$, allow the characterization of the equilibrium as follows. Nominal wages are equal within a particular location. Profits are zero. Since there are no economies of scope, each firm produces a single variety. All firms hire the same amount of labor irrespective of the variety they produce and their location, then the level of production across varieties is equal. Within a particular location, mill prices are equal across varieties, and hence they can be denoted without the $n$ as in Equation (10.4). Agents consume all varieties. Within a particular location, consumption across agents is identical, where the consumption level in location $j$ is equal across all varieties produced in $j'$, $n_{j'}$. By knowing this characterization and given $L_1, \ldots, L_j$, then the short-run equilibrium can be redefined as a vector: $\{n_j^*, w_j^*, q^*, l^*, p_j^*, c_{1j}^*, \ldots, c_{Jj}^*\}$ for $j = 1, \ldots, J$ such that

(e.1) $\{c_{1j}^*, \ldots, c_{Jj}^*\} Max U(c_{1j}, \ldots, c_{Jj})$ $s.t.$
$Y_j = L_j w_j^* \geq Ljn_1^* c_{1j} T_{1j} p_1^* + \cdots + L_j c_{Jj} n_J^* T_{Jj} p_J^*$ for all $j = 1, \ldots, J$,

(e.2) $\{q^*\} Max p_j^* q - w^*(F + vq)$, for any $j = 1, \ldots, J$,
(e.3) $q^* = L_1 c_{n1}^* + \cdots + L_J c_{nJ}^*$ for all $n = 1, \ldots, J$ and
(e.4) $(n_1^* + \cdots + n_J^*) l^* = L = 1$.

(e.1) is the optimal consumption of the representative agent in location $j$. The maximization of their utility is subject to a budget condition, where their income can be expressed either individually $w_j$ or aggregated $L_j w_j$. Individual consumption in location $i$ of all varieties produced in location $j$ is denoted by $n_j c_{ji}$. (e.2) is the level of production by any firm. The assumptions of the model allow one to obtain $q^*$ irrespective of the price and wage associated with a particular variety. (e.3) is the equilibrium condition in the product market and (e.4) is the equilibrium condition in the labor market.

The model does not have a closed-form solution. For $j = 1, \ldots, J$, the equilibrium must satisfy the following system of $Jx2$ non-linear equations instead:

$$G_j = \left[ \sum_{s=1}^{J} {}_s (w_s T_{js})^{(1-\sigma)} \right]^{\frac{1}{(1-\sigma)}} \tag{10.6}$$

and

$$w_j = \left[ \sum_{s=1}^{J} Y_s (T_{js})^{1-\sigma} G_s^{\sigma-1} \right]^{\frac{1}{\sigma}}. \tag{10.7}$$

Equation (10.6) represents a price index in location $j$. Equation (10.7) is the wage equation, which generates zero profits given prices, income and trade costs. Real wages across locations might be different.

When real wages are different, labor moves from regions with a low real wage to regions with higher real wages. Fujita *et al.* (1999) define

$$\varpi = \sum_{j=1}^{J} L_j \omega_j. \tag{10.8}$$

The labor share dynamics over time for $j = 1, \ldots, J$ are

$$\Delta k_j = \gamma(\omega_j - \varpi) L_j. \tag{10.9}$$

When Equations (10.6) and (10.7) are satisfied there is no interaction among locations. Put another way, it is the Dixit and Stiglitz (1977) setting for multiple regions. Then, Equation (10.9) is added up to connect locations by equalizing it to zero. More precisely, under this law of motion, any initial difference in real wages among regions implies that Equation (10.9) is positive, driving over time a population distribution different from the original. By using discrete choice theory the size of regions may depend upon other factors different from monetary (wage) considerations. Particularly, there are two departures to explain migration. One, is to assume taste heterogeneity among workers (Murata, 2003). The other is to assume that regions exhibit several features (Tabuchi and Thisse, 2002).

In order to relate urban agglomeration and international trade openness, three assumptions are incorporated. First, there are two countries termed, foreign and home. Only one location or city is located in the foreign country and three in the home country. Trade among three cities in the home country involves the same Samuelson (1952) type iceberg trade costs, $T$. But trade costs between a particular city in the home country and the unique city in the foreign country $i$ are $T_0$. Second, it is assumed that migration is allowed between cities within the home country but not across countries. Third, a centrifugal force of concentration, such as a non-linear congestion cost, is also included: a non-linear congestion diseconomy to the city size. Then, real wages are defined as

$$\omega_j = \frac{w_1(1 - L_j)^\delta}{G_j}, \tag{10.10}$$

where $\delta$ is a congestion parameter.

Our contribution here is to add a third secondary city to this setting, making it a richer model that can be exploited to explain the population dynamics among secondary cities. It is assumed that the value of the parameters are $L_0 = 2$ (population in the foreign city), $L_1 + L_2 + L_3 = 1$ (population within the home country normalized to one), $\delta = 0.1$ (congestion), $\sigma = 5$ (love for variety) and $T = 1.25$ (internal trade costs). The distribution of the population over time

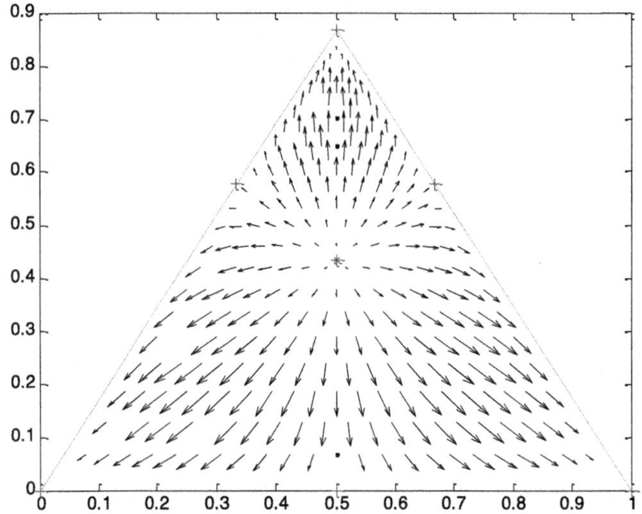


**Figure 10.2.** Long-run equilibria given three local cities and $T_0 = 1.9$.

*Note*: Calculations carried out in MATLAB.

and across domestic cities is represented in the unit simplex in Figures 10.2 and 10.3. What happens in the foreign city is neglected because the size of the unique foreign city never changes.

In Figures 10.2 and 10.3, the center represents equal distribution of the population across cities. Points (0, 0), (0.5, 0.86) and (1, 0) mean that the whole domestic population is concentrated in cities 1, 2 or 3, respectively. The middle point between the line that joins points (0, 0) and (0.5, 0.86) means that total population is equally divided between cities 1 and 2. In these figures, the initial point of an arrow is a point, which represents a short-term equilibrium given a particular distribution of the population. This means that while real wages might be different across cities, then labor migration is expected to generate a new distribution. The length of the arrow represents the magnitude of labor movements over time across cities ($\Delta L_1$, $\Delta L_2$, $\Delta L_3$) and the direction represents the sign of these changes ($\Delta L_j \geq 0$ or $\Delta L_j < 0$).

Figure 10.2 shows that for high levels of international trade costs ($T_0 = 1.9$), partial concentration in one city is a stable long-run

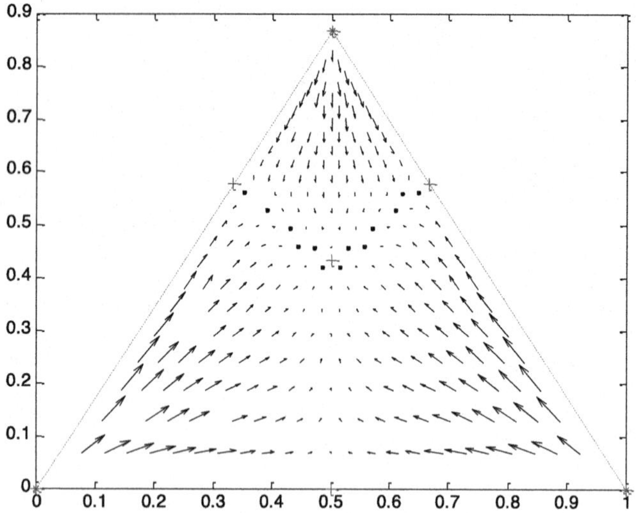


**Figure 10.3.** Long-run equilibria given three local cities and $T_0 = 1$.

*Note*: Calculations carried out in MATLAB.

equilibrium. It should be pointed out that concentration in one city is not total because a small fraction of the total population is distributed across the rest of the cities. Equal distribution between three or two cities implies an unstable equilibrium. Internal and international trade takes place and all varieties produced in the economy are consumed in all cities. The main city produces a large variety of goods and the secondary cities produce a limited variety of goods and trade between cities is balanced. Figure 10.3 shows that, the equal distribution of population in the domestic country is a stable long-run equilibrium for high levels of trade openness. Partial concentration in one or two cities is unstable.

With high international trade costs, both firms and workers, by focusing their expenditure on national goods, magnify the market size effects of agglomeration through prices and nominal wages. In other words, an extra worker in a particular city represents a higher demand and such a benefit always offsets fiercer competition in the labor market. Thus, equilibrium is reached when congestion costs are high enough to prevent further agglomeration. For lower trade costs ($T_0 = 1$) the weight of imports in agents' expenditure is large enough such that any deviation from the dispersed equilibrium is associated with weak market size effects.

Despite the fact that NEG models are highly stylized, their results are quite compelling. Furthermore, adding one domestic city to Fujita *et al.* (1999) allows a richer model in order to consider the following hypotheses to be tested:

**Hypothesis 1:** Trade openness reduces the size of main cities and increases the size of secondary cities.

**Hypothesis 2:** Trade openness reduces the size of the main city and increases the size of secondary cities given that these cities represent a substantial fraction of the urban population.

**Hypothesis 3:** Trade openness reduces the size of the main city and increases the size of secondary cities given that these ones are heavily populated.

Hypothesis 1 cannot be theoretically established with two cities in the home country because the population in the secondary city is the residual from the main city. In the case of three cities, trade openness predicts competition for workers between cities instead, due to their incentives to take advantage of agglomeration. Hypothesis 2 is based on the fact that secondary cities may have some degree of primacy although the main city is overwhelmingly large. Hypothesis 3 is generated by the lack of implications of the size of the urban population: the model works for any size. For example, given the parameters used in Figure 10.2 (high trade costs: $T_0 = 1.9$), it is not entirely unexpected that the majority of the population would live in one city, as happens to be the case for either Dublin or San Jose. However, the model does not work, for instance, for India because in equilibrium, hundreds of million people would be expected to live in Bombay.

## 10.4. Model Specification and Method of Estimation

Behrens and Thisse (2007) suggest spatial econometrics is a road in empirical regional economics. Nevertheless, they claim that its application to multi-regional trading is "practically non-existent".

For this reason among others, in this section we propose three basic reduced-form specifications to test the hypotheses set out in the previous section. The first one is linear, cross-sectional, and first-order dependences are incorporated as a regressor in the form of a spatially lagged dependent variable, because cities in the model are interconnected, and their size is determined simultaneously within a country. The first model, referred to as spatial lag, is expressed as:

$$\boldsymbol{Y} = \boldsymbol{X\beta} + \rho \boldsymbol{WY} + \boldsymbol{\varepsilon}, \tag{10.11}$$

where $\boldsymbol{Y}$ is an $n \times 1$ vector of observations of the dependent variable. $\boldsymbol{X}$ is an $n \times k$ matrix of observations on $k$ exogenous variables. $\boldsymbol{W}$ is an $n \times n$ spatial weights matrix of known constants. $\boldsymbol{\varepsilon}$ is an $n \times 1$ vector of i.i.d error terms. $\boldsymbol{\beta}$ is a $k \times 1$ vector of regression coefficients. $\rho$ is a scalar autoregressive parameter. The spatial lag term $\boldsymbol{WY}$ is correlated with $\boldsymbol{\varepsilon}$, therefore it must be treated as an endogenous variable. $\boldsymbol{W}$ captures the spatial interdependence underlying Figures 10.2 and 10.3. The second specification is given by defining a particular spatial structure for the disturbance terms. Hence

$$\boldsymbol{Y} = \boldsymbol{X\beta} + \boldsymbol{\varepsilon} \tag{10.12}$$

and

$$\boldsymbol{\varepsilon} = \boldsymbol{\lambda W \varepsilon} + \boldsymbol{\xi}, \tag{10.13}$$

where $\boldsymbol{\xi}$ is an i.i.d random variable and $\lambda$ is the spatial autoregressive coefficient for the error lag $\boldsymbol{W\varepsilon}$. Equation (10.12) is referred to as the spatial error model. This model is applied when the political divisions do not match economic divisions. The third specification assumes $\rho = 0$ in (10.11). We also carried out estimations of the panel data versions of Equations (10.11) and (10.12), see Elhorst (2003), where the general form is usually written as:

$$\boldsymbol{Y_t} = \boldsymbol{X_t\beta} + \rho \boldsymbol{WY_t} + \boldsymbol{\varepsilon_t} \tag{10.14}$$

and

$$\boldsymbol{\varepsilon_t} = \boldsymbol{\lambda W \varepsilon_t} + \boldsymbol{\xi_t}. \tag{10.15}$$

The assumptions made concerning $\boldsymbol{W}$, are that $w_{ij} = b_{ij}^{\phi}/d_{ij}^{\alpha}$, where $d_{ij}$ is the distance between city $i$ and $j$. $\alpha$ and $\phi$ are parameters equal to one, $b_{ij}$ is equal to one if cities $i$ and $j$ belong to the same country and equal to zero otherwise.

Equations (10.11) and (10.12) are not specified directly from theory due to the non-linearities that arise from the assumptions on preferences that impede an analytical solution. Following Anselin (1999, 2003), (1) and (2) partially capture the behavior of NEG models. By assuming that both sorts of innovations, $\boldsymbol{\xi}$ and $\boldsymbol{\varepsilon}$, are distributed as a $\boldsymbol{N}(0,\sigma^2\boldsymbol{I})$ the three models can be estimated by applying the method of maximum likelihood due to Anselin and Bera (1998). The linear and spatial lag model estimates are obtained by using our programs written in MATLAB and the spatial error lag model by using James Le Sage's web page programs. Ordinary Least Squares (OLS) estimates from the first model will be biased and inconsistent, and inefficient from the second model. $\boldsymbol{Y}$ is a vector of the values of the log of city size. The estimation strategy associated with testing the first hypothesis covers the five most important cities in 84 countries. In this case, every country has the same number of observations. The second hypothesis is tested using a sample consisting of cities whose size represents a fraction larger than 0.05 of the urban population. To test the third hypothesis, the sample is selected in terms of absolute population. It consists of cities with a population over a million. Hence the number of observations across countries is not equal to test these last two hypotheses. Some countries have just one observation, such as Costa Rica or Ireland and other countries such as the US and Brazil have many observations. The estimation is for the periods 1970–1985 and 1985–2000, and for panel data with time fixed effects. By invoking Zipf's (1949) law, which states that the number of cities with a population larger than $S$ is approximately proportional to $S^{-p}$, where $p$ is close to 1, samples one and three might be very similar if countries' main city sizes were equal.

We carry out tests for spatial dependence using the Rao score criterion (Anselin and Bera, 1998). In the first model, the null hypotheses are $H_0$: $\rho = 0$ ($RS\rho$) and $H_0$: $\rho = 0$ in the presence of local mis-specification involving a spatial-dependent error process ($RS^*\rho$). In the second model the null hypotheses are $H_0$: $\lambda = 0$ ($RS\lambda$) and

$H_0$: $\lambda = 0$ in the presence of local mis-specification involving spatial lag dependence ($RS^*\lambda$). A third test is also carried out for both models where the null hypothesis is $H_0$: $\lambda = 0$ and $\rho = 0$ ($RS\rho\lambda$). We also obtain the value of the log-likelihood function as goodness of fit. This class of test only requires estimation of the model under the null and also allow for the distinction between a spatial error and a spatial lag alternative. These tests are also implemented using MATLAB routines. All of them converge to a $\chi^2(1)$ distribution.

## 10.5. Trade Openness Definitions

NEG models specifically define international trade openness as low international trade costs, which are an abstraction based on transport costs, tariffs, subsidies, taxes, non-tariff barriers, etc. Empirically, then, what are the variables associated with trade openness? Are these variables correlated? Do high trade volumes mean trade openness? Rodríguez and Rodrik (2000) claim that trade openness indicators have been problematic as measures of trade barriers. For example, "simple tariff averages underweight high tariff rates because the corresponding import levels tend to be low". Pritchett (1996) addresses the implications of different indicators of trade policy stance to capture a common element that foster growth.

Yanikkaya (2003) points out that this definition is not unique and has evolved over time from "one extreme to another". On the one hand, trade liberalization can be achieved by lowering the degree by which the protective structure in a country is biased against exports. For example, subsidizing exports or encouraging export schemes. According to this definition an open economy could have very high import tariffs in order to foster import substitution. On the other hand, Harrison (1996) considers that trade openness is linked to the idea of neutrality, the indifference between earning a unit of foreign exchange by exporting and saving a unit of foreign exchange through import substitution.

Back to Yanikkaya (2003), trade openness can be divided into four categories. First, trade shares in GDP (imports plus exports relative to GDP). Second, trade barriers that include average tariff rates, export taxes, total taxes on international trade and indices of non-tariff barriers. According to Baldwin (1989), the former falls under the category of an outcome-based measure and the latter under the category of an incidence-based measure. Third, bilateral payments arrangements (BPAs) can be used as a measure of trade orientation. A BPA is an agreement that describes the general method of settlement of trade balances between two countries. Fourth, the exchange rate black market premium is the most commonly used measure to show the severity of trade restrictions. Nevertheless, it measures a combination of bad policies rather than being a reference to just trade policy.

It is worth mentioning that Limão and Venables (2001) show that trade costs do not depend only on artificial or administrative barriers as Yanikkaya (2003) states, but also on countries' geography and on their level of infrastructure. Remote and landlocked countries trade less than coastal economies. Countries with a poor transport and communications infrastructure have limited participation in global trade.

Earlier empirical work on the cross-country relationship between city size and trade openness does not take into account the implications of using different definitions of trade openness, where trade share in GDP and import barriers have been the standard measures. Anderson and van Wincoop (2004) survey the measurement of trade costs. They acknowledge that tariffs are less important than other policies.

In this chapter, three other measures are used: the weighted share of trade with the US; the share of trade with Japan, Germany and the US jointly; and an instrumental variable.

## 10.6. Data

The data set covers information on 84 countries over two time periods: 1970–1985 as in Ades and Glaeser (1995) and Nitsch (2006), and 1985–2000 as in Nitsch (2006). Ades and Glaeser's (1995) sample covers 85 countries; however, as shown in the appendix, Table 10.A2, only 84 countries are listed. In addition, former European communist

**Table 10.1.** City size (in thousands).

| Sample | Period | Maximum | Minimum | Median | Mean |
|---|---|---|---|---|---|
| By ranking (top five) | 1970–1985 | 27,192 (Tokyo, Japan) | 13 (Tipitapa, Nicaragua) | 463 | 1,346 |
| | 1985–2000 | 32,718 (Tokyo, Japan) | 37 (Carnot, Central African Republic) | 722 | 1,821 |
| Main city | 1970–1985 | 27,192 (Tokyo, Japan) | 111 (Kigali, Rwanda) | 1,005 | 2,675 |
| | 1985–2000 | 32,718 (Tokyo, Japan) | 260 (Bujumbura, Burundi) | 1,558 | 3,624 |
| Over million | 1970–1985 | 27,192 (Tokyo, Japan) | 223 (Sana'a, Yemen) | 1,126 | 2,085 |
| | 1985–2000 | 32,718 (Tokyo, Japan) | 706 (Faridabad, India) | 1,712 | 2,846 |
| Over 5% of total urban population | 1970–1985 | 27,192 (Tokyo, Japan) | 20 (Mzuzu, Malawi) | 621 | 1,739 |
| | 1985–2000 | 32,718 (Tokyo, Japan) | 67 (Mzuzu, Malawi) | 988 | 2,359 |

*Data source*: UN (2003). World Urbanization Prospects.

countries are not included because their size heavily depended upon the decisions of central planners (see Clayton and Richardson, 1989). In the case of China, from 1953 to 1978, industrial location depended upon three principles: geographical proximity to mountains, dispersion and concealment (see Wen, 2004).

Table 10.1 shows the cities used in this study. Both the dependent and explanatory variables for period $t$ are constructed by averaging observations over five-year intervals. For example, the 1970–1985 period averages information for the years 1970, 1975, 1980 and 1985. However, for some variables information is not always available for all years.

Three sample criteria are applied to validate the hypotheses of this chapter. The first sample consists of the five most populous cities in 2000, and consists of 355 observations. This ranking is invariable over time with the exception of two countries. The Netherlands' main city in the period 1970–1985 was Rotterdam and it was Amsterdam in the period 1985–2000. Syria's main city in the former period was Aleppo and Damascus in the latter period. In both periods, the largest city is Tokyo and the smallest one is Tipitapa in Nicaragua in the period 1970–1985. The second sample contains information on 224 cities with a population over a million in 2000. Faridabad in India and Sana'a in Yemen are the smallest cities of the sample for the first and second periods, respectively. The third sample contains 183 cities that represent a fraction larger than five percent with regard to urban population in 2000. African cities are the smallest cities in this sample.

Information at the country level changes for three countries: Germany, Yemen and Ethiopia. The first two countries experienced a process of unification, West and East Germany, and South and North Yemen; and the last one split into Ethiopia and Eritrea. For the first period, information on West Germany, South Yemen and Ethiopia is used. In the second period, information for these "new" countries is used, although Eritrea is ignored in this sample. For panel data estimation these countries are not included. Some countries do not have complete information on their most important cities. For example, there is only information for one city in Costa Rica. Furthermore, information on cities is not clearly defined. A natural question is what are the city bounds? For example, in the case of either Germany or Japan there is information on a system of cities that jointly are considered as a single city. In other words the political or administrative divisions do not coincide with the actual economic bounds. This is considered a nuisance in spatial econometrics. For that reason, we assume in one of the model specifications a stochastic process in the spatial error structure. The Organisation for Economic Co-operation and Development (OECD) dummy excludes Turkey and Mexico because they are outliers in terms of income and other economic and social indicators. The central location dummy is 1 when the distance between the city and the country's central point is less than the square root of the land area. Dummies related to central location and access by sea are important determinants of agglomeration as natural advantages of locations (see Kim, 1999; Ellison and Glaeser, 1999). The lack of political rights and civil liberties dummy is 1 when each component is above 3.5 (seven means no "democracy"), and 0 otherwise. The road index denotes the ratio of road network over the square root of land area.

We use five definitions of trade openness: share of trade in GDP (STG); weighted by distance share of trade with the US in GDP (WUS); share of trade with Japan, the US and Germany (JUG); import duties as a fraction of total imports (ID), and an instrumental variable (IV). The weights related to bilateral trade with the US are the distance between the geographic centers of the US and the corresponding country. Therefore, a dollar exported (imported) to (from) Canada has less weight than a dollar exported (imported) to (from) Australia. Trade with Japan, the US and Germany is not weighted by distance because it is assumed that they are equidistant and their volume of trade is similar. For observations related to cities from Japan, Germany and the US, trade information with economies of similar size of these countries is used, respectively. We use information issued by statistical offices of Japan, Germany and the US.

The instrumental variable is constructed by following Frankel and Romer's (1999) estimation strategy and information of bilateral trade between 165 countries (see Appendix 10.A1). This is a way to overcome endogeneity problems that arise from the correlation between the error term and the trade openness variable. Telephone mainlines is a proxy variable of information technologies (IT).

The main data sources are the UN World Urbanization Prospects, World Bank Indicators, The CIA World Fact-book, Vernon Henderson's Web page, Statitisches Bundesamt Deutschland, Freedom in the World, Yanikkaya (2003) and John Helliwell's bilateral trade data set. See 10.A3 for further details on our data set.

## 10.7. Results

Our econometric estimates are reported in Tables 10.2–10.8. The analysis is conducted by sampling. Regarding the five most important cities: on the one hand the estimates without assuming spatial dependence show that city size is positively related to trade openness;

**Table 10.2.** Cities by ranking, 1 to 5.

| Dependent variable: Log of city population | OLS | | | Lag-ML | | | Err-ML | | |
|---|---|---|---|---|---|---|---|---|---|
| | 1970–1985 | 1985–2000 | Panel data | 1970–1985 | 1985–2000 | Panel data | 1970–1985 | 1985–2000 | Panel data |
| **1) Intercept** | −3.295*** | −3.067*** | −2.904 | −2.431** | −2.088*** | −2.084*** | −2.869* | −2.470** | −2.446*** |
| | *(1.08)* | *(0.86)* | *(4.39)* | *(0.99)* | *(0.77)* | *(0.61)* | *(1.48)* | *(1.25)* | *(0.94)* |
| **2) Main city dummy** | 1.554*** | 1.681*** | 1.605 | 1.702*** | 1.855*** | 1.765*** | 1.569*** | 1.699*** | 1.626*** |
| | *(0.26)* | *(0.25)* | *(8.84)* | *(0.24)* | *(0.23)* | *(0.17)* | *(0.21)* | *(0.19)* | *(0.14)* |
| **3) Capital city dummy** | 0.601*** | 0.545*** | 0.561 | 0.677*** | 0.636*** | 0.641*** | 0.652*** | 0.638*** | 0.625*** |
| | *(0.15)* | *(0.15)* | *(5.04)* | *(0.14)* | *(0.13)* | *(0.10)* | *(0.12)* | *(0.12)* | *(0.09)* |
| **4) Log of nonurbanized population** | 0.715*** | 0.614*** | 0.668 | 0.498*** | 0.400*** | 0.449*** | 0.701*** | 0.600*** | 0.653*** |
| | *(0.05)* | *(0.04)* | *(22.32)* | *(0.06)* | *(0.05)* | *(0.04)* | *(0.07)* | *(0.06)* | *(0.04)* |
| **5) Log of land area** | 0.125*** | 0.150*** | 0.133 | 0.091*** | 0.105*** | 0.096*** | 0.130** | 0.160*** | 0.142*** |
| | *(0.04)* | *(0.04)* | *(5.16)* | *(0.03)* | *(0.03)* | *(0.02)* | *(0.05)* | *(0.05)* | *(0.04)* |
| **6) Log of real GDP per capita** | 0.297*** | 0.481*** | 0.342 | 0.198** | 0.276*** | 0.207*** | 0.266** | 0.410*** | 0.295*** |
| | *(0.08)* | *(0.08)* | *(6.00)* | *(0.08)* | *(0.07)* | *(0.05)* | *(0.12)* | *(0.11)* | *(0.08)* |
| **7) Share of the labor force outside the agriculture** | 1.654*** | 0.645** | 1.032 | 1.192*** | 0.602* | 0.829*** | 1.727*** | 0.888* | 1.195*** |
| | *(0.36)* | *(0.35)* | *(4.10)* | *(0.34)* | *(0.31)* | *(0.23)* | *(0.50)* | *(0.51)* | *(0.36)* |
| **8.1) Share of trade in GDP** | 0.418 | 0.294 | 0.325 | 0.308 | 0.207 | 0.246 | 0.229 | 0.084 | 0.151 |
| | *(0.37)* | *(0.31)* | *(1.41)* | *(0.34)* | *(0.27)* | *(0.21)* | *(0.41)* | *(0.34)* | *(0.26)* |
| **9.1) Share of trade in GDP × main city dummy** | −0.38344 | −0.48737 | −0.38256 | −0.472 | −0.607* | −0.481* | −0.471 | −0.643** | −0.504** |
| | *(0.44)* | *(0.37)* | *(1.35)* | *(0.41)* | *(0.33)* | *(0.26)* | *(0.36)* | *(0.28)* | *(0.22)* |
| **10) Port city dummy** | 0.391* | 0.321 | 0.368 | 0.343 | 0.257 | 0.306** | 0.342 | 0.306 | 0.331** |
| | *(0.23)* | *(0.23)* | *(2.32)* | *(0.21)* | *(0.20)* | *(0.14)* | *(0.22)* | *(0.20)* | *(0.15)* |
| **11) Port city dummy × share of trade in GDP** | −0.65227 | −0.689** | −0.68428 | −0.499 | −0.420 | −0.469** | −0.358 | −0.299 | −0.350 |
| | *(0.41)* | *(0.34)* | *(2.68)* | *(0.38)* | *(0.30)* | *(0.23)* | *(0.39)* | *(0.31)* | *(0.24)* |

(*Continued*)

**Table 10.2.** (*Continued*)

| Dependent variable: Log of city population | OLS | | | Lag-ML | | | Err-ML | | |
|---|---|---|---|---|---|---|---|---|---|
| | 1970–1985 | 1985–2000 | Panel data | 1970–1985 | 1985–2000 | Panel data | 1970–1985 | 1985–2000 | Panel data |
| **12) Central location dummy** | 0.044 | −0.001 | 0.005687 | 0.029 | −0.019 | 0.013 | 0.025 | −0.065 | −0.001 |
| | (*0.21*) | (*0.22*) | (*0.04*) | (*0.19*) | (*0.20*) | (*0.14*) | (*0.20*) | (*0.21*) | (*0.14*) |
| **13) Central location dummy × share of trade in GDP** | 0.005 | 0.065 | 0.031 | 0.030 | 0.067 | 0.023 | 0.103 | 0.175 | 0.101 |
| | (*0.38*) | (*0.34*) | (*0.13*) | (*0.34*) | (*0.30*) | (*0.22*) | (*0.36*) | (*0.31*) | (*0.23*) |
| **14) Lack of political rights and civil liberties dummy** | −0.254* | 0.484*** | 0.054 | −0.195 | 0.270* | 0.009 | −0.289 | 0.398 | 0.006 |
| | (*0.14*) | (*0.17*) | (*0.54*) | (*0.13*) | (*0.16*) | (*0.09*) | (*0.19*) | (*0.25*) | (*0.14*) |
| **15) OECD country dummy** | −0.302* | −0.25638 | −0.35585 | −0.203 | −0.142 | −0.213* | −0.263 | −0.194 | −0.297* |
| | (*0.17*) | (*0.21*) | (*2.82*) | (*0.15*) | (*0.19*) | (*0.12*) | (*0.23*) | (*0.30*) | (*0.18*) |
| **16) Log of telephone mainlines (per 1000 people)** | 0.003 | 0.037 | 0.06161 | 0.001 | 0.022 | 0.034 | −0.003 | 0.030 | 0.049 |
| | (*0.04*) | (*0.04*) | (*2.17*) | (*0.03*) | (*0.03*) | (*0.03*) | (*0.05*) | (*0.06*) | (*0.04*) |
| **17) 1985–2000 dummy** | | | | | | 0.125** | | | 0.188** |
| | | | | | | (*0.06*) | | | (*0.09*) |
| **18) City interaction parameter** (*rho*) | | | 0.178 | 0.300 | 0.349 | 0.325 | | | |
| | | | (*2.85*) | (*5.77*) | (*7.13*) | (*8.89*) | | | |
| **19) City interaction parameter** (*lambda*) | | | | | | | 0.366 | 0.425 | 0.388 |
| | | | | | | | (*6.96*) | (*8.74*) | (*10.47*) |
| **RS***rho* | | | | 36.01 | 44.57 | 77.64 | | | |
| **RS*** *rho* | | | | 1.64 | 1.14 | 3.40 | | | |
| **RS***lambda* | | | | | | | 50.99 | 61.18 | 110.08 |
| **RS*** *lambda* | | | | | | | 16.63 | 17.76 | 35.83 |
| **RS***lambdarho* | | | | 52.64 | 62.32 | 113.47 | 52.64 | 62.32 | 113.47 |
| **Log-likelihood** | −323.88 | −309.69 | −605.73 | −308.90 | −289.84 | −572.76 | −302.89 | −281.49 | −559.21 |
| **R2** | 0.78 | 0.76 | 0.77 | | | | | | |
| **Number of observations** | 305 | 305 | 580 | 305 | 305 | 580 | 305 | 305 | 580 |

Standard deviation reported below the estimated coefficients. ***significant at 1% level; **significant at 5% level; *significant at 10% level.

**Table 10.3.** Cities by ranking, 1 to 5 (other definitions of trade openness).

| Dependent variable: Log of city population | OLS | | | Lag-ML | | | Err-ML | | |
|---|---|---|---|---|---|---|---|---|---|
| | 1970–1985 | 1985–2000 | Panel data | 1970–1985 | 1985–2000 | Panel data | 1970–1985 | 1985–2000 | Panel data |
| **8.2) Weighted share of trade with the U.S. in GDP** | 201.290 | 290.650 | 784.350 | 156.600 | 106.940 | 419.980 | 586.880 | 24.832 | 629.240 |
| | *(663.78)* | *(385.30)* | *(630.56)* | *(608.86)* | *(343.14)* | *(577.45)* | *(733.84)* | *(412.99)* | *(678.44)* |
| **9.2) Weighted share of trade with the U.S. in GDP × main city dummy** | −667.280 | −278.540 | −699.970 | −689.100 | −388.510 | −854.250 | −681.110 | −464.410 | −945.410 |
| | *(846.85)* | *(473.53)* | *(781.59)* | *(775.81)* | *(421.34)* | *(714.14)* | *(684.18)* | *(355.57)* | *(618.48)* |
| **City interaction parameter** | | | | 0.293 | 0.356 | 0.325 | 0.365 | 0.441 | 0.401 |
| | | | | *(5.59)* | *(7.27)* | *(8.86)* | *(6.93)* | *(9.28)* | *(11.01)* |
| **RS***rho* | | | | 34.03 | 47.01 | 78.45 | | | |
| **RS*** *rho* | | | | 1.78 | 1.52 | 5.07 | | | |
| **RS***lambda* | | | | | | | 48.32 | 64.23 | 112.81 |
| **RS*** *lambda* | | | | | | | 16.07 | 18.74 | 39.43 |
| **RS***lambdarho* | | | | 50.10 | 65.74 | 117.88 | 50.10 | 65.74 | 117.88 |
| **Log-likelihood** | −323.56 | −313.17 | −608.27 | −309.39 | −292.50 | −575.28 | −303.26 | −283.06 | −560.32 |
| **R2** | 0.78 | 0.76 | 0.77 | | | | | | |
| **Number of observations** | 305 | 305 | 580 | 305 | 305 | 580 | 305 | 305 | 580 |
| **8.3) Share of trade with Jap+Ger+U.S. in GDP** | −0.656 | 0.314 | 0.581** | −0.336 | 0.301 | 0.469* | −0.368 | 0.159 | 0.508 |
| | *(0.46)* | *(0.28)* | *(0.29)* | *(0.42)* | *(0.25)* | *(0.26)* | *(0.55)* | *(0.36)* | *(0.37)* |
| **9.3) Share of trade with Jap+Ger+U.S. in GDP × main city dummy** | −1.160 | −0.775 | −0.744 | −1.174 | −0.817* | −0.815* | −1.053 | −0.675* | −0.726* |
| | *(0.83)* | *(0.49)* | *(0.52)* | *(0.76)* | *(0.44)* | *(0.47)* | *(0.70)* | *(0.39)* | *(0.41)* |
| **City interaction parameter** | | | | 0.295 | 0.355 | 0.328 | 0.355 | 0.425 | 0.399 |
| | | | | *(5.65)* | *(7.25)* | *(8.99)* | *(6.66)* | *(8.74)* | *(10.92)* |
| **RS***rho* | | | | 34.08 | 46.86 | 80.51 | | | |
| **RS*** *rho* | | | | 1.76 | 1.36 | 4.20 | | | |
| **RS***lambda* | | | | | | | 48.60 | 59.83 | 114.25 |
| **RS*** *lambda* | | | | | | | 16.28 | 13.33 | 37.93 |
| **RS***lambdarho* | | | | 50.36 | 60.19 | 118.45 | 50.36 | 60.19 | 118.45 |
| **Log-likelihood** | −323.12 | −312.02 | −608.83 | −308.82 | −291.42 | −575.01 | −302.79 | −283.84 | −561.26 |
| **R2** | 0.78 | 0.76 | 0.77 | | | | | | |
| **Number of observations** | 305 | 305 | 580 | 305 | 305 | 580 | 305 | 305 | 580 |

*(Continued)*

**Table 10.3.** (*Continued*)

| Dependent variable: Log of city population | OLS | | | Lag-ML | | | Err-ML | | |
|---|---|---|---|---|---|---|---|---|---|
| | 1970–1985 | 1985–2000 | Panel data | 1970–1985 | 1985–2000 | Panel data | 1970–1985 | 1985–2000 | Panel data |
| **8.4) Import duties as percent of Imports** | −0.225 | 0.235 | 0.055 | −0.099 | 0.450 | 0.191 | −0.520 | −0.223 | −0.256 |
| | (*1.18*) | (*1.09*) | (*0.81*) | (*1.09*) | (*0.98*) | (*0.74*) | (*1.36*) | (*1.32*) | (*0.95*) |
| **9.4) Import duties × main city dummy** | 2.138* | 2.455** | 2.026** | 2.316** | 2.541** | 2.130*** | 2.144** | 2.360*** | 1.942*** |
| | (*1.25*) | (*1.16*) | (*0.87*) | (*1.14*) | (*1.04*) | (*0.80*) | (*1.03*) | (*0.92*) | (*0.71*) |
| **City interaction parameter** | | | | 0.285 | 0.332 | 0.313 | 0.352 | 0.411 | 0.375 |
| | | | | (*5.12*) | (*6.23*) | (*8.00*) | (*6.25*) | (*7.87*) | (*9.50*) |
| **RS***rho* | | | | 28.88 | 36.09 | 67.23 | | | |
| **RS*** *rho* | | | | 0.31 | 0.19 | 1.71 | | | |
| **RS***lambda* | | | | | | | 37.79 | 45.77 | 90.35 |
| **RS*** *lambda* | | | | | | | 9.19 | 9.86 | 24.84 |
| **RS***lambdarho* | | | | 38.07 | 45.96 | 92.06 | 38.07 | 45.96 | 92.06 |
| **Log-likelihood** | −290.51 | −276.16 | −552.84 | −278.40 | −260.18 | −524.91 | −273.95 | −254.19 | −514.18 |
| **R2** | 0.79 | 0.78 | 0.78 | | | | | | |
| **Number of observations** | 275 | 275 | 530 | 275 | 275 | 530 | 275 | 275 | 530 |
| **8.5) Constructed share of trade in GDP** | −3.111 | −1.739 | −1.978 | −1.852** | −1.118 | −1.121 | −2.888 | −2.165 | −2.116 |
| | (*1.43*) | (*1.12*) | (*1.60*) | (*0.92*) | (*0.79*) | (*0.97*) | (*1.11*) | (*1.15*) | (*1.46*) |
| **9.5) Constructed share of trade in GDP × main city dummy** | −1.071 | −1.318 | −0.956 | −1.367** | −1.546 | −1.190 | −1.143 | −1.436 | −1.266 |
| | (*0.42*) | (*0.74*) | (*0.66*) | (*0.58*) | (*0.95*) | (*0.89*) | (*0.54*) | (*1.02*) | (*1.09*) |
| **City interaction parameter** | | | | 0.271 | 0.318 | 0.296 | 0.334 | 0.402 | 0.365 |
| | | | | (*0.05*) | (*0.05*) | (*0.04*) | (*0.06*) | (*0.05*) | (*0.04*) |
| **RS***rho* | | | | 25.66 | 36.03 | 60.29 | | | |
| **RS*** *rho* | | | | 0.98 | 0.09 | 0.98 | | | |
| **RS***lambda* | | | | | | | 36.84 | 46.38 | 83.44 |
| **RS*** *lambda* | | | | | | | 12.16 | 10.43 | 23.92 |
| **RS***lambdarho* | | | | 37.82 | 46.47 | 83.31 | 37.82 | 46.47 | 84.55 |
| **Log-likelihood** | −302.65 | −301.88 | −582.88 | −291.46 | −285.63 | −556.66 | −285.55 | −279.28 | −553.42 |
| **R2** | 0.78 | 0.78 | 0.78 | | | | | | |
| **Number of observations** | 290 | 305 | 570 | 290 | 305 | 570 | 290 | 305 | 580 |

Standard deviation reported below the estimated coefficients. ***significant at 1% level; **significant at 5% level; *significant at 10% level.

**Table 10.4.** Cities with a share of urban population over 5%.

| Dependent variable: Log of city population | OLS | | | Lag-ML | | | Err-ML | | |
|---|---|---|---|---|---|---|---|---|---|
| | 1970–1985 | 1985–2000 | Panel data | 1970–1985 | 1985–2000 | Panel data | 1970–1985 | 1985–2000 | Panel data |
| **1) Intercept** | −2.278** | −1.153 | −2.045*** | −2.299** | −1.178 | −2.058*** | −2.111* | −0.808 | −1.629** |
| | *(1.03)* | *(0.91)* | *(0.65)* | *(0.99)* | *(0.87)* | *(0.63)* | *(1.14)* | *(0.96)* | *(0.74)* |
| **2) Main city dummy** | 0.514** | 0.653*** | 0.601*** | 0.504** | 0.630*** | 0.589*** | 0.585*** | 0.615*** | 0.666*** |
| | *(0.23)* | *(0.21)* | *(0.14)* | *(0.22)* | *(0.21)* | *(0.14)* | *(0.19)* | *(0.18)* | *(0.12)* |
| **3) Capital city dummy** | 0.804*** | 0.728*** | 0.755*** | 0.795*** | 0.707*** | 0.743*** | 0.813*** | 0.761*** | 0.743*** |
| | *(0.11)* | *(0.11)* | *(0.08)* | *(0.11)* | *(0.11)* | *(0.08)* | *(0.09)* | *(0.09)* | *(0.06)* |
| **4) Log of nonurbanized population** | 0.689*** | 0.582*** | 0.678*** | 0.692*** | 0.586*** | 0.680*** | 0.681*** | 0.575*** | 0.658*** |
| | *(0.05)* | *(0.05)* | *(0.03)* | *(0.05)* | *(0.05)* | *(0.03)* | *(0.06)* | *(0.05)* | *(0.04)* |
| **5) Log of land area** | 0.135*** | 0.139*** | 0.117*** | 0.135*** | 0.140*** | 0.117*** | 0.130*** | 0.139*** | 0.116*** |
| | *(0.04)* | *(0.03)* | *(0.02)* | *(0.04)* | *(0.03)* | *(0.02)* | *(0.04)* | *(0.04)* | *(0.03)* |
| **6) Log of real GDP per capita** | 0.179 | 0.406*** | 0.286*** | 0.181** | 0.406*** | 0.287*** | 0.204** | 0.397*** | 0.286*** |
| | *(0.09)* | *(0.09)* | *(0.06)* | *(0.09)* | *(0.08)* | *(0.06)* | *(0.10)* | *(0.10)* | *(0.07)* |
| **7) Share of the labor force outside the agriculture** | 2.516*** | 1.257*** | 1.466*** | 2.524*** | 1.273*** | 1.474*** | 2.427*** | 1.240*** | 1.551*** |
| | *(0.39)* | *(0.39)* | *(0.28)* | *(0.37)* | *(0.38)* | *(0.27)* | *(0.44)* | *(0.44)* | *(0.33)* |
| **8.1) Share of trade in GDP** | 0.254 | −0.203 | −0.097 | 0.245 | −0.214 | −0.105 | 0.071 | −0.339 | −0.310 |
| | *(0.39)* | *(0.30)* | *(0.22)* | *(0.37)* | *(0.29)* | *(0.22)* | *(0.39)* | *(0.30)* | *(0.23)* |
| **9.1) Share of trade in GDP × main city dummy** | 0.1125 | −0.15566 | −0.063953 | 0.125 | −0.129 | −0.050 | −0.108 | −0.187 | −0.117 |
| | *(0.37)* | *(0.29)* | *(0.21)* | *(0.36)* | *(0.28)* | *(0.21)* | *(0.31)* | *(0.24)* | *(0.17)* |
| **10) Port city dummy** | 0.762*** | 0.610*** | 0.641*** | 0.755*** | 0.601*** | 0.633*** | 0.596** | 0.556*** | 0.460*** |
| | *(0.24)* | *(0.22)* | *(0.15)* | *(0.24)* | *(0.21)* | *(0.15)* | *(0.24)* | *(0.21)* | *(0.15)* |
| **11) Port city dummy × share of trade in GDP** | −0.931** | −0.605** | −0.723*** | −0.923** | −0.603** | −0.718*** | −0.569 | −0.444 | −0.402* |
| | *(0.40)* | *(0.30)* | *(0.22)* | *(0.39)* | *(0.28)* | *(0.21)* | *(0.40)* | *(0.29)* | *(0.22)* |
| **12) Central location dummy** | 0.185 | −0.079 | −0.22652 | 0.177 | −0.092 | −0.233 | 0.059 | −0.143 | −0.283* |
| | *(0.24)* | *(0.23)* | *(0.15)* | *(0.23)* | *(0.22)* | *(0.15)* | *(0.23)* | *(0.22)* | *(0.15)* |

*(Continued)*

**Table 10.4.** (*Continued*)

| Dependent variable: Log of city population | OLS | | | Lag-ML | | | Err-ML | | |
|---|---|---|---|---|---|---|---|---|---|
| | 1970–1985 | 1985–2000 | Panel data | 1970–1985 | 1985–2000 | Panel data | 1970–1985 | 1985–2000 | Panel data |
| **13) Central location dummy × share of trade in GDP** | −0.375 | 0.146 | 0.191 | −0.362 | 0.162 | 0.200 | −0.171 | 0.194 | 0.260 |
| | *(0.39)* | *(0.30)* | *(0.22)* | *(0.38)* | *(0.29)* | *(0.22)* | *(0.38)* | *(0.30)* | *(0.22)* |
| **14) Lack of political rights and civl liberties dummy** | 0.013 | 0.331** | 0.126 | 0.017 | 0.343** | 0.132 | 0.033 | 0.260 | 0.117 |
| | *(0.14)* | *(0.16)* | *(0.10)* | *(0.14)* | *(0.15)* | *(0.10)* | *(0.16)* | *(0.18)* | *(0.12)* |
| **15) OECD country dummy** | −0.359** | −0.480** | −0.526*** | −0.359** | −0.474** | −0.524*** | −0.371* | −0.511** | −0.513*** |
| | *(0.17)* | *(0.21)* | *(0.13)* | *(0.16)* | *(0.20)* | *(0.12)* | *(0.19)* | *(0.23)* | *(0.15)* |
| **16) Log of telephone mainlines (per 1000 people)** | −0.008 | −0.030 | 0.062* | −0.008 | −0.030 | 0.062* | −0.010 | −0.023 | 0.051 |
| | *(0.04)* | *(0.04)* | *(0.03)* | *(0.04)* | *(0.04)* | *(0.03)* | *(0.04)* | *(0.05)* | *(0.04)* |
| **17) 1985–2000 dummy** | | | 0.243*** | | | 0.242*** | | | |
| | | | *(0.06)* | | | *(0.06)* | | | |
| **18) City interaction parameter** (*rho*) | | | | −0.002 | −0.005 | −0.003 | | | |
| | | | | *(0.21)* | *(0.47)* | *(0.40)* | | | |
| **19) City interaction parameter** (*lambda*) | | | | | | | 0.225 | 0.235 | 0.255 |
| | | | | | | | *(3.50)* | *(3.68)* | *(0.08)* |
| **RS***rho* | | | | 0.04 | 0.22 | 0.16 | | | |
| **RS*** *rho* | | | | 0.44 | 0.90 | 1.76 | | | |
| **RS***lambda* | | | | | | | 8.82 | 11.12 | 41.06 |
| **RS*** *lambda* | | | | | | | 9.92 | 11.80 | 42.67 |
| **RS***lambdarho* | | | | 9.26 | 12.02 | 42.83 | 9.26 | 12.02 | 42.83 |
| **Log-likelihood** | −152.38 | −146.34 | −284.76 | −151.99 | −145.86 | −284.47 | −147.12 | −140.04 | −263.35 |
| **R2** | 0.83 | 0.81 | 0.83 | | | | | | |
| **Number of observations** | 183 | 183 | 352 | 183 | 183 | 352 | 183 | 183 | 352 |

Standard deviation reported below the estimated coefficients. ***significant at 1% level; **significant at 5% level; *significant at 10% level.

**Table 10.5.** Cities with a share of urban population over 5% (other definitions of trade openness).

| Dependent variable: Log of city population | OLS | | | Lag-ML | | | Err-ML | | |
|---|---|---|---|---|---|---|---|---|---|
| | 1970–1985 | 1985–2000 | Panel data | 1970–1985 | 1985–2000 | Panel data | 1970–1985 | 1985–2000 | Panel data |
| **8.2) Weighted share of trade with the U.S. in GDP** | 210.230 | 51.061 | 401.660 | 211.880 | 60.375 | 410.970 | 186.230 | −20.258 | 204.990 |
| | *(423.92)* | *(236.43)* | *(376.51)* | *(404.62)* | *(225.37)* | *(367.04)* | *(417.47)* | *(228.16)* | *(366.51)* |
| **9.2) Weighted share of trade with the U.S. in GDP × main city dummy** | −250.000 | 23.061 | −447.300 | −238.670 | 45.926 | −426.530 | −365.800 | −110.250 | −475.310 |
| | *(392.92)* | *(226.62)* | *(365.77)* | *(375.42)* | *(216.84)* | *(357.32)* | *(350.11)* | *(190.81)* | *(296.72)* |
| **City interaction parameter** | | | | −0.006 | − 0.010 | −0.006 | 0.240 | 0.284 | 0.210 |
| | | | | *(0.56)* | *(1.00)* | *(0.84)* | *(3.77)* | *(4.62)* | *(0.08)* |
| **RS***rho* | | | | 0.32 | 0.99 | 0.69 | | | |
| **RS*** *rho* | | | | 1.24 | 2.50 | 3.55 | | | |
| **RS***lambda* | | | | | | | 13.06 | 15.76 | 51.97 |
| **RS*** *lambda* | | | | | | | 13.98 | 17.27 | 54.83 |
| **RS***lambdarho* | | | | 14.30 | 18.26 | 55.52 | 14.30 | 18.26 | 55.52 |
| **Log-likelihood** | −155.11 | −155.26 | −295.00 | −154.58 | −154.39 | −294.44 | −148.17 | −146.07 | −268.49 |
| **R2** | 0.83 | 0.79 | 0.82 | | | | | | |
| **Number of observations** | 183 | 183 | 352 | 183 | 183 | 352 | 183 | 183 | 352 |
| **8.3) Share of trade with Jap+Ger+U.S. in GDP** | −0.816 | 0.175 | 0.165 | −0.836* | 0.176 | 0.160 | −0.521 | 0.274 | 0.158 |
| | *(0.53)* | *(0.23)* | *(0.21)* | *(0.51)* | *(0.22)* | *(0.21)* | *(0.50)* | *(0.22)* | *(0.22)* |
| **9.3) Share of trade with Jap+Ger+U.S. in GDP × main city dummy** | 0.170 | −0.071 | 0.073 | 0.195 | −0.073 | 0.077 | 0.041 | −0.155 | −0.010 |
| | *(0.58)* | *(0.20)* | *(0.21)* | *(0.55)* | *(0.19)* | *(0.20)* | *(0.51)* | *(0.16)* | *(0.19)* |
| **City interaction parameter** | | | | −0.008 | −0.009 | −0.006 | 0.234 | 0.296 | 0.202 |
| | | | | *(0.75)* | *(0.87)* | *(0.78)* | *(3.66)* | *(4.86)* | *(0.08)* |
| **RS***rho* | | | | 0.56 | 0.75 | 0.60 | | | |
| **RS*** *rho* | | | | 1.57 | 2.18 | 3.39 | | | |
| **RS***lambda* | | | | | | | 10.82 | 17.44 | 52.68 |
| **RS*** *lambda* | | | | | | | 11.82 | 18.87 | 55.47 |
| **RS***lambdarho* | | | | 12.39 | 19.62 | 56.07 | 12.39 | 19.62 | 56.07 |
| **Log-likelihood** | −154.19 | −154.44 | −296.26 | −153.54 | −153.69 | −295.74 | −148.28 | −144.53 | −269.83 |
| **R2** | 0.83 | 0.79 | 0.82 | | | | | | |
| **Number of observations** | 183 | 183 | 352 | 183 | 183 | 352 | 183 | 183 | 352 |

*(Continued)*

**Table 10.5.** (*Continued*)

| Dependent variable: Log of city population | OLS | | | Lag-ML | | | Err-ML | | |
|---|---|---|---|---|---|---|---|---|---|
| | 1970–1985 | 1985–2000 | Panel data | 1970–1985 | 1985–2000 | Panel data | 1970–1985 | 1985–2000 | Panel data |
| **8.4) Import duties as percent of Imports** | 2.441 | 3.173* | 2.765** | 3.232* | 3.516** | 3.313*** | 1.125 | 1.872 | 1.237 |
| | *(1.77)* | *(1.63)* | *(1.28)* | *(1.71)* | *(1.56)* | *(1.27)* | *(1.72)* | *(1.67)* | *(1.31)* |
| **9.4) Import duties × main city dummy** | −0.005 | 1.010 | 0.403 | −0.302 | 0.790 | 0.127 | 1.378 | 1.626* | 1.012 |
| | *(1.41)* | *(1.28)* | *(0.91)* | *(1.33)* | *(1.22)* | *(0.90)* | *(1.19)* | *(0.97)* | *(0.75)* |
| **City interaction parameter** | | | | −0.008 | −0.013 | −0.014 | 0.271 | 0.385 | 0.205 |
| | | | | *(0.75)* | *(1.15)* | *(1.70)* | *(4.15)* | *(6.42)* | *(0.08)* |
| **RS***rho* | | | | 3.36 | 1.29 | 2.84 | | | |
| **RS*** *rho* | | | | 5.77 | 3.76 | 6.58 | | | |
| **RS***lambda* | | | | | | | 12.44 | 27.28 | 32.81 |
| **RS*** *lambda* | | | | | | | 14.85 | 29.75 | 36.56 |
| **RS***lambdarho* | | | | 18.21 | 31.03 | 39.39 | 18.21 | 31.03 | 39.39 |
| **Log-likelihood** | −138.73 | −133.38 | −254.92 | −136.58 | −132.29 | −253.24 | −131.17 | −117.42 | −237.11 |
| **R2** | 0.84 | 0.80 | 0.83 | | | | | | |
| **Number of observations** | 164 | 158 | 310 | 164 | 158 | 310 | 164 | 158 | 310 |
| **8.5) Constructed share of trade in GDP** | −4.318* | −2.915 | −3.245** | −4.387** | −2.980* | −3.283** | −4.174* | −2.621 | −3.794** |
| | *(2.31)* | *(1.82)* | *(1.47)* | *(2.22)* | *(1.75)* | *(1.44)* | *(2.40)* | *(1.87)* | *(1.59)* |
| **9.5) Constructed share of trade in GDP × main city dummy** | 0.851 | 0.517 | −0.638 | 0.934 | 0.593 | −0.598 | −0.046 | 0.083 | −0.943 |
| | *(2.13)* | *(1.50)* | *(1.28)* | *(2.05)* | *(1.44)* | *(1.25)* | *(1.76)* | *(1.23)* | *(1.04)* |
| **City interaction parameter** | | | | −0.003 | −0.003 | −0.002 | 0.233 | 0.235 | 0.302 |
| | | | | *(0.25)* | *(0.33)* | *(0.23)* | *(3.51)* | *(3.68)* | *(0.09)* |
| **RS***rho* | | | | 0.06 | 0.11 | 0.05 | | | |
| **RS*** *rho* | | | | 0.57 | 0.69 | 1.24 | | | |
| **RS***lambda* | | | | | | | 11.55 | 11.81 | 32.66 |
| **RS***lambda | | | | | | | 12.05 | 12.39 | 33.85 |
| **RS***lambdarho* | | | | 12.11 | 12.50 | 33.90 | 12.11 | 12.50 | 33.90 |
| **Log-likelihood** | −136.05 | −146.67 | −283.29 | −135.61 | −146.24 | −283.03 | −129.95 | −140.07 | −265.94 |
| **R2** | 0.84 | 0.81 | 0.81 | | | | | | |
| **Number of observations** | 168 | 183 | 330 | 168 | 183 | 330 | 168 | 183 | 330 |

Standard deviation reported below the estimated coefficients. ***significant at 1% level; **significant at 5% level; *significant at 10% level.

**Table 10.6.** Cities with a population over a million.

| Dependent variable: Log of city population | OLS | | | Lag-ML | | | Err-ML | | |
|---|---|---|---|---|---|---|---|---|---|
| | 1970–1985 | 1985–2000 | Panel data | 1970–1985 | 1985–2000 | Panel data | 1970–1985 | 1985–2000 | Panel data |
| **1) Intercept** | 4.556*** | 4.371*** | 4.279*** | 5.782*** | 5.696*** | 5.398*** | 4.461*** | 4.578*** | 4.358*** |
| | *(1.49)* | *(1.23)* | *(0.90)* | *(1.45)* | *(1.20)* | *(0.88)* | *(1.46)* | *(1.16)* | *(0.87)* |
| **2) Main city dummy** | 2.150*** | 2.128*** | 2.033*** | 2.053*** | 1.992*** | 1.905*** | 2.141*** | 2.130*** | 2.037*** |
| | *(0.28)* | *(0.27)* | *(0.19)* | *(0.26)* | *(0.25)* | *(0.18)* | *(0.27)* | *(0.26)* | *(0.19)* |
| **3) Capital city dummy** | 0.296** | 0.264** | 0.368*** | 0.430*** | 0.397*** | 0.519*** | 0.304** | 0.250* | 0.365*** |
| | *(0.14)* | *(0.13)* | *(0.10)* | *(0.14)* | *(0.13)* | *(0.10)* | *(0.14)* | *(0.13)* | *(0.10)* |
| **4) Log of nonurbanized population** | 0.407*** | 0.343*** | 0.424*** | 0.320*** | 0.267*** | 0.348*** | 0.410*** | 0.337*** | 0.422*** |
| | *(0.06)* | *(0.05)* | *(0.04)* | *(0.06)* | *(0.05)* | *(0.04)* | *(0.06)* | *(0.04)* | *(0.04)* |
| **5) Log of land area** | −0.039 | 0.002 | −0.017 | −0.038 | −0.003 | −0.022 | −0.037 | −0.003 | −0.019 |
| | *(0.04)* | *(0.04)* | *(0.03)* | *(0.04)* | *(0.04)* | *(0.03)* | *(0.04)* | *(0.04)* | *(0.03)* |
| **6) Log of real GDP per capita** | 0.077 | 0.366*** | 0.159** | 0.075 | 0.321*** | 0.147** | 0.078 | 0.359*** | 0.156** |
| | *(0.10)* | *(0.11)* | *(0.07)* | *(0.10)* | *(0.10)* | *(0.06)* | *(0.10)* | *(0.10)* | *(0.06)* |
| **7) Share of the labor force outside the agriculture** | 2.397*** | 0.677 | 1.848*** | 1.850*** | 0.340 | 1.455*** | 2.411*** | 0.701 | 1.859*** |
| | *(0.57)* | *(0.54)* | *(0.39)* | *(0.57)* | *(0.51)* | *(0.38)* | *(0.56)* | *(0.51)* | *(0.38)* |
| **8.1) Share of trade in GDP** | 2.229*** | 1.379*** | 1.543*** | 1.922*** | 1.157*** | 1.269*** | 2.214*** | 1.397*** | 1.553*** |
| | *(0.63)* | *(0.48)* | *(0.38)* | *(0.60)* | *(0.45)* | *(0.37)* | *(0.61)* | *(0.45)* | *(0.37)* |
| **9.1) Share of trade in GDP × main city dummy** | −2.850*** | −2.320*** | −2.394*** | −2.249*** | −1.719*** | −1.759*** | −2.823*** | −2.331*** | −2.411*** |
| | *(0.57)* | *(0.47)* | *(0.36)* | *(0.56)* | *(0.46)* | *(0.36)* | *(0.55)* | *(0.45)* | *(0.35)* |
| **10) Port city dummy** | 0.586*** | 0.431** | 0.4639*** | 0.597*** | 0.466** | 0.488*** | 0.578*** | 0.448** | 0.470*** |
| | *(0.19)* | *(0.20)* | *(0.14)* | *(0.18)* | *(0.18)* | *(0.13)* | *(0.19)* | *(0.19)* | *(0.13)* |
| **11) Port city dummy × share of trade in GDP** | −1.145** | −0.557 | −0.621* | −1.112** | −0.627 | −0.633** | −1.114** | −0.604 | −0.638** |
| | *(0.49)* | *(0.42)* | *(0.32)* | *(0.46)* | *(0.39)* | *(0.30)* | *(0.48)* | *(0.40)* | *(0.31)* |
| **12) Central location dummy** | 0.320* | 0.151 | 0.221* | 0.405** | 0.241 | 0.312** | 0.315* | 0.165 | 0.226* |
| | *(0.19)* | *(0.18)* | *(0.13)* | *(0.18)* | *(0.17)* | *(0.12)* | *(0.18)* | *(0.17)* | *(0.13)* |

*(Continued)*

Table 10.6. (*Continued*)

| Dependent variable: Log of city population | OLS | | | Lag-ML | | | Err-ML | | |
|---|---|---|---|---|---|---|---|---|---|
| | 1970–1985 | 1985–2000 | Panel data | 1970–1985 | 1985–2000 | Panel data | 1970–1985 | 1985–2000 | Panel data |
| **13) Central location dummy × share of trade in GDP** | −0.708 | −0.266 | −0.470 | $-1.047^{**}$ | −0.537 | $-0.801^{***}$ | −0.689 | −0.312 | −0.488 |
| | *(0.48)* | *(0.39)* | *(0.30)* | *(0.46)* | *(0.37)* | *(0.30)* | *(0.46)* | *(0.38)* | *(0.30)* |
| **14) Lack of political rights and civl liberties dummy** | 0.039 | $0.362^{**}$ | $0.159^{*}$ | 0.001 | $0.326^{**}$ | $0.143^{*}$ | 0.038 | $0.360^{**}$ | $0.159^{*}$ |
| | *(0.13)* | *(0.16)* | *(0.09)* | *(0.12)* | *(0.15)* | *(0.08)* | *(0.13)* | *(0.15)* | *(0.08)* |
| **15) OECD country dummy** | −0.185 | $-0.337^{*}$ | $-0.405^{***}$ | −0.120 | −0.247 | $-0.348^{**}$ | −0.188 | $-0.328^{*}$ | $-0.404^{***}$ |
| | *(0.19)* | *(0.20)* | *(0.15)* | *(0.18)* | *(0.19)* | *(0.14)* | *(0.19)* | *(0.19)* | *(0.14)* |
| **16) Log of telephone mainlines (per 1000 people)** | −0.059 | −0.067 | $-0.111^{**}$ | −0.049 | −0.058 | $-0.119^{***}$ | −0.059 | −0.070 | $-0.113^{***}$ |
| | *(0.06)* | *(0.06)* | *(0.04)* | *(0.06)* | *(0.06)* | *(0.04)* | *(0.06)* | *(0.06)* | *(0.04)* |
| **17) 1985–2000 dummy** | | | $0.205^{***}$ | | | $0.235^{***}$ | | | $0.206^{***}$ |
| | | | *(0.07)* | | | *(0.06)* | | | *(0.06)* |
| **18) City interaction parameter** (*rho*) | | | | 0.049 | 0.049 | 0.051 | | | |
| | | | | *(3.37)* | *(3.96)* | *(5.24)* | | | |
| **19) City interaction parameter** (*lambda*) | | | | | | | 0.029 | −0.057 | −0.026 |
| | | | | | | | *(0.31)* | *(0.59)* | *(0.37)* |
| **RS***rho* | | | | 10.83 | 57.13 | 26.58 | | | |
| **RS****rho* | | | | 10.85 | 15.83 | 27.51 | | | |
| **RS***lambda* | | | | | | | 0.06 | 0.16 | 0.05 |
| **RS****lambda* | | | | | | | 0.08 | 0.86 | 0.98 |
| **RS***lambdarho* | | | | 10.91 | 15.99 | 27.57 | 10.91 | 15.99 | 27.57 |
| **Log-likelihood** | −209.04 | −188.46 | −375.04 | −203.26 | −180.56 | −361.50 | −208.70 | −188.04 | −374.82 |
| **R2** | 0.48 | 0.43 | 0.49 | | | | | | |
| **Number of observations** | 224 | 224 | 417 | 224 | 224 | 417 | 224 | 224 | 417 |

Standard deviation reported below the estimated coefficients. $^{***}$significant at 1% level; $^{**}$significant at 5% level; $^{*}$significant at 10% level.

**Table 10.7.** Cities with a population over a million (other definitions of trade openness).

| Dependent variable: Log of city population | OLS 1970–1985 | OLS 1985–2000 | OLS Panel data | Lag-ML 1970–1985 | Lag-ML 1985–2000 | Lag-ML Panel data | Err-ML 1970–1985 | Err-ML 1985–2000 | Err-ML Panel data |
|---|---|---|---|---|---|---|---|---|---|
| **8.2) Weighted share of trade with the U.S. in GDP** | −404.640 | −0.843 | 407.790 | −380.950 | −103.410 | 99.346 | −461.560 | −61.100 | 216.540 |
| | *(662.10)* | *(462.94)* | *(721.42)* | *(609.71)* | *(421.38)* | *(675.36)* | *(659.08)* | *(451.66)* | *(727.11)* |
| **9.2) Weighted share of trade with the U.S. in GDP × main city dummy** | −496.270 | −121.320 | −684.590 | −467.850 | −51.904 | −573.680 | −452.530 | −92.712 | −582.060 |
| | *(701.03)* | *(480.88)* | *(754.18)* | *(645.52)* | *(437.49)* | *(702.12)* | *(660.17)* | *(460.86)* | *(730.48)* |
| **City interaction parameter** | | | | 0.064 | 0.062 | 0.063 | 0.150 | 0.072 | 0.118 |
| | | | | *(4.59)* | *(5.22)* | *(6.66)* | *(1.68)* | *(0.78)* | *(1.79)* |
| **RS***rho* | | | | 20.02 | 25.10 | 42.29 | | | |
| **RS*** *rho* | | | | 18.58 | 24.83 | 40.41 | | | |
| **RS***lambda* | | | | | | | 1.92 | 0.29 | 2.15 |
| **RS*** *lambda* | | | | | | | 0.48 | 0.02 | 0.27 |
| **RS***lambdarho* | | | | 20.50 | 25.12 | 42.56 | 20.50 | 25.12 | 42.56 |
| **Log-likelihood** | −225.48 | −205.46 | −407.62 | −215.11 | −192.33 | −385.88 | −224.04 | −204.95 | −405.80 |
| **R2** | 0.40 | 0.33 | 0.41 | | | | | | |
| **Number of observations** | 224 | 224 | 418 | 224 | 224 | 418 | 224 | 224 | 418 |
| **8.3) Share of trade with Jap+Ger+U.S. in GDP** | 1.844* | 0.963 | 1.710*** | 1.269 | 0.591 | 1.299** | 1.683 | 0.970 | 1.682*** |
| | *(1.08)* | *(0.71)* | *(0.61)* | *(1.00)* | *(0.66)* | *(0.57)* | *(1.07)* | *(0.68)* | *(0.61)* |
| **9.3) Share of trade with Jap+Ger+U.S. in GDP × main city dummy** | −3.240*** | −1.429* | −1.935*** | −2.533** | −0.816 | −1.292** | −3.051*** | −1.436** | −1.880*** |
| | *(1.12)* | *(0.74)* | *(0.66)* | *(1.05)* | *(0.70)* | *(0.62)* | *(1.09)* | *(0.72)* | *(0.65)* |
| **City interaction parameter** | | | | 0.061 | 0.058 | 0.059 | 0.115 | −0.009 | 0.073 |
| | | | | *(4.39)* | *(4.75)* | *(6.23)* | *(1.27)* | *(0.09)* | *(1.08)* |
| **RS***rho* | | | | 18.15 | 21.01 | 37.15 | | | |
| **RS*** *rho* | | | | 17.30 | 21.46 | 36.37 | | | |
| **RS***lambda* | | | | | | | 0.95 | 0.00 | 0.78 |
| **RS*** *lambda* | | | | | | | 0.10 | 0.45 | |
| **RS***lambdarho* | | | | 18.25 | 21.46 | 37.15 | 18.25 | 21.46 | 37.15 |
| **Log-likelihood** | −220.15 | −201.83 | −400.90 | −210.67 | −190.82 | −381.66 | −219.24 | −201.53 | −399.82 |
| **R2** | 0.43 | 0.35 | 0.43 | | | 0 | | | |
| **Number of observations** | 224 | 224 | 418 | 224 | 224 | 418 | 224 | 224 | 418 |

*(Continued)*

**Table 10.7.** (*Continued*)

| Dependent variable: Log of city population | OLS | | | Lag-ML | | | Err-ML | | |
|---|---|---|---|---|---|---|---|---|---|
| | 1970–1985 | 1985–2000 | Panel data | 1970–1985 | 1985–2000 | Panel data | 1970–1985 | 1985–2000 | Panel data |
| **8.4) Import duties as percent of Imports** | 0.130 | 0.171 | 0.469 | −0.173 | 0.033 | 0.329 | 0.181 | 0.177 | 0.569 |
| | (*1.37*) | (*1.16*) | (*0.89*) | (*1.27*) | (*1.05*) | (*0.83*) | (*1.41*) | (*1.13*) | (*0.91*) |
| **9.4) Import duties × main city dummy** | 0.809 | 1.305 | 1.020 | 1.701 | 2.295** | 1.739* | 0.866 | 1.328 | 1.103 |
| | (*1.27*) | (*1.14*) | (*0.89*) | (*1.19*) | (*1.05*) | (*0.90*) | (*1.21*) | (*1.09*) | (*0.92*) |
| **City interaction parameter** | | | | 0.067 | 0.066 | 0.065 | 0.163 | 0.046 | 0.124 |
| | | | | (*4.27*) | (*5.05*) | (*6.25*) | (*1.72*) | (*0.46*) | (*1.75*) |
| **RS***rho* | | | | 17.37 | 23.54 | 37.31 | | | |
| **RS***** *rho* | | | | 16.04 | 23.60 | 35.45 | | | |
| **RS***lambda* | | | | | | | 1.75 | 0.09 | 2.20 |
| **RS***** *lambda* | | | | | | | 0.43 | 0.14 | 0.34 |
| **RS***lambdarho* | | | | 17.79 | 23.69 | 37.65 | 17.79 | 23.69 | 37.65 |
| **Log-likelihood** | −211.87 | −190.80 | −379.56 | −202.84 | −178.47 | −360.73 | −210.45 | −190.40 | −378.07 |
| **R2** | 0.38 | 0.33 | 0.40 | | | | | | |
| **Number of observations** | 206 | 205 | 382 | 206 | 205 | 382 | 206 | 205 | 382 |
| **8.5) Constructed share of trade in GDP** | 20.198*** | 9.929*** | 10.337*** | 18.144*** | 9.326*** | 8.269*** | 20.040*** | 9.938*** | 10.191*** |
| | (*4.81*) | (*2.97*) | (*2.69*) | (*4.59*) | (*2.75*) | (*2.57*) | (*4.65*) | (*2.84*) | (*2.66*) |
| **9.5) Constructed share of trade in GDP × main city dummy** | −22.267*** | −10.383*** | −12.259*** | −18.112*** | −7.692*** | −7.847*** | −22.087*** | −10.434*** | −12.029*** |
| | (*4.23*) | (*2.55*) | (*2.29*) | (*4.22*) | (*2.43*) | (*2.29*) | (*4.06*) | (*2.47*) | (*2.23*) |
| **City interaction parameter** | | | | 0.044 | 0.054 | 0.058 | 0.030 | −0.048 | 0.050 |
| | | | | (*3.00*) | (*4.47*) | (*5.72*) | (*0.32*) | (*0.50*) | (*0.73*) |
| **RS***rho* | | | | 8.57 | 18.75 | 31.47 | | | |
| **RS***** *rho* | | | | 8.57 | 19.50 | 31.27 | | | |
| **RS***lambda* | | | | | | | 0.06 | 0.11 | 0.30 |
| **RS***** *lambda* | | | | | | | 0.05 | 0.86 | 0.10 |
| **RS***lambdarho* | | | | 8.63 | 19.62 | 31.57 | 8.63 | 19.62 | 31.57 |
| **Log-likelihood** | −205.28 | −192.16 | −385.86 | −200.64 | −182.34 | −369.58 | −204.94 | −191.77 | −385.20 |
| **R2** | 0.48 | 0.41 | 0.46 | | | | | | |
| **Number of observations** | 222 | 224 | 416 | 222 | 224 | 416 | 222 | 224 | 416 |

Standard deviation reported below the estimated coefficients. ***significant at 1% level; **significant at 5% level; *significant at 10% level.

**Table 10.8.** Main cities.

| Dependent variable: Log of city population | OLS | | |
|---|---|---|---|
| | 1970–1985 | 1985–2000 | Panel Data |
| **1) Intercept** | 2.024* | 2.752*** | 2.520*** |
| | *(1.21)* | *(1.04)* | *(0.75)* |
| **2) Main city dummy** | | | |
| **3) Capital city dummy** | 0.390*** | 0.313** | 0.330*** |
| | *(0.12)* | *(0.13)* | *(0.09)* |
| **4) Log of nonurbanized population** | 0.242** | 0.165* | 0.201*** |
| | *(0.09)* | *(0.09)* | *(0.06)* |
| **5) Log of land area** | −0.027 | 0.015 | −0.008 |
| | *(0.04)* | *(0.04)* | *(0.03)* |
| **6) Log of real GDP per capita** | 0.137 | 0.239** | 0.160** |
| | *(0.10)* | *(0.10)* | *(0.07)* |
| **7) Share of the labor force outside the agriculture** | 0.845* | 0.033 | 0.328 |
| | *(0.46)* | *(0.41)* | *(0.30)* |
| **8.1) Share of trade in GDP** | −0.667 | −0.535 | −0.563* |
| | *(0.51)* | *(0.48)* | *(0.32)* |
| **9.1) Share of trade in GDP × main city dummy** | | | |
| **10) Port city dummy** | 0.098 | 0.279 | 0.203 |
| | *(0.28)* | *(0.27)* | *(0.18)* |
| **11) Port city dummy × share of trade in GDP** | 0.152 | −0.147 | −0.035 |
| | *(0.52)* | *(0.42)* | *(0.29)* |
| **12) Central location dummy** | 0.245 | 0.041 | 0.15567 |
| | *(0.28)* | *(0.26)* | *(0.17)* |
| **13) Central location dummy × share of trade in GDP** | −0.285 | 0.006 | −0.167 |
| | *(0.50)* | *(0.37)* | *(0.26)* |
| **14) Lack of political rights and civl liberties dummy** | 0.286* | 0.242 | 0.262** |
| | *(0.15)* | *(0.17)* | *(0.11)* |
| **15) OECD country dummy** | −0.246 | −0.381* | −0.286** |
| | *(0.19)* | *(0.22)* | *(0.14)* |
| **16) Log of telephone mainlines (per 1000 people)** | 0.032 | 0.022 | 0.066* |
| | *(0.04)* | *(0.05)* | *(0.03)* |
| **17) Log of urbanized population** | 0.454*** | 0.455*** | 0.455*** |
| | *(0.09)* | *(0.09)* | *(0.06)* |
| **18) 1985–2000 dummy** | | | 0.131* |
| | | | *(0.07)* |
| **Log-likelihood** | −35.96 | −34.46 | −375.04 |
| **R2** | 0.89 | 0.86 | 0.49 |
| **Number of observations** | 84 | 84 | 417 |

Standard deviation reported below the estimated coefficients. ***significant at 1% level; **significant at 5% level; *significant at 10% level.

on the other hand, the impact of international trade on city size for different definitions of trade openness barely changes from our benchmark trade openness' definition. In particular, using STD, WUS, JGU and ID, we find that main cities decrease in size and secondary cities increase in size in both periods as a result of openness to trade. Recall that higher ID means lower levels of trade openness. But a higher value of ID for the second period implies that all cities increase in size as well. However, using IV, the estimation predicts that both main and secondary cities decrease in size for higher levels of trade openness for the first and second periods, and panel data as well.

MLE is the method of estimation when the sample is selected by city ranking and the specification model is spatial lag, these results being reported in Tables 10.2 and 10.3. In sum, a 10% increase in the share of trade in GDP increases the size of the top five cities by three percent for the period 1970–1985 and two percent for the period 1985–2000, after controlling for the main city status. Both main and secondary cities are larger if they have access by seaports. But if they are located close to the center of the country such a condition does not have a significant impact on their size. Political liberties and civil rights negatively impact on the size of cities in the period 1970–1985 but not in the period 1985–2000. It is worth mentioning that countries in Latin America have turned to democratic regimes since 1985. Even some OECD countries such as Spain, Portugal, Greece, Korea, Turkey and Mexico have noticeably increased their levels of civil liberties since the mid-1970s as well. A positive $\rho$ can be interpreted as people leaving the main city and going to cities of immediate lower ranking as a consequence of international trade. OECD countries have smaller cities. Over time cities grew by 12%. Regarding main cities, trade openness has a negative net impact on main cities' size. In the first period, a 10% increase in trade openness reduces size by approximately 1.7% and four percent in the second period.

For the error lag specification, MLE is also the method of estimation. The results are similar to the spatial lag specification. Here we focus our attention on the trade openness variables. The results are consistent over all definitions, except the IV, where secondary cities are negatively related to trade openness. Regarding ID, restrictive policies reduce the size of secondary cities but increase the size of main cities. The instrumental variable associated with the 1970–1985 period must be treated carefully because it is weakly correlated (0.5) with the actual share of trade in GDP and its explanatory power is relatively low ($R^2 = 0.24$).

Rao tests show that the error lag model is the more appropriate because in the spatial lag model we fail to reject the null hypothesis $\rho = 0$ given $\lambda \neq 0$. Besides we reject the null hypothesis $\lambda = 0$ given $\rho \neq 0$. This happens to be true with a 0.975 confidence for all definitions of trade openness in both periods and panel data.

If the sample includes cities whose population is above five percent of the urban population the effects of trade openness are not clear. The results of this sample are reported in Tables 10.4 and 10.5. By analyzing the first model the effects of international trade openness on city size are mixed over time. For the period 1970–1985 it is positive, but negative for the second. Lack of political rights and civil liberties positively affects city size in both periods. The IT variable affects city size little. A similar pattern is observed in the spatial lag model. In the spatial error model trade openness positively affects city size except main cities. The coefficient associated with the central location times STG dummy is negative in the first period and positive in the second period under the three basic specifications. Using other definitions of trade openness, the results are also mixed. The message is that under this sample there is little support for saying anything about secondary cities. There is empirical support for a negative impact on main cities.

The results related to the sample of cities with a population over a million in 2000 are reported in Tables 10.6 and 10.7. Regarding the linear specification with no spatial dependence, main cities' size reduces and secondary cities' size increases if a country experiences a process of trade liberalization. In particular, a 10% increase in the share of trade in GDP pushes up the population of cities by around 22 and 13% in the first and second periods respectively; however, in both periods the net effect on main cities is negative. OECD cities are smaller, port and central cities on average are larger. Populous cities are more sensitive to trade openness *versus* the previous samples. These results are significant at the 10% level or less. The lack of political rights and civil liberties positively affects the size of cities.

The results are similar for the spatial lag and spatial error models, however, the effects of trade openness on city size are attenuated. With respect to city interaction the parameter is not significant. However, the log likelihood is higher for the model where we assume spatial dependence. Recall that $\boldsymbol{W}$ is not symmetric at the country level: the number of cities in the sample is not equal across countries.

Our estimates are consistent with different definitions of trade openness, except ID and WUS. In this case, cities reduce their size for higher levels of trade openness, except the main cities. Regarding the model that fits better, the spatial lag has the maximum likelihood. Besides we fail to reject the null hypothesis $\lambda = 0$ given that $\rho \neq 0$.

By construction, there is no spatial dependence regarding the sample consisting of only main cities around the world. In this case, for Equation (10.1) given $\rho = 0$ is estimated by OLS and the results are reported in column 1 of Tables 10.2–10.5. The most noteworthy results are that a 10% increase in the share of trade in GDP reduces city size by 6.6 and 5.3% in the 1970–1985 and 1985–2000 periods, respectively. However, neither of the estimates are statistically significant. On the other hand, panel data estimates show that a 10% share of trade of GDP causes a city size reduction by 5.6%. In the first period, lack of political rights and civil liberties on average increase the size of a city by 28% and they are 39% larger if they are capitals, and similar results arise for the period 1985–2000, however, these coefficients show a lower value. Both types of variable respectively summarize political instability and rent seeking opportunities. In sum, the Ades and Glaeser (1995), and Henderson (1974) results are confirmed.

The OECD main cities are smaller in both periods, which might suggest that a higher level of taste heterogeneity in OECD countries attenuates urban agglomeration as Murata (2003) suggests. Cities of OECD countries are 25% smaller. There is evidence that main cities' sizes are positively related to non-urbanized population outside of the city. This could be explained by agricultural workers flowing to cities as in Gaviria and Stein (2000), Puga (1998), Picard and Zeng (2005) claim. With respect to geographic variables, main cities at ports or close to the center of the country are expected to be larger. In both periods, cities' size reaction to trade openness is slightly positive if they fall within the port category, which is consistent with Fujita and Mori (1996). Also their reaction is negative if the city is close to the center, which coincides with Hanson's (1998) results and the Frankel and Romer (1999) rationale. The variable related to IT indicates that by doubling up the telephone lines per 1,000 people, city size increases by 22 and 32% in each period respectively. It is worth pointing out that within the regional science literature there is a no consensus on the effects of IT on urban structure (see Sohn *et al.* (2002). When using panel data main cities are on average 13% larger in the second period. Only under this sample the log of urbanized population outside the city is taken as an explanatory variable because in the other models the equivalent to this variable is $\boldsymbol{WY}$.

## 10.8. Summary and Conclusions

Within the literature there are several ways to explain agglomeration. One of them is through non-price interactions where technological externalities are generated in a perfectly competitive environment, e.g., Bel and Fageda (2008). In the NEG approach, however, the explanation is based upon micro foundations where the effects of concentration are transmitted through prices and wages. By increasing the international exposure of an economy, the incentives of firms and workers to cluster together are weakened and a balanced urban system is generated. Several predictions of Fujita *et al.* (1999) have been tested in this chapter. The hypothesis that main cities reduce in size and secondary cities increase in size can be validated provided that they are top ranked. The implication of this result is that poverty, crime, pollution and congestion associated with top-ranked cities can be partially attacked by fostering international trade. Besides, urban planners must pay attention to urban growth in secondary cities.

For different definitions of trade openness, big cities, in terms of urban primacy, are not so clearly affected by trade openness. The other results related to hypothesis 3 are that heavily populated cities are more sensitive to trade because economies of scale play a more important role. In this case, results are similar and significant to the sample consisting of top ranked cities with the exception of IV. An advantage of assuming spatial dependence opens the possibility that cities compete for workers. In this chapter, the coefficients related to city interaction are positive suggesting that a struggle arises in the labor market. In Puga (1998), however, city size is also explained as a result of migration from rural areas. Da Mata *et al.* (2005), for example, find that city growth in Brazil is driven by rural population supply and inter-regional transport improvements and spillover effects of knowledge accumulation. Regarding the sample, which consists of cities that represent more than five percent of urban population, our results are not consistent with our theoretical framework.

The consequences of using different definitions of trade openness is that those related to volumes of trade affect city size but a clear link to tariffs is not robust. One answer is that tariffs are biased; in other words, they do not entirely capture real trade costs. Another explanation is that tariff elasticity of imports and exports are low. Trade deflated by distance is a significant explanatory variable. But joint trade with Germany, Japan and the US might not affect city size because it does not necessarily imply trade openness.

The main focus of this chapter is the effect of trade openness on the whole urban system. The effect can be disentangled into two parts: first, more openness of an economy to trade reduces dramatically the incentives to cluster together: economies of agglomeration (centripetal forces) are offset by high costs of congestion (centrifugal forces). Second, the size of a particular city is an explanatory variable of the size of the other cities, since we find interaction among cities. Both results are entirely expected in our NEG framework. Nevertheless, political factors (political rights or civil liberties), first nature geographic conditions (access to sea or geographic location) and economic structure (share of labor force outside the agricultural sector) also explain city size.

One limitation of this chapter is that we do not connect variables across countries. For instance, political factors in one country affect the size of cities in other country. Or the size of one city affects the size of a city in a different country. One way forward is to assess the effects of variables across countries.

## References

Ades, AF and EL Glaeser (1995) Trade and circuses: Explaining urban giants, *Quarterly Journal of Economics* 110, 195–227.

Alonso-Villar, O (2001) Large metropolises in the third world: An explanation, *Urban Studies* 38, 1359–1371.

Anderson, JE and E van Wincoop (2003) Gravity with gravitas: A solution to the border puzzle, *American Economic Review* 93, 170–192.

Anderson, JE and E van Wincoop (2004) Trade costs, *Journal of Economic Literature* 42, 691–751.

Anselin, L (1999) *Spatial Econometrics.* Dallas, TX: Bruton Center, University of Texas.

Anselin, L (2003) Spatial externalities, spatial multipliers and spatial econometrics, *International Regional Science Review* 26, 153–166.

Anselin, L and AK Bera (1998) Spatial dependence in linear regression models with an introduction to spatial econometrics. In *Handbook of Applied Economic Statistics.* A Ullah and D Giles (Eds.). New York: Marcel Dekker, 237–289.

Baldwin, RE (1989) Measuring non-tariff trade policies. *Working Paper No.* 2978, National Bureau of Economic Research.

Behrens, K and J-F Thisse (2007) Regional economics: A new economic geography perspective, *Regional and Urban Economics* 37, 457–465.

Behrens, K, CG Gianmarco, IP Ottaviano and J-F Thisse (2007) Countries, regions and trade: On the welfare impacts of economic integration, *European Economic Review* 51, 1277–1301.

Bel, G and X Fageda (2008) Getting there fast: Globalization, intercontinental flights and location of headquarters, *Journal of Economic Geography* 8, 471–495.

Central Intelligence Agency. *The World Fact-Book.* Available at www.cia.gov. Accessed on March 27, 2013.

Christaller, W (1933) *Central Place in Southern German.* Jena, Germany: Fisher (English translation by CW Baskin, London: Prentice Hall, 1966).

Clayton, E and T Richardson (1989) Soviet control of city size, *Economic Development and Cultural Change* 38, 155–165.

Da Mata, D, U Deichman, JV Henderson, SV Lall and HG Wang (2005) Determinants of city growth in Brazil. *Working Paper No.* 11585, National Bureau of Economic Research.

Dixit, AK and JE Stiglitz (1977) Monopolistic competition and optimum product diversity, *American Economic Review* 67, 297–308.

Edwards, S (1993) Openness, trade liberalization, and growth in developing countries, *Journal of Economic Literature* 21, 1358–1393.

Elhorst, JP (2003) Specification and estimation of spatial panel data models, *International Regional Science Review* 26, 244–268.

Ellison, G and EL Glaeser (1999) The geographic concentration of industry. Does natural advantage explain agglomeration? *American Economic Review Papers and Proceedings* 89, 311–316.

Frankel, JA and D Romer (1999) Does trade cause growth, *American Economic Review* 89, 379–399.

Freedom House. *Freedom in the World: Country Ratings.* Available at www.freedomhouse.org. Accessed on April 20, 2013.

Fujita, M and T Mori (1996) The role of ports in the making of major cities: Self-agglomeration and hub-effect, *Journal of Development Economics* 49, 93–120.

Fujita, M and J-F Thisse (1996) Economics of agglomeration, *Journal of the Japanese and International Economies* 10, 339–378.

Fujita, M, P Krugman and AJ Venables (1999) *The Spatial Economy: Cities, Regions and International Trade.* Cambridge, MA: MIT Press.

Gaviria, A and E Stein (2000) The evolution of urban concentration around the world: A panel approach. *Working Paper No.* 414, Inter-American Development Bank.

Hanson, GH (1996) Integration and location of activities: Economic integration, intra industry trade, and frontier regions, *European Economic Review* 40, 941–949.

Hanson, GH (1997) Increasing returns, trade and the regional structure of wages, *The Economic Journal* 107, 113–133.

Hanson, GH (1998) North American economic integration and industry location, *Oxford Review of Economic Policy* 14, 30–43.

Harrison, AE (1996) Openness and growth: A time series, cross country analysis for developing countries, *Journal of Development Economics* 48, 419–447.

Heavens Above. Available at www.heavens-above.com. Accessed on February 27, 2006.

Helliwell, JF. Home Page. *World Trade Data Set.* Available at www.econ.ubc.ca/helliwell/. Accessed on February 6, 2006.

Henderson, JV. Home Page. *World Cities Data.* Available at www.econ.brown.edu/faculty/henderson. Accessed on June 1, 2013.

Henderson, JV (1974) The sizes and types of cities, *American Economic Review* 64, 640–656.

Henderson, JV, Z Shalizi and AJ Venables (2001) Geography and development, *Journal of Economic Geography* 1, 81–105.

Hotelling, H (1929) Stability in competitions, *Economic Journal* 39, 41–57.

Ionnides, YM (2004) Economic geography and the spatial evolution of wages in the United States. In *Advances in Spatial Econometric.* L Anselin, RJGM Florax and SJ Rey (Eds.). Berlin: Springer, 335–357.

Kim, S (1999) Regions, resources and economics geography: Sources of US regional comparative advantage, 1880–1987, *Regional Science and Urban Economics* 29, 1–32.

Kresl, PK and EH Fry (2005) *The Urban Response to Internationalization.* Cheltenham: Edward Elgar.

Krueger, AO (1997) Trade policy and economic development: How we learn, *American Economic Review* 87, 1–20.

Krugman, P (1991) Increasing returns and economic geography, *Journal of Political Economy* 99, 137–150.

Krugman, P and R Livas (1996) Trade policy and the third world metropolis, *Journal of Development Economics* 49, 137–150.

Le Sage JP. Home page. Available at www.spatial-econometrics.com. Accessed on March 27, 2006.

Limão, N and AJ Venables (2001) Infrastructure, geographical disadvantage, transport costs, and trade, *World Bank Economic Review* 15, 451–479.

Lösch, A (1940) *The Economics of Location.* Jena, Germany: Fischer (English translation, New Haven, CT: Yale University Press, 1954).

Mansori, KS (2003) The geographic effects of trade liberalization with increasing returns in transportation, *Journal of Regional Science* 43, 249–268.

Ministry of Finance of Japan. Available at www.mof.go.jp. Accessed on February 20, 2013.

Murata, Y (2003) Product diversity, taste heterogeneity, and geographic distribution of economic activities: Market *vs.* non-market interactions, *Journal of Urban Economics* 53, 126–144.

Nitsch, V (2006) Trade openness and urban concentration: New evidence, *Journal of Economic Integration* 21, 340–362.

Picard, PM and D-Z Zeng (2005) Agricultural sector and industrial agglomeration, *Journal of Development Economics* 77, 75–106.

Pritchett, L (1996) Measuring outward orientation in LDCs: Can it be done? *Journal of Development Economics* 49, 307–335.

Puga, D (1998) Urbanized patterns: European *versus* less developed countries, *Journal of Regional Science* 38, 231–252.

Puga, D (2010) The magnitude and causes of agglomeration economies, *Journal of Regional Science* 50, 203–219.

Rauch, JE (1991) Comparative advantage, geographic advantage and the volume of trade, *The Economic Journal* 101, 1230–1244.

Richardson, HW and C-H Bae (2005) *Globalization and Urban Development.* Berlin: Springer.

Rodriguez, F and D Rodrik (2000) Trade policy and economic growth: A skeptic's guide to the cross-national evidence. *Unpublished Manuscript*, University of Maryland and Harvard University.

Rosen, KT and M Resnick (1980) The size distribution of cities: An examination of the Pareto law and primacy, *Journal of Urban Economics* 8, 165–186.
Rossi-Hansberg, E (2006) A spatial theory of trade, *American Economic Review* 95, 1464–1491.
Samuelson, PA (1952) The transfer problem and transport costs: The terms of trade when impediments are absent, *Economic Journal* 62, 278–304.
Sohn, J, TJ Kim and GJD Hewings (2002) Information technology impacts on urban spatial structure in the Chicago region, *Geographical Analysis* 34, 313–329.
Statitisches Bundesamt Deutschland. Available at www.destatis.de. Accessed on March 27, 2013.
Tabuchi, T and J-F Thisse (2002) Taste heterogeneity, labor mobility and economic geography, *Journal of Development Economics* 69, 155–177.
UN (2003) *World Urbanization Prospects.* Available at www.esa.un.org/unup. Accessed on March 20, 2013.
US Census Bureau. Available at www.census.gov/foreign-trade. Accessed on March 27, 2013.
Venables, AJ (1998) The assessment: Trade and location, *Oxford Review of Economic Policy* 14, 1–6.
Von Thünen, JH (1826) *Der IsolierteStaat in Beiziehung au Landschaft und Nationalökonomie.* Hamburg (English translation by CM Wartenberg, *von Thünen's Isolated State*, Oxford: Pergamon Press, 1966).
Weber, A (1909) *Theory of Location of Industries.* Chicago, IL: University of Chicago Press.
Wen, M (2004) Relocation and agglomeration of Chinese industry, *Journal of Development Economics* 73, 329–347.
World Bank Indicators. Available at www.worldbank.org. Accessed on August 7, 2013.
Yanikkaya, H (2003) Trade openness and economic growth: A cross country empirical investigation, *Journal of Development Economics* 72, 57–89.
Zipf, GK (1949) *Human Behavior and the Principle of Least Effort.* New York: Addison Wesley.

## Appendices

### 10.A1. Construction of the Instrumental Variable

We construct the instrumental variable as follows. First, we estimate the coefficients of the gravity Equation (10.6) from Frankel and

Romer (1999),

$$\ln(\tau_{ij}/GDP_i) = a_0 + a_1 \ln D_{ij} + a_2 \ln N_i + a_3 \ln N_j + a_4(L_i + L_j) + B_{ij}a_5 + B_{ij}a_6 \ln D_{ij} + a_7 B_{ij} \ln N_i + a_8 B_{ij} \ln N_j + a_9 B_{ij} + a_{10} B_{ij}(L_i + L_j), \tag{10.A1}$$

where $\tau_{ij}/GDP_i$ is the share of trade between country $i$ and $j$ in $GDP$ at country $i$; $D_{ij}$ is the distance between country $i$ and country $j$; $N_i$ and $N_j$ denote the population in country $i$ and country $j$, respectively; $L_i$ and $L_j$ denote a dummy if country $i$ and $j$ have access to sea, respectively, see Anderson and van Wincoop (2003) for a critique of the gravity equation. The information is obtained for 1970 and 1985 for 165 countries. The potential number of observations is $165^2$, however there are missing observations in both periods. Information was obtained from John Helliwell's data set. The instrumental variable is then calculated using

$$\hat{T}_i = \sum_{j \neq i} e^{\hat{a} X_{ij}}.$$

Table 10.A1 contains the results of a regression of the actual share of trade in GDP on the instrumental variable. The sample only includes the 84 countries. They are correlated and $R^2$ are relatively high.

**Table 10.A1.** Regression on the constructed variable.

| Dependent variable: Actual share of trade in GDP | 1985 | 1970 |
|---|---|---|
| 1) Intercept | 3.220 | 3.016 |
| | *7.345* | *4.892* |
| 2) Constructed share of trade in GDP | 0.355 | 0.33.8 |
| | *8.397* | *7.656* |
| Coefficient of correlation | 0.630 | 0.494 |
| $R^2$ | 0.397 | 0.244 |
| Number of observations | 84 | 76 |

*Note*: Calculations carried out in MATLAB; $t$-values reported below estimated coefficients.

**Table 10.A2.** World cities sample.

| Region | Country: Cities |
|---|---|
| **North America** | **1. Canada:** Toronto, Montreal, Vancouver, Ottawa and Calgary. |
| | **2. United States:** NY, LA, Chicago, Philadelphia, Miami, Dallas-Fort Worth, Boston, Washington, D.C., Detroit, Houston, Atlanta, San Francisco-Oakland, Phoenix-Mesa, Seattle, San Diego, Minneapolis, Baltimore, St. Louis, Tampa-St. Petersburg, Denver-Aurora, Cleveland, Pittsburgh, Portland, San Jose, Riverside-San Bernardino, Cincinnati, Sacramento, Virginia Beach, Kansas City, Las Vegas, San Antonio, Milwaukee, Indianapolis, Providence, Orlando, Columbus and New Orleans. |
| | **3. Mexico:** Mexico City, Guadalajara, Monterrey, Toluca, Puebla, Tijuana, León, Ciudad Juárez and Torreón. |
| **Central America and the Caribbean** | **4. Costa Rica:** San José. |
| | **5. Dominican Republic:** Santo Domingo, Santiago, Romana, San Pedro de Macoris and San Francisco de Macorís |
| | **6. El Salvador:** San Salvador, Apopa, San Miguel, Santa Ana and Nueva San Salvador. |
| | **7. Guatemala:** Guatemala City and Quetzaltenango. |
| | **8. Haiti:** Port-au-Prince and Cape Haitien. |
| | **9. Honduras:** Tegucigalpa, San Pedro Sula, La Ceiba and Choloma. |
| | **10. Jamaica:** Kingston. |
| | **11. Nicaragua:** Managua, León, Chinandega, Masaya and Tipitapa. |
| | **12. Panama:** Panama City, Colon and David. |
| **South America** | **13. Argentina:** Buenos Aires, Córdoba, Rosario, Mendoza, San Miguel de Tucumán. |
| | **14. Bolivia:** La Paz, Santacruz, Cochabamba, Oruro and Sucre. |
| | **15. Brazil:** Sao Paulo, Río de Janeiro, Belo Horizonte, Porto Alegre, Recife, Salvador, Fortaleza, Brasilia, Curitiba, Campiñas, Belem, Goiania, Santos, Grande Vitoria, Manaus. |
| | **16. Chile:** Santiago, Concepción, Viña del Mar, Antofagasta and Valparaíso. |
| | **17. Colombia:** Santa Fe de Bogota, Medellín, Cali, Barranquilla and Bucaramanga. |

(*Continued*)

**Table 10.A2.** (*Continued*)

| Region | Country: Cities |
|---|---|
| | **18. Ecuador:** Guayaquil, Quito, Cuenca, Santo Domingo and Machala. |
| | **19. Paraguay:** Asunción and Ciudad del Este. |
| | **20. Peru:** Lima, Arequipa, Trujillo, Chiclayo and Iquitos. |
| | **21. Uruguay:** Montevideo and Salto. |
| | **22. Venezuela:** Caracas, Maracaibo, Valencia, Maracay and Barquisimeto. |
| **Asia** | **23. India:** Bombay, Calcuta, Delhi, Madras, Bangalore, Hyderabad, Ahmadabad, Pune, Surta, Kanpur, Jaipur, Lucknow, Nagpur, Patna, Indore, Vadodara, Bhopal, Coimbatore, Ludhiana, Kochi, Viskhapatnam, Agra, Varanasi, Madurai, Meerut, Nashik, Jabalpur, Jamshedpur, Asansol, Dhanbad, Allahabad and Faridabad. |
| | **24. Indonesia:** Jakarta, Bandung, Surabaja, Medan and Palembang. |
| | **25. Israel:** Tel Aviv-Jaffa, Haifa, Jerusalem, Beér Sheva ad Ashgelon. |
| | **26. Japan:** Tokyo, Osaka-Kobe, Nagoya, Fukuoka-Kitakyushu, Kyoto and Sapporo. |
| | **27. Jordan:** Amman, Zarqa, Irbid, Russeifa and Wad-as-Sir. |
| | **28. Korea:** Seoul, Pusan, Taegu, Inchón, Taejon, Kwangju and Ulsan. |
| | **29. Malaysia:** Kuala Lumpur, Klang, JohoreBharu, Ipoh and Petaling Jaya. |
| | **30. Nepal:** Katmandu, Biratnagar, Lalitpur, Pokhara and Birgunj. |
| | **31. Pakistan:** Karachi, Lahore, Faisalabad, Rawalpindi, Multan, Gujranwala, Hyderabad and Peshawar. |
| | **32. Philipines:** Metro Manila, Davao, Cebu, Zamboanga and Cagayan de Oro. |
| | **33. Saudi Arabia:** Riyadh, Jidda, Mecca, Medina and Damman. |
| | **34. Sri Lanka:** Colombo, Dehiwala/Mt. Lavinia, Moratuwa, Jaffna and Negombo. |
| | **36. Thailand:** Bangkok, Nontaburi, Nakhon-Ratchasima, Chon Buri and Chiang Mai. |
| | **37. Yemen:** Aden, Sanaá, Taiz, Al-Hudaydah and Ibb. |
| | **35. Syria:** Damascus, Aleppo, Homs, Lattakia and Hama. |

(*Continued*)

Table 10.A2. (*Continued*)

| Region | Country: Cities |
|---|---|
| **Europe** | **38. Austria:** Vienna, Linz, Graz, Salzburg ad Innsbruck. |
| | **39. Belgium:** Brussels, Antwerpen, Liège, Cherleroi and Gent. |
| | **40. Denmark:** Copenhagen, Arhus, Odense and Aalborg. |
| | **41. Finland:** Helsinki, Tampere, Turku, Oulu and Lahti. |
| | **42. France:** Paris, Lyon, Marseille-Aix-en- Provence, Lille and Nice-Cannes. |
| | **43. Germany:** Rhein-Ruhr North, Rhein- Main, Berlin, Rhein-Ruhr Middle, Rhein-Ruhr South, Sttutgart, Hamburg, Munich, Rhein-Neckar, Bielefeld, Hannover, Nuremberg and Aachen. |
| | **44. Greece:** Athens, Thessaloniki, Pátrai, Irákilon and Vólos. |
| | **45. Ireland:** Dublin and Cork. |
| | **46. Italy:** Milan, Naples, Rome, Turin and Genoa. |
| | **47. The Netherlands:** Rotterdam, Amsterdam, The Hague, Ultrech and Eindhoven-Tivoli. |
| | **48. Norway:** Oslo, Bergen, Stavanger, Trondheim and Frederikstad. |
| | **49. Portugal:** Lisbon, Porto, Penisula of Setubal, Braga and Funchal. |
| | **50. Spain:** Madrid, Barcelona, Valencia, Sevilla and Málaga. |
| | **51. Swiss:** Zürich, Geneve, Basel, Bern and Lausanne. |
| | **52. Turkey:** Istambul, Ankara, Izmir, Bursa and Adana. |
| | **53. United Kingdom:** London, Birmingham, Manchester, Leeds and Tyneside. |
| **Africa** | **54. Argelia:** Algiers, Oran, Constantine, Annaba and Batna. |
| | **55. Benin:** Cotonou, Djougu, Porto- Novo and Parakou. |
| | **56. Burkina Faso:** Ouagadougu, Koudogou and Bobo-Dioulasso. |
| | **57. Burundi:** Bujumburi. |
| | **58. Camerun:** Douala, Yaoundé, Garova, Marova and Bamenda. |
| | **59. Central Afircan Republic:** Bangui, Berberati, Bouar, Carnot and Bambari. |
| | **60. Chad:** NĎjamena. |
| | **61. Egypt:** Cairo, Alexandria, Port Said, Suez, and Al-Mahalla al-Kubra. |
| | **62. Ethiopia:** Addis Ababa, Dire Dawa, Nazret, Gondar and Dessie. |

(*Continued*)

**Table 10.A2.** (*Continued*)

| Region | Country: Cities |
|---|---|
| | **63. Ghana:** Accra, Kumasi, Secondi Takoradi, Tamale ad Ashaiman. |
| | **64. Ivory Coast:** Abidjan, Bouake, Yamoussoukro, Daloa and Korhogo. |
| | **65. Kenya:** Nairobi, Mombasa, Kisumo, Nakuro and Eldoret. |
| | **66. Liberia:** Monrovia. |
| | **67. Madagascar:** Antananarivo, Toamasino, Antsirabe, Fianarantsoa ad Mahajanga. |
| | **68. Malawi:** Blantyre- Lymbe, Lilongwe and Mzuzu. |
| | **69. Mali:** Bamako and Sikasso. |
| | **70. Morocco:** Casablanca, Rabat, Fès, Marrakech ad Agadir. |
| | **71. Niger:** Niamey, Maradi and Zinder. |
| | **72. Nigeria:** Lagos, Kano, Ibadan, Kaduna and Benin City. |
| | **73. Rwanda:** Kigala. |
| | **74. Senegal:** Dakar, Thies, Kaolak, Ziguinchor and Saint Louis. |
| | **75. Sierra Leone:** Freetown. |
| | **76. Somalia:** Mogadishu and Merca. |
| | **77. Sudan:** Khartoum, Port Sudan, Nyala, Kassala and Al Obeid. |
| | **78. Tanzania:** Dar es Salaam, Arusha, Mbeya, Mwanza and Zanzíbar. |
| | **79. Togo:** Lomé. |
| | **80. Tunisia:** Tunis, Sfax, Sousse, Dejerba ad Kairouan. |
| | **81. Uganda:** Kampala, Gulu, Jinja and Lira. |
| | **82. Dem. Rep. Congo:** Kinshasa, Lubumbashi Mbuji-Mayi, Boma and Kisangani. |
| | **83. Zambia:** Lusaka, Kitwe, Ndola, Kabwe and Chingola. |
| **Oceania** | **84. Australia:** Sydney, Melbourne, Brisbane, Perth and Adelaide. |

**Table 10.A3.** Data sources.

| Variable | Units | Period | Source |
|---|---|---|---|
| Capital city dummy | 1 or 0 | NA | 1999 Encarta Encyclopedia |
| Central location dummy | 1 or 0 | | CIA World Fact-book |
| Distance from city $i$ to city $j$ | Kms | NA | Own calculations using longitude and latitude from Vernon Henderson's web site; and Heavens-above.com |
| GDP per capita in 2000 prices | US $ | Average 1970, 1975, 1980 and 1985<br>Average 1985, 1990, ..., 2000<br>Average 70, ..., 2000 | World Bank Indicators |
| Import duties as a fraction of Imports | (0, 1) | Average 1970 and 1980<br>Average 1980 and 1990<br>Average 1970, ..., 1990 | Yanikkaya (2003) |
| Lack of Civil Liberties and Political Rights (goes from 1 to 7 each one) Dummy | 1 if both are higher than 3.5 and 0 otherwise | Average 1972, 1973, ..., 1985<br>Average 1985, 1986, ..., 2000<br>Average 1970, 1971 ..., 2000 | Freedom in the World of Freedom House |
| Log of land area | Thousands of Hectares | Average 1970, 1975, 1980 and 1985.<br>Average 1985, 1990, ..., 2000.<br>Average 70, ..., 2000 | World Bank Indicators |
| Log of non-urbanized population | Thousands | Average 1970, 1975, 1980 and 1985.<br>Average 1985, 1990, ..., 2000.<br>Average 70, ..., 2000 | UN World Urbanization Prospectus: Revision 2003 |

(*Continued*)

**Table 10.A3.** (*Continued*)

| Variable | Units | Period | Source |
|---|---|---|---|
| Log of urbanized population outside the $i$ most populated cities | Thousands | Average 1970, 1975, 1980 and 1985. Average 1985, 1990, ..., 2000. Average 70, ..., 2000 | UN World Urbanization Prospects: Revision 2003 |
| OECD dummy | 0 or 1 | NA | OECD web site |
| Population in the 5 largest cities | Thousands | Average 1970, 1975, 1980 and 1985 Average 1985, 1990, ..., 2000 | UN World Urbanization Prospectus: Revision 2003 |
| Port city dummy | 1 or 0 | NA | 1999 Encarta Encyclopedia |
| Roads, total network | Kms | Average 1970, 1975, 1980 and 1985 Average 1985, 1990, ..., 2000 Average 70, ..., 2000 | World Bank Indicators |
| Share of Imports in GDP | (0, 1) | Average 1970, 1975, 1980 and 1985 Average 1985, 1990, ..., 2000. Average 70, ..., 2000 | World Bank Indicators |
| Share of the non-agricultural labor force | (0, 1) | Average 1970, 1975, 1980 and 1985 Average 1985, 1990, ..., 2000 | World Bank Indicators |
| Share of trade, imports and exports in GDP | (0, 1) | Average 1970, 1975, 1980 and 1985 Average 1985, 1990, ..., 2000 Average 70, ..., 2000 | World Bank Indicators |

(*Continued*)

**Table 10.A3.** (*Continued*)

| Variable | Units | Period | Source |
|---|---|---|---|
| Share of trade, imports and exports with Japan + US + Germany in GDP | (0, 1) | Average 1970, 1975, 1980 and 1985<br>Average 1985, 1990, ..., 2000<br>Average 1970, 1975, ..., 2000 | Foreign Trade Statistics. US Census Bureau.<br>Federal Statistics Office of Germany.<br>Trade Statistics of Japan. Ministry of Finance.<br>John F. Helliwell data set. |
| Telephone mainlines (per 1,000 people) | (0, 1) | Average 1970, 1975, 1980 and 1985<br>Average 1985, 1990, ..., 2000<br>Average 70, ..., 2000 | World Bank Indicators |
| Weighted share of trade, imports and exports with US in GDP | (0, 1) | Average 1970, 1975, 1980 and 1985<br>Average 1985, 1990, ..., 2000<br>Average 1970, 1975, ..., 2000 | Foreign Trade Statistics. US Census Bureau.<br>CIA The World Fact-book. |

# Chapter 11

# Infrastructure and the International Export Performance of Turkish Regions

*Mehmet Guney Celbis*, Peter Nijkamp† and Jacques Poot‡*

**UNU-MERIT, Maastricht Graduate School of Governance, Maastricht University*

*†Department of Spatial Economics, Free University of Amsterdam*

*‡National Institute of Demographic and Economic Analysis, University of Waikato*

*We estimate the Anderson and van Wincoop model of trade by using the data on the bilateral export flows from 26 Turkish regions to 180 countries for the years 2002–2010. Regional transportation and communication infrastructure capacity, the positioning of point infrastructure in a region, and geography are explicitly accounted for. Our results highlight that land infrastructure, air transport capacity, and private maritime infrastructure presence, together with the distance of regional economies to exit nodes such as ports and airports, are important determinants of export performance. Based on our preferred regression where multilateral resistance terms are accounted for, we estimate that increases in the current land infrastructure, air transport capacity, and number of private ports of 1% increases exports approximately by 0.38%, 0.14%, and 0.045% respectively.*

## 11.1. Introduction

Since the early 2000's, Turkey has been ambitiously investing in its transportation infrastructure. This period of increase in infrastructure investment has been accompanied by a surge in export performance, but at the same time has been coinciding with an increase in the current accounts deficit. Roughly at the same time as this upward trend in infrastructure investments and exports in Turkey, the economic literature focusing on the relationship between infrastructure and trade has also become enriched with many new research results. A positive effect of infrastructure on trade through the reduction of transport costs has been documented by: Bougheas *et al.* (1999) for a sample of European countries; Limao and Venables (2001), Nordas and Piermartini (2004), Carrre (2006), Iwanow and Kirkpatrick (2009) and Portugal-Perez and Wilson (2012) for samples consisting of a range of countries around the world, Vijil and Wagner (2012) for a sample of developing countries, and Celbis *et al.* (2015a) by means of meta-analysis, among others. In accordance with these results, the 2009 OECD/WTO report on aid for trade underlines the significance of infrastructure as "one of the most important regional public goods with enormous potential to facilitate cross-border trade, growth and development" (OECD/WTO, 2009).

A recent study on Turkey by Kustepeli *et al.* (2012) found no significant relationship between country-wide highway infrastructure[1] and international trade. However, the authors also point out that there is a negative correlation between highway infrastructure investment and highway length.[2] Considering that road infrastructure represents only a part of all trade-related infrastructure,[3] and that infrastructure is not uniformly distributed among regions, it would be beneficial to focus on the infrastructure-trade relationship with explicit emphasis on different infrastructure categories and on the positioning of infrastructure in space. Therefore, this study aims to answer the following two questions: first, how much of the

[1]The authors measure infrastructure interchangeably in two ways: the share of highway expenditures in the public budget, and highway length.

[2]We assume that a possible reason for their finding could be that investment could have been made for removing older, curvier roads, and replacing them with straighter roads (or for example, building a tunnel) which would reduce the length of a highway from one point to another.

[3]As of 2009, the distribution of Turkish exports by modes of transportation were as follows: Roads 41.7%, Sea 46.0%, Air 9.5%, Rail 0.9%, and other modes 1.8% (Karacadag Development Agency, 2011).

recent expansion and the sub-regional differences in Turkey's export performance can be attributed to trade-related infrastructure? Second, how did the different types of infrastructure impact on exports? The answer to these questions can potentially provide some valuable information not only for Turkey but also for other emerging economies and LDC's where infrastructure deprivation remains as a crucial issue. Additionally, we note that many trade studies measure point infrastructure in terms of traffic (such as port or airport traffic). We aim to answer the above questions with a focus on capacity rather than traffic in order to reduce endogeneity concerns.

## 11.2. Theoretical Framework

We follow the Anderson and van Wincoop (2003) (henceforth AvW) gravity model of trade, in which consumers in region $j$ maximize the following utility function:

$$U_j = \left( \sum_{i=1}^{n} \beta_i^{\frac{1-\sigma}{\sigma}} c_{ij}^{\frac{\sigma-1}{\sigma}} \right)^{\frac{\sigma}{\sigma-1}}, \quad i \neq j, \tag{11.1}$$

subject to:

$$\sum_{i=1}^{n} c_{ij} \tau_{ij} p_i = y_j, \tag{11.2}$$

where $\sigma$ is the elasticity of substitution, $c_{ij}$ is the consumption of the unique product of region $i$ by the consumers in region $j$, $\beta_i > 0$ is a distribution parameter for determining the weight assigned by consumers in $j$ on the unique product of $i$, and the supply price of the exporter is $p_i$. AvW define $p_{ij}$ as the price for goods of region $i$ that the consumers in $j$ face. The supply price $p_i$ is scaled by a trade cost factor ($t_{ij} > 1$) that applies to the trade from $i$ to $j$ such that $p_i t_{ij} = p_{ij}$.[4] Consequently, the budget constraint for region $j$ in the AvW model is $\sum_i c_{ij} t_{ij} p_i = y_j$. In our adaptation of the AvW

[4]The AvW model assumes frictionless intra-regional trade such that $t_{ii} = 1$.

model, we define $\tau_{ij}$ as the trade costs divided by the export capacity of region $i$ denoted by $s_i$:

$$\tau_{ij} = \frac{t_{ij}}{s_i}, \tag{11.3}$$

where $0 < s_i < 1$. If $s_i$ could equal to 1, then the export capacity of region $i$ is at a maximum, so that the c.i.f. price to consumers in region $j$ is at a minimum. Alternatively, if $s_i$ is close to zero, region $i$ has virtually no capacity to export and the cost of exporting from $i$ to $j$ would be prohibitively high. Therefore, exports from $i$ to $j$ are subject to two constraints: (1) the budget constraint of region $j$ and (2) the export capacity constraint of region $i$. The following market clearing condition is imposed:

$$y_j = \sum_{i=1}^{n} x_{ji}, \tag{11.4}$$

where $x_{ji}$ is the value of exports of $j$ to $i$ and $p_j \tau_{ji} c_{ji} = x_{ji}$.

Equation (11.4) says that the income of region $j$ is the sum of all exports of $j$ to all other regions $i$. Solving the above defined model leads to the gravity equation:

$$x_{ij} = \frac{y_j y_i}{y_w} \left( \frac{t_{ij}/s_i}{P_j P_i} \right)^{1-\sigma}, \tag{11.5}$$

where $y_w$ is the world income. A common proxy for $t_{ij}$ in trade literature is the distance between origin and destination economies. However, it has been emphasized by Beckerman (1956) that *relative distance* should be taken into consideration rather than absolute distance when examining the impact of distance on trade flows. Beckerman (1956) also suggested using prices in the origin and destination economies for measuring the relative distances. The author highlights two distance elements and defines them as follows: "the relative distance of every other country to the given country, which will influence the import pattern of the given country in one way" and "the relative distance of the given country to each other country, which will affect the export pattern of each other country and will thereby also have an effect on the import pattern of the given country" Beckerman (1956, p. 36). In the Anderson and van Wincoop

(2003) model this concept is refined as "multilateral resistance" and formalized as price indices in the terms $P_j$ and $P_i$ where:

$$P_j^{1-\sigma} = \sum_{i=1}^{n} \left(\frac{\tau_{ij}}{P_i}\right)^{1-\sigma} \frac{y_i}{y_w}, \tag{11.6}$$

$$P_i^{1-\sigma} = \sum_{j=1}^{n} \left(\frac{\tau_{ij}}{P_j}\right)^{1-\sigma} \frac{y_j}{y_w}. \tag{11.7}$$

AvW assumes symmetry of trade barriers ($\tau_{ij} = \tau_{ji}$). This condition translates to our adaptation as $\frac{t_{ij}}{s_i} = \frac{t_{ji}}{s_j}$ which assumes that the trade costs that $i$ and $j$ face relative to their own export capacities are equal.

The log-linearization of (11.5) yields:

$$\begin{aligned} \ln X_{ij} &= \ln y_j + \ln y_i - \ln y_w + (1-\sigma)\ln t_{ij} \\ &\quad - (1-\sigma)\ln s_i - (1-\sigma)\ln P_j - (1-\sigma)\ln P_i. \end{aligned} \tag{11.8}$$

Assuming that $\sigma > 1$, the closer region $i$ is to its full capacity to export, the higher the export flows from $i$ to $j$ conditional on the level of income of the consumers in $j$.

Trade costs $t_{ij}$ are defined by Anderson and van Wincoop (2004) as:

$$t_{ij} = \prod_{m}^{M} (z_{ij}^m)^{\gamma_m}, \tag{11.9}$$

where $z_{ij}^m$ is the $m$'th observable factor for regions $i$ and $j$ that is associated with trade costs $t_{ij}$, and $\gamma_m$ is the parameter measuring the role of the $m$'th factor in trade costs. Substituting (11.9) into (11.8) gives:

$$\begin{aligned} \ln X_{ij} &= \ln y_j + \ln y_i - \ln y_w + (1-\sigma)\sum_{m}^{M} \gamma_m \ln z_{ij}^m \\ &\quad + (\sigma-1)\ln s_i - (1-\sigma)\ln P_j - (1-\sigma)\ln P_i \end{aligned} \tag{11.10}$$

which yields our regression equation to be estimated after adding an error term to the right hand side. Section 11.4 explicitly shows the variables corresponding to each term in Equation (11.10).

## 11.3. Data and Descriptive Statistics

The system of reporting the regional output data for Turkey has gone through several modifications in the last decade. The spatial scale has been changed to NUTS 2 from NUTS 3[5] and the indicator of output has been changed to gross value added from gross domestic product. This change in reporting also corresponds time-wise to a two year gap in the data between 2001 and 2004. Moreover, the regional public investments data are reported only if province (NUTS 3) specific, but not if an investment was directed to more than one NUTS 3 level province. To cope with these issues in the data, we use the adjusted NUTS 2 level GVA and public investment figures compiled by Celbis *et al.* (2015b). To summarize, the adjusted series for both these variables account for the differences in spatial scale in the officially reported data by (1) aggregating NUTS 3 (provincial) figures to NUTS 2 (regional) ones, (2) adjusting for the change of measurement from GDP to GVA, and (3) imputing the two consecutive missing years. Celbis *et al.* (2015b) also show for a sample of three regions, that inflating the public investment figures by an estimated amount[6] for each region in order to account for the unreported province-specific investments cause roughly a parallel shift upwards in the investment trend lines for these regions and advocate that using the officially reported data should not cause *biases*.[7]

Table 11.A.2 lists the 26 regions that form the basis of the empirical analysis. The boundaries of these regions are displayed in Figure 11.1.[8] Table 11.1 presents the sources and definitions of

[5]NUTS stands for "Nomenclature of Units for Territorial Statistics".

[6]This estimation is the result of meticulous extraction of investment figures reported separately by project name with attached locational information.

[7]Celbis *et al.* (2015b) use the GVA data for the year 2011 in their adjustments while in our study their adjustment process is replicated including the GVA figures up to the year 2010.

[8]These regions are not administrative units but only statistical regions. The largest administrative sub-national units in Turkey are provinces. All regions consist of at least two provinces, except for Istanbul, Ankara, and Izmir which are provinces and regions at the same time.

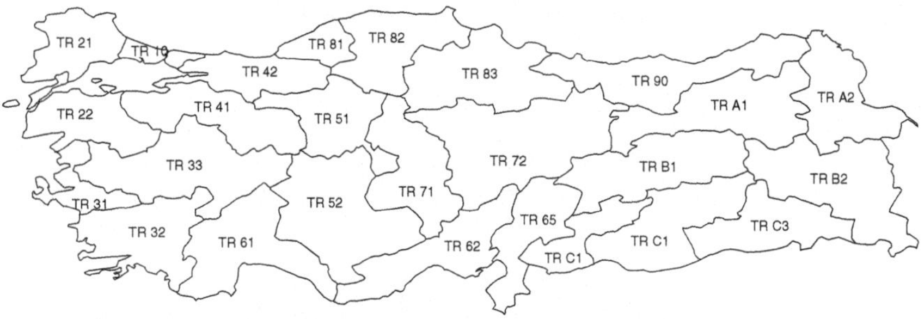


**Figure 11.1.** NUTS-2 level regional map of Turkey.

the variables used in the estimations. We use a set of covariates that consist of both continuous and dummy variables. Several of the variables, especially the geographical ones and some of the infrastructure capacity variables are either completely time invariant, or only exhibit very small changes over time. In our estimations this causes some information to be lost or some coefficients to be estimated imprecisely if regional fixed effects are included. Additionally, some variables such as *Air capacity* and *EU customs union* are constant for some regions or countries throughout the time range while some variation is present for other trading units. This implies that the fixed effects estimation would still keep such variables even though for many observations in the sample the figures would be absorbed by the fixed effects. Therefore, in our fixed effects estimations, we manually drop such "mostly constant" variables for consistency. We employ distance based variables as in Granato (2008) from regional cores to exit nodes as a component of transport costs. These variables are also constant since they are defined in terms of Euclidean distance rather than road distance.

The descriptive statistics of the variables in our panel are presented in Table 11.2(a and b) for region specific and general variables respectively. All summaries are based on observations for nine years.[9] These tables show that for some regions certain types of

[9]The continuous variables that enter the estimations in natural logarithms are transformed to ln form after adding one if they include minimum values of zero in order to avoid values of ln(0).

Table 11.1. Variable definitions.

| Name | Year Coverage | Description |
|---|---|---|
| $Exports_{ij,t}$ | 2002–2010 | Bilateral value of regional total exports of region $i$ to country $j$ in constant 2005 100,000 USD. *Source*: Turkstat. |
| *Regional (exporter)* $GVA_{it}$ | 2002–2010 | Regional gross value added in constant 2005 100,000 USD. Modified as specified in the Appendix. *Source*: Turkstat |
| *Country (importer)* $GVA_{jt}$ | 2002–2010 | Partner country gross value added constant 2005 100,000 USD. Modified as specified in the Appendix. *Source*: UN: http://unstats.un.org/unsd/snaama/Introduction.asp. |
| $Distance_{ij}$ | Constant | Euclidean distance between the most populous province of the region and the capital of the partner country. *Source* (for region coordinates): http://www.tageo.com/index-e-tu-cities-TR.htm. Coordinates for Sakarya, Artvin, Agri, Ardahan, Tunceli are obtained from www.wikipedia.org. *Source* for country coordinates: UN: http://esa.un.org/unup/CDROM/Urban-Agglomerations.htm. The coordinate for Belgium is from www.wikipedia.org, converted to decimal degrees using webtool at: http://transition.fcc.gov/mb/audio/bickel/DDDMMSS-decimal.html..[10] |
| *Partner country exchange* $rate_{jt}$ | 2002–2010 | Partner country exchange rate to Turkish Lira. *Source*: Penn world Table 7.1 (Version 2 for China). |

(*Continued*)

[10]The center of a region is taken as its most populous city of the region in 2008 (Turkstat). Generated from coordinates using Stata command *spmat* (Drukker *et al.*, 2011). MRT corrected as suggested by Baier and Bergstrand (2009).

Table 11.1. (*Continued*)

| Name | Year Coverage | Description |
|---|---|---|
| *Land transport infrastructure$_{it}$* | 2002–2010 | Index made from highway, road, and railroad lengths per 1000 square meters. National export shares that go through these type of infrastructure are used as the weights. |
| *Avg. min. euclidean distance to major airports$_{it}$* | constant | Regional average distance of each provincial center to the closest major airport. Added 1 km in cases where the point infrastructure is at the provincial center in order to avoid values of ln(0). *Source*: Airport data and coordinates from www.dhmi.gov.tr/havaalanlari.aspx. Coordinates for Sabiha Gokcen airport added from: www.istanbulairports.com/general-informations.htm. Data for Adiyaman airport is from http://en.wikipedia.org/wiki/Ad%C4%B1yaman_Airport. |
| *Avg. min. euclidean distance to major ports$_{it}$* | constant | Regional average distance of each provincial center to the closest major port. Added 1 km in cases where the point infrastructure is at the provincial center in order to avoid values of ln(0). *Source*: Port coordinates are obtained from http://www.searates.com/maritime/Turkey.htm, converted to decimal degrees using webtool at http://transition.fcc.gov/mb/audio/bickel/DDDMMSS-decimal.html (Mersin Port Administration was privatizated on 11.05.2007). |
| *Public port capacity$_{it}$* | constant (as of 2006) | Port handling capacity in major ports in 100,000 tons (General cargo and dry bulk). |
| *Air capacity$_{it}$* | 2002–2010 | Total passenger capacity (in 100,000 persons) of the region's airports. Compiled from the information on area and establishment dates available at several websites of the Republic of Turkey: Ministry of Transport, Maritime Affairs and Communication. |
| *Similar language$_{ij}$* | constant | Equals to 1 if parner country has a Turkic language as an official language, zero otherwise. |
| *EU customs union$_{ij,t}$* | 2002–2010 | Dummy = 1 if the partner country is an EU member, therefore being in customs union with Turkey. |

(*Continued*)

**Table 11.1.** (*Continued*)

| Name | Year Coverage | Description |
|---|---|---|
| *DSL lines*$_{it}$ | 2002–2010 | Number of DSL/ADSL lines in the PTT offices per 1000 persons. *Source*: Republic of Turkey–General Directorate of PTT. Values for 2002 and 2005 are imputed as shown in the Appendix. |
| *Country (importer) population*$_{jt}$ | 2002–2010 | Partner country population (100,000 persons). *Source*: World Bank. |
| *Regional (exporter) population*$_{it}$ | 2002–2010 | Regional population (100,000 persons). *Source*: OECDstat. |
| *Common open border*$_{ij}$ | constant | Equals to 1 if the region and the partner country share a common border that is open to trade, zero otherwise. |
| *Partner country is landlocked*$_j$ | constant | Equals to 1 if the partner country is landlocked, zero otherwise. |

air and, naturally, maritime infrastructure does not exist at all. The summarized variables in levels enter the econometric estimations in natural logarithms as suggested by the theoretical model presented in Section 11.2 (except the dummy variables).

Figures 11.2 to 11.4 show the trends in country-wide exports, public investments in transportation and communication, and gross value added respectively for the years 2002–2010. A general upwards trend can be observed for all three indicators. Figure 11.5 plots the relationship between exports and public investments in transportation and communication observed during the nine-year period. A positive association is present, however higher values of investment are not always corresponding to higher values of exports. This can be attributable to a possible satiation effect: After a certain point, investments and exports may no longer be strongly related. It is also important to note that no implication on causation can be made at this point. In order to explore the spatial dimension for these figures, we plot the regionally disaggregated trend lines for the five

**Table 11.2.** Summary statistics.

| Variable | Mean | Std. Dev. | Min. | Max. | N |
|---|---|---|---|---|---|
| (a) Exporting regions | | | | | |
| *Regional Exports*$_{it}$ | 1764.69 | 5156.16 | 0 | 47666.66 | 1620 |
| *Regional (Exporter) GVA*$_{it}$ | 133058.42 | 178652.48 | 19622.32 | 1072149.75 | 234 |
| *Land transport infrastructure*$_{it}$ | 75.73 | 17.57 | 50.78 | 139.82 | 234 |
| *DSL lines per cap.*$_{it}$ | 0.046 | 0.038 | 0.0005 | 0.31 | 234 |
| *Air capacity*$_{it}$ | 35.03 | 59.92 | 0 | 285 | 234 |
| *Public port capacity*$_{i}$ | 6.57 | 11.21 | 0 | 32.47 | 234 |
| *Number of private ports*$_{i}$ | 2.42 | 5.36 | 0 | 27 | 234 |
| *Avg. min. dist. to major airports*$_{i}$ | 3.61 | 3.08 | 0.14 | 10.24 | 234 |
| *Avg. min. dist. to major ports*$_{i}$ | 2.40 | 1.85 | 0.09 | 6.98 | 234 |
| *Region (exporter) Population*$_{it}$ | 27.32 | 20.36 | 7.33 | 129.15 | 234 |
| (b) Importing countries | | | | | |
| *Country (importer) GVA*$_{jt}$ | 2379450.86 | 10587286.74 | 955.01 | 132041000 | 1620 |
| *distance*$_{ij}$ | 5897.20 | 4061.41 | 449.86 | 17401.78 | 1620 |
| *MRT corrected dist.*$_{ij}$ | 0.0002 | 0.00004 | 0.0001 | 0.0003 | 1620 |
| *Exchange rate*$_{ij,t}$ | 384.62 | 1486.86 | 0.19 | 21226.34 | 1548 |
| *EU customs union*$_{ij,t}$ | 0.11 | 0.32 | 0 | 1 | 1620 |
| *Similar language*$_{ij}$ | 0.028 | 0.16 | 0 | 1 | 1620 |
| *Country (importer) Population*$_{jt}$ | 345.41 | 1337.89 | 0.28 | 13378.25 | 1620 |
| *landlocked importer*$_{j}$ | 0.22 | 0.42 | 0 | 1 | 1620 |
| *Common open border*$_{ij}$ | 0.028 | 0.16 | 0 | 1 | 1620 |

economically largest regions[11] in natural logarithms:[12] Figures 11.6 and 11.7 show the trends in exports and investments respectively for these regions. The largest economy of the country, Istanbul, is

[11] As of 2008.

[12] We use the logarithmic transformation to avoid a large gap in the graph between the region with the highest GVA and the other four.

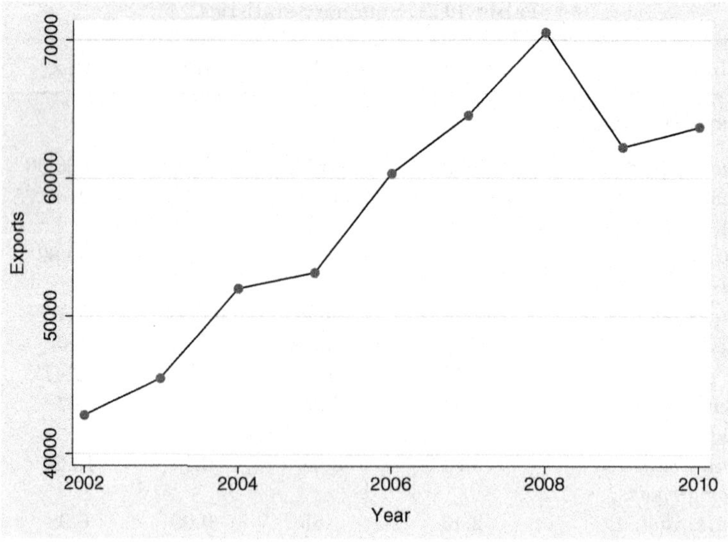


**Figure 11.2.** Exports, Turkey (constant 2005 millions of USD).

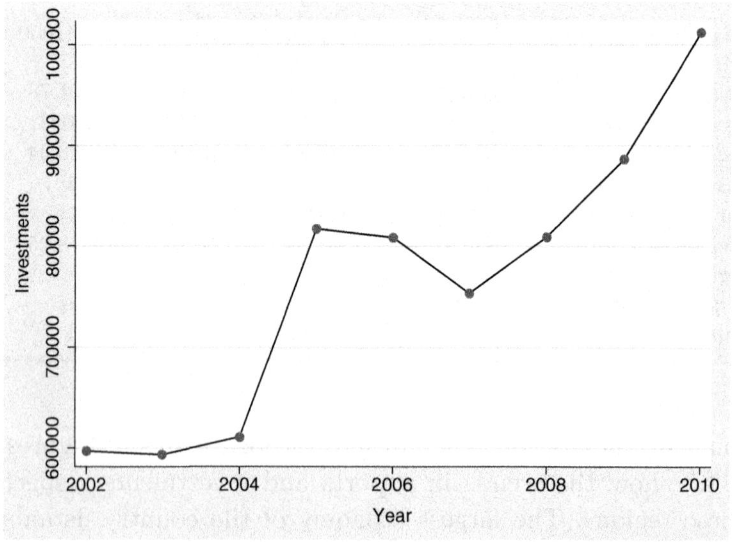


**Figure 11.3.** Public investments in transportation and communication, Turkey (constant 2005 millions of USD).

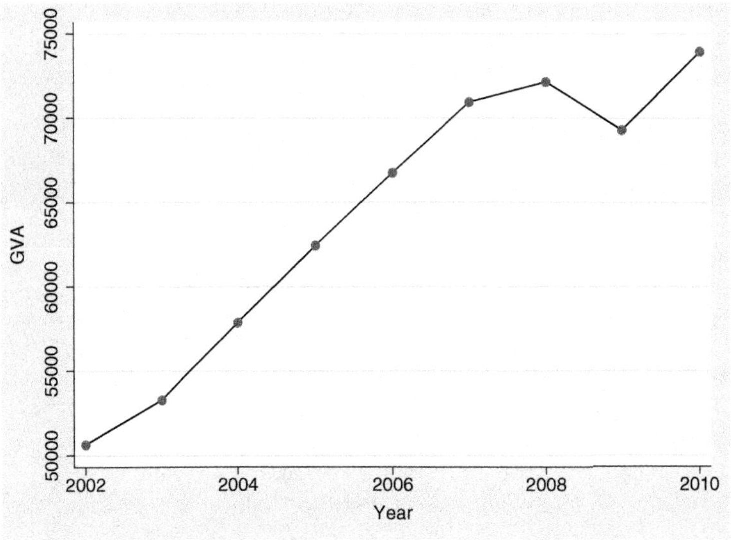


**Figure 11.4.** Gross value added, Turkey (constant 2005 billions of USD).

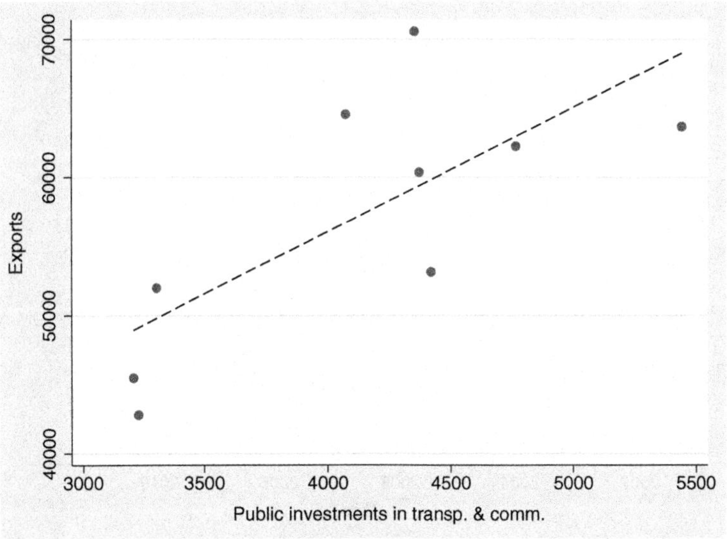


**Figure 11.5.** Exports and public investment in transportation and communication, Turkey (constant 2005 millions USD).

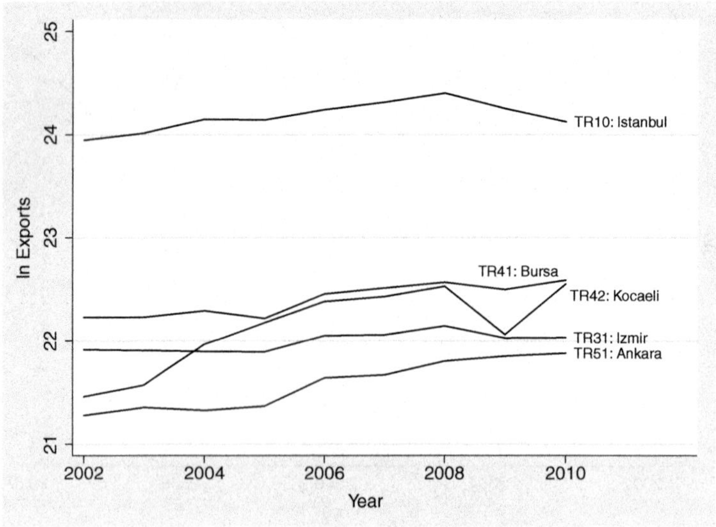


**Figure 11.6.** The natural logarithm of regional exports for the five largest regions, Turkey (constant 2005 millions of USD).

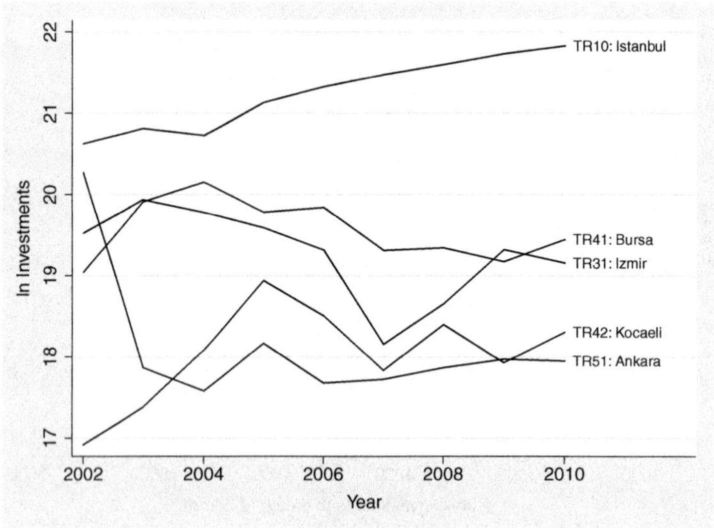


**Figure 11.7.** The natural logarithm of public investments in transportation and communication for the five largest regions, Turkey (constant 2005 millions of USD).

persistently higher than the other four largest economies in both exports and investments. While for exports, smoother trend lines are observed, the trend lines for investments are rather erratic except for Istanbul. Since the investment allocation is subject to central decision-making in Turkey where the decision-makers consider a range of factors before directing regional public investments (Celbis *et al.*, 2015b), relatively smooth trends would have implied that investment decisions are mostly unchanged from one year to another while this figure suggests otherwise.

The spatial variation in the export and investment figures for the years 2002 and 2010 are presented in Figures 11.8(a), 11.8(b), 11.9(a) and 11.9(b) respectively. These maps which present a snapshot of the geographic distribution for the first and last years of the sample

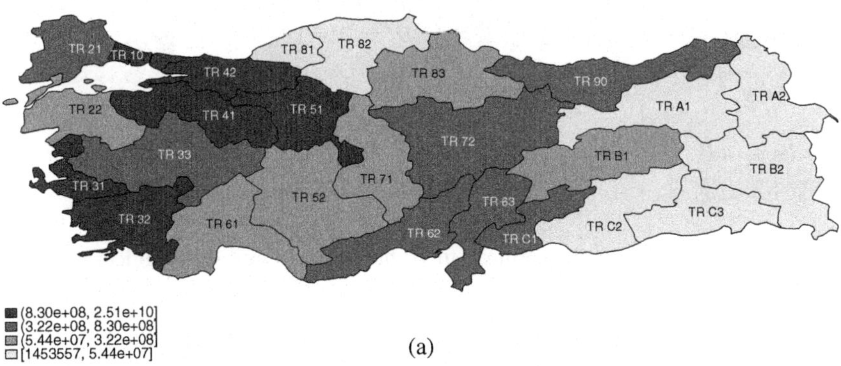


(a)

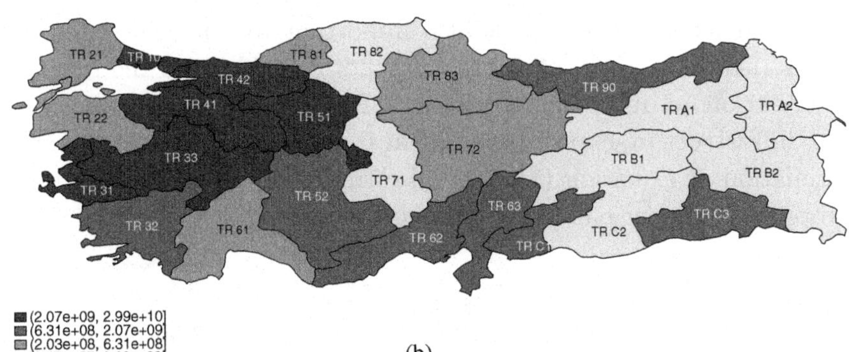


(b)

**Figure 11.8.** Regional exports.

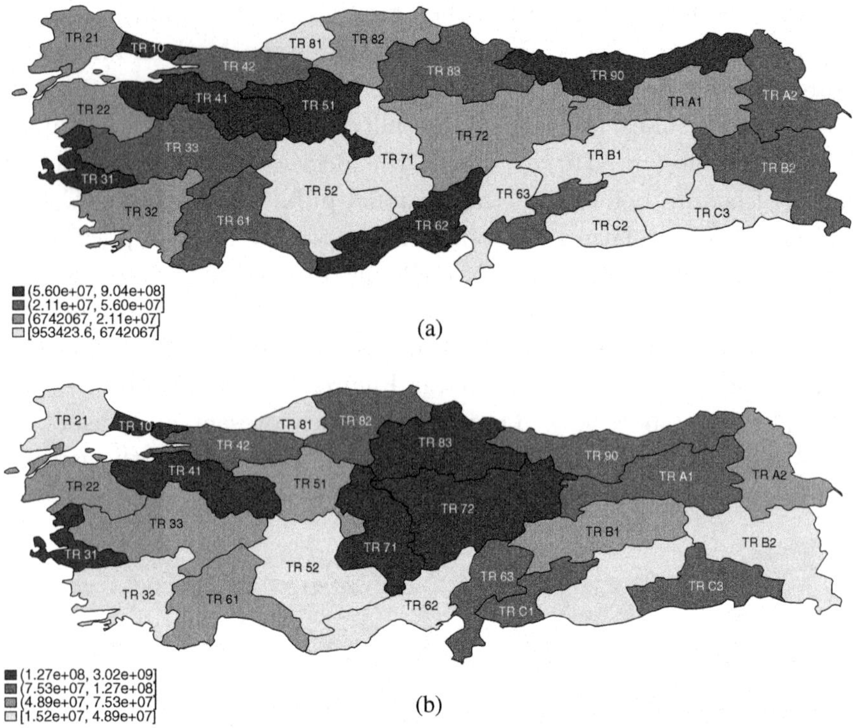


**Figure 11.9.** Public investment in transportation and communication.

suggest that the relative export performances of the regions did not change drastically[13,14] while for investments there is not such a persistence over time. It is also important to underline that the infrastructure investment figures may not coincide with the regional distribution of infrastructure stock. For a closer examination of the infrastructure-export relationship, Section 11.4 discusses the estimation of Equation (11.10). All estimations are conducted after dropping importer partner countries that have zero imports through

[13]Except for region TRC: 3 in the south-east.

[14]All maps have been made by using the *spmap* command in Stata developed by Pisati (2007). NUTS 3 provinces in the originally available shapefile have been aggregated to NUTS 2 regions using the Stata module *mergepoly* by Picard and Stepner (2012).

the covered nine years with 23 or more of the regions of Turkey. We are then left with 180 countries in our data set out of the original 186 countries.[15]

## 11.4. Estimation and Empirical Results

There are two methods that are common in the trade literature for controlling for the unobservable multilateral resistance terms $P_j$ and $P_i$, namely by estimating the gravity model with importer and exporter fixed effects or by implementing the approach suggested by Baier and Bergstrand (2009) for approximating the MRT's expressed as price indices in Equation (11.5). The Baier and Bergstrand (2009) method is adapted to our split-sample (non-symmetric trade matrix) case for the distance variable as follows; replacing their GDP-share weighted averages with simple averages (*i.e.*, there is no GDP weighting of the variables in our study), we adjust the distance variable for MRT's as: $\ln \, MRT \ adjusted \ distance_{ij} = \ln Distance_{ij} - \left(\frac{1}{n}\right)\sum_j^n \ln Distance_{ij} - \left(\frac{1}{m}\right)\sum_i^m \ln Distance_{ij} + \left(\frac{1}{mn}\right)\sum_i^m \sum_j^n \ln Distance_{ij}$ where $n$ is the number of importing countries and $m$ is the number of exporting regions. The first term on the right-hand-side is the unadjusted ln distance of the exporting region $i$ to the importing country $j$, the second term is the average ln distance of the exporting region $i$ to all importing countries, the third term is the average ln distance of all exporting regions to the importing country $j$, and the fourth term is the average ln distance of all exporting regions to all importing countries. Additionally, if a random distribution of multilateral resistances is assumed, the specification can be estimated using a random effects model (Shepherd, 2012). We use all three approaches in our estimations. However, a pair random effect estimation is ruled out in favor of fixed effects estimation by the Hausman test statistic reported in Table 11.4.

[15] Among the six countries dropped, Sudan has been dropped due to missing years in the data.

We define the terms in Equation (11.10) as functions of several empirical variables as follows:

$$\begin{aligned}
X_{ij} &= Exports_{ij}, \\
y_i &= Region\ (exporter)\ GVA_i \\
z_{ij}^m &= f(Distance_{ij}, Average\ minimum\ distance\ to\ major \\
&\quad airports_i,\ Average\ minimum\ distance\ to\ major\ ports_i, \\
&\quad Common\ open\ border_{ij}), \\
s_i &= g(Land\ transport\ infrastructure_i,\ Public\ port\ capacity_i, \\
&\quad Air\ capacity_i,\ DSL\ lines\ per\ capita_{it}).
\end{aligned}$$

As the parameter $\sigma$ is associated with the terms $\sum_m^M \gamma_m \ln z_{ij}$ and $\ln s_i$ in Equation (11.10), and these terms are determined by a multitude of empirically specified variables, we do not attempt an explicit estimation of this parameter of the structural model. In order to augment the theoretical gravity model with variables that account for region and country characteristics and their connectivity, the following variables are added to the specification: *Partner country exchange rate*$_j$, *Similar language*$_{ij}$, *EU customs union*$_{ij}$, *Country (importer) population*$_j$, *Regional (exporter) population*$_i$, *and Partner country is landlocked*$_j$.

After including the time index $t$, constant and error terms, the final specification is:

$$\begin{aligned}
&\ln Exports_{ij,t} \\
&\quad = a + \beta_1 \ln Regional\ (exporter)\ GVA_{it} \\
&\qquad + \beta_2 \ln Country\ (importer)\ GVA_{jt} \\
&\qquad + \beta_3 \ln Distance_{ij} + \beta_4 \ln(Partner\ country\ exchange\ rate)_{jt} \\
&\qquad + \beta_5 EU\ customs\ union_{jt} + \beta_6 Similar\ language_j \\
&\qquad + \beta_7 Land\ transport\ infrastructure_{it} + \beta_8 \ln DSL\ per\ capita_{it} \\
&\qquad + \beta_9 \ln Air\ capacity_{it} + \beta_{10} \ln Public\ port\ capacity_i \\
&\qquad + \beta_{11} Number\ of\ private\ ports_i
\end{aligned}$$

$$+\beta_{12} \ln Average\ minimum\ distance\ to\ major\ airports_i$$
$$+\beta_{13} \ln Average\ minimum\ distance\ to\ major\ ports_i$$
$$+\beta_{14} \ln Regional\ (exporter)\ population_{it}$$
$$+\beta_{15} \ln Country\ (importer)\ population_{jt}$$
$$+\beta_{16} Partner\ country\ is\ landlocked_j$$
$$+Common\ open\ border_{ij} + \epsilon_{ij,t}. \quad (11.11)$$

Table 11.3 presents estimation results of pooled OLS models with and without year dummies, and of an OLS model with MRT adjusted distance variable. Additionally, because in our data set 19,379 observations of zero exports exist, which is 46% of all trade flows, we also report the results of a Heckman sample selection model developed by Heckman (1979) to cope with possible selection *bias*.[16] We hypothesize that the adjacency of two economies would increase their probability to trade, but would not impact the amount of trade once trade has begun. Therefore, the variable *Common open border*$_{ij}$ is the only selection term we employ.[17] We separately discuss this estimation in (Appendix 11.A).

### 11.4.1. *Transport costs and export capacity*

Our results highlight the importance of air transportation infrastructure in enhancing export performance. ln *Aircapacity* is significant and positive in all models at Tables 11.3 and 11.4. As mentioned earlier, we include the variables that are measured in terms of distance as proxies for the trade costs $t_{ij}$. Therefore, role of air transport infrastructure accessibility is also examined by the variable ln (*Avg. min. distance to airports*). This variable yields negative but insignificant results in our estimations; we do not observe conclusive evidence that economies which are further away from airports export less than those that are closer to these exit nodes, but we find robust evidence that the transport capacity of these nodes are important.

[16]These results are presented in Table 11.A.1 in the Appendix.
[17]The Heckman model is estimated by maximum likelihood.

**Table 11.3.** Estimation results for Equation (11.11).

| | (1) OLS | (2) OLS | (3) MRT |
|---|---|---|---|
| ln *Regional (exporter)* $GVA_{it}$ | 0.442*** (0.0969) | 0.337*** (0.117) | 0.377*** (0.128) |
| ln *Country (importer)* $GVA_{jt}$ | 0.311*** (0.0166) | 0.309*** (0.0166) | 0.343*** (0.0172) |
| ln $(Distance)_{ij}$ | −0.777*** (0.0326) | −0.779*** (0.0327) | |
| ln $(Exchange\ rate)_{jt}$ | −0.0659*** (0.00872) | −0.0663*** (0.00870) | −0.0807*** (0.00963) |
| $EU\ customs\ union_{ij,t}$ | 0.319*** (0.0900) | 0.314*** (0.0906) | 0.792*** (0.0872) |
| $Similar\ language_{ij}$ | 1.153*** (0.144) | 1.152*** (0.144) | |
| ln $(Land\ transport\ infrastructure)_{it}$ | 0.406*** (0.151) | 0.390*** (0.151) | 0.382** (0.161) |
| ln $(DSL\ per\ capita)_{it}$ | 0.220 (0.394) | −1.467*** (0.521) | −1.394** (0.553) |
| ln $(Air\ capacity)_{it}$ | 0.141*** (0.0173) | 0.141*** (0.0173) | 0.137*** (0.0189) |
| ln $(Public\ port\ capacity)_{i}$ | −0.145*** (0.0290) | −0.147*** (0.0291) | −0.152*** (0.0324) |
| $Number\ of\ private\ ports_{i}$ | 0.0427*** (0.00577) | 0.0453*** (0.00596) | 0.0453*** (0.00680) |
| ln $(Avg.\ min.\ distance\ to\ airports)_{i}$ | −0.0107 (0.0358) | −0.0580 (0.0412) | −0.0585 (0.0455) |
| ln $(Avg.\ min.\ dist.\ to\ major\ ports)_{i}$ | −0.325*** (0.0540) | −0.326*** (0.0542) | −0.339*** (0.0602) |
| ln *Regional (exporter)* $Population_{it}$ | 0.427*** (0.111) | 0.491*** (0.123) | 0.445*** (0.133) |
| ln *Country (importer)* $Population_{jt}$ | 0.0733*** (0.0162) | 0.0742*** (0.0161) | 0.0944*** (0.0172) |
| $Landlocked\ importer_{j}$ | −0.484*** (0.0534) | −0.486*** (0.0533) | 0.0765 (0.0539) |

*(Continued)*

**Table 11.3.** (*Continued*)

| | (1) OLS | (2) OLS | (3) MRT |
|---|---|---|---|
| *Common open border*$_{ij}$ | 0.870*** | 0.867*** | 2.132*** |
| | (0.162) | (0.163) | (0.154) |
| ln (*MRT corrected distance*)$_{ij}$ | | | −1.360*** |
| | | | (0.204) |
| Constant | −4.634*** | −3.491*** | −22.36*** |
| | (1.059) | (1.209) | (2.150) |
| Observations | 42120 | 42120 | 42120 |
| Number of pairs | 4680 | 4680 | 4680 |
| Year Dummies | No | Yes | Yes |
| Standard errors clustered by | Pair | Pair | Pair |
| $R$-squared | 0.471 | 0.472 | 0.422 |

Standard errors in parentheses.
$^{*}p < 0.10$, $^{**}p < 0.05$, $^{***}p < 0.01$.

Port infrastructure related variables present interesting results. While ln *Public port capacity* is negative and significant in all our models, *Number of private ports* yields positive and significant coefficients. This could be a sign of a crowding-out effect, or could underline that regions with more privately operated ports are much more efficient while those with a high public port capacity are adversely affected. Our results show that distance to ports also has a negative impact on regional exports, further highlighting the importance of this infrastructure type in export performance. This observed difference in the role of distance for airports and ports is easy to explain; distance would matter for ports because of bulky and heavy goods being transported, but not for airports because of high-value but small-volume exports.

The land infrastructure index is associated significantly and positively with regional export performance according to our results except in the models with importer and exporter fixed effects and pair fixed effects. These results provide evidence supporting the importance of road, highway, and railroad stocks for regional export

**Table 11.4.** Additional estimation results for Equation (11.11).

| | (1) Importer FE | (2) Imp-exp FE | (3) Pair FE |
|---|---|---|---|
| ln *Regional (exporter) GVA*$_{it}$ | 0.309*** | −0.103 | −0.103 |
| | (0.105) | (0.164) | (0.164) |
| ln *Country (importer) GVA*$_{jt}$ | 0.701*** | 0.701*** | 0.701*** |
| | (0.0900) | (0.0898) | (0.0895) |
| ln *(Distance)*$_{ij}$ | −1.327*** | −1.360*** | |
| | (0.164) | (0.161) | |
| ln *(Exchange rate)*$_{jt}$ | −0.250*** | −0.250*** | −0.250*** |
| | (0.0674) | (0.0671) | (0.0669) |
| *EU customs union*$_{ij,t}$ | 0.315*** | 0.315*** | 0.315*** |
| | (0.0690) | (0.0688) | (0.0686) |
| *Similar language*$_{ij}$ | 0.905* | | |
| | (0.465) | | |
| ln *(Land transport infrastructure)*$_{it}$ | 0.395*** | −0.378 | −0.378 |
| | (0.137) | (0.270) | (0.269) |
| ln *(DSL per capita)*$_{i}$ | −1.519*** | 0.408 | 0.408 |
| | (0.461) | (0.360) | (0.359) |
| ln *(Air capacity)*$_{it}$ | 0.143*** | | |
| | (0.0149) | | |
| ln *(Public port capacity)*$_{i}$ | −0.143*** | | |
| | (0.0249) | | |
| *Number of private ports*$_{i}$ | 0.0454*** | | |
| | (0.00535) | | |
| ln *(Avg. min. distance to airports)*$_{i}$ | −0.0576 | | |
| | (0.0369) | | |
| ln *(Avg. min. dist. to major ports)*$_{i}$ | −0.316*** | | |
| | (0.0483) | | |
| ln *Regional (exporter) Population*$_{it}$ | 0.524*** | 0.992*** | 0.992*** |
| | (0.111) | (0.172) | (0.171) |
| ln *Country (importer) Population*$_{jt}$ | 0.0163 | 0.0163 | 0.0163 |
| | (0.225) | (0.223) | (0.223) |
| *Landlocked importer*$_{j}$ | −0.461 | | |
| | (0.431) | | |

(*Continued*)

**Table 11.4.** (*Continued*)

| | (1) Importer FE | (2) Imp-exp FE | (3) Pair FE |
|---|---|---|---|
| *Common open border*$_{ij}$ | −0.630 | | |
| | (0.479) | | |
| Constant | −2.043 | 6.759** | −7.180*** |
| | (2.172) | (3.159) | (2.414) |
| Observations | 42120 | 42120 | 42120 |
| Number of pairs | 4680 | 4680 | 4680 |
| Year Dummies | Yes | Yes | Yes |
| Standard errors clustered by | Pair | Pair | Not clustered |
| $R$-squared | 0.534 | 0.547 | 0.2556 |
| Hausman test statistic | | | 141.005 |

Standard errors in parentheses.
$^{*}p < 0.10$, $^{**}p < 0.05$, $^{***}p < 0.01$.

performance with an estimated elasticity of approximately 0.38%. This finding is not very far from the estimated infrastructure elasticity of trade of about 0.42% for a developing economy estimated in the meta-analytic study of Celbis *et al.* (2015a). Our estimations suggest that for Turkey, land infrastructure is the type of infrastructure that has the most impact on regional exports, which is another result that is consistent with the above mentioned meta-analytic study. This finding may also be related to the fact that Turkey is adjacent to a trade block such as the EU to which it is connected mainly through land routes. Therefore, regions within Turkey can be seen as heavily reliant on land infrastructure regarding their trade with the EU.

Our estimations present inconclusive results considering the impact of communication infrastructure, represented by *DSL per capita*. Contrary to expectations, we observe a negative sign on the elasticities obtained from the OLS model with time dummies, OLS model with multilateral resistance terms, and the regression results with importer fixed effects while models 2 and 3 in Table 11.4 yield positive but insignificant results.

Finally, distance between trading pairs, as expected, is always found to impact on exports negatively and significantly. This result is consistent with the common findings in the trade literature such as those by Limao and Venables (2001) who find a positive effect of distance on trade costs and a negative impact on trade flows, Carrre and Schiff (2005) who observe that for a majority of countries the impact of distance on trade has become increasingly important over time, Berthelon and Freund (2008) who attribute the increasing effect of distance on industrial distance sensitivities, and the meta-analytic studies of Linders (2005) and Disdier and Head (2008), among others.

### 11.4.2. *Geography*

*Common open border* positively and significantly affects exports according to most of our results from the models estimated by OLS, OLS with time dummies, and OLS with multilateral resistance terms. This variable is dropped from the model in the importer–exporter and pair fixed effects estimations as it is bilaterally constant through our sample period. Results suggest that adjacency of a region and a country significantly and positively affects regional exports and that it is a relevant control variable. There is also some evidence based on our results from the OLS models with and without year dummies that if a partner country is landlocked, regional exports are negatively affected. However, this effect is no longer observable if multilateral resistances or importer fixed effects are taken into account in column 3 of Table 11.3 and column 1 of Table 11.4 respectively.

### 11.4.3. *Regional demographic characteristics and other core gravity variables*

Coefficients on regional population are positive and significant in all our models, suggesting that agglomeration economies export more. On the other hand, while destination country population yields positive estimates, out of these coefficients, those estimated using importer, importer and exporter, and pair fixed effects respectively in the columns of Table 11.4 are not significant.

The remaining variables are other commonly used factors in trade studies that stem from the theoretical gravity model. We observe the expected positive and significant coefficients for importer country GVA, emphasizing on the role of the destination demand. On the other hand, some evidence is also observed for the positive effect of the origin GVA.

As expected, the larger the value of the Turkish Lira in the currency of the trading partner, the less are the export flows. On the other hand, if a country enters into a EU customs union agreement with Turkey, regional exports are positively impacted according to the majority of our results. Finally, language similarity exhibits the expected positive impact.

## 11.5. Concluding Remarks

Celbis *et al.* (2015a) conducted a meta-analysis on the infrastructure elasticities of trade obtained from 36 previous studies. According to their results, estimations that used a land transport infrastructure variable found significantly higher infrastructure elasticities of trade relative to estimations using other infrastructure types. Our results in Tables 11.3 and 11.4 are in line with this observation except for the models using importer–exporter and pair fixed effects, which yield insignificant elasticities of land transport infrastructure. The authors also find that estimations focusing on maritime or air transport infrastructure find a significantly higher estimate of the impact of importer's infrastructure. While in our study, we focus on only exporter's infrastructure, our results regarding these two types of infrastructure reinforce the conclusion that they play an important role in trade facilitation, except for public port capacity, as seen in both Tables 11.3 and 11.4. Therefore, the continuation of public investments in these types of public infrastructure are recommended. Results on ports yield a different story; as the number of private ports exhibit a positive impact on exports, public port capacity does not. This may point to certain efficiency differences between publicly and privately managed ports. However, access to public ports measured in terms of distance still has a positive effect on regional exports.

Thus, our results also show that the location of point infrastructure is important for regions regardless of a public-private distinction. As a result, the findings of this study underline the roles of land, port, and air transport infrastructures in the exports of Turkey, and also the importance of the spatial distribution of point infrastructures as exit nodes for exports.

## 11.A. Appendix

### 11.A.1. *Additional estimation results*

Column 1 in Table 11.A.1 presents the results of the panel estimation with random effects. While most of the coefficients are similar to those from our previous results, the earlier reported Hausman test suggests that we favor the pair fixed effects results reported in column 3 of Table 11.4. On the other hand, the pair fixed effects regression drops many key variables due to them being constant, causing loss of valuable information.

Sample selection *bias* can potentially arise in trade research as only those countries that engage in trade are used in the regression analyses (Helpman *et al.*, 2008). We conduct a maximum likelihood estimation of a Heckman sample selection model for our empirical specification.[18] Column 2 of Table 11.A.1 suggests that sample selection is not an issue in our analyses, as the inverse Mill's ratio is insignificant. The selection variable is *Open common border* as mentioned in Section 11.4. The neighbors of Turkey are Georgia, Armenia, the Nakhchivan enclave of Azerbaijan,[19] Iran, Syria, Iraq, Bulgaria, and Greece. Due to political frictions, the border between Armenia and Turkey is closed, hence the name Common *open* border for this variable. On the other hand, Armenia is dropped from

[18]Puhani (2000) suggests that the full-information maximum likelihood estimator can be preferred over the two-step method of Heckman (1979) if collinearity problems are not present.

[19]We do not consider Azerbaijan as a neighbor of Turkey as the enclave represents only a very small part of its economy.

**Table 11.A.1.** Pair RE and Heckman estimation results for Equation (11.11).

| | (1) | (2) | |
|---|---|---|---|
| | | Heckman MRT | |
| | Pair RE | Outcome | Selection |
| ln *Regional (Exporter)* $GVA_{it}$ | 0.0508<br>(0.0989) | 1.185***<br>(0.200) | 0.775***<br>(0.113) |
| ln *Country (importer)* $GVA_{jt}$ | 0.325***<br>(0.0163) | 0.452***<br>(0.0307) | 0.295***<br>(0.0138) |
| ln $(distance)_{ij}$ | −0.770***<br>(0.0318) | | |
| ln $(Exchange\ rate)_{jt}$ | −0.0658***<br>(0.00866) | −0.139***<br>(0.0162) | −0.00769<br>(0.00764) |
| $EU\ customs\ union_{ij,t}$ | 0.319***<br>(0.0575) | 0.940***<br>(0.0899) | 0.577***<br>(0.0589) |
| $Similar\ language_{ij}$ | 1.156***<br>(0.144) | | |
| ln $(land\ transport\ infrastructure)_{it}$ | 0.133<br>(0.138) | 0.232<br>(0.255) | 0.0627<br>(0.136) |
| ln $(DSL\ per\ capita)_i$ | 0.295<br>(0.346) | 0.691<br>(0.816) | 1.543***<br>(0.431) |
| ln $(Air\ capacity)_{it}$ | 0.110***<br>(0.0173) | 0.114***<br>(0.0307) | −0.0182<br>(0.0147) |
| ln $(Public\ port\ capacity)_i$ | −0.195***<br>(0.0289) | −0.287***<br>(0.0486) | −0.208***<br>(0.0229) |
| $Number\ of\ private\ ports_i$ | 0.0530***<br>(0.00573) | 0.0518***<br>(0.00886) | −0.00124<br>(0.00425) |
| ln $(Avg.\ min.\ distance\ to\ airports)_i$ | −0.111***<br>(0.0376) | 0.197***<br>(0.0604) | −0.00594<br>(0.0396) |
| ln $(Avg.\ min.\ dist.\ to\ major\ ports)_i$ | −0.426***<br>(0.0533) | −0.564***<br>(0.0891) | −0.608***<br>(0.0423) |
| ln *Regional (exporter)* $Population_{it}$ | 0.833***<br>(0.106) | 0.253<br>(0.214) | −0.0111<br>(0.118) |
| ln *Country (importer)* $Population_{jt}$ | 0.0627***<br>(0.0161) | 0.292***<br>(0.0301) | 0.119***<br>(0.0138) |

(*Continued*)

**Table 11.A.1.** (*Continued*)

| | (1) | (2) | |
|---|---|---|---|
| | | Heckman MRT | |
| | Pair RE | Outcome | Selection |
| *landlocked importer*$_j$ | −0.468*** | 0.203** | −0.0550 |
| | (0.0536) | (0.0925) | (0.0423) |
| *Common open border*$_{ij}$ | 0.883*** | | 1.289*** |
| | (0.163) | | (0.120) |
| ln (*MRT corrected distance*)$_{ij}$ | | −1.720*** | −0.450*** |
| | | (0.285) | (0.151) |
| Constant | −0.122 | −35.63*** | −16.03*** |
| | (1.142) | (3.178) | (1.615) |
| Observations | 42120 | 42120 | |
| Censored observations | | 18226 | |
| Uncensored observations | | 23894 | |
| Number of pairs | 4680 | 4680 | |
| Year Dummies | Yes | Yes | |
| Standard errors clustered by | Not clustered | Pair | |
| Log likelihood | | −70703.7 | |
| Lambda (Inverse Mill's ratio) | | 0.0488 | |
| SE Lambda (SE of Inverse Mill's ratio) | | (0.130) | |

Standard errors in parentheses.
$^{*}p < 0.10$, $^{**}p < 0.05$, $^{***}p < 0.01$.

the sample due to too little trade in the procedure detailed in Section 11.3. Therefore the term "open" in this variable is no longer relevant in the analysis. The most important difference of the results from the Heckman estimation compared to our other results is that communication infrastructure has the expected positive and significant coefficient. On the other hand, land transport infrastructure has an insignificant coefficient.

### 11.A.2. *Conversion to constant prices*

The GVA and public investment (PI) data has been compiled in terms of 1998 national currency. According to the T.R. Ministry of Development, the external currency deflator to 2005 from

**Table 11.A.2.** Region codes and names.

| |
|---|
| TR10: Istanbul |
| TR21: Tekirdag, Edirne, Kirklareli |
| TR22: Balikesir, Canakkale |
| TR31: Izmir |
| TR32: Aydin, Denizli, Mugla |
| TR33: Manisa, Afyon, Kutahya, Usak |
| TR41: Bursa, Eskisehir, Bilecik |
| TR42: Kocaeli, Sakarya, Duzce, Bilecik |
| TR51: Ankara |
| TR52: Konya, Karaman |
| TR61: Antalya, Isparta, Burdur |
| TR62: Adana, Mersin |
| TR63: Hatay, Kahramanmaras, Osmaniye |
| TR71: Kirikkale, Aksaray, Nigde |
| TR72: Kayseri, Sivas, Yozgat |
| TR81: Zonguldak, Karabuk, Bartin |
| TR82: Kastamonu, Cankiri, Sinop |
| TR83: Samsun, Tokat, Corum, Amasya |
| TR90: Trabzon, Ordu, Giresun, Rize |
| TRA1: Erzurum, Erzincan, Bayburt |
| TRA2: Agri, Kars, Igdir, Ardahan |
| TRB1: Malatya, Elazig, Bingol, Tunceli |
| TRB2: Van, Mus, Bitlis, Hakkari |
| TRC1: Gaziantep, Adiyaman, Kilis |
| TRC2: Sanliurfa, Diyarbakir |
| TRC3: Mardin, Batman, Sirnak, Siirt |

1998 (national currency) is 0.1415.[20] The regional GVA and PI figures were divided by this deflator to convert them to 2005 prices. The USD conversion rate specified in the same source was 1 USD = 1.67 TL for 2005. Therefore the GVA and PI values in 2005 constant national currency were divided by 1.67 and converted to dollars.

[20]Retrieved from: www2.dpt.gov.tr/kamuyat/2005/2005deflator.xls.

### 11.A.3. *Land infrastructure index construction*

The weights presented in Footnote 3 were used to create the land infrastructure index using road length, highway length, and railroad length per 1000 sqm as follows: The total share of road and railroad in exports in 2009 was $0.417 + 0.09 = 0.507$ (so about half of total exports in were made through these types of infrastructure). $0.417 \div 0.507 = 0.82249$ is the weight of roads in land infrastructure and $0.09 \div 0.507 = 0.17751$ is the weight of railroads in land infrastructure. The index "land" is calculated as follows:

$$\begin{aligned} land = {} & 0.822485207100592 \\ & \times [\ln(road\ per\ area) + \ln(highway\ per\ area)] \\ & + 0.177514792899408 \times [\ln(railroad\ per\ area)]. \end{aligned}$$

### 11.A.4. *Exchange rates*

Exchange rates to USD for each partner country are from Penn World Table 7.1 (Heston *et al.*, 2012).[21] Each country's exchange rate to USD was divided by Turkey's exchange rate to USD in a given year so that all observations express the amount of the corresponding foreign currency one Turkish Lira can buy within a specific year.

### 11.A.5. *DSL data imputation*

The observations for 2002 and 2005 for each region is missing for the DSL (or ADSL) data.[22] The missing values were imputed using the regional public investments in transportation and communication (TPI) by predicting the missing values for each region $i$ using the coefficients from the OLS estimation of the below equation:

$$\ln(adsl)_t = a + \beta(TPI)_{t-1} + \epsilon.$$

[21] The rates for China are from "version 2" of this table.

[22] For 2003, the figure is reported as "DSL" where as for the rest of the years they are reported as "ADSL".

## References


Anderson, JE and E van Wincoop (2003) Gravity with gravitas: A solution to the border puzzle, *American Economic Review* 93(1), 170–192.

Anderson, JE and E van Wincoop (2004) Trade costs, *Journal of Economic Literature* 42(3), 691–751.

Baier, SL and JH Bergstrand (2009) Bonus vetus ols: A simple method for approximating international trade-cost effects using the gravity equation, *Journal of International Economics* 77(1), 77–85.

Beckerman, W (1956) Distance and the pattern of intra-European trade, *The Review of Economics and Statistics* 38(1), 31–40.

Berthelon, M and C Freund (2008) On the conservation of distance in international trade, *Journal of International Economics* 75(2), 310–320.

Bougheas, S, PO Demetriades, and EL Morgenroth (1999) Infrastructure, transport costs and trade, *Journal of International Economics* 47(1), 169–189.

Carrre, C (2006) Revisiting the effects of regional trade agreements on trade flows with proper specification of the gravity model, *European Economic Review* 50(2), 223–247.

Carrre, C and M Schiff (2005) On the geography of trade. Distance is alive and well, *Revue Conomique* 56(6), 1249–1274.

Celbis, MG, P Nijkamp and J Poot (2015a) Infrastructure and trade: A meta-analysis, *Region* 1(1), 25–64.

Celbis, MG, D de Crombrugghe and J Muysken (2015b) Public investment and regional politics: The case of Turkey, Centre d'Economie de la Sorbonne & Paris School of Economics Seminar "Economie Publique, Institutions & Organisations," http://ces.univ-paris1.fr/membre/seminaire/EPIO/SEPIO.htm. Available at http://laep.univ-paris1.fr/SEPIO/SEPIO150303Celbis.pdf.

Disdier, AC and K Head (2008) The puzzling persistence of the distance effect on bilateral trade, *The Review of Economics and Statistics* 90(1), 37–48.

Drukker, DM, H Peng, I Prucha, and R Raciborski (2011) SPPACK: Stata module for cross-section spatial-autoregressive models, *Statistical Software Components*, Boston College Department of Economics. Available at https://ideas.repec.org/c/boc/bocode/545/245.html.

Granato, MF (2008) Regional export performance: First nature, agglomeration and destiny? The role of infrastructure *Mimegraph.*

Heckman, JJ (1979) Sample selection bias as a specification error, *Econometrica: Journal of the Econometric Society* 153–161.

Helpman, E, M Melitz and Y Rubinstein (2008) Estimating trade flows: Trading partners and trading volumes, *The Quarterly Journal of Economics* 123(2), 441–487.

Heston, A, R Summers, and B Aten (2012) Penn world table version 7.1. *Center for International Comparisons of Production, Income and Prices at the University of Pennsylvania*, November 2012.

Iwanow, T and C Kirkpatrick (2009) Trade facilitation and manufactured exports: Is Africa different? *World Development* 37(6), 1039–1050.

Karacadag Development Agency (2011) Sanliurfa sanayisinin yeniden yapilandirilmasi icin teknik destek projesi–lojistik sektor analiz raporu. *Industry report* TR 06 02.08-02/001, Karacadag Development Agency Sanlurfa Investment Support Office. Available at http://www.investinurfa.org.tr/tr/dokumanmerkezi/Documents/Sektor%20Raporlari/Bilesen%20E_Lojistik%20Sektoru%20Kapsam%20Gelistirme%20Calismasi.pdf.

Kustepeli, Y, Y Gulcan, and S Akgungor (2012) Transportation infrastructure investment, growth and international trade in Turkey, *Applied Economics* 44(20), 2619–2629.

Limao, N and AJ Venables (2001) Infrastructure, geographical disadvantage, transport costs, and trade, *The World Bank Economic Review* 15(3), 451–479.

Linders, G-JM (2005) Distance decay in international trade patterns — A meta-analysis, *ERSA Conference Papers* ersa05p679, European Regional Science Association.

Nordas, HK and R Piermartini (2004) Infrastructure and trade. *WTO Staff Working Paper ERSD*-2004-04, Economic Research and Statistics Division WTO.

OECD and World Trade Organization (2009) *Aid for Trade at a Glance 2009: Main-taining Momentum*, OECD Publishing, ISBN: OECD-978-92-64-06903-9.

Picard, R and M Stepner (2012) MERGEPOLY: Stata module to merge adjacent polygons from a shapefile. *Statistical Software Components*, Boston College Department of Economics. Available at http://ideas.repec.org/c/boc/bocode/s457574.html.

Pisati, M (2007) SPMAP: Stata module to visualize spatial data. *Statistical Software Components*, Boston College Department of Economics. Available at http://ideas.repec.org/c/boc/bocode/s456812.html.

Portugal-Perez, A and JS Wilson, (2012) Export performance and trade facilitation reform: Hard and soft infrastructure, *World Development* 40(7), 1295–1307.

Puhani, P (2000) The Heckman correction for sample selection and its critique, *Journal of Economic Surveys* 14(1), 53–68.

Shepherd, B (2012) The gravity model of international trade: A user guide. *Manual by UNESCAP and ARTNeT Gravity Modeling Initiative, United Nations — Economic and Social Commission for Asia and the Pacific*, (ST/ESCAP/2645).

Vijil, M and L Wagner (2012) Does aid for trade enhance export performance? Investigating the infrastructure channel, *The World Economy* 35(7), 838–868.

# Chapter 12

# Trade in Services and Regional Specialization: Evidence and Theory

*Hamid Beladi* and Saibal Kar†*

**University of Texas at San Antonio, USA*

*†Centre for Studies in Social Sciences, Calcutta, India; IZA, Bonn, Germany*

## 12.1. Introduction

World trade in services in the recent times has been a little under US$ 2 trillion. This is approximately a quarter of world trade in goods and the ratio continues to be so over the last five decades affecting growth and distribution in a significant manner (see Bhagwati, 1987; Francois, 1990; Jones and Ruane, 1990; Hoekman, 2006; Lipsey, 2009; Markusen and Strand, 2007; etc.). An important facet of current trends of globalization is the growing scope and quantitative importance of cross-border commercial service transactions, and of cross-border investments in the services sector. Figure 12.1 provides an indication of how the growth-wise best performing countries in the world, namely China, India and Brazil account for the trade in services as a whole. Quite clearly, the trend for India seems to be significantly higher than that of China and Brazil despite recent slowdown.

Previously, it has been argued that unless the cross-border service trade takes off, the impediments to trade in commodities would not be minimized, in particular when international fragmentation of production has become considerably important (Deardorff, 2001). Owing to this complementarity between trade in goods and services, or due to factors such as the cost advantage and improved technological capabilities following structural changes in respective countries, the

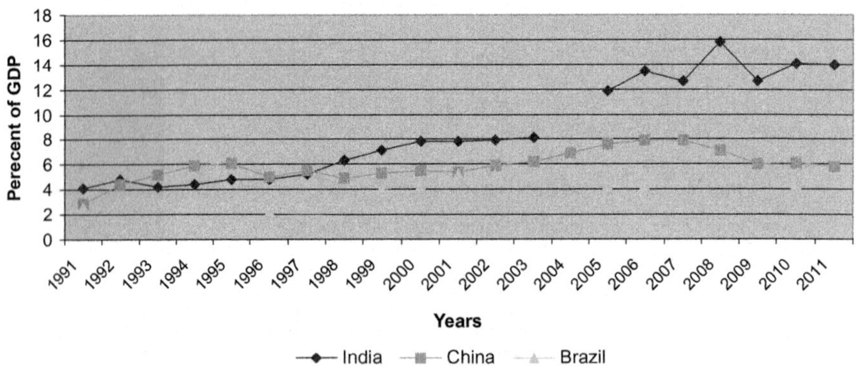


**Figure 12.1.** Trade in services as % of gross domestic product (GDP).
*Source*: World Bank. World Development Indicators (WDI).

share of service sector in (GDP), employment and investments is presently substantial and further increasing in many Asian countries.

This chapter looks into regional specialization in service trade within India, but of a specific variety — namely, the trade in health services of which medical tourism is an important component. The subject of regional trade arises from two sources. First, the demand for health tourism catered to by India arises from certain regional blocs. Although, we show that India receives tourists from almost all over the world, the importance of all regional blocs is not symmetric. Second, within India, the supply of health tourism is significantly region specific. Now, before we devote ourselves to this specific aspect, the following figures may be useful for emphasizing the general importance of the service sector in India. Figures 12.2 and 12.3 provide the shares of agriculture, industry and service sectors in India and the sectoral growth rates *vis-à-vis* the GDP growth rate, respectively. The growing importance of the service trade for India is reflected in the country's economic growth that has been largely driven by the growth of the service sector in recent years. Rapid improvements in total factor productivity (TFP) in the service sector (for example, see Verma, 2008), coupled with an increasing share of this sector in aggregate output, have accelerated the overall pace of growth of the Indian economy. Macroeconomic

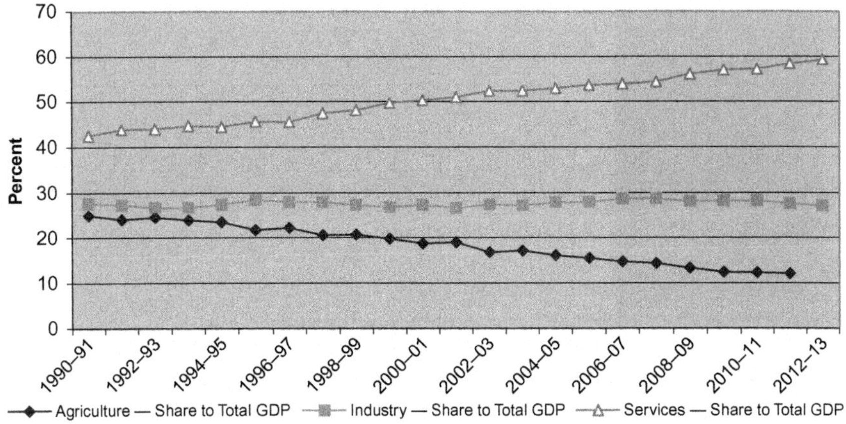


**Figure 12.2.** Sectoral shares in GDP for India.

*Source*: Reserve Bank of India. Handbook of Statistics on Indian Economy.

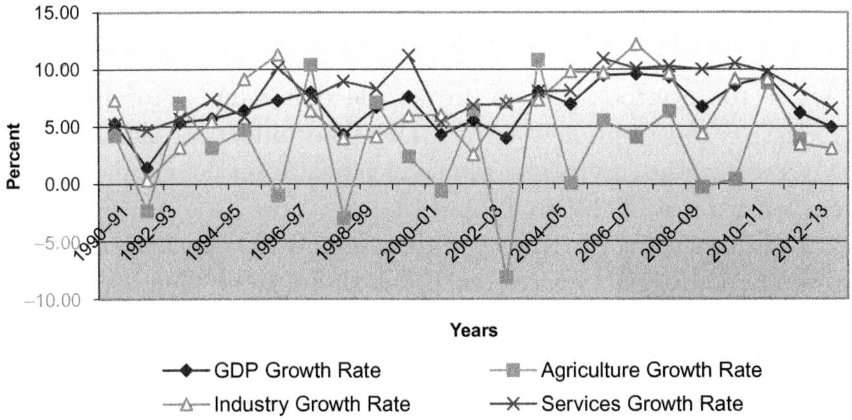


**Figure 12.3.** GDP and sectoral growth rates in India (%).

*Source*: Reserve Bank of India. Handbook of Statistics on Indian Economy.

data shows that during the last 10 years, Indian GDP registered an average annual growth rate of 7.16%, while the growth rate of output of the service sector was recorded at 8.93% and have been consistently higher till date. The service sector's share in GDP, which was about 55.40% in 1999–2000, reached 64.36% in 2008–2009.

**Table 12.1.** Industrial classification within services.

| 2-Digit SIC Code | Industry |
|---|---|
| 51 | Wholesale trade |
| 52 | Retail trade |
| 55 | Hotels and restaurants |
| 62 | Air, land and water transport |
| 64 | Post and telecom |
| 65 | Finance, insurance and auxiliary financial intermediation |
| 70 | Real estate activities |
| 71 | Renting of machinery and other businesses |
| 72 | Computer and related activities |
| 75 | Public administration and defense |
| 80 | Education |
| 85 | Health and social work |
| 91 | Activities of membership organizations |
| 92 | Entertainment and recreations |
| 98 | Other diversified activities |

*Source*: Standard Industrial Classification (SIC) for services, Government of India (GOI).

This sector overtook agriculture as the dominant sector in terms of relative contribution toward GDP. The industrial classification (NIC) within the service sector, of which health services is an integral component, is available in Table 12.1.

According to World Trade Organization (WTO), in 2005, the total value of commercial services trade was US$ 4,760 billion, equivalent to 23% of global merchandise trade. Since six of the top 20 leading countries exporting and importing services around the world are from Asia, it seems that service trade in general have acquired an important role in the intra-Asian and global economic linkages. Several Asian countries, including India, are proposing or negotiating bilateral and regional comprehensive economic partnership agreements that aim at liberalizing and facilitating international trade in commercial services. For example, India has a bilateral agreement with Singapore, called the Comprehensive Economic Cooperation Agreement that includes liberalization of service trade. Likewise, India and Japan are also pursuing broader economic agreements, which include services.

As mentioned above, we look at the supply of and demand for health services in India, which reportedly generate billions of dollars in revenue under the behest of the medical tourism (featuring under codes 85 and 92 *vide* Table 12.1). The medical tourism has been a relatively new 'avatar' of the transfer of health services from the developed to the developing countries.[1] It largely follows an early definition by Hill (1977) where services refer to simultaneous location of production and consumption. The definition seems to appropriately characterize the large market created for medical tourism where patients travel to low-cost developing countries for health services. The very definition tends to preclude international, even inter-regional, trade. In this case, however, it is the cross-border movement of the subjects that allow such transactions to take place consequently generating 'export' of health services from the host country. As later pointed out by Melvin (1989), this definition refers largely to 'contact' services and of course is not the only form so far as the conceptual issues in defining services are concerned. A number of other services permit separation of the location of production and consumption both over time and space. In fact, some of the categories we will register here also fall within the latter definition, such as the services rendered in the form of medical transcription and telemedicine. Presently, a large number of studies for India and for competing nations mainly in Asia, report substantive revenue generations from the export of health services (see Guiry and Vequist, 2011) on quality issues; Cattaneo (2010) for the analysis of health care markets in developing countries; Vijaya (2010) for health tourism as a channel for international transfer of healthcare problems; Chanda and Smith (2006) on the aspects of trade in health services under the General Agreement on Trade in Services (GATS); Ernst (2006) on East and South Asian experiences with health tourism, etc.).

As one would expect, health tourism is not the forte of all the states and union territories (federally administered regions) in India,

[1]See Freire (2012) discussing the advantages and disadvantages of medical tourism in foreign countries.

but is limited to the major urban centers with substantial health facilities available in the locality to accommodate domestic and foreign patients (or 'tourists') alike, or sometimes rationing access for locals as foreign patients are priced at a higher level. Despite our best efforts we did not have sufficient information to analyze the price behavior, which is reportedly discriminatory against foreigners (analogous to substantially higher ticket prices for non-residents in tourist locations such as the Taj Mahal, museums, royal palaces, jungle safaris, etc.). While facilities offering Thai spa or Indian Ayurveda are obviously not as uncommon as the Taj, the tourists usually find the discriminatory charges plus the cost of travel lower than what they would end up paying in the source country. If it concerns dental treatment, eye care, surrogate mothers, artificial limbs, clinical trials, etc., the prices in the host country reflect both comparative advantage and the absence of insurance for many of these treatments in the developed countries. It subsequently implies that health facilities accessed by foreigners choosing to undergo treatment of a serious nature (the list follows) or as part of tourist activity (such as Ayurveda, health spa, rejuvenation clinics, etc.), will have regional concentration. That in turn suggests that some degree of disparity across regions may appear given that the share of such activities is considerable. The regions as we will show with a brief theoretical model shall draw upon resources available in other regions, which do not have the comparative advantage for catering to such facilities. In essence, the liberalization of cross-border service trade and the regional concentration of specific service-related activities within a country may engender regional factor flows that would not take place under autarky.

The data shall delineate the outreach and the extent of medical health and tourism services produced and consumed in India and the product variety involved in this activity. The primary survey and the results, which we describe in Section 12.2, have been able to capture only a small share of the overall activities but even that seems a reasonably stable source of export earnings generated at the regional level in India. Section 12.3 develops the model and Section 12.4 concludes.

## 12.2. Data and Methodology

A pilot survey was conducted in eight cities in India, namely, Kolkata, Chennai, Bengaluru, Hyderabad, Trivandrum, Mumbai, Pune and Delhi in the years 2009–2010. These cities are considered to be the prime locations for international trade (mainly, export) in health services originating in India. In the absence of secondary data on the prevailing extent of participation and distribution of activities in health care services in these cities, the pilot survey tried to identify the major suppliers, types and the overall scope of trade in health services. It should be immediate that a survey of this nature also intends to document and estimate the level of financial transactions associated with these activities. To this end, the study engaged in using unit level questionnaires to conduct a survey based on purposive sampling of medical and allied facilities in these cities. The study focused on questions/issues on (including, but not limited to):

a. Product-wise and country-wise information for service provided by each unit.
b. Value of export and import of services by destination/source country for each category.
c. The share of foreign exchange in total revenue of each unit surveyed.
d. Listing of various services under broad medical categories, as identified in the schedule.
e. Employment of personnel catering to these facilities and break-ups according to specializations and types of services.
f. Medical transcriptions — by type of activity.
g. Clinical trials.
h. Contract research.

The collected data typically concentrates on the flow of trade in health services between India (eight major urban centers) and the rest of the world for the categories mentioned above. We provide extensive information on the supply of health services originating from India through a large number of major and minor units engaged in one or more of these activities. We report on the volume and quality of services and the associated pricing and revenue information as a novel contribution to the expanding literature. It should be noted that, the survey was not meant to be a census and therefore possibly excludes many units that also contribute to the export earnings of India.

Notwithstanding the fact that the study leaves out many possibilities other than what the survey has been able to account for, the financial implications of these activities seem reasonably large. The revenue generated from 'export' of direct and indirect health services appear substantial despite possibilities of general under-reporting tendencies even by formal and registered service providers. Since there is not sufficient information on service types by units, we started off with enumeration (generating a 'census' of facilities is still under process). The survey mainly enquired (and checked official records) on whether a unit has inducted and 'registered' a patient of foreign origin or not. Note that, it is a legal requirement on the part of the facilities to keep a copy of the identification document (passport) of the patient when admitted to and released from the hospital. Reportedly however, the Non-Resident Indians (NRI's) and People of Indian Origin (PIO's) often use the address and identification of a relative or a friend living as a permanent resident in India in order to get admitted to hospitals and avail of charges applying to locals.[2] Second, many facilities do not wish to record the citizenship of a patient owing to complexity of the reporting procedure with the local police station, unless the patient has done so already. This is fairly common for seafarers arriving through various ports in India. However, from our subsequent calculations we figured that the total revenue from foreign sources accumulated at the level of the facilities is higher than what the major country blocs contribute, such that, a large portion of the revenues had to be denoted as generated from 'unreported countries'.

[2]We are not aware of the exact procedure by which the requirement is bypassed, but usually the hospitals ask for the address and phone number of the person (relative or friend) accompanying a patient. NRIs may also have ration cards or voter identification cards that would be acceptable as residence proof.

Moreover, patients from neighboring countries who speak the local language are difficult to identify as a typical foreign patient or a medical tourist. This includes individuals from Bangladesh seeking treatment in Kolkata, West Bengal; Tamil patients from Sri Lanka visiting Chennai, Tamil Nadu or those from Maldives and Middle East arriving in Trivandrum, Kerala, all of who speak the local languages. Since, many of the facilities do practice differential pricing and charge foreign tourists more, it pays off to speak local languages and take the benefit of domestic prices. However, these should still be considered as export revenue although it is expected to be lower than that earned from patients without such connections and advantages. Thus, the survey listed and approached a total of 412 units, of which 380 are hospitals, 17 are Ayurveda centers and 15 are Business Process Outsourcing (BPOs)/Transcription/Clinical research centers. Of these 58 belong to National Accreditation Board for Hospitals and Healthcare Providers (NABH, 100 total all-India) and 8 belong to Joint Commission International (JCI, incomplete list, 25 all-India). The overall sample is 40% of enumerated units in India with proportional shares selected from each city. The survey enquired regarding induction of at least one foreign patient during the previous fiscal year. From the sample, approximately 35% in Bengaluru, 20% in Chennai, 37% in Delhi, 27% in Hyderabad, 67% in Kolkata, 13% in Mumbai, 54% in Pune and 78% in Trivandrum provided us with the data.[3] The documentation of the BPOs dealing

[3]Information was collected from some of the major hospitals as chosen destinations for a large number of foreign patients, namely, Fortis Hospital in Bengaluru; Fortis Malar Hospital, Santosh Hospitals Pvt. Ltd. and Apollo Hospitals in Chennai; Holy Angel Hospital in Delhi; Pranaam Hospitals Pvt. Ltd., Anupama Hospital, Ravi Hospital in Hyderabad; Kokilaben Dhirubhai Ambani Hospital & Medical Research Centre, Nefron Hospital in Mumbai; Hardikar hospital, Jeewan Jyot Hospital in Pune; Dr. Franklin's Panchakarma Institute, Chaithanya Eye Hospital & Research Institute, Kerala, Institute of Medical Sciences, Somatheeram Ayurveda Group, etc. in Trivandrum; and Apollo Gleneagles, Medica Superspeciality hospital and Peerless Hospital in Kolkata, to name a few. In addition, we collected data from the BPO units engaged with medical transcription and related activities. Information on clinical trials conducted in India by foreign pharmaceutical companies was strictly withheld by facilitating agencies.

with medical transcriptions and foreign exchange has been a rather difficult exercise. Once again, using an incomplete list available from the Associated Chamber of Commerce and Industry of India (ASSOCHAM) and from scattered sources, we approached a total of 115 units, and obtained data on export of services from 15 units only.

It should be noted that our main concern with the primary survey was to locate and collect information on export of medical services provided to foreign patients or firms directly or indirectly, depending on the nature of the services. The survey was also instrumental in capturing the level of activity and the turnovers related to most common activities under medical tourism, offered in the form of Ayurvedic therapies, cosmetic surgery, eye and dental care, naturopathy, etc., where our focus was exclusively on how many foreign patients have been catered to and the value of export recorded by these units. Based on the data we analyzed some of the major variables, namely, '*Total Export of Health Services*' and '*Export of Medical/Health Tourism*' by the medical units as shown through following tables. Besides, participation from major countries with the information about the number of patients country-wise and medical discipline-wise has also been reported in subsequent tables. For the survey, the financial information pertains to 2010–2011, i.e., 1st April 2010 to 31st March 2011. All the data are reported in thousands of Rupees ('000 INR, US$ 1 = INR 50, approximately).

### 12.2.1. *The results*

This section elaborates the findings of our survey of the eight cities. Table 12.2 shows that approximately 26% of the hospitals in the targeted cities cater to NRIs, PIO and foreign nationals. The concept of 'export' therefore refers to who is being served.[4] It should be noted that in four cities, namely Bengaluru, Chennai, Hyderabad and Pune we documented lesser number of NRI/foreign patients compared to the all-India average for reasons mentioned in Section 12.2. Rest of

[4]Since we do not have any record on what currency was used for payments, we use the 'country of origin' of the patients/tourists as a proxy for international transactions.

**Table 12.2.** Number of units with and without foreign patients (city-wise).

| Cities | No. of units with foreign revenues | No. of units without foreign revenues | Total no. of units surveyed | Percentage of units with foreign patients |
|---|---|---|---|---|
| Bengaluru | 12 | 44 | 56 | 21 |
| Chennai | 8 | 32 | 40 | 25 |
| Delhi | 18 | 42 | 60 | 30 |
| Hyderabad | 13 | 45 | 58 | 22 |
| Kolkata | 23 | 52 | 75 | 30 |
| Mumbai | 12 | 30 | 42 | 29 |
| Pune | 8 | 35 | 43 | 19 |
| Trivandrum | 14 | 21 | 35 | 40 |
| Total | 108 | 301 | 409 | 26 |

*Data source*: Primary survey data.

the cities, however, i.e., Delhi, Kolkata, Mumbai and Trivandrum cater to relatively large number of NRI/foreign patients compared to the all-India average. Out of these cities, Trivandrum registered the largest occurrence in terms of patients of foreign origin (40%), whereas for Pune, the rate of incidence is fairly low at 19%. The actual numbers and percentages are reported in Table 12.2.

Table 12.3 shows the total exports of health services by categories during 2010–2011 (in INR '000). The data exhibits that the major sources of revenue are medical or health tourism (8,28,430.419 INR), medical transcription (50,173.727 INR), medical billing (20,000.000 INR) and contract research (33,749.757 INR). It is to be noted that '0' in some of the facilities offered in other categories indicates non-availability of data. The total export of health services according to the overall calculations from units surveyed is 9,32,353.903 INR. Once again, all the above figures in Table 12.3 are reported in thousands of Indian Rupees ('000 INR).

Next, Table 12.4 shows exports of health services to major trading partners during 2010–2011. The table reveals that during the above mentioned time period the total export earning from the health service sector was INR 9,32,353.903 or approximately US$ 200 million. The trading partners have been classified into five

**Table 12.3.** Export of health services by categories during 2010–2011 (in '000 INR).

| Service category | Export |
|---|---|
| Medical or health tourism | 8,28,430.419 |
| Telemedicine | 0 |
| Medical transcription | 50,173.727 |
| Medical coding | 0 |
| Medical billing | 20,000.000 |
| Health claims processing | 0 |
| Clinical trials | 0 |
| Contract research | 33,749.757 |
| Distant health education | 0 |
| Temporary overseas movement of personnel | 0 |
| Others | 0 |
| **Total** | **9,32,353.903** |

*Data source*: Primary survey data.

blocs namely America consisting of countries in North America, U.S.A., Canada; South America consisting of Costa Rica, Brazil etc.; Africa comprising of South Africa, Nigeria, Kenya etc.; Europe which consists of Russia, Germany, the UK etc.; West Asia which consists of Iraq, U.A.E., Israel, etc.; and finally, Asian & Australian bloc which includes countries from South Asia, South East Asia and East Asia along with Australia. Export earnings from each country is reported in detail.

Table 12.4 shows that 31% of export earnings comes from the European Bloc. In this respect, contribution of the African Block is the least (5%). Asian and Australian Block (excluding countries of West Asia) contribute 23% of the total export revenue. As already mentioned, it should be further noted that due to the lack of proper information it was not possible to identify the sources for approximately 25% of the export revenue. For the American Block, not surprisingly, U.S.A. is the largest contributor and for those originating in South America, Honduras occupies the lowest position. Further, distribution within the African Block suggests that Nigeria contributes the highest amount to our aggregate export earnings from Africa, whereas, Gambia's contribution is the lowest. Among

**Table 12.4.** Exports and imports of health services by major trading partners (in '000 INR).

| Bloc | Trading partners | Export ('000 INR) |
|---|---|---|
| America | Mexico | 911.800 |
| | USA | 95,507.169 |
| | Canada | 4,284.241 |
| | Nicaragua | 180.000 |
| | Barbados | 61.141 |
| | Costa Rica | 92.059 |
| | Honduras | 32.000 |
| | Venezuela | 429.001 |
| | Brazil | 2,302.905 |
| Africa | Gambia | 0.800 |
| | Ghana | 820.116 |
| | Malawi | 304.665 |
| | Uganda | 10.974 |
| | Tanzania | 3,399.319 |
| | Kenya | 4,253.175 |
| | S. Africa | 4,105.492 |
| | Nigeria | 19,579.851 |
| | Congo | 7,000.000 |
| | Burundi | 5,000.000 |
| | Egypt | 660.800 |
| | Mauritius | 45.932 |
| | Zambia | 18.140 |
| | Ethiopia | 27.750 |
| | Gabon | 4.953 |
| **Block-wise Share of Export Revenue: Total = 9,32,353.903 ('000 INR) = US$ 200 million.**<br>Americas — 12%<br>Africa — 5%<br>Europe — 30%<br>West Asia — 5%<br>Australia, New Zealand,<br>East & South East Asia — 23%<br>Unreported — 25% | | |
| Europe | Russia | 56,863.595 |
| | Switzerland | 10,417.202 |
| | Germany | 40,053.293 |
| | UK | 29,055.012 |
| | Italy | 31,245.353 |
| | Norway | 37,495.265 |

(*Continued*)

**Table 12.4.** *Continued*

| Bloc | Trading partners | Export ('000 INR) |
|---|---|---|
| | Austria | 12,071.916 |
| | Ireland | 1,248.282 |
| | Ukraine | 2,040.472 |
| | Denmark | 3,603.192 |
| | France | 54,200.884 |
| | Bosnia | 150.000 |
| | Estonia | 48.762 |
| | Spain | 4,374.527 |
| | Belgium | 1,282.815 |
| | Hungary | 3.065 |
| | Monaco | 2.100 |
| | Poland | 2,282.000 |
| | Portugal | 453.580 |
| | Romania | 7.855 |
| | Turkey | 1,446.961 |
| West Asia | Bahrain | 12.600 |
| | Iraq | 4,085.351 |
| | Iran | 1,100.641 |
| | Israel | 4,571.971 |
| | Oman | 786.600 |
| | Qatar | 1,452.187 |
| | U. Arab Emirates | 25,427.525 |
| | Kazakhstan | 12,500.000 |
| South Asia, South East Asia, East Asia & Australia | Afghanistan | 1,040.501 |
| | Bangladesh | 70,106.065 |
| | Bhutan | 36,701.853 |
| | Maldives | 15,946.235 |
| | Nepal | 2,553.524 |
| | Pakistan | 6,352.451 |
| | Sri Lanka | 16,114.900 |
| | Myanmar | 33,337.329 |
| | Japan | 9,517.426 |
| | Korea | 900.000 |
| | China | 773.254 |
| | Indonesia | 3,503.516 |
| | Singapore | 290.405 |
| | Malaysia | 11,834.673 |
| | Australia | 3,544.137 |
| | New Zealand | 2,917.266 |
| | Solomon Islands | 2.926 |
| Unreported | | 2,29,602.153 |

*Data source*: Primary survey by authors.

countries of the European Block, Russia is the highest contributor to the export earnings while Monaco is the lowest. Out of eight countries of West Asia U.A.E. is the biggest contributor to the export and Bahrain generates the lowest. The Asian Block (excluding the West Asian Countries) consists of seventeen countries in which Bangladesh is the largest export partner, while Singapore contributes the lowest amount of export revenue from within this block, and from the Australian Block, Australia contributes the largest share. Regardless of the size of the contribution what is interesting is that India, notwithstanding how poor the per-capita health facilities are for the natives, receives patients whether stranded air passengers or tourists or those on intended medical treatments from almost all over the world.

We found that the main reason for visiting India for regular medical requirements is the substantially lower cost of medical care compared to those in the advanced countries, despite possibility of encountering lower quality aspects in some of the areas. In other words, there seems to be a clear cost advantage that drives patients of Indian origin living in foreign countries or those of foreign origin to consider regular and exotic health care choices available in India and to particular locations therein. For some of the other countries, like those neighboring India, the unavailability of advanced health care provisions and critical care is the prime reason why the trade in health services at all occurs. This should be of interest to researchers and policy makers in the area of international economics, where there seems to be at least one major commodity/service for which the south–south transactions are as potent as the north–south trade relations.

The extended Table 12.4 shows that the total export revenue earned from medical tourism alone is about US$ 200 million for the years 2009–2010, which is still an underestimate because the sample has only covered 40% of all such units which potentially cater to foreign patients. In addition, the units earning export revenues *via* medical transcription, contract research and clinical trials or agencies dealing with surrogacy, etc. have also been sparsely covered in this survey. Overall, the estimate of this primary survey is commensurate with the reports by the Confederation of Indian Industries (CII) and McKinsey which estimates a total of US$ 2.2 billion export revenue from these sources during 2009–2012. The revenue estimates if realized would still be less than 1% of the budget allocation for health services in India, which is quite poor even among developing countries. Notwithstanding, the table shows that U.S.A. generates the largest amount of revenue for health services, while Bangladesh occupies the second highest position. Russia is also a major contributor to the export earnings and not unexpectedly, the revenue generation is low from medically advanced countries that also offer generous welfare programs to their citizens, as those in the Scandinavia.

Finally, let us provide a brief overview of the number and percentage of patients arriving from the major blocs (Table 12.5) as defined above and the medical discipline-wise treatments (Table 12.6) that are offered by the medical units surveyed. The reason for invoking such information in the present chapter is primarily to offer an idea about the use of skilled workers and capital deployment at the level of the service facilities. Indirectly, these should motivate the description of regional idiosyncrasies relating to the availability of the factors of production.

Section 12.3 develops the model with some of these features as part of it.

**Table 12.5.** Number and percentage of patients arriving from different blocs.

| Blocs | Number of patients | Percentage |
|---|---|---|
| America | 401.00 | 0.62 |
| Africa | 360.00 | 0.56 |
| Europe | 8,619.00 | 13.38 |
| West Asia | 7,822.00 | 12.15 |
| East-South East-South-Asia–Australia | 47,197.00 | 73.29 |
| Total | 64,399.00 | 100.00 |

*Source*: Primary survey.

**Table 12.6.** Country-bloc wise and discipline-wise distribution of patients.

| Geographical bloc | America | Africa | Europe | West Asia | South, South East, East Asia and Australia | Total |
|---|---|---|---|---|---|---|
| discipline | | | | | | |
| Cardiology | 12 | 20 | 05 | 06 | 575 | 618 |
| ENT | 00 | 02 | 01 | 05 | 571 | 579 |
| Gastro entrology | 00 | 00 | 11 | 00 | 1,071 | 1,082 |
| Surgery | 02 | 06 | 01 | 18 | 974 | 1,001 |
| General medicine | 07 | 07 | 03 | 04 | 1,636 | 1,657 |
| Opthalmology | 00 | 00 | 00 | 00 | 7,422 | 7,422 |
| Orthopedics | 02 | 03 | 01 | 08 | 870 | 884 |
| Respiratory medicine | 00 | 00 | 01 | 00 | 687 | 688 |
| Gynaecology | 05 | 01 | 00 | 00 | 493 | 499 |
| Ayurveda & Yoga | 50 | 02 | 526 | 29 | 35 | 642 |
| Multidiscipline | 300 | 255 | 8,044 | 7,709 | 31,137 | 47,445 |
| Others | 23 | 64 | 26 | 43 | 1,726 | 1,882 |
| Total | 401 | 360 | 8,619 | 7,822 | 47,197 | 64,399 |

*Data source*: Primary survey data.

## 12.3. A Model

Consider a developing country with $j$ regions indexed in a continuum $[0, 1]$. Each region of the country has the potential to produce two goods: a traditional industrial product $X_j(L_j)$, $X_j' > 0, X_j'' < 0$, where $L_j$ is the availability of unskilled labor in region $j$ and a modern service. The country produces the modern service sector output $Y_j$, which uses $S$ as the input of skilled labor and infrastructure $(I)$.[5] Unlike the region-specific endowment of unskilled labor, the supply of skilled labor depends on the availability of infrastructure in region $j$. This is given by $S_j^s$ as in equation (12.3). Let us define $w_{Sj}$ as the skilled wage determined in region $j$; $w_j$ is the unskilled wage determined in region $j$ and $k_j$ is the price per unit of infrastructure in region $j$. The autarkic prices of commodity $X$ and $Y$ be given by

[5]See Grubel (1987) arguing the importance of human capital in service trade.

$(P_X, P_Y)$, obtained at the equilibrium from the supply of the two commodities and respective demands. The following set of equations depicts this economy closely:

$$X_j = (L_j)^\beta \quad 0 < \beta < 1, \quad X_j' > 0, X_j'' < 0, \tag{12.1}$$

$$Y_j = S_j^\alpha I_j^{1-\alpha} \quad 0 < \alpha < 1, \tag{12.2}$$

$$S_j^s = (\widetilde{I}_j)^{\sigma+1} \quad 0 < \sigma < 1, \quad S_j^{s\prime} > 0, \quad S_j^{s\prime\prime} > 0, \tag{12.3}$$

$$L_j^s = (\widetilde{L}_j), \tag{12.4}$$

$$I_j^s = (\widetilde{I}_j), \tag{12.5}$$

and the utility function for the representative consumer in this economy (also see Giannetti, 2002) is given by:

$$U(X, Y) = X^\theta Y^{1-\theta} \quad 0 < \theta < 1. \tag{12.6}$$

Under these assumptions, the budget constraint of a representative consumer in region $j$ is given by $P_X X + P_Y Y = w_j^* L_j^* + w_{Sj}^* S_j^*$. We assume homothetic preferences such that only total income and the relative prices of the two goods are relevant for determining aggregate demand. The autarkic equilibrium prices are derived from the supply and demand schedules directly.

Equations (12.1) and (12.2) determine the output levels of the two commodities based on the endowments of unskilled labor in Equation (12.4) and the supply of skilled labor as in Equation (12.3). Equation (12.6) on the other hand offers the aggregate demand for commodities $X$ and $Y$ subject to maximization of the utility functions for each skill type. We begin by solving the equilibrium employment levels of $L_j$ and $S_j$. From Equations (12.1) and (12.4) taking $w_j^*$ as the equilibrium wage rate in region $j$, we maximize output in $X$ by choosing optimal unskilled employment.

Thus, $[\max_{L_j} \pi_{Xj} = P_X L_j^\beta - w_j L_j]$ yields the optimal employment of unskilled labor in region $j$:

$$L_j^d = \left(\frac{w_j}{\beta P_X}\right)^{\frac{1}{\beta-1}}, \quad \text{such that,} \quad \frac{\delta L_j^d}{\delta w_j} < 0. \tag{12.7}$$

The equilibrium unskilled wage in region $j$ is a result of $L_j^d = \left(\frac{w_j}{\beta P_X}\right)^{\frac{1}{\beta-1}} = \tilde{L}_j$, i.e.,

$$w_j^* = \left(\tilde{L}_j\right)^{\beta-1} \beta P_X. \tag{12.8}$$

Relation (12.8) shows that as the endowment of unskilled labor rises in the $j$th region, the equilibrium wage falls, whereas the rise in price of commodity $X$ raises the same. The unskilled labor is freely mobile across all regions of the country since commodity $X$ is produced everywhere. This further implies that regions where $w_j^*$ is low owing to larger stock of unskilled workers will send workers out to regions where $w_j^*$ is higher. This should determine one common wage and employment level throughout the country.

The case for skilled workers is however, different. Let the total cost of producing $Y_j$ be given by $C = w_{Sj} S_j + k_j I_j$, where $w_{Sj}$ is the skilled wage and $k_j$ is the price per unit of infrastructure in region $j$. Thus, constrained profit maximization in $Y_j$ is written as:

$$\begin{aligned} \max_{S_j, I_j} \pi_{Y_j} &= P_{Yj} S_j^{\alpha} I_j^{1-\alpha} - w_{Sj} S_j - k_j I_j \\ &\quad + \lambda_S (S_j - m_S^2 - S_j^s) + \lambda_I (I_J - m_I^2 - I_j^s), \end{aligned} \tag{12.9}$$

where, the standard condition is well known; $g_j(T) \geq b_j \Rightarrow g_j(T) - m = b_j$; $m_S$ and $m_I$ are slack variables (squared) defining the distance between the constraint and the amount used; $\lambda_S$ and $\lambda_I$ are Lagrange multipliers for the two constraints used in the production of $Y_j$. The endowments of infrastructure and skilled labor for a region $j$ are derived from Equations (12.3) and (12.5) respectively. Non-zero values of $\lambda_S$ and $\lambda_I$ would imply that the constraints are binding. Solving Equation (12.9) with respect to $S_j, I_j, \lambda_S, \lambda_I, m_S, m_I$, and by obtaining standard first order conditions, we get

$$S_j^* = \left[\frac{w_{Sj} - \lambda_S}{\alpha P_{Yj} I_j^{1-\alpha}}\right]^{\frac{1}{\alpha-1}} \tag{12.10}$$

and

$$I_j^* = \left[\frac{k_j - \lambda_I}{(1-\alpha) P_{Yj} S_j^{\alpha}}\right]^{-\frac{1}{\alpha}}. \tag{12.11}$$

Further,

$$m_S^2 = -S_j^s + \left[\frac{w_{Sj} - \lambda_S}{\alpha P_{Yj} I_j^{1-\alpha}}\right]^{\frac{1}{\alpha-1}} \neq 0, \tag{12.12a}$$

$$m_I^2 = -I_j^s + \left[\frac{k_j - \lambda_I}{(1-\alpha) P_{Yj} S_j^{\alpha}}\right]^{\frac{1}{\alpha}} \neq 0. \tag{12.12b}$$

The complementary slackness conditions show that the slack variables being non-zero, the Lagrangian multipliers must be zero from $\frac{\delta \pi_{yj}}{\delta m_S} = 0$ and $\frac{\delta \pi_{yj}}{\delta m_I} = 0$. Thus, $\lambda_S = 0 = \lambda_I$ can be substituted back in Equations (12.10)–(12.12b) to generate the final set of solutions. Thus, regions that fall short of the available infrastructure cannot draw in skilled workers to productive use, even though the solution for the unconstrained version of Equation (12.9) shows that the wage offered in equilibrium must be higher.

In other words, if Equation (12.9) is maximized without the constraints, i.e.,

$$\max_{S_j, I_j} \pi_{Y_j} = P_{Yj} S_j^{\alpha} I_j^{1-\alpha} - w_{Sj} S_j - k_j I_j. \tag{12.13}$$

The optimal solutions lead to:

$$w_{Sj} = \frac{\alpha}{1-\alpha} \frac{I_j^*}{S_j^*} k_j. \tag{12.14}$$

Under the constrained case, however, $I_j^* > \tilde{I}_j$. This implies that, $w'_{Sj} > w_{sj}$, where $w'_{Sj}$ is the constrained wage. Despite such potential wage differences prevailing across regions, mobility of skilled workers will not take place toward the unconstrained region because infrastructure cannot be transferred along with skilled workers. The regional wage differential may therefore prevail even in autarky.

Finally, let us introduce trade in this model. Equation (12.10) shows that with a rise in the equilibrium wage the optimal employment of $S$ falls ($0 < \alpha < 1$), but with a rise in the price of $Y_j$, the same rises. The second result is particularly interesting. Given that so far we have dealt with autarky, introduction of trade should raise the price of the exportable. In other words, as the country opens up to trade $P_{Yj}$ rises. Consequently

$$\frac{\delta S_j^*}{\delta P_{Yj}} = -\frac{1}{\alpha - 1}\left[\frac{w_{Sj}}{\alpha P_{Yj} I_j^{1-\alpha}}\right]^{\frac{2-\alpha}{\alpha-1}} \left[\frac{\alpha I_j^{1-\alpha}}{\left(\alpha P_{Yj} I_j^{1-\alpha}\right)^2}\right] > 0. \quad (12.15)$$

This means that the optimal skill requirement in region $j$ rises with trade. Thus, all regions that possess higher endowments of skill, as determined by higher endowments of infrastructure shall be the ones that supply $Y_j$. The regional concentration of the service facility is therefore an outcome of higher returns to the sector, but supported only by adequate availability of infrastructure. Such regions also enjoy the comparative advantage in cost as we derived in the model. This seems consistent with the flow of foreign patients to the major centers in the country, because they have the adequate infrastructure to attract urban skilled workers. The coexistence of skilled workers and infrastructure is a pre-requisite for this pattern of regional concentration of activities despite higher per unit returns to skill in many other regions that do not have the support of infrastructure facilities.

## 12.4. Concluding Remarks

The regional and city-wise concentration of health-related service facility in India and lower prices per unit has led to a near revolution in the countries of the south. The international trade in health services makes use of the cost advantage in the south, where almost same quality of treatment is offered at much lower prices than the north countries. At some point in the history of trade in health services it was also shown that a very small country like Cuba offered much better treatments compared to that in the US. In a famous documentary it was argued that the capture of private health facilities in the US by the profiteering motives of pharmaceutical companies keep the prices way above the tolerance limit of a regular patient. The data we explored for India do not speak of public facilities either, and yet the prices are significantly lower in order to attract foreign patients. There should be little doubt that catering to foreign patients creates pressure on the capacity of the domestic units to serve the locals, and that there has been an upward movement in the prices. The price differential that exits nonetheless is potent enough to sustain trade. It should also be pointed out that the patients that come to India originate in various blocs around the world. Except for the South American countries, almost every country in the world contributed to the trade revenue from health services in India. While Bangladesh, Myanmar or Nepal sends patients owing to poorer health services in such countries, the patients from the Organisation for Economic Co-operation and Development (OECD) countries unambiguously take advantage of the significant price gap for common as well as specific health care services.

Moving from the global trade to regional concentration of these activities, we showed that eight major cities account for the lion's share of revenue generation in the country. The departments of general medicine as well as gastroenterology alongside typical components of health tourism like health spas and Ayurveda continue to be biggest attractions in the country and these services have regional specialization as well. In this regard, India witnesses a movement of patients internationally as well as domestically to such regions where specialized treatments have achieved the quality of the developed nations at a much lower price. This seems to be the source of the comparative advantage at the core of the trade in health services. In future, development of data sets over a longer time horizon and spanning various other service facilities that the present pilot could not do justice to may offer robustness checks on the issue.

## Acknowledgments

The authors wish to thank Dipankar Sinha and Amitava Saha of the Directorate General of Commercial Intelligence and Statistics, Ministry of Commerce, Government of India for the grant enabling a pilot survey on the export of health services from India. We wish to thank several officials who have helped in the process of data collection. Without the support of the administration in charge of health care services in various states the data collection would have not been feasible. We are also indebted to Ayan Kumar Banerjee and Sumit Dutta for excellent research assistance. The survey results have benefited from presentations at the DGCI & S; NSSO; Planning Commission of India, etc. Discussion with Rittwik Chatterjee has been extremely helpful.

## References

Bhagwati, JN (1987) International trade in services and its relevance for economic development. In *The Emerging Service Economy, Services World Economy Series* 1. O Giarini (Ed.). New York: Pergamon Press, 3–34.

Cattaneo, O (2010) Health without borders: International trade for better health systems and services. In *International Trade in Services: New Trends and Opportunities for Developing Countries*. Washington DC: World Bank, 99–140.

Chanda, R and R Smith (2006) International trade in health services and the GATS: Current issues and debates. In *Trade and Development Series*. Washington DC: World Bank, 245–304.

Deardorff, AV (2001) International provision of trade services, trade, and fragmentation, *Review of International Economics* 9(2), 233–248.

Ernst, D (2006) *Medical Tourism: Why Americans Take Medical Vacations Abroad*. San Francisco: Pacific Research Institute.

Francois, JF (1990) Trade in producer services and returns due to specialization under monopolistic competition, *Canadian Journal of Economics* 23, 109–124.

Freire, N (2012) The emergent medical tourism: Advantages and disadvantages of the medical treatments abroad, *International Business Research* 5(2), 41–50.

Giannetti, M (2002) The effects of integration on regional disparities: Convergence, divergence or both? *European Economic Review* 46(3), 539–567.

Grubel, HG (1987) All traded services are embodied in materials or people, *The World Economy* 10, 319–330.

Guiry, M and D Vequist (2011) Traveling abroad for medical care: US medical tourists' expectations and perceptions of service quality, *Health Mark Quarterly*, 28(3), 253–269.

Hill, TP (1977) On goods and services, *Review of Income and Wealth* 23(4), 315–338.

Hoekman, B (2006) Liberalization of trade in services: A survey. *World Bank Policy Research Paper, WPS* No. 4030. Washington DC.

Jones, RW and F Ruane (1990) Appraising the options for international trade in services, *Oxford Economic Papers, New Series* 42(4), 672–687.

Lipsey, R (2009) Measuring international trade in services. In *International Trade in Services and Intangibles in the Era of Globalization*. M. Reins and M. Slaughter (Eds.). Cambridge, Mass: NBER Press, 27–74.

Markusen, JR and BB Strand (2007) Trade in business services in general equilibrium. *NBER Working Paper No.* w12816. Cambridge, Mass.

Melvin, JR (1989) Trade in producer services: A Heckscher–Ohlin Approach, *Journal of Political Economy* 97(5), 1180–1196.

Reserve Bank of India. *Handbook of Statistics on Indian Economy*. Various issues.

Verma, R (2008) The service sector revolution in India: A quantitative analysis. UNU-WIDER Research Paper No. 2008/72, Helsinki.

Vijaya, R (2010) Medical tourism: Revenue generation or international transfer of healthcare problems? *Journal of Economic Issues* 44(1), 53–69.

World Bank. *World Development Indicators*, 1991–2013.

# Index

CPSIA information can be obtained at www.ICGtesting.com
Printed in the USA
BVOW11*0527220615

405276BV00006B/9/P

9 789814 520157